The English School of Int———————————————

What is the English School of Int
an accelerating growth of interes
leading commentators, provide
distinctive approach to the stud
coexistence and cooperation, a
between sovereign states. In the first book-length volume of its kind, the authors present a comprehensive discussion of the rise and development of the English School, its principal research agenda, and its epistemological and methodological foundations. The authors further consider the English School's position on progress in world politics, its relationship with Kantian thought, its conception of a sociology of states-systems, and its approach to good international citizenship as a means of reducing harm in world politics. Lucidly written and unprecedented in its coverage, this book is essential reading for anyone interested in International Politics and Politics worldwide.

ANDREW LINKLATER is the Woodrow Wilson Professor of International Politics at the University of Wales, Aberystwyth. He is the author of *The Transformation of Political Community* (1998), *Beyond Realism and Marxism* (1990), and *Men and Citizens in the Theory of International Relations* (2nd edition, 1990).

HIDEMI SUGANAMI is Professor of International Politics at the University of Wales, Aberystwyth. Previous publications include *On the Causes of War* (1996) and *The Domestic Analogy and World Order Proposals* (1989).

CAMBRIDGE STUDIES IN INTERNATIONAL RELATIONS: 102

The English School of International Relations

Editorial Board

Steve Smith (*Managing editor*)
Thomas Biersteker Phil Cerny Michael Cox
A.J.R. Groom Richard Higgott Kimberley Hutchings
Caroline Kennedy-Pipe Steve Lamy Michael Mastanduno
Louis Pauly Ngaire Woods

Cambridge Studies in International Relations is a joint initiative of Cambridge University Press and the British International Studies Association (BISA). The series will include a wide range of material, from undergraduate textbooks and surveys to research-based monographs and collaborative volumes. The aim of the series is to publish the best new scholarship in international studies from Europe, North America and the rest of the world.

CAMBRIDGE STUDIES IN INTERNATIONAL RELATIONS

(List continues at the end of book)

The English School of International Relations

A Contemporary Reassessment

Andrew Linklater
and
Hidemi Suganami

CAMBRIDGE
UNIVERSITY PRESS

CAMBRIDGE UNIVERSITY PRESS
Cambridge, New York, Melbourne, Madrid, Cape Town, Singapore, São Paulo

Cambridge University Press
The Edinburgh Building, Cambridge CB2 2RU, UK

Published in the United States of America by Cambridge University Press, New York

www.cambridge.org
Information on this title: www.cambridge.org/9780521675048

First published 2006

Printed in the United Kingdom at the University Press, Cambridge

A catalogue record for this book is available from the British Library

Library of Congress Cataloging-in-Publication Data
Linklater, Andrew.
The English school of international relations: a contemporary reassessment / Andrew
Linklater and Hidemi Suganami.
   p. cm.
Includes bibliographical references and index.

1. International society. 2. International relations–Study and
teaching. I. Suganami, Hidemi. II. Title.
JZ1237.L55 2006
327.1′01–dc22
2005022419

ISBN-13: 978-0-521-85835-9 hardback
ISBN-10: 0-521-85835-6 hardback
ISBN-13: 978-0-521-67504-8 paperback
ISBN-10: 0-521-67504-9 paperback

Contents

Acknowledgements

We are grateful to Tim Dunne, Nick Wheeler and Ian Hall for their helpful comments on the draft chapters they read, to Monica Ingber for consolidating our two separately grown bibliographies, and also to the two anonymous referees of the manuscript for their criticisms.

Introduction

The present volume, written in close collaboration by Hidemi Suganami and Andrew Linklater, is the first book-length attempt to detail the essential features of the so-called English School of International Relations and to demonstrate how some of its key texts and ideas can provide a basis for a historically informed and normatively progressivist understanding of contemporary international relations.

Our initial idea to produce a collaborative work on the theme of the English School emerged while we taught together in the Department of International Relations at Keele University. The subject was an obvious choice for our collaboration. Since his arrival in the UK in 1970 as a graduate student, Suganami has been closely acquainted with several scholars, and their works, whose names it has become customary to relate to the label, 'the English School'. Although his own interests in the study of international relations go beyond the traditional research parameters of English School writers (see, e.g., Suganami, 1996), some of their early publications (e.g., Manning, 1975) had a formative influence on his understanding of the institutional structure of contemporary international society (see Suganami, 1982, 1983, 1989, 2001a). Over the same period, Linklater had dedicated much of his scholarly work to developing a cosmopolitan perspective, arguing for the necessity and possibility of reducing the areas in which the institutional distinction between citizens and outsiders is treated as morally relevant in the practice of world politics (see, in particular, Linklater 1982, 1990, 1998). In this process, he had come to see in some key works of the English School – especially historical ones emanating from the British Committee on the Theory of International Politics – a rich source of insight and inspiration.

The present volume is also a response to an accelerating growth of interest, especially marked in the past few years, in the English School, its works, future potential and role in the disciplinary history of International Relations. Indeed, contemporary analysts frequently rely on the School's principal themes to understand continuity and change in the structure of international politics (see, for instance, Fawn and Larkins, 1996a; Roberson, 1998). The lasting significance of its inquiry into the relationship between international order and the aspiration for human justice is evident in many analyses of the changing relationship between state sovereignty, the global human rights culture and the norm of humanitarian intervention which emerged in the context of the post-Cold War era (Roberts, 1993; Wheeler and Dunne, 1998; Mayall, 2000c; Wheeler, 2000). The English School's pathbreaking analysis of the expansion of international society has been extended in studies of the failed state in the world's most violent regions (Jackson, 1990, 2000). A related concern with the revolt against the West, and with the need for understanding between different and often clashing cultural world-views in a uniquely multicultural international society, has lost none of its importance following the events of 11 September (Shapcott, 2000; Linklater, 2002a). Moreover, students of the history of the discipline continue to discuss and debate the significance of the English School in the study of international relations (Dunne, 1998; Suganami, 2001a; Bellamy, 2005).

Past areas of neglect on the part of the English School, such as European integration, international political economy and global environmental politics, are now being brought onto the agenda of research by scholars who self-consciously follow in the footsteps of earlier English School thinkers (see Buzan, 2001). As the agenda of the School has broadened, so has its scholarly worth come to be recognized by a wide range of writers (Der Derian, 1987; Linklater, 1998; Krasner, 1999). Inquiries into the relationship between the English School and constructivism have asked whether the former to some extent pre-empted the latter in recognizing the importance of norms in international relations and whether it might learn from the latter's methodological sophistication. These considerations have had a central place in recent international relations theory (Dunne, 1995b; Reus-Smit, 1999, 2002; Suganami, 2001d).

Investigations of this kind are closely connected with the growing interest in forging connections between historical sociology and International Relations. The historical-sociological turn in the discipline has

2

many different influences, among the most important being Watson's panoramic analysis of the different global configurations of power in world history and Wight's grand vision of a comparative sociology of states-systems (Wight, 1977; Watson, 1992; see also Buzan and Little, 2000; Hobden and Hobson, 2002; Linklater, 2002a). In summary, over the last five to ten years, the English School has become more influential in global debates and discussions about the movement of world politics, about the prospects for, and constraints on, the development of fairer global arrangements, and about the methodologies which are best suited to improve understanding on those fronts.

It was against this background of the renaissance of interest in the English School that our idea of producing a jointly authored volume was implemented. The division of labour between us reflected our respective interests and strengths. Suganami wrote the first three chapters of this volume, aimed, respectively, to show: (1) who can plausibly be considered as the central figures of the English School; (2) what types of questions they have investigated and how their suggested answers constitute a closely interwoven set of knowledge-claims; and (3) on the basis of what sorts of assumptions about the nature of International Relations (IR) as an intellectual pursuit they have conducted their inquiries. These reflect Suganami's special interest in meta-disciplinary engagement with substantive knowledge-claims advanced by leading IR scholars.

Linklater wrote the next four chapters. These cumulatively demonstrate how a critical and constructive reading of some selected English School texts yields a rich perspective on world politics. This perspective (1) points to progressive potentials embedded in anarchical states-systems; (2) accommodates the Kantian tradition of international relations theory as a foundation of its substantive contentions; (3) produces a historical-sociological research project on past states-systems, with special reference to how different kinds of harm are brought under normative constraint; and (4) is capable of formulating some basic normative guidelines regarding the conduct of foreign policy in a number of contexts prevailing in the contemporary world. These reflect Linklater's long-standing interest in normative theorizing about international relations which articulates the progressive direction the contemporary society of states is capable of taking towards an ethically more satisfactory social universe.

Both of us revised our respective chapters a number of times, and on every occasion we each took into account the other's criticisms and responses until we were both satisfied that they have been dealt with appropriately given what each of us sets out to achieve. Primary responsibility for the claims made in Chapters 1–3 rests with Suganami and that for those in Chapters 4–7 with Linklater. We are jointly responsible for the introduction and conclusion.

In the process of mutual scrutiny, we became aware that our strategies of reading texts are somewhat different. Suganami has tended to focus on extracting a rationally defensible core from a given text, cutting out ambiguities, inconsistencies and not fully developed points. By contrast, Linklater has been more tolerant of ambiguities, inconsistencies and underdeveloped points in a given text, and has been concerned with developing the English School in a more critical and normative direction. It is our hope, however, that our division of labour and mutual ciriticisms have produced a balanced and fruitful interpretation of the texts that we discuss in the main body of this volume. The reader may notice that we are somewhat different in our writing styles too. But it was not our aim to attempt to produce a stylistically more unified volume. Naturally, we paid close attention to the clarity and intelligibility of our expositions, and we hope we are united in our styles in those respects. In the remaining part of this introduction, the overall argument of the book is outlined to indicate where we begin, how we end and through what route.

It was mentioned above that Linklater's interest in the English School is focused on the number of works emanating from the British Committee on the Theory of International Politics, especially those of Martin Wight, Adam Watson and Hedley Bull. He highlights these in his chapters as the main source of inspiration and insight. The British Committee has been seen as the institutional home of the English School by some leading commentators on its life and works (see Dunne, 1998), and has effectively been treated as its other name (Little, 1995; Watson, 2001). The association of the two bodies is nowhere more apparent than in Barry Buzan's call in 1999 to 'reconvene the English School' (Buzan, 2001) – to enhance intellectual collaboration among like-minded International Relations (IR) specialists on the model of the British Committee with a view to making scholarly contributions further along the lines set out by some of the School's classical texts. But this view of the English School's identity is at odds with an earlier conception of it, according to which the School had evolved from 'that intimate intellectual grouping, based at the LSE in the 1950s and 60s, which inaugurated and first developed the [international society] approach' (Wilson, 1989: 55) to the study and teaching of international relations under the intellectual leadership of C. A. W. Manning.

A closer examination of a series of key pronouncements concerning the English School in the IR literature reveals that there are in fact considerable discrepancies in the ways its identity has been construed. This can cause a problem for a volume such as the present one whose subject-matter is nothing other than the English School, its achievements and potentials. Chapter 1 therefore attempts to resolve this problem by a detailed critical examination of the history of *the idea* of 'the English School'. The upshot of the critical exposition is that 'the English School' is itself a historically constructed entity, through the process of historical recounting, in which a number of partly overlapping, and more or less equally plausible, stories are told about its origins, development and identity. Neither the more recent 'British Committee view' of the English School, led by Dunne (1991), nor the older 'LSE view' of it, initiated by Roy Jones (1981), can be said to monopolize full truths about the School's identity. The realization that 'the English School' is a historically con-structed idea enables us to adopt a broad and flexible picture of its identity, according to which C. A. W. Manning, Martin Wight, Hedley Bull, Alan James, John Vincent, Adam Watson and a few others, includ-ing more recent contributors, such as Andrew Hurrell, Nicholas Wheeler, Tim Dunne and Robert Jackson, are all seen to play a key role in its origins and continuing evolution.

Chapter 2 outlines the arguments of the English School. This gives further credence to the claim that the above-mentioned authors form a school, as the questions they pose and the answers they deliver are seen to form a closely interwoven tapestry of knowledge-claims about international relations with regard to a number of interrelated issues. These are divided into structural, functional and historical dimensions, and several key English School contributors' arguments are expounded in the light of this tripartite division.

The purpose of this chapter is to give an accurate account of the key English School authors' substantive contentions about international relations in some detail, paying attention to interconnections between them put forward over a diverse range of issues. One important section of this chapter discusses the contrast between 'pluralism' and 'solidarism'. This distinction was introduced by Hedley Bull in one of his earliest works (1966b) against the background of the failure of the United Nations' collective security mechanism during the Cold War, but has come to be used in a rather different way in connection with the evolving practice of humanitarian intervention in the post-Cold War period (see Wheeler 2000). Pluralism and solidarism, which at the beginning referred mainly to two contrasting empirical interpretations about whether there was sufficient solidarity or potential solidarity to make law-enforcement workable in the existing international society, have now come by and large to be taken to mean two contrasting normative positions, one aiming at a minimalist goal of the orderly coexistence of states, and the other going beyond this to include a more demanding goal of the international protection of human rights standards globally. How this shift of meaning was possible, given some ambiguity in Bull's initial writing (1966b), and how the empirical and the normative are related in formulating one's position along the pluralist-solidarist axis are explained in the chapter. This discussion is important in that the distinction between pluralism and solidarism in the more recent sense plays a key role in the later chapters of this volume.

Having revealed close similarities and intricate interconnections in the English School authors' substantive arguments about their subject-matter, Suganami moves, in Chapter 3, to examine the methodological and epistemological parameters within which their substantive works on international relations have been produced. The purpose of this chapter is partly to see whether, at this deeper level too, there may be some unity in the School's thinking, and partly also to explain what kind of intellectual enterprise theirs is when they produce knowledge-claims about international relations. There is a need to engage in this type of examination because English School authors have not themselves been very explicit about the epistemological nature of their contentions, and the more methodologically self-conscious parts of the IR community have therefore found English School works difficult to incorporate into their research. As one North American critic has put it: 'for many American scholars, simply figuring out what its methods *are* is a challenge' (Finnemore, 2001: 509; emphasis Finnemore's).

The discussion in this chapter is conducted in response to this remark in the light of the three key questions. (1) English School writers are united in their appreciation of the relevance of historical knowledge to the study of international relations, but what precisely is it that they think the former can do for the latter? The discussion reveals considerable ambiguity and uncertainty on the part of the English School about the nature of historical knowledge and its relevance to IR. (2) English School writers are united in their scepticism towards a scientific study of international relations, but what do they offer in its place and what do they fail to give sufficient attention to in their studies? The discussion points to the English School writers' emphasis on explaining what goes on internationally by penetrating the minds, and uncovering the assumptions and motives, of the key actors, and also to their almost total neglect of causal mechanisms for political change. (3) English School writers have exhibited notable ambivalence towards normative or ethical questions, but what explains this, how have they circumvented such questions, and how satisfactory is this situation? The discussion points to the absence of any serious meta-ethical reflections within the English School; and its writers' tendency to insist either that they are only making a factual observation about the presence of certain values within a society, or that their evaluation of the desirability of particular international norms pertains only to their instrumental appropriateness, and not to the ultimate validity of the ends thereby sought. Despite such weaknesses, the English School's approach to the study of international relations is shown to have considerable merits: it does not fail to draw attention to the institutional dimension of modern world politics organized as a society of states; it is historically informed; and it aims to produce substantive understanding of international relations without deviating too far into meta-theoretical disputations. Further, despite their general emphasis on the goal of order in world politics, they, or Bull in particular, do not lose sight of the fact that order is not the only value pursued by humankind.

What emerges from these three chapters is a clear picture of the English School as a broad church. Its works are closely interconnected, yet they cover a wide range of subjects. There are certain ambiguities and uncertainties in their methodological and epistemological assumptions, yet even at this level there are common parameters and tendencies in their thoughts and orientations. Future works that self-consciously take the English School's achievements as their point of departure may cover diverse issues. Among them are: a more detailed empirical study of the historical evolution of social arrangements in inter-societal relationships; a normative theory of international relations which is more reflective of its meta-ethical foundations; an analysis of world historical narratives from the viewpoint of their relations to different traditions of thought about the nature of international politics. The next four chapters of this volume, written by Linklater, go on to underline, and give some substance to, these suggestions.

The starting point of Linklater's engagement with the English School writings is his judgement that the most fundamental question in IR is: 'How far can world politics be changed for the better?' He considers that English School authors have provided a judicious perspective on this question – that there can be and has been more progress than the realists think possible, but nothing so far-reaching as the radical revolutionists would like.

In Linklater's four chapters, the reader will find that his idea of progressive transformation is expressed in the light of a number of key concepts: 'system, society and community', 'pluralist society' and 'solidarist society', 'international harm conventions and cosmopolitan harm conventions', and 'a good international citizen' in different kinds of social contexts. The underlying idea is that relations between political communities can progress from one in which they treat one another as simply a brute fact to take into account in deciding how to act ('a system') towards a more fully societal one in which they share interest in governance through common institutions ('a society'). Societal relations can in turn develop from a minimalist ('pluralist') one, in which the common goal is restricted to the maintenance of the orderly coexistence of separate political communities, towards a more advanced ('solidarist') one, in which the goal increasingly incorporates the protection of human rights across separate communities. When the evolution progresses to an exceptionally high point where the society can no longer appropriately be said to consist of separate political communities which are determined to maintain their sovereignty or independence, the label 'community' comes to be used. A pluralist society of states is concerned with reducing inter-state harm and incorporates 'international harm conventions' within its institutional framework, whereas a solidarist society of states incorporates 'cosmopolitan harm conventions', designed to reduce harm done to individual citizens located in separate communities. 'International good citizens' are states, or governments acting for the states, who act to protect the respective social goals of the pluralist, solidarist and other interrelations.

English School writers have not analysed historical states-systems with a view to producing a general theory of the evolution of international society along such a path. However, some of them (e.g., Watson, 1992) have drawn attention to the historical tendencies for a crude system of inter-state interaction to develop into a more fully developed societal one, and also to the fact that the modern states-system, in particular, has come to embrace transcultural values (e.g., Bull and Watson, 1984). At the same time, English School writers do not lose sight of the danger of the destruction of international society and the constant need to protect and strengthen the element of international society in world politics.

Against this background, Chapter 4 extrapolates from a number of English School sources an explanation – which is in principle applicable transhistorically – of how states under anarchy may evolve their relations from a mere system, via the most basic post-systemic form, towards an increasingly more societal, and morally less deficient, kind, and how such a process may come to embrace the entire world. In the Cold War period, English School writings have been characterized by their stress on prudence, caution and the pursuit of pluralist values. There are followers of the English School tradition who are still inclined to draw attention to the dangers of trying to go much beyond an orderly coexistence of states towards a more solidarist goal (e.g., Jackson, 2000). But, in Linklater's view, the important function of the English School as a whole has been to alert us to the progressive potentials embedded in anarchical states-systems and possibilities for further progress immanent in the contemporary society of states.

The purpose of the four chapters by Linklater, therefore, is to explore how English School writings may be read, reread and exploited to sketch out a progressive perspective on international relations which draws on the resources of critical international theory. Such a stance, however idealistic in its intent and orientation, is not a utopian project. To the extent that it offers normative guidelines on how states ought to behave in various contexts to sustain and enhance the moral quality of life internationally, it is meliorist, gradualist and builds on what can plausibly be interpreted to be already present as trends and potentialities within the existing reality of international politics. The older generation of English School writers were somewhat hesitant to offer such normative guidelines very explicitly, adamant that, as an academic observer, they should focus on representing the world as it actually is in a detached manner. But, it is submitted, there is no way to represent the world without necessarily offering an interpretation of it and there is no way to do so without, however marginally, affecting, or contributing to, the way the world goes on. This is especially so where the interpretation proffered relates to the possibilities and limits of change.

The earlier English School inclination to focus on the limits of progress went side by side with their disdainful view of radical revolutionism, which they tended to depict as verging on fanaticism, totally lacking in prudence. One unfortunate victim – unfortunate not only for the victim, but also for the development of the English School as a serious intellectual movement imbued with a deep understanding of the traditions of international thought – is Immanuel Kant. Contrary to the well-publicized English School view, Kant's international theory, as demonstrated in Chapter 5, is best described as solidarism – within the rationalist tradition which is characterized as a *via media* between realism and revolutionism by Wight (1991). And when this point is appreciated, and Kant restored to his rightful place, it becomes easier to begin to appreciate the potential of English School writings as a resource for developing a more explicitly normative and progressivist perspective on world politics. Chapter 5 demonstrates this by pointing, among other things, to an important parallelism between, on the one hand, Kant's view of the possibility of progress in reaching agreements about duties not to injure others in domestic, international and transnational spheres of human relations, and, on the other, Bull's claim that *international* order is to be judged in the end by the extent to which it contributes to *world* order.

Progressivism, underlying the argument of the four chapters by Linklater, however, should not be taken to imply belief in the inevitability of progress. What is sought and offered is an interpretation of anarchical states-systems as having a potential to progress beyond mere systemic relations, an assessment of the modern states-system as perhaps uniquely capable of progressing far, and a judgement about the current phase of world politics as embracing discernible trends and possibilities for further progress towards solidarist goals. A characteristically English School way – because of the British Committee's pioneering interest in a comparative study of states-systems – to pursue this line of inquiry is to engage in a historical sociology of states-systems with special reference to the development of international and cosmopolitan harm conventions. An outline of such a project is given in some detail in Chapter 6. It argues that the fatalistic sociology which we find in Wight's writings does not exhaust the English School's resources, and that a sociology of states-systems which points to progressive potentials is already present in Wight's own essays.

In outlining the latter type of project, Linklater distinguishes between different forms of harm in world politics, and identifies some ways of answering the question of whether the modern states-system is different from earlier ones because the former takes notions of human solidarity more seriously than did the latter. He suggests that in some respects the modern states-system may have incorporated more demanding tests of human conduct, but acknowledges that various moral deficits remain, not least because of widening global inequalities, opportunities for exploitation of the poor, and so on. A civilizing process of humankind is not a straightforward unilinear one, which was also Kant's view.

The focus on norms and values is a distinctive feature of the English School's approach to the study of world politics, and there is a marked difference between that and the neorealists' view of inter-state relations. For the latter, international order reproduces itself through the operation of the invisible hand under anarchy. For the former, states-systems are rare achievements and require 'tremendous *conscious* effort' (Butterfield, quoted in Dunne, 1998: 126) to sustain and develop them. It is consistent with this that English School writings are agent-centric and normative; instead of working out causal mechanisms of transformation, they tend to discuss how states ought to behave to sustain international order and, more recently, how humanitarian goals may be achieved without at the same time seriously jeopardizing order among states.

Given this, it is apt that the final chapter of this volume should be dedicated to spelling out, on the basis of a number of key English School texts, what principles ought to guide states' conduct in various kinds of international contexts. This is done by focusing on three questions: (i) what states should do, to count as 'good international citizens', in an environment marked by pluralism; (ii) what they should do to one another as like-minded solidarists; and (iii) what those located in a solidarist environment should do to those in a pluralist environment when the concerns of the two kinds of societies clash – most characteristically when serious human rights abuse takes place within a pluralist (and non-interventionist) state which shocks the conscience of the solidarists. These principles are extrapolated mainly from English School writings, and are presented as a set of guidelines about what states should be aiming for if they are genuine about good international citizenship. At a maximum, they contain a vision of the most decent forms of world political organization attainable for our time.

1 The idea of 'The English School' as a historical construct

The idea of the English School, or the view that such an entity exists, is now firmly established in the community of scholars specializing in International Relations across the world, especially since Barry Buzan's call, at the 1999 annual conference of the British International Studies Association, to 'reconvene the English School'. This has resulted in a dramatic rise in the volume of conference papers and published works on a wide variety of themes associated with the School's key texts and its research agenda (Buzan, 2001; www.leeds.ac.uk/polis/englishschool/). But the *idea* of the English School is itself only about twenty years old. The purpose of this chapter is to trace the formation of this idea in the specialized academic discourse of International Relations. It is in this branch of knowledge that the idea can be said to find its home, even though the tradition of international thought which the School represents in broad outline is arguably as old as the Westphalian states-system itself.[1]

The need to trace the emergence and evolution of the idea of the English School stems from the fact that, during the twenty years or so since the first reference was made to the School's presence (Jones, 1981), there has been some deep discrepancy, as well as convergence, among the chief commentators' views on the School's existence, identity and contributions. Here are some noteworthy examples, listed at this point to reveal a wide diversity of views on the subject, which may

---

[1] Where in the traditions of international thought the central argument of the English School lies is discussed later in this chapter in connection with Wight's (1991) well-known tripartite classification of these traditions, Bull's (1977) incorporation of it in his discussion of world politics, and, above all, Richard Little's claim (2000) that the English School stands for pluralism, representing *all* the three traditions of thought.

be somewhat bewildering to those who have yet to locate themselves in the intellectual map of British, or mainly British, International Relations.

'There is a school of thought, constituting the mainstream in the study of International Relations in Britain, united by the general similarities of disposition, initiated by C. A. W. Manning, and followed by Alan James, F. S. Northedge and Hedley Bull. There are a substantial number of teachers and students who were either directly or indirectly influenced by the teaching of those four scholars.'

(Suganami, 1983: 2363)

'To see these British scholars [Manning, Wight, Bull, Northedge and Donelan] as a "school" is to see them as they did not see themselves.' (Grader, 1988: 42)

'Without doubt the idea [of international society] occupies a central place in their [English School writers'] thinking. Uncovering the *nature* of international society is the focus of Manning's principal work. Similarly, the question, "What is the nature of international society?" was the central question in Wight's International Theory. In *The Anarchical Society* the idea of international society is central to Bull's theory of how order is maintained in world politics . . . Much of Alan James's work on international relations theory has been aimed at demonstrating that it is both accurate and illuminating to conceive the collectivity of states in terms of a society . . . The concept of international society occupies a central place in the methodology of Vincent's recent study of human rights . . . Finally, and in a direct fashion, Mayall, after noting the failure of the attempt to develop value-free scientific theories of international relations, has "re-asserted" the concept of international society as "central to international theory" . . . Northedge was a principal member of that intimate intellectual grouping, based at the LSE in the 1950s and 60s, which inaugurated and first developed the [international society] approach . . . [His] works – particularly his *International Political System*, and his essay on transnationalism – read very much like other works of the English school.' (Wilson, 1989: 54–5)

'The idea of international society goes back at least as far as Hugo Grotius. It is rooted in the classical legal tradition and the notion that international law constitutes a community of those participating in the international legal order. Within the discipline of international relations, the concept has been put forward and developed by writers of the so-called English school, including E. H. Carr, C. A. W. Manning, Martin Wight, Hedley Bull, Gerrit Gong, Adam Watson, John Vincent, and James Mayall.' (Buzan, 1993: 328)

'The School includes Martin Wight, Herbert Butterfield, Hedley Bull and Adam Watson among others . . . The members of the School came together initially at the instigation of Kenneth Thompson and was identified as the British Committee on the Theory of International Relations [*sic*].'　　　　　　　　　　(Little, 1995: 32, note 1)

'Any book devoted to the concept of International Society must necessarily acknowledge its debt to the Department of International Relations at the London School of Economics. Coming from the site of International Society's birth and early nurturing in the writings of Charles Manning, Hedley Bull, Martin Wight and, all too briefly, R. J. Vincent, this volume hopes to build on their valuable intellectual legacy' (Fawn and Larkins, 1996a: xi). 'However, at the same time, one of the assumptions of the book is that the notion of International Society has traditionally been limited by its association with the concerns of the so-called English School.'

(Fawn and Larkins, 1996b: 1)

'To sum up: the "English School" as represented by Carr or Butterfield could be understood as a version of classical realism – in the case of Carr (1946) a secular version, in the case of Butterfield (1953) a Christian version. But as represented by Wight (1991) and Bull (1977), the "English School" is a more comprehensive academic enterprise which emphasises the interactive relationship between all three of these basic human inclinations in international relations (i.e., Realism, Rationalism and Revolutionism of Wight). Rationalism or "Grotianism" is, of course, at the heart of that relationship.'

(Jackson, 1996: 213)

'The "English School" is unfortunately named, given that its major figure in recent years, Hedley Bull, was indisputably Australian, albeit an Australian who built his career in London, and later, at Oxford. The name also implies that most International Relations theorists in England (or, more appropriately, Britain) were members of the school, which has certainly not been the case – E. H. Carr, C. A. W. Manning, and F. S. Northedge are but three leading British theorists of the last half-century who would not qualify as members of the English School. It is best defined as a group of scholars – most notably Martin Wight, Adam Watson, R. J. Vincent, James Mayall, Robert Jackson, and recent rising stars such as Timothy Dunne and Nicholas Wheeler, in addition to Bull – whose work focuses on the notion of a "society of states" or "international society".'

(Brown, 1997: 52)

'One of the most significant moments in British International Relations thinking occurred in the late 1950s when a group of scholars gathered to form a Committee to investigate the fundamental questions of "international theory". The first formal meeting of the British Committee, in January 1959, signifies the symbolic origins of the English School' (Dunne, 1998: xi). 'The affinity between the English School and the British Committee effectively displaces Charles Manning from being a member of the School, as he was never invited to participate in the Committee's proceedings' (Dunne, 1998, 12). 'Perhaps the best way to describe Carr's role is that of a dissident in the School' (Dunne, 1998: 13). 'More than any substantive intellectual contribution, it is this pivotal role in organising The British Committee on the Theory of International Politics which marks out Herbert Butterfield as one of the founder members of the English School' (Dunne, 1998: 73). 'While I remain ambivalent as to Manning's contribution, I have no doubt that Carr remains critical to the formation of the English School.' (Dunne, 2000: 233)

'I have followed Dunne in defining the English school primarily around a Wight-Bull-Vincent axis, leaving C. A. W. Manning to the side.' (Epp, 1998: 48)

'Rather than linking the English school to a *via media* and, in particular, to the idea of international society, it is argued [in this article] that the school, from an early stage, has been committed to developing a pluralistic approach to the subject, expressed in both ontological and methodological terms' (Little, 2000: 395). 'Certainly the English school has acknowledged the importance of rationalist ideas but this is not to the exclusion of realist and revolutionist ideas.' (Little, 2000: 398)

Here then is some considerable diversity. According to some commentators, the English School's main contribution has been to articulate the international society perspective on world politics, Manning being a founding figure, and the Department of International Relations at LSE its initial institutional base (Suganami, 1983; Wilson, 1989; Fawn and Larkins, 1996a, 1996b). According to some others, the English School has indeed to do with the international society perspective, but not with Manning (Brown, 1997; Dunne, 1998). In some commentators' view, however, the School has to do mainly or even exclusively with the British Committee on the Theory of International Politics led by Butterfield and Wight (Little, 1995; Dunne, 1998). Some writers consider E. H. Carr to belong to the English School (Buzan, 1993; Jackson, 1996; Dunne, 1998), while others do not (Suganami, 1983; Wilson, 1989; Brown, 1997). In the view of some commentators, even the international society perspective is not what the English School is centrally about (Little, 2000, 2003; Buzan, 2001), while according to another, there is no such thing as the English School in any case (Grader, 1988).

Such a striking disunity of views, exhibited by those who claim to know about the English School, its identity and contributions, appears quite disconcerting, even standing in the way (unless sorted out at the outset) of proceeding with a volume, such as the present one, whose subject-matter is none other than the English School itself, its way of thinking, and how we may build upon its achievements. The presence of these contending interpretations, however, will not be especially damaging to such an enterprise if we appreciate their similarities, as well as differences; if we do not suppose any of these interpretations to convey the truth about the identity of the School exclusively and exhaustively; and if, above all, we understand that the idea of the English School has a history.

It is a central contention of this chapter that, when these differing interpretations are subjected to a critical textual and contextual scrutiny, and efforts are made to conciliate as well as adjudicate between them, the identity of the English School will reveal itself – although, importantly, as a historically constituted and evolving cluster of scholars with a number of inter-related stories to tell about them. A survey of the English School's classical texts and their descendants, conducted in Chapter 2, will demonstrate exceptionally close interconnections among these works and add credence to the claim that their authors can be seen to form a school. In Chapter 3, it will further be argued that, despite a considerable diversity and uncertainties in their presuppositions about the nature of International Relations as an intellectual pursuit, there are certain reasonably clear parameters within which English School writers have traditionally operated. The overall aim of these three chapters is to establish what kind of entity the English School is, who its key architects are, and what they stand for – both in terms of their substantive contentions about world politics and in terms of their understandings of the nature of International Relations as an intellectual pursuit.

The following discussion will first focus on the debate about the identity of the English School which took place in the 1980s. It will be noted that, during this phase, those who believed in the existence of such a school focused their attention primarily upon 'that intimate intellectual grouping, based at the LSE in the 1950s and 60s, which inaugurated and first developed the approach' (Wilson, 1989: 55) to the study of international relations, of which C. A. W. Manning, a juris-prudence expert, was a leading figure. This is followed by an exposition of a new trend in the 1990s which, while not doubting the existence of the English School, began to see it in a rather different light, drawing attention to the research agenda and output of the British Committee on the Theory of International Politics, led in its early stages by historians, Herbert Butterfield and Martin Wight. The concluding discussion of this chapter draws attention to the nature of the English School as a historical construct. A number of implications follow from this (at times neglected) feature of the entity in question. It will be suggested that a more comprehensive appreciation of the English School as an intellectual movement can only come from a thorough examination of a wide range of texts emanating from this broad church in the study of international relations – an examination of the kind that will be attempted in the subsequent two chapters.

The English School debate in the 1980s

After the publication, in 1981, of Roy Jones' polemical article in *Review of International Studies*, memorably titled 'The English School of International Relations: A Case for Closure', there followed in the same decade a few sporadic contributions to what might be called 'the English School debate'. This was a discussion about: (1) whether there is indeed such a school; if so, (2) whether 'the English School' is an appropriate name for it; (3) who its leading members are; (4) how they differ from other schools of thought about international relations; and (5) what their main strengths and weaknesses are. These contributions include a piece by Suganami (1983), a critical response to Jones and Suganami by Sheila Grader (1988), and a reply to Grader by Peter Wilson (1989).

The questions comprising the English School debate are not of equal importance in substance. Question (3), for example, has struck many as not warranting a lengthy debate (Dunne, 2000; Hurrell, 2001: 489; Little, 2003: 444). Questions (4) and (5) are the more important ones from the viewpoint of engaging critically with some standard works in the field. Yet without a considered view on (3), questions (4) and (5) could not be addressed. Clearly, who one considers to be the School's central figures shapes what one identifies as the School's major texts and tenets, and hence one's assessment of the School's achievements. Question (3) has a procedural significance and cannot be dismissed as unworthy. Question (2), admittedly, would seem insignificant; yet it was, in Jones' case, closely associated with his position on the more substantive question (5) – for, as explained below, he had chosen the 'English School' label specifically to point to what he saw as its key members' serious inadequacies.

Roy Jones (1981) on the English School

It is well known that Hedley Bull, a member of Jones' English School, had launched an attack on the scientific approach to the study of international relations, then in ascendancy in the United States. He did so in defence of what he called a 'classical' approach (1969), and he no doubt had in mind here the kind of enterprise he was pursuing with his colleagues in the British counterpart of the American Committee on the Theory of International Politics (Dunne, 1998: 116ff). Nonetheless, Jones did not think it appropriate to give the label 'classical' or 'British' to what appeared thus to be presenting itself as a 'British' 'classical' alternative to the 'American' 'scientific' approach. Jones preferred the label 'English' for the following reasons.

First, he lamented that, for the most part, his English School authors have cut themselves off from the fundamental concern of the *classical* theory of politics, from Plato onwards, 'which is to form a view of the best relationship which should exist between individual men in terms of the common authority among them' (1981: 1). This therefore ruled out the label 'classical' for him. Second, he was dismayed that their work shows little evidence of any commitment to 'the truly *British* liberal tradition of economic and political studies, founded largely in the eighteenth century, to which numbers of outstanding Scotsmen and even one or two Welshman made significant contributions' (1981: 2; emphasis added). Thus, for Jones, the School did not deserve the title 'British', either. To these, he added one other reason: 'For the most part they also share a common academic provenance in the department of international relations at the London School of Economics and Political Science' (1981: 1).

That Jones was a Welshman writing from Cardiff may explain his association of 'London' specifically with 'England'. 'The reference to an "English" School was made first by a Welshman (Jones, 1981) who was critical of the way that international relations was taught in England', commented Richard Little (1995: 32, note 1). Jones' largely idiosyncratic reasons for his choice of the label, however, related to his two pertinent criticisms: English School authors' lack of interest in *doing* political theory and their neglect of economic dimensions of international relations. The latter point is noted often enough (see, for example, O'Hagan, 2002: 121). As for the former, it is quite untrue, of course, that English School writers were not interested in the arguments of classical political thinkers, especially those who discussed problems arising in the context of inter-state relations. But it is the case that they fell short of producing a well-developed political theoretical argument themselves concerning – as such an argument would centrally address – the duties of citizens and their governments in the world of sovereign states.

Looking back at the past twenty years or so, we may well doubt that the argument of the Jones article has ever been taken seriously. In any case, his rather tenuous reasoning for his pejoratively intended label most certainly did not stay in the collective consciousness of the IR profession, even within Britain. But the name – 'the English School' – did, and with it gradually arose an awareness that there was a distinct community of scholars whose works exhibited a close family resemblance. By advocating its closure, Jones had inadvertently contributed to the School's coming into existence in the popular awareness of the IR community at large.

The 'seminal thinkers' of this school, according to Jones, were Manning and Wight, (Jones, 1981: 1). 'Hedley Bull, Michael Donelan, F. S. Northedge, Robert Purnell and others' were 'the core of its extant membership' 'still in its prime', and, he added, 'young recruits [were] constantly coming forward' (1981: 1). In his judgement, these scholars exhibited a number of similarities. They appear, he wrote, 'to share a broad commitment to international relations as a distinct, even autonomous, subject' (1981: 1). He added:

> Their principal professional task they perceive to be that of examining and describing such measure of order as the world *as a whole* may, in their view, be expected to maintain on the basis of the structure of relations between what they habitually call 'sovereign nation-states'. Their style is easily recognizable, if only for what it leaves out: few statistics, no geometry and less algebra; and no vulgar agonizing over so-called world problems of poverty, commodity prices, monetary reform and such. Though often given to philosophical allusion, their own philosophical position is not distinguished by its scope and completeness. (1981: 1; italics original)

It is difficult to summarize Jones' article as a whole as he did not develop his argument very systematically. A few pertinent observations are made, but they are mingled with dismissive assertions against Manning and Wight in particular, in a manner that tends more to reveal Jones' exasperation with these writers' approaches and arguments than expound them helpfully to the reader. He appears to have been curious about why Manning and Wight, who had both passed away by then, were held in so much awe *personally* by some of their former students and colleagues. But when he read the writings of Manning and Wight as well as those of their followers, he clearly found their views on international society of sovereign states, international theory and international history muddled, unpalatable and impoverished. Jones' two main criticisms aimed at their works were reasonable – their neglect of economics and of serious political theorizing. However, other more detailed criticisms were to a great extent based on his inadequate attention, as was his inclusion into his English School of Michael Donelan, whose central aim was the application of natural law to the conduct of international relations. His views, therefore, were considerably at odds with those of the rest listed by Jones (see, in particular, Bull, 2000e).

The primary role that the Jones article performed in the history of International Relations as an academic discipline was to make the community of IR specialists begin to think that there was a distinct school about their subject-matter: –'the English School'. It is difficult to judge what impact, if any, Jones' call to close the school had in the 1980s. The 'extant members' and 'young recruits' of Jones' English School went on, regardless, to produce some of their most significant works in this period (Bull and Watson, 1984; James, 1986a; Vincent, 1986), although Bull died in 1985, and Vincent in 1989, both tragically young.

Suganami (1983) on the British institutionalists

A similar set of features to the ones noted by Jones were also found significant in grouping together Manning and a few others by Suganami (1983), who characterized them as 'the institutionalists', then occupying the mainstream position in the British study of international relations. Alan James, F. S. Northedge and Hedley Bull were counted as among Manning's 'followers', and it was noted that there were 'a substantial number of teachers and students who were either directly or indirectly influenced by the teaching of those four scholars' (Suganami, 1983: 2362). The common features identified were: (1) their aspiration or declared intent to pursue *Wertfreiheit* (or 'value-freedom'), which subsumed a number of inter-related attitudes on their part towards values and norms in the academic study of international relations; (2) their rejection of behaviourism and scientism; (3) their reliance on certain sociological methods, for example, ideal-type analysis, and particular stress on the method of *Verstehen* (or 'understanding') in the light of the institutional or cultural framework of international society; (4) their recognition of the unity as well as the specificity of the states-system, based on their rejection of the domestic analogy, and consequent assertion of the independence of International Relations as an academic discipline; and (5) their positive estimate of the degree of order in the states-system, and negative estimate of the possibility of altering its basic structure, resulting in their rejection of utopianism. Some of these themes will be examined further in Chapter 3.

This article, like Jones', had been written against the background of a succession of publications in the 1960s and 1970s. In 1962, Manning's *The Nature of International Society* had appeared, based on what he had taught in the previous thirty years at the LSE (Suganami, 2001a). This was followed, in 1966, by the publication of *Diplomatic Investigations: Essays in the Theory of International Politics*, edited by Herbert Butterfield and Martin Wight. In it were found some of the most important early texts of the English School, such as Wight's 'Why Is There No International Theory?' and 'Western Values in International Relations', and Bull's 'Society and Anarchy in International Relations' and 'The Grotian Conception of International Society'. This was a collection of essays written by the members of the British Committee on the Theory of International Politics, but little was known about its activities at that time.[2]

Six years after the publication of the Butterfield and Wight volume came, in 1972, another collection of essays, *The Aberystwyth Papers*, edited by Brian Porter, a former student of Manning and Wight. In it was found a chapter on 'The Theory of International Politics 1919–1969' by Bull, then well known for championing what he called the

---

[2] The British Committee was founded in 1958 by the Rockefeller Foundation as a British counterpart of an American committee (Butterfield and Wight, 1966: Preface). Chaired successively by Butterfield, Wight, Watson and Bull, the Committee, comprising a number of academics and some officials, and holding weekend meetings three times a year, collectively produced *Diplomatic Investigations* (1966) and, in its later phase, Bull and Watson's *The Expansion of International Society* (1984). Separate publications by Wight (1977), Bull (1977) and, later, Watson (1992) owe much to the work of the Committee, whose central importance as a site of the English School's evolution is now evident, thanks mainly to the work of Tim Dunne (1998).

classical approach against the concerted move, gaining preponderance especially in the United States, to transform the study of international relations into a scientific enterprise (Bull, 1969). There was also a chapter by Manning, entitled 'The Legal Framework in the World of Change', which expounded his unchanging view of the nature and role of international law in the society of states. Herbert Butterfield, who had written on 'The Balance of Power' and 'The New Diplomacy and Historical Diplomacy' for the Butterfield and Wight volume, now contributed a chapter on 'Morality and an International Order'.

A year later, in 1973, *The Bases of International Order* was published in honour of C. A. W. Manning edited by Alan James, much of whose effort in undergraduate teaching at the LSE and later at Keele University was focused on developing Manning's ideas (Manning, 1951a, 1951b, 1954; Suganami, 2001a). The James volume contained chapters by Manning's former students and colleagues, including Northedge, Goodwin, Wight, Bull and the editor himself. In 1974, John Vincent's *Nonintervention and International Order* was published, based on his doctoral dissertation supervised by Hedley Bull and J. D. B. Miller at the Australian National University. In 1975, Manning's *The Nature of International Society* was reissued with a new preface, followed by his former pupil, Northedge's publication, in 1976, of *The International Political System*, based, in turn, on his undergraduate lectures at the LSE. This annual succession culminated in 1977 in the publication of Bull's major work, *The Anarchical Society: A Study of Order in World Politics*. The same year also saw Wight's *Systems of States*, based on his work at the British Committee, posthumously edited by the Committee's co-member and Wight's great admirer, Bull. This was followed, in 1978, by *Power Politics* also by Wight edited by Hedley Bull and Carsten Holbraad, a former doctoral student of Wight.

By the close of the 1970s, then, it was possible to see, if one took note of it, that a network of scholars was gaining a momentum in the British teaching and study of International Relations as reflected in these publications by old and young – all saying broadly similar things, under similar titles, about international relations and the way to study it, and everyone related to everyone else through some overlapping personal connections. Suganami's piece (1983) had been presented at the 1980 Annual Conference of the British International Studies Association – in a panel on 'The British Establishment in International Relations'. James, Northedge and Bull each expressed their broad agreement with the argument of the paper, James stressing, however, that there were significant differences among them as well as similarities, and Bull pointing out that the main weakness of the paper was its neglect of Wight's work and his influence particularly upon Bull's own thinking about international relations. In Bull's view, though not in James', the article exaggerated Manning's formative influence on British International Relations.[3]

Grader (1988) and Wilson (1989) on the English School

The theme of internal differences, to which James drew attention, was developed by Grader (1988) in what appears to be the only work published to respond point by point to Jones' criticisms of the English School. But Grader's main argument – partly also directed at Suganami (1983) – was that there were such fundamental 'philosophical' differences among those scholars Jones and Suganami had bracketed together, that it was in fact meaningless to consider them as forming a school. There was merit in the suggestion, she acknowledged, that the identity of the 'English School' coalesced around the idea of international society (1988: 38). She maintained, however, that the views of Manning, Bull, and Northedge on international society were quite diverse – for 'Manning's society is metaphysical, Bull's is empirical and normative, and Northedge's view tends towards discounting international society in favour of the international system of states' (1988: 38). Grader conceded that the members of Jones' English School were also similar in rejecting behaviouralism dominant in the American study of international relations, but she rightly noted that this was not a feature unique to them (1988: 40–1). 'To see these British scholars as a "school" is to see them as they did not see themselves', she concluded (1988: 42).

There does seem to be some truth in this last contention. Before the Jones article appeared (by which time Manning and Wight, the two leading figures of his English School, were already dead), there was as

---

[3] This is based on Suganami's memory of his conversation with Bull, James, and Northedge at the time the paper was presented. At the conference, Bull said of the paper that it was a 'decent' one, criticized its neglect of Wight's input, and expressed his view that it was not a bad thing that a school of thought (called 'institutionalism' in the paper) asserted its existence and articulated its views because, he said, others not belonging to the school can formulate their respective positions in opposition to the school's lines. This is in accord with Wight's notion of international theory as a conversation between different strands of thought, and betrays Bull's endorsement of intellectual pluralism. It is important to note, however, that Bull (or James or Northedge) did not object to being characterized in the paper as an institutionalist.

yet no well-articulated, common understanding on the part of the IR community at large – or even perhaps on the part of those whom Jones had chosen to call 'the English School' – that a line demarcating them from others in the field, give or take one or two, constituted a particularly significant boundary. This was what Grader, a former student of Manning and others at the LSE, was pointing to. By 1989, however, Wilson was able to cite a number of articles published in the immediate past (Vincent, 1983; Lyons, 1986; Hoffman, 1987) as evidence of 'increasing acceptance among International Relations scholars that there [was] a group of writers which should be recognized as constituting a distinct school of thought' – more often than not called the English School (Wilson, 1989: 49). Wilson himself took the view that there was a school of thought here, but primarily in the sense that 'the thought of the scholars in question is sufficiently similar for them to be grouped together, and thereby distinguished from other International Relations scholars' (1989: 52).

The way Wilson arrived at this conclusion was initially through rejecting Grader's claim that Manning and his supposed associates were not talking about the same thing when they discussed international society. In particular, Wilson rejected as superficial Grader's key assertion that 'Manning's "society" [was] metaphysical whilst Bull's [was] empirical and normative' (1989: 52). As Wilson rightly noted, 'international society' was ideational and norm-based either for Manning or for Bull, and they both took the view that its rules and principles ought to be defended and made more effective (1989: 52–3). Wilson went on to observe that there was 'no difference in the ontological status of the international society, as the concept [was] employed by Manning, Wight, Bull, James and by more recent recruits to the school such as R. J. Vincent and James Mayall', adding that 'this [was] not surprising given Manning's well-known intellectual influence, either directly or indirectly, upon' the others (1989: 54). Wilson also demonstrated that the concept of international society was central to the theory of international relations advanced by Manning, Wight, Bull, James, Vincent and Mayall (1989: 54–5), adding that even though Northedge preferred the term 'international political system' to 'international society', his methods of analysis and central arguments about international relations were very similar to those of the rest. After all, he added, Northedge was 'a principal member of that intimate intellectual grouping, based at the LSE in the 1950s and 60s, which inaugurated and first developed the approach' (1989: 55).

Ultimately, Wilson concluded, it is this sharing of certain methods and arguments that united the English School, and separated them from all others in the discipline. He maintained that their methods and arguments were similar in the following four respects: (1) their assertion of the orderliness of the relations of states; (2) their stress on the institutional bases of international order; (3) their rejection of utopian schemes for the radical restructuring of the international system; and (4) their dismissal of the behavioural or scientific methodology in favour of the empathetic understanding and interpretation (1989: 55–6). These are virtually identical to Suganami's list of similarities, noted earlier, presented as distinguishing the works of Manning and his associates from those of others. Further, although Wilson did not treat this as a defining feature of the English School, he maintained, as did Jones earlier, that the institutional basis of the English School was at the London School of Economics and Political Science.

Development in the 1990s

After Bull's untimely death in 1985, followed by Vincent's four years later, a number of academics followed in their footsteps and also those of Wight, who had passed away earlier in the 1970s. Among them were Andrew Hurrell, one of the last of Bull's students at Oxford, Tim Dunne, a former doctoral student of Hurrell at Oxford, Nicholas Wheeler, Dunne's close collaborator, and Robert Jackson, then of the University of British Columbia, who discovered the works of Manning, Wight, Bull, James, Vincent and others through his British colleagues (see Hurrell, 1990, 1992, 1998; Jackson, 1990, 2000; Wheeler, 1992, 2000; Dunne, 1995a, 1995b, 1998; Wheeler and Dunne, 1996; Alderson and Hurrell, 2000). By now the 'English School debate' appeared to have been settled in so far as the issue of the School's *existence* was concerned. Meanwhile, attention of the IR community at large came to be focused on the debates between the neo-realists and their critics emanating from North America (Waltz, 1979; Keohane, 1986a; Der Derian and Shapiro, 1989; Linklater, 1990a; Buzan, Jones and Little, 1993). Against the background of the momentous changes in the world scene, however, the beginning of the 1990s also saw a number of IR scholars revisit ideas and arguments about 'international society' and 'world order' embodied in some of the key writings that had come to be associated with the label, 'the English School'.

A special 'Winter 1992' issue of *Millennium*, edited by Rick Fawn and Jeremy Larkins, later published as *International Society after the Cold War: Anarchy and Order Reconsidered* (1996a), demonstrated this, as did the 1992 Limerick Workshop, convened to reconsider the idea of international society after the end of the Cold War. This resulted in a volume edited by Barbara Roberson: *International Society and the Development of International Relations Theory* (1998). This coincided with the publication of Dunne's *Inventing International Society: A History of the English School* (1998), based on his doctoral thesis, submitted in 1993.

So far, Dunne's book has done the most to remind the IR world of the existence of the English School and alert the profession to its collective achievements. His 'English School', however, took on an identity which was significantly different from that of the School discussed in the 1980s by Jones, Suganami and Wilson. Whereas their pieces drew attention specially to the legacies of Manning in the British study of International Relations, Dunne focused on the work of the British Committee on the Theory of International Politics. However, this shift of focus was already underway in some of the contributions to the Roberson volume (1998: 2, 17, 85) and the two notable publications of this period by Buzan (1993) and Little (1995) respectively. Before turning to Dunne's work, pivotal in the history of the English School debate, the two leading authors' treatment of the School is examined below.

Buzan (1993) and Little (1995, 2000)

Buzan's article on the English School appeared in an influential American journal, *International Organization* (1993) and Little's in the first issue of the *European Journal of International Relations* (1995). Apart from his inclusion of Carr, Buzan's characterization of the English School's identity is basically in accord with the prevailing view of the 1980s. But when one compares Buzan's argument developed at length in his article with the works of Manning, Bull and Watson (counted by Buzan as the leading members of the English School) as well as those of James (whom it does not appear to be Buzan's wish to exclude from the School), one finds that his understanding of the English School thinking was selective.[4] In particular, he appears insufficiently aware that, according to some of the leading English School writers themselves, *pragmatic needs* were a strong enough motive for sovereign states, even

---

[4] Buzan, in his more recent discussions of the English School (Buzan, 2004), refers to James' ideas fairly extensively in illustrating the School's views.

in the absence of *common culture*, to subject themselves to some basic common institutions of international society.

This argument is fundamental to Manning, for whom states' need to pay formal deference to the authority of international law as law was in the nature of 'a situationally generated pragmatic inevitability' (1972: 328). Bull and Watson would ultimately agree with this line since in their view, the states of Asia and Africa perceived strong interests in accepting the rules and institutions of international society, originating in the West, because they *could not do without* them even in their relations with one another (1984: 433–43). James is even more outspoken:

> to me it seems that when independent political units come into regular contact with each other certain requirements present themselves almost as a matter of logical necessity: some rules are necessary for the regulation of their intercourse, and also, therefore, some agreement on how these rules are to be established or identified; there must be some means of official communication, and with it an understanding that official agents must be personally respected and privileged; and if the collectivity of units is deemed to form a society this carries with it the concept of membership, and hence the necessity for some criterion whereby this political unit is identified as a member and that not. These requirements would seem to be valid whatever the cultural complexion or geographical location of the political entities who establish or later join an international society. (1986b: 466)[5]

That this 'almost logical necessity' thesis only points at best to a potential force embedded in inter-societal dynamics – that, therefore, the supposed near-necessity may not materialize regularly in world-historical terms – is less pertinent here than the fact that James had thought along such ahistorical and mechanistic lines.[6] This, and the

---

[5] This line of thinking is an application to the international sphere of H. L. A. Hart's argument about what he called 'the minimum content of natural law' (Hart, 1961: 189–95). The same source also inspired Bull (1977). Hart's line is basically that, given the characteristics of human beings, their wish to survive, and the nature of the environment in which they live, it is rational, or pragmatically necessary, that social norms governing different societies are found to have a few basic principles in common, which are the sorts that used to be spoken of as natural law principles.

[6] Adam Watson's observation (1992: 318) is pertinent here: 'We may conclude that regulatory arrangements always come into being between civilized polities when the volume of contacts becomes worth regulating. Anything more intimate, a society that goes beyond rules and institutions to shared values and assumptions, has hitherto always developed within a cultural framework, even if some of the values and assumptions are later adopted by communities outside the culture.'

other observations just made, show that the argument from pragmatic needs (rather than cultural commonality) was already an important element in some English School thinkers' view of the emergence of norm-based cooperation in inter-state relations. But Buzan appears to think that this is a special insight that he brings from the American neo-realist camp to the English School (1993: 327). He expresses this point in terms of the distinction between the *Gemeinschaft* and the *Gesellschaft* (1993: 333ff). The former, according to him, is a society that grows out of a common culture, and, unlike the latter, is not built on pragmatic considerations on the part of the units. Further, he sees the English School conception of international society as *Gemeinschaft*-like, and contrasts it to the neo-realist conception which is *Gesellschaft*-like. But his interpretation of the English School's conception of international society probably derives from his focused reading of Wight, according to whom all historical states-systems grew out of a common culture (Wight, 1977: 33), and also his relative neglect of the details, in particular, of Manning's ideas and James' writings.

A similar bias is found more conspicuously in Little, Buzan's close collaborator. According to him:

> At the end of the 1950s, a group of individuals who came later to be known collectively as the English School (ES) began to develop a research programme which offers a radical alternative to established thinking about international relations. (1995: 10)

> The School includes Martin Wight, Herbert Butterfield, Hedley Bull and Adam Watson and others . . . The members of the School came together initially at the instigation of Kenneth Thompson and was identified as the British Committee on the Theory of International Relations [*sic*]. The reference to an English School was made first by [Jones]. (1995: 32, note 1)

Thus, in Little's version, Jones was the first to refer to '*an* English School', but it was really the British Committee on the Theory of International Politics that came later to be known as '*the* English School'.[7] Much as one needs to appreciate the importance of the British Committee as a key contributory factor to the evolution of the English School – after all, two central texts of the English School, *Diplomatic Investigations* (1966) and *The Expansion of International Society* (1984), were direct products of the Committee – Little's literal identification of

---

[7] While himself not equating the two entities, Buzan (2001: 472ff), too, suggests that Jones (1981) was only depicting '*an* English School' (2001: 471; emphasis added).

the two entities is somewhat surprising. Other than mentioning Jones' article in passing, in which, incidentally, he had in fact referred to '*the* English School' rather than '*an* English School', Little pays no attention to the English School debate of the 1980s in which the School's institutional base was seen to be located at the LSE. More importantly, Little does not elaborate on his assertion that the British Committee 'came later to be known as the English School': he simply presents it as if a matter of common knowledge. One noteworthy consequence of this identification of the two bodies is that James, not being a member of the British Committee, is not only excluded from Little's 'English School', but counted among the School's *critics* (1995: 11).

But the issue of the inclusion or exclusion of one particular scholar or another is not a very serious matter – for it would in any case be a mistake to think of the English School as a club-like entity demarcating its members *clearly* from the outsiders. That is, of course, one reason why the English School could *not* be equated with the British Committee, which was an exclusive club. More importantly, Little's idea of the English School's identity and his resultant focus on the works of Wight and Bull at the expense of certain other writers, as well as a slight slant he gave to his reading of those two scholars, led him to argue that the English School's approach should *not* be identified exclusively with the international society perspective on world politics, but that they should, in fact, be seen as advocating pluralism, the international society perspective being only one of the three perspectives they offer.

There is undeniably some truth in Little's contention here. To appreciate this, it is necessary at this point to remind ourselves of Wight's well-known tripartite classification of the traditions of international thought (or 3Rs) and Bull's incorporation of it in his discussion of world politics, and to try to locate the central tenet of the English School in the greater scheme of things.

According to Wight, there are three traditions of international thought: 'Rationalism', 'Realism' and 'Revolutionism'. Wight's 'Rationalism' (also referred to by the label 'Grotian') should not be confused with the doctrine, also called 'rationalism' in the American political science of international relations, according to which states, the key actors in the arena of world politics, are rational utility-maximizers (Keohane, 1989b). The Rationalist tradition of international thought, in Wight's terminology, takes the view that, despite the formally anarchical structure of world politics, inter-state relations are governed by normative principles in the light of which states can, and to a remarkable degree do, behave reasonably towards one another (Wight, 1991, 13–14). Now, the Rationalist paradigm was a third view, the *via media*, juxtaposed to two others: Realism and Revolutionism, also known as the 'Machiavellian' (or 'Hobbesian') and the 'Kantian' traditions respectively in Wight's nomenclature. Realism sees in the anarchical structure of the states-system that emerged from Western Christendom a condition under which war is a perpetual possibility between any states, where therefore 'political action is most regularly necessitous' (Wight, 1966a: 26), and which thus makes plausible an interpretation of international politics as 'the realm of recurrence and repetition' (Wight, 1996a: 26). Revolutionism, by contrast, advances an entirely different – progressivist – interpretation of world history. It is distinguished from the other two by its insistence that 'it was only at a superficial and transient level that international politics was about relations among states at all' (Bull, 1991: xii). As Bull explains:

> [According to Revolutionism] at a deeper level [international politics] was about relations among human beings of which states were composed. The ultimate reality was the community of mankind, which existed potentially, even if it did not exist actually, and was destined to sweep the system of states into limbo.   (Bull, 1991: xii)

At the end of this historical process, according to Revolutionism, lay a world of justice and peace.[8]

Wight, who popularized this tripartite understanding of international thought in Britain,[9] seems to have been somewhat of an enigma to his students: which tradition did *he* fall under? To this, Bull answers as follows, resisting the temptation to force Wight into any one pigeonhole:

> It is a truer view of him to regard him as standing outside the three traditions, feeling the attraction of each of them but unable to come to rest within any one of them, and embodying in his own life and thought the tension among them.   (Bull, 1991)

In his *The Anarchical Society*, Bull has translated this Wightianism, or what, in Bull's interpretation, was Wight's position, to a related claim that there are three elements in modern world politics, captured by the Realist, Rationalist, and Revolutionist representations of the world.

---

[8] For a detailed critique of Wight's and Bull's treatment of Kant as a Revolutionist in their sense, see Chapter 5.

[9] See, for example, the taken-for-granted way in which Wight's tripartite classification is used in Goodwin (1973).

According to Bull, just as no single tradition of thought is to be favoured at the expense of the others, no single model of world politics – power-political states-system, regulated international society, or transnational solidarity and conflict – can be said fully and accurately to depict the world (1977: 41–2).

It is these parallel claims of Wight, as interpreted by Bull, and of Bull himself that give considerable plausibility to Little's interpretation that pluralism is the essence of the English School. It may even be that, as Little (2000) maintains, these three approaches, Realism, Rationalism and Revolutionism embody, or can be interpreted as embodying, distinct social scientific methodologies, positivism, hermeneutics and critical social theory. But, as Little himself acknowledges, the English School writers 'have seen it as one of their central tasks to create the conceptual space needed to examine international society' (2000: 396). Certainly, this was 'not to the exclusion of realist and revolutionist ideas' (Little, 2000: 398). Indeed, the English School's view of international politics overlaps to some extent with a moderate version of Realism, which is unsurprising when we note that, according to Wight himself, the three categories dovetail and are indistinctive at the edges (Wight, 1991: 158). It remains the case, however, that the English School writers tended to see themselves as drawing special attention to those aspects of world politics which are best captured by Rationalism or the international society perspective.

This is particularly true of Manning and James (James, 1964, 1973a, 1986a, 1989, 1993; Manning, 1975). For Little, however, this observation would not undermine his contention since these two scholars, not being members of the British Committee, were outside of *his* English School. But, as was already noted, Little does not defend his view that the English School was just another name for the British Committee. In any case, even though Bull and Wight, the two main figures of Little's English School, never suggested that the international society or Rationalist perspective captured *everything* about world politics, it is clear from their writings as a whole that their emphasis was on the key importance of that particular perspective. Thus, while they never entirely rejected Realist depictions of international relations, they did not articulate the Realist perspective in the way they, or Bull in particular, elaborated on the Rationalist one. In any case, they were quite unsympathetic to Revolutionism (Bull, 1977, 2000b; Wight, 1991), and their discussion of world society (see, in particular, Bull, 1977) was seriously underdeveloped, as Little (2000) is himself aware. Wight confessed that his 'prejudices are Rationalist' (1991: 268) and that he became 'more Rationalist and less Realist' (1991: 268) in the course of the lectures on International Theory he gave at the LSE. Bull would not have written so extensively in defence of the international society of states and its historically evolved institutions, nor would he have written so approvingly of Grotius's contribution to making it possible to conceive of sovereign states as forming a society (Bull, 1990), had he not thought that the Rationalist perspective was of particular significance. Indeed, according to Bull, the Rationalist perspective 'provides the constitutional principle in terms of which international relations today are in fact conducted' (1990: 93).[10]

In this connection, we may recall the following observation by Jackson (1996: 213): 'as represented by Wight [1991] and Bull [1977], the "English School" is a more comprehensive academic enterprise [than Realism] which emphasises the interactive relationship between all three of these basic human inclinations in international relations [i.e., Realism, Rationalism and Revolutionism of Wight]'. But Jackson also added: 'Rationalism or "Grotianism" is, of course, at the heart of that relationship' (1996: 213). This can be understood to mean that, in Jackson's view, the English School, as represented by Wight and Bull, saw in Rationalism a particularly significant way to represent world politics in the modern period. By comparison, Little's characterization of the English School as advocating pluralism tends to give a misleading impression that all the three elements of world politics were held by them to be of equal significance, and cannot therefore be accepted without seriously qualifying what is meant by 'advocating pluralism'.[11]

---

[10] Here is Bull's assessment: 'The importance of Grotius lies in the part he played in establishing the idea of international society – an idea that provides one of the several paradigms in terms of which we have thought about international relations in modern times, and that, for better or worse, provides the constitutional principle in terms of which international relations today are in fact conducted' (1990: 93).

[11] See, in this connection, also Buzan (2001). Buzan's argument is that whereas '[t]he main thrust of the English School's work has been to uncover the nature and function of international societies, and to trace their history and development' (2001: 477), the School's approach is intrinsically pluralistic, and its Realist and Revolutionist elements, focusing on the working of the international system and the evolution of world society, respectively, can be developed further. To the extent that this implies that the English School's work on international society was just a phase in their research programme, it does not strike as an accurate representation of the intentions of the School's central figures. To the extent that this shows a commitment to engage constructively with the potentials of the English School, it is to be commended. See Buzan (2004) for the latest development.

32

In any event, Little's pronouncement in 1995 that the British Committee had *come to be known as* the English School is considerably at odds with the rough consensus that existed in the 1980s in the IR profession regarding the identity of the English School. It appears, however, that he characterized the English School in that manner under the influence of a new interpretation that was emerging in some quarters which culminated in Dunne's publication of his book (1998) with a subtitle *A History of the English School*.

Dunne (1998) on the English School

Dunne is the author who has done most to make the IR community appreciate the importance of the British Committee in the evolution of the English School. Even though, unlike Little, he does not literally equate the British Committee with the English School, he offers a picture of the School in which key members of the Committee are given high positions, and which thereby challenges the older view of its identity. For example, according to his considered view, 'Manning and Northedge are not members of the School' (1998: 15). It needs to be noted of course that, in line with the prevailing view, Wight, Bull and Vincent remain the central figures of Dunne's English School, but Butterfield is given a prominent place because of his chairmanship of the British Committee, and, much more doubtfully, Carr is treated as a member because of 'the importance key thinkers like Bull and Vincent attached to his work' (Dunne, 1998: 36).

Dunne's guidelines for identifying the members of his English School are threefold: (1) self-identification with a particular tradition of inquiry; (2) an interpretive approach; and (3) international theory as normative theory (1998: 6–9). In the abstract, these criteria do not seem so efficacious in making his idea of the English School diverge much from the older conception. If anything, they appear too general to be capable of delineating his subject-matter clearly. However, in translating his first membership criterion into 'awareness of a body of literature, a set of central questions and a common agenda' (1998: 6), what he had in mind in more concrete terms appears to be a collaborative grouping of researchers working together on a set project – of the sort exemplified well by the British Committee. The outsiders to the Committee are therefore liable to be excluded even if they had belonged to the same *tradition of inquiry* in a broader sense. The second membership criterion is reminiscent of the stress on empathetic understanding and interpretation treated by Suganami (1983) and Wilson (1989) as a distinctive methodological feature of the English School. But what they were pointing to was the approach that straightforwardly insisted that we must understand the cultural and institutional assumptions of those who speak and act in the name of the states in order to be able to make sense of what goes on in international relations. By contrast, what Dunne has in mind, in substance, is the approach associated with Wight's 'international theory', which profoundly influenced Bull – namely an attempt to interpret what goes on in world politics in the light of the three or more Western traditions of international thought identified in the ideas of international lawyers, political philosophers, diplomats and state leaders. Those who stressed an interpretive approach as indispensable to the study of international relations in Suganami's and Wilson's sense, but did not share Wight's interests in patterns of international thought (and practice), such as Manning in particular, are therefore liable to be excluded from the list.[12]

There is much to be said for the representation of the English School that highlights the work of the British Committee and treats it as an institutional base for the School's achievements, an important site in the history of the evolution of the English School's research agenda. Still, Dunne's exclusion of Manning and inclusion of Carr cannot go unchallenged. Of course, as was remarked earlier, the issue of the inclusion or exclusion of one particular scholar or another may not be a very serious matter. However, Manning had been such a central figure in the earlier conception of the School that Dunne's exclusion of him is not of marginal significance. Nor is Dunne's inclusion of Carr inasmuch as this extremely influential scholar had never seriously been treated as a member of the English School in earlier discussions, Buzan's brief reference to him (1993) as belonging to the School being one exception to this rule. Clearly, the combined effect of Manning's exclusion and Carr's inclusion is not of negligible significance, and therefore each case deserves some re-examination.

As for Manning, even though he was not invited to join the British Committee, he certainly was a key figure – a foundational figure even – in the cluster of thinkers in twentieth-century Britain who contributed to making international society the central focus of academic speculation

---

[12] The sense in which Dunne attributes 'normative' theorizing to the English School – his third membership criterion – is rather unclear. The School's attitude towards the issues of values and norms in the study of international relations will be discussed fully in Chapter 3.

about international relations. We should note here that making the society of states the central focus of IR is precisely what Dunne means by 'inventing international society' (1998: xii), which is said by him to be the central concern of the English School (1998: xii).

Of course, international society was never 'invented'. Rather, it gradually came to be grounded in thought and practice through a very long process of sedimentation. Classical writers on international law, such as Grotius, Pufendorf, Wolff and Vattel, as well as positivist writers of the nineteenth and early twentieth centuries who stressed the 'specific character of international law', all made their intellectual contributions to this process.[13] But the concept of international society, and a particular conception of it, which drew attention to its unique character as a realm formally anarchical but substantively orderly, became a focal point of the university teaching of International Relations in Britain. This is largely due to Manning's formative influence. He obtained a chair of International Relations at the LSE in 1930, and for over thirty years he was the head of the undergraduate programme in IR. Wight and Bull, who made very important contributions in furthering the study of international society, had been invited by Manning to join the LSE, where he was very keen to build a united vehicle of undergraduate education in International Relations (Suganami, 2001a). If, as Dunne rightly acknowledges, the primary aim of the English School was to make international society a central concern of the study of international relations, stories of the School that do not include Manning as a major figure are seriously incomplete.

It is worth noting at this juncture that Nicholas Wheeler, while quoting Dunne's book as an authoritative source on the English

---

[13] Grotius ([1646]1925) argued that despite the absence of a higher authority, the relations of sovereigns are subject to legal constraints and in so doing he contributed to the emergence of the idea of a society of states. This idea (of sovereign states, rather than sovereigns, forming a society) can, however, be said to have arisen only after states came to be seen as moral persons coexisting in an international state of nature. Manning shows his awareness of this point when he distinguishes the (early modern) Grotian concept of the society of sovereigns from what he called the (modern) 'neo-Grotian' idea of the society of sovereign states (Manning, 1975: 69). This idea, stemming from Hobbes's ([1651]1962) analogy of the state of nature with the relations of sovereigns, was gradually worked out by Pufendorf ([1688]1935) and Wolff ([1764]1934), culminating in Vattel's ([1758]1916) conception of a society of states. Positivist international lawyers and legal theorists of the nineteenth century and early twentieth century considered international law as a law of a specific kind – between states, not above states. The idea that international society, despite its formal anarchy, is still societal corresponds to the view that international law, while decentralized, is still a legal system (Jellinek, 1922: 379; Kelsen, 1967).

School, has nevertheless considered it appropriate to include Manning among those 'usually' treated as its members (2000: 6); and further that Chris Brown, in the second edition of his *Understanding International Relations* (2001), dropped his earlier reference to Manning being an outsider to the English School – even though he has not found it fit to include him in his account of the School.

Inasmuch as Dunne's exclusion of Manning can be seen as a minor corollary to his serious revisionist attempt to shift the focus away from the traditional centre of attention towards the then relatively unknown, but crucially important factor, the British Committee, there is little to be said against him – except that the exclusion of Manning from the English School is not a necessary corollary. A discussion of the English School that pays full attention to the writings, emanating from the collaborative work within the Committee, need by no means neglect the works of those who were not invited to join the Committee – as the discussion in Chapter 2 will demonstrate.[14]

Dunne's inclusion of Carr in the English School is also problematic. It is curious that, unlike in the case of Manning, the fact that Carr, too, was never invited to join the British Committee (Dunne, 1998: 93) is not made to count. Thus Dunne treats Carr ultimately as a member, though 'a dissident' (1998: 38), of the English School, despite his judgement that he does not satisfy a key condition of the membership of a school, that is, 'the conscious act of identification with a particular community of scholars' (1998: 12–13). This move is significant to note in that Dunne had treated Manning as an outsider substantially because of his judgement that he did not satisfy this particular 'necessary condition' (1998: 6), Manning's exclusion from the British Committee being a key manifestation, for Dunne, of this lack of sense of community.[15]

---

[14] For Dunne, 'the clinching reason for being suspicious of Manning's inclusion in the English School concerns the racial exclusions built in to his conception of international society, something Wight rejected on Christian grounds, and Bull and Vincent because of their belief in racial equality' (2000: 233). It is doubtful, however, that racial exclusions – a racist principle – can be said to be built into Manning's conception of international society as any constitutionally independent political community, regardless of race, was included in international society as he saw it. See Suganami (2003) for a more detailed discussion of racism/West-centricity in Manning and other English School writers.

[15] It may be added here that the idea of someone being 'a dissident' within a community *without* the conscious act of identification with it makes little sense.

Dunne's chief reason for considering Carr as a member of the English School is the importance its key members like Bull and Vincent attached to his work (Dunne, 1998: 36). But this is not a strong enough argument for including Carr specifically in the English School – for it is difficult to think of a key member of the entire IR community of the generation of Bull and Vincent who did *not* attach considerable significance to Carr's thinking about international relations. Furthermore, there is not the slightest doubt that Manning was far more important than Carr when judged specifically in terms of their respective contributions towards answering what Dunne identifies at one point as the central question for English School international theory – 'what is international society?' (Dunne, 1998: 8). As Bull rightly noted, '[t]he idea of international society – of common interests and common values perceived in common by modern states, and of rules and institutions deriving from them – is scarcely recognized in [Carr's] *The Twenty Years' Crisis* (Bull, 2000c: 137). In that book, Carr has a very short section on international community, but his argument concerning its ideational and constructed nature (1946: 162), noted by Dunne (1998: 34), is in fact strongly reminiscent of the line Manning had taken with increasing stress at least since 1936 (Manning, 1936: 1975). If one of them influenced the other in this area, it is more likely that Manning influenced Carr than Carr did Manning. It may also be added that Carr, in the Preface to the first edition of *The Twenty Years' Crisis* (1939), acknowledged his indebtedness to Manning.

Perhaps unsurprisingly, the publication of Dunne's book temporarily reopened the 'English School debate' (Dunne, 2000a, 2001; Knudsen, 2000, 2001; Makinda, 2000, 2001; Suganami, 2000, 2001c). Nonetheless, there is no doubt at all that his book has made a major impact on the way the IR community now thinks of the English School. Roger Epp's statement, quoted earlier, that he 'followed Dunne in defining the English school primarily around a Wight-Bull-Vincent axis, leaving C. A. W. Manning to the side' (1998: 48), illustrates this well. In any case, a critical discussion of Dunne's specific claims about Manning and Carr is not meant to undermine the value of his contributions, and in particular the attention he has drawn to the work of the British Committee, untouched in the 1980s discussions about the English School. Dunne's book certainly added a new – and indispensable – insight into our understanding of the School's contributions.

Within the IR profession, not only in Britain but also in other parts of the world, the existence of the English School is no longer seriously in doubt, and there is a broad consensus about who its leading figures are.[16] There is also a strong interest now, partly orchestrated by Buzan's call (2001) to 'reconvene the English school', or to enhance intellectual collaboration on the model of the British Committee with a view to making scholarly contributions further along the lines set out by some of the School's classical texts. Twenty years after the Jones article, the School now appears alive and well again – with, one may add, 'the core of its extant membership' 'still in its prime' and 'young recruits constantly coming forward'.

The English School approach, however, is no longer seen primarily as embodied in the ahistorical perspective of Manning or the study of the formal structure of contemporary international society which developed under his intellectual leadership. More historically based works stemming from collaboration within the British Committee are now highlighted as containing the English School's key achievements.[17] But this by no means entails that, in our engagement with the English School tradition, all that we should concern ourselves with is the legacy of historical scholarship of the leading British Committee members. For one thing, as will be examined closely in Chapter 3, the attitudes towards history they exhibit are not always very clear-cut or consistent. Furthermore, as will be shown in Chapter 2, English School works are closely interwoven, forming a tapestry of arguments extending from the more ahistorical and formal, through functional and normative, to the more historical and historical-sociological. A more comprehensive appreciation of the English School as an intellectual movement, if this is to be desired, can only come from a thorough examination of a wide range of texts emanating from this exceptionally close-knit, yet to some extent also diverse, community of scholars in the study of international relations.

---

[16] Buzan's most recent work (2004) treats Manning as among his English School authors, but excludes Carr, whom he considers a Realist (Buzan, 2004: 30–1) – in turn a distorted representation given Carr's overall argument in his classic work (see Carr, 1939).

[17] 'Forum on the English School', published in *Review of International Studies* 27(3), has 'Foreword' by Adam Watson (2001), one of the surviving members of the British Committee. It is clear that Watson takes Buzan's call to 'reconvene the English School' as meaning 'relaunching the British Committee'.

The nature of the English School

In the light of the foregoing analysis of the formation of the idea of the English School, it is possible to offer a number of important observations about the School's key characteristics.

First, those who discuss the English School think of it more than just a school of thought united simply by the outward similarities of views expressed on a particular set of issues. They have in mind a group of scholars the similarities of whose views are attributable in varying degrees to intellectual influences, interactions and collaborations, based on the particularly intimate personal or professional relationships amongst them. This is a specially strong theme in Dunne's conception of the English School. Even Wilson, according to whom the English School formed a school of thought primarily in the sense that 'the thought of the scholars in question is sufficiently similar for them to be grouped together, and thereby distinguished from other International Relations scholars' (1989: 52), rightly draws attention to the fact that the scholars in question formed an '*intimate* intellectual grouping' (1989: 55; emphasis added).

Secondly, however, the English School is more cluster-like than club-like as an entity. Thus Dunne, who pays considerable attention in his book to the membership issue, suggests nevertheless, that the English School does not have fixed or immutable boundaries (Dunne, 1998: 5). This means that it is a mistake to think of the English School as having clear insiders and outsiders. The British Committee on the Theory of International Politics had a very strong sense of exclusiveness from the beginning, but, as Dunne (2000a: 229) rightly notes, the Committee and the English School cannot be equated, even though some leading members of the Committee were also those who came to be treated as central figures of the English School.

Thirdly, the *historicity* of the English School must be recognized. This means a number of things. The first is that it is anachronistic to suppose the School to have been a well-defined entity from the start. Such a supposition leads one to assume that a clear set of membership criteria applied from the beginning or that there must have been a collective understanding on the part of the members from the start that they formed a group. But the English School did not come into existence on a particular day by self-proclamation or confirmation of its identity on the part of its supposed members. Rather, it had an uncertain beginning, in which there was no clear awareness either on the part of those supposedly within or without that the line dividing them was necessarily any more significant than any other plausible boundaries. What stimulated the emergence of the English School was an external proclamation – by Roy Jones. Thus Dunne, who stresses the element of self-identification as a key to the presence of a school, notes in passing that Jones 'helped to create' the English School (1998: 3).

What has happened is a gradual formation of the English School in the collective consciousness of the IR community: the English School, not easily or uncontroversially recognizable earlier, has come to be more readily seen and treated as an entity. A number of factors contributed to this historical process of emergence. First, there really were some overlapping connections and similarities among some of those whom Jones first wrote of as forming a school and a few others he did not mention. Second, a sufficient number of commentators in the IR profession began to talk of 'the English School' as forming a distinct grouping in the study of international relations. Third, most of those who were said to form this grouping, and were still alive, accepted, or did not strongly resist, this labelling. The English School is an entity that emerged historically as people – the 'IR people' – gradually came to think of it as an entity.

Given such a process of its emergence, it is not surprising that there is some dispute as to the School's pre- or early history. There were some objectively present similarities and connections, but depending on which particular connections are stressed and which similarities are highlighted, different stories are constructed as to the origins of the English School – either by its historians or by its subsequently self-identifying members. This is another sense, a very important sense, in which the historicity of the English School must be recognized – it is a historically constituted entity, *through the act of historical recounting*.

The disagreement regarding the centrality or otherwise of certain figures arises from the fact that who one includes in, or excludes from, one's discussion of the early life and works of the English School is inevitably a function of what story one wants to tell about that entity. However, what story one feels able to tell about the subject is to some extent also a function of who one thinks were the School's more central figures. And although there is no point in discussing 'who was in and who was out' in a categorical way, because there never has been any rigid boundary to the English School that would make such a question meaningful to raise in the first place, it does not follow that any interpretation of the centrality or otherwise of a particular scholar is as good as any other, or that it does not matter who is considered central or peripheral.

Finally, the historicity of the English School also means that it takes on the character of an intellectual *tradition*, thereby forcing the School to transform itself from a particular grouping who worked together at one time, towards a succession of scholars who identify themselves as part of the biography of a subject, called the English School, in which they depict themselves as learning from and attempting to modify the methods and arguments of the earlier scholars. At this stage, the 'we' feeling uniting the School becomes a historical consciousness. There is little doubt that many of those working in response to Buzan's initiative to reconvene the English School share such a consciousness, though again it would be a mistake to consider that such an awareness had a clear beginning. It gradually grew through a historical, and historicizing, process.[18]

The English School, it appears on the basis of the foregoing discussion, is best seen as a historically evolving cluster of (so far) mainly UK-based contributors to International Relations. They were initially active in the latter part of the twentieth century and broadly agree in treating Rationalism, in Wight's sense, as a particularly important way to interpret world politics. Their views and intellectual dispositions share a family resemblance due partly to the very conspicuous personal or professional ties. These ties were initially formed at the London School of Economics, but later extended to other academic institutions, and were also, to a large extent independently, cultivated within the exclusive British Committee on the Theory of International Politics. The School being a *cluster* – sharing a pattern of thought and involving personal or professional connections – rather than an exclusive *club*, as the British Committee clearly was, there is no rigid boundary between its 'insiders and outsiders'. There are many IR scholars worldwide whose views also share some family resemblance with the opinions of those associated with the English School – though, in their case, not due to close personal or professional ties (Nardin, 1983).

Such a characterization of the English School suggests (and accords with the view) that C. A. W. Manning, Martin Wight, Hedley Bull, Alan James, John Vincent and Adam Watson have a strong case to be

---

[18] See Carr (1986) on how (historical) identity is produced by (historicizing) narrative.

treated as the School's central figures in its early stages, though this is not in the least to insist that there are no others, or that there will not be a slightly different, but perhaps equally plausible, conception of the English School. Herbert Butterfield, in particular, would seem to have a reasonably good case to be included in the list, though his direct contribution to the study of international relations is somewhat limited (Butterfield, 1966a, 1966b, 1972).[19] Butterfield would not have objected to being counted as an important figure in the English School as this has come to be constructed in the dominant narratives of the 1990s; but of course these narratives had placed the British Committee, and with it, Butterfield himself, as their key subjects (see, in particular, Dunne, 1998: 73).

One way to characterize these writers would be to label them 'institutionalists', for their main or initial focus of attention is the institutional structure of the relations of states, which, to them – hence their label 'Rationalists' – are marked by a considerable degree of order and some degree of justice (Suganami, 1983). But the label 'institutionalists' is more commonly used to refer to a group of North American writers led by Robert Keohane and others, and 'Rationalists', unfortunately, is an ambiguous title. In any case, the name 'the English School' has already taken root within the IR community worldwide. What its leading authors' main concerns and arguments are regarding the nature of world politics is the subject of the next chapter.

---

[19] See Hall (2002) for an excellent discussion on Butterfield. See also Hall (2001).

2 The argument of the English School

There are three basic and inter-related orientations in the English School's investigations into world politics. They may be labelled 'structural', 'functional' and 'historical'. Manning's *The Nature of International Society* (1975), James' *Sovereign Statehood* (1986a), and parts of Bull's *The Anarchical Society* (1977) are examples of the first type. Their main contributions are in the identification of the institutional structure of contemporary international society. The second type is illustrated by parts of Bull's *The Anarchical Society*, which added to a structural study an extended investigation into the workings and relative merits of the existing institutional structure. Vincent's *Nonintervention and International Order* (1974) and *Human Rights and International Relations* (1986a) also fall into this second category, although in the latter Vincent's focus has shifted from the instrumental to the more explicitly ethical. The third type advances the study of the historical evolution of the institutional structure of international relations. Wight's *Systems of States* (1977), Bull and Watson's *The Expansion of International Society* (1984), Gong's *The Standard of Civilization in International Relations* (1984), and Watson's *The Evolution of International Society* (1992) exemplify this type of study. Among the more recent works, Wheeler's *Saving Strangers* (2000) and Jackson's *The Global Covenant* (2000) are notable contributions to the second type of inquiry as Buzan and Little's *International Systems in World History* (2000) is to the third.[1]

---

[1] Wheeler (2000) and Jackson (2000) deal with both functional and normative issues; the latter is treated under the general rubric of the functional analysis in this chapter because to say that a certain value ought, or ought not, to be pursued by states in international society is to suggest that international society is or is not a framework which functions well for the purpose of achieving such values. The ambivalence of earlier English School writers towards normative questions is discussed further in Chapter 3.

These texts are closely interwoven, adding further credence to the claim that the phenomenon we are dealing with here deserves to be discussed under the rubric of a school – even though the Buzan and Little volume is arguably more of a corrective to Waltz's neo-realist picture of the world than a work that belongs straightforwardly to the English School tradition. This chapter aims to present an intellectual portrait of the English School through a detailed interrogation of a number of these key texts which have emerged in the past few decades.

The structural study of international society

Alexander Wendt has remarked that '[w]hen IR scholars today use the word structure they almost always mean Waltz's materialist definition as a distribution of capabilities' (1999: 249). This is not so in the British study of international relations where Rationalism, in Wight's sense, has been a dominant interpretation of world politics. In spite of the formally anarchical structure of the world of states, international relations are governed by rules, and therefore, substantively, the interactions of states exhibit a degree of order that could not, under anarchy, normally be expected. This is the essence of Rationalism, and one of the central tenets of the English School, as captured in the title of Bull's chief work, *The Anarchical Society*. The relative dominance of Rationalism over Realism in Britain has meant that the word 'structure' is more closely associated with the institutional framework of the world than with its polarity, the pattern of the distribution of national capabilities in a brute sense. Characteristically, where the English School authors discuss 'great powers', they invariably have in mind the socially recognized status of a small number of powerful states, rather than merely their outstanding military capabilities (see e.g., Bull, 1977). Integral to the English School's institutional orientation in the study of international relations is their view, explained below, that a world of states is an entity markedly different from an ordinary domestic society.

Against the domestic analogy: Manning, Wight and Bull

The Anarchical Society was a culmination of a decade of thinking on the part of its author, who, in one of his earliest essays, had formulated his central preoccupation in a brief but significant footnote as follows:

Anarchy: 'Absence of rule; disorder; confusion' (*O.E.D.*) The term here is used exclusively in the first of these senses. The question with which the essay is concerned is whether in the international context it is to be identified also with the second and the third.

(1966a: 35, note 2)

In the immediately preceding footnote, Bull acknowledges his indebtedness to Wight and Manning (1966a: 35, note 1). Bull's deep indebtedness to Wight is clearly visible throughout this article, which freely makes use of the body of literature and categories now familiar to the readers of Wight's posthumously published work, *International Theory: The Three Traditions* (1991). Bull's indebtedness to Manning, by contrast, centres on just one key concept, the domestic analogy, of whose validity in the study of international relations the two scholars were highly sceptical. In a lecture delivered at the Geneva Institute of International Relations in August 1935, presaging much of what he subsequently taught about the nature of international society, Manning had stated as follows:

> Given, then, a milieu where the units are persons only in idea, where the foundation of ordinary intercourse is the notion of sovereignty, and where law is not even superficially an instrument of social control, the problem of promoting collectivism must, I conceive, be one where analogies drawn from domestic experience may admit, at best, of only the most hesitant application. (1936: 165)

In the same lecture, Manning (1936: 174) went on to use the term 'the domestic analogy' to refer to the application of ideas based on domestic experience to the discussion of international relations. Notwithstanding his support for the League of Nations, he was critical of an unreflective, and what was to him an excessive, reliance on this analogy. In fact, he considered the society of states to be *sui generis*, which was also his reason for believing in International Relations as a distinct academic discipline, to be distinguished, in particular, from Politics within states (Suganami, 2001a). Exactly thirty years after Manning's Geneva lecture, Bull's 'Society and Anarchy in International Relations' appeared in Butterfield and Wight's *Diplomatic Investigations*. Bull's article begins with a clear formulation of one of the central themes of International Relations, which is worth quoting in full:

> Whereas men within each state are subject to a common government, sovereign states in their mutual relations are not. This anarchy it is possible to regard as the central fact of international life and the starting-point of theorizing about it. A great deal of the most fruitful

reflection about international life has been concerned with tracing the consequences in it of this absence of government. We can, indeed, give some account in these terms of what it is that distinguishes the international from the domestic field of politics, morals, and law.

One persistent theme in the modern discussion of international relations has been that as a consequence of this anarchy states do not form together any kind of society; and that if they were to do so it could only be by subordinating themselves to a common authority. One of the chief intellectual supports of this doctrine is what may be called the domestic analogy, the argument from the experience of individual men in domestic society to the experience of states, according to which the need of individual men to stand in awe of a common power in order to live in peace is a ground for holding that states must do the same. The conditions of an orderly social life, on this view, are the same among states as they are within them: they require that the institutions of domestic society be reproduced on a universal scale. (Bull, 1966a: 35)

In this article, Bull demonstrated why the domestic analogy was not a fruitful line to follow, and argued that, despite anarchy, international society could, and did, exist. In his other contribution to the Butterfield and Wight volume, entitled 'Grotian Conception of International Society', Bull discussed what type of legal regime should govern the society of states, and here, too, he expressed his serious reservations about the reliance on the domestic analogy, arguing that the twentieth-century tendency in international law to emulate the standards of domestic law was misconceived and counterproductive from the viewpoint of enhancing the orderly coexistence of states (Bull, 1966b). A similar point was made also by Manning, who remarked as follows in one of his last major essays:

It is, submittedly, more realistic to see international law as law of a different species, than as merely a more primitive form of what is destined some day to have the nature of a universal system of non-primitive municipal law. (1972: 319)

Bull's rejection of the domestic analogy led him to argue that international society, while anarchical in structure, had its own historically grown, indigenous, non-domestic-type institutions, through the working of which, order was maintained in world politics at the inter-state level. According to Bull (1977), these institutions were: the balance of power, international law, diplomacy, war and the concert of great powers. In his identification of these 'institutions', Bull may have been influenced by Wight, who had suggested that the institutions of international society were 'according to its nature' – 'diplomacy, alliances, guarantees, war and neutrality' (1978: 111; emphasis added) – and also that – following Lassa Oppenheim (1912, 1:80) – the balance of power was a precondition for the effective functioning of international law (Wight, 1966c: 172). But, unlike Wight, who seems to have been interested more in the writings of some classical jurists than in the operation of international law in the contemporary world, Bull rightly counted international law as one of his five institutions of international society. But the person who put a real stress on international law as the backbone of international order was Manning, a student of Jurisprudence who had turned to International Relations (Suganami, 2001a).

Manning on international society

There seems little doubt that the prevalence of Rationalism among the British academic specialists in International Relations is due, to some extent, to Manning's foundational effort to draw attention to the uniqueness of international society as a formally anarchical but substantively orderly social environment (Suganami, 2001a). Whereas Wight was inclined to treat this particular stance as one of the three main traditions of thought about international politics, and expended much energy in gathering specimens of Rationalist thinking from Grotius onwards, there was no explicit attempt on Manning's part to build his understanding of international relations by recourse to the classical literature. Manning always presented his picture of the world as something he himself saw, or understood to be, out there. Out there in the world, according to him, were states – personified entities, as he stressed – whose governments acted in their names, and carried on interacting with one another on the basis of a certain set of assumptions, a primary one being that sovereign states were members of an international society. Another important assumption was that the sovereign states were bound by international law and international morality (Manning, 1972: 318–19; 1975).

Herein, incidentally, lies Manning's simple solution to the (at times confused) discussion regarding the relationship between sovereign statehood and international legal obligation. There is, according to him, no conceptual contradiction between them. It is a fundamental principle of international society, *as it has historically evolved*, that international law creates rights and duties for the states; and although the states, which are members of international society, are called 'sovereign' states, the meaning of the word 'sovereign' in this context differs from that of the same word when used to refer to 'sovereign' person(s) within the state; the term 'sovereign states' simply refers to their status as 'constitutionally insular', or 'constitutionally independent'; in fact, it is only these entities that fully enjoy the rights and duties under international law; and all this is no more than a matter of conventional assumption or what Manning called 'socially prevalent social theory' of international relations, which it was one of his chief aims to expose (Manning, 1972: 305–10; 1975: xxi–xxii, ch. 9).

It was, according to Manning, the prevalence, as orthodox, of such a set of assumptions that made it possible for states to interact with one another in a relatively orderly manner.[2] However, the realm in which this set of assumptions prevailed – the society of states – was at the same time the realm which this very set of assumptions made possible. International society, to Manning, therefore was a socially constructed social reality. International society, as a social reality, provides a context in which particular states formulate and implement their foreign policies; hence Manning's insistence (1954: 67) that the study of the context is indispensable to the study of the interactions of the states. But the context, in turn, is not a naturally given, but a socially constructed environment, subject therefore to interpretation, reinterpretation and reshaping. He wrote:

> Omar Khayyam, when he sang of 'this sorry scheme of things', did not thereby imply that he would have been happier without one . . . And we, too, like him, shall perceive that there already exists a scheme, a sorry one perhaps, but given, and a going concern . . . Yet, while perceiving it as given, we should not mistake its genesis. This scheme was not the work of Nature . . . It is artificial, man-developed – a 'socio-fact' in the jargon of some. What this generation can hope to affect is not so much the present inherited structure of the given scheme of things, man-created though it be; but, the manner in which the coming generation comes to read, re-interpret, and, in reinterpreting, to remould, the scheme. (1975: 8–9)

Thus, in Manning, we find an early example of constructivism in International Relations, predating the current rise of interest in constructivism by a few decades, although neither he nor any other English School writer produced such a detailed work as, for example, Wendt's (1999) on the social construction of international reality (Suganami, 2001d).

---

[2] Wight (1966b: 97), too, spoke of an international social consciousness as a presupposition of international society.

Manning took very seriously the contribution international law made to international order. To him, an orderly coexistence of sovereign states was effectively synonymous with their lawful coexistence, and what was particularly important, from his viewpoint, was to keep alive the orthodox diplomatic assumption that international law is a binding system of norms. As far as this assumption prevailed, he thought, the game of international relations could go on without an umpire; if it were to crumble, civilized intercourse of states would be seriously undermined (Manning, 1972; 1975: preface to the reissue).

Manning's analysis was at the beginning of the formal structure study of international relations in Britain. His approach was followed closely by his former student and colleague, Alan James, whose *Sovereign Statehood* (1986a) is a contribution on that subject that exemplifies well the English School's interest in the formal structure study of world politics. In legal matters, too, James' line (1973b) is very close to Manning's, emphasizing the importance of the binding nature of international law for the maintenance of international order. Perhaps it was in reaction against what was seen as Manning's excessive legalism and the emphasis some of his close followers placed on international law and organizations that Bull advanced a line of argument which deflated the claim of international law and organizations to be the master institutions of international society.

From Manning to Bull

Introducing his *The Anarchical Society*, Bull remarked:

> the approach to order in world politics that is developed here is one that does not place primary emphasis upon international law or international organisation, and which, indeed, treats order as something that can exist and has existed independently of both. Order, it is contended here, does depend for its maintenance upon rules, and in the modern international system (by contrast with some other international systems) a major role in the maintenance of order has been played by those rules which have the status of international law. But to account for the existence of international order we have to acknowledge the place of rules that do not have the status of law. We have also to recognise that forms of international order might exist in the future, and have existed in the past, without rules of international law. It is, I believe, one of the defects of our present understanding of world politics that it does not bring together into common focus those rules of order or coexistence that can be derived from

international law and those rules that cannot, but belong rather to the sphere of international politics.   (1977: xiii–xiv)

The reference here to 'the modern international system' and 'some other international systems' betrays the extent to which, under the influence of Wight, Bull came to be interested in a comparative study of historical states-systems – a dimension conspicuously absent from the writings of Manning and James. But it would be a mistake to interpret the above passage as indicating a major difference between Manning and Bull. Manning certainly placed much emphasis on international law, but he too acknowledged the primacy of international politics to international law, as the following passage reveals:

> The title of this essay ['The Legal Framework in a World of Change'] notwithstanding, it never was the law that provided a framework, even in the most metaphorical sense, for international politics, but always the other way about. At any moment international law is what it is because the facts of international politics are what they are. It is the political framework which reflects itself in the law – and not the law which determines the political framework . . . If international politics occur within and in terms of a framework, it is scarcely within a framework of law. At most it is within a framework of shared diplomatic assumptions, the common premises of all international debate. And this framework, as it happens, cannot fundamentally be considered to have changed [in the fifty-year period of 1919–69, on which Manning was invited to write].
>
> (1972: 318)

What Bull has attempted in *The Anarchical Society* is to identify the content of these 'common premises of all international debate' or the 'framework of shared diplomatic assumptions' within the modern international system in a much more detailed way than Manning had done. In Bull's interpretation (1977: 67–70), such common premises or shared diplomatic assumptions comprise three sets of rules: 'the fundamental or constitutional normative principle of world politics' in the present era, 'the rules of coexistence', and 'the rules concerned to regulate co-operation among states – whether on a universal or on a more limited scale'. The fundamental principle, according to Bull, 'identifies the idea of a society of states, as opposed to such alternative ideas as a universal empire, a cosmopolitan community of individual human beings, or a Hobbesian state of nature or state of war, as the supreme normative principle of the political organisation of mankind' (1977: 67–8). This is identical in substance to Manning's oft-repeated point that international society is made possible by the prevalence of the orthodox diplomatic assumption that sovereign states form an international society. Bull's 'rules of coexistence' (1977: 69) relate to such basic issues as the control of the use of force by states or making valid agreements between them, and are embodied in general international law, and in a less precise form, in conventional moral ideas about inter-state relations. Bull's 'rules of co-operation' comprise various rules 'that facilitate co-operation, not merely of a political and strategic, but also of a social and economic nature' (1977: 70), and are in fact hard to imagine existing outside of international legal conventions and treaties. Effectively, therefore, Bull's argument is a more complex version of Manning's simple argument (1975: xxi–xxii, 110–11) that international order is sustained by the prevalence of the orthodox diplomatic assumption that sovereign states are bound by international law and international morality.

Bull's already quite complex argument does not end here, however. According to him, the mere recognition of the existence of rules is not sufficient for the maintenance of international order. To be effective, rules must be communicated, administered, interpreted, enforced, legitimized, adapted and protected, and Bull argues that these functions have been fulfilled by what he calls the institutions of international society – the balance of power, international law, diplomacy, war and the concert of the great powers (1977: 56–7, part 2).

Here Bull appears to follow his Oxford teacher, H. L. A. Hart (1961), who suggested that an advanced legal system is characterized by a combination of primary and secondary rules, or rules about behaviour and rules about rules. In a parallel fashion, Bull has suggested that international order has been sustained by a combination of 'rules' *and* 'institutions'.[3] To the extent that Bull's analysis of international order is

---

[3] Bull's own comment on this point was that he did not consciously follow Hart's theory, but that, having the similarity pointed out to him, he could now see that there was a parallel. See Suganami (1983: 2375, n. 43). Buzan's argument (2004: 169) that Bull's 'institutions' derive from his 'rules of co-existence' and that that is why Bull's 'institutions' are (necessarily) 'pluralist', rather than 'solidarist', is hard to fathom. It is clear that 'international law', in particular, is an institution that can embody rules of cooperation, as well as rules of coexistence and constitutional rules. Indeed, it is difficult to imagine, as already noted, Bull's rules of cooperation outside of the international legal system. 'Diplomacy', another of Bull's 'institutions', may be directed towards the achievement of goals associated with 'co-existence', but need not be; it is also an indispensable institution for the attainment of those goals that come under the rubric of 'co-operation' in Bull's scheme. Similarly, 'great powers' may concert for all kinds of goals, not just for those of 'co-existence'. Only 'the balance of power' and 'war' may be said to relate specifically to 'co-existence', and not 'co-operation', in Bull's scheme.

an application of Hart's theory of domestic order, there is a degree of *domestic analogy* in Bull's structure of thought. However, Bull's rejection of that analogy can be seen in his insistence that international order exists despite the absence of institutions at the international level analogous to those of a domestic society, and that international order is maintained by the functioning of those institutions that are peculiar to international relations.

In moving from the discussion of rules to that of institutions, Bull makes an important observation that in the anarchical, or decentralized, world of inter-state relations, it is sovereign states themselves that are chiefly responsible for making the rules effective. States make the rules, and communicate, administer, interpret, enforce, legitimize, adapt and protect them (Bull, 1977: 71–3). This corresponds to James' basic point (1986a) that international society is a society of sovereign states, where only those entities which satisfy the criterion of sovereign statehood, understood as constitutional independence, can enjoy international rights and duties fully as society members. Bull's conception of the role of the states in an anarchical international society also parallels Hans Kelsen's idea (1967: 101–5) of the role of the states in the decentralized international legal order, and was developed further in one of Bull's most important essays, 'The State's Positive Role in World Affairs' (2000b).[4] In noteworthy contrast to Waltz's neo-realist conception (1979), which effectively equates self-help with self-preservation by military means, Bull's conception of self-help under anarchy has to do with 'helping to make the rules effective' – or socialized collaboration in what Manning had heuristically called the game of 'let's-play-sovereign-states' (1975: xxviii). Identifying the constitutive and regulative rules of this 'game' has been the English School writers' first objective. Manning, James, Wight and Bull, taken together, pursued this objective with considerable thoroughness.

International system, international society and world society

It may have been noted that Manning's 'international society' is essentially an idea adopted by those who act and talk in the name of the states to guide and make sense of their own interactions. For him, 'international society' was the name of the game sovereign states

---

[4] Bull, however, considered Kelsen's idea of the decentralized social monopoly of force as wishful thinking. See Bull (1986: 329).

played, and he was keenly aware that the game could deteriorate into a less orderly one (1975: Preface). A similar point could be conveyed by employing Bull's distinction between 'international system' and 'international society'. For him, an 'international system' can already be said to exist when 'states are in regular contact with one another, and where in addition there is interaction between them sufficient to make the behaviour of each a necessary element in the calculations of the other' (1977: 10). By contrast, 'international society' only exists 'when a group of states, conscious of certain common interests and common values, form a society in the sense that they conceive themselves to be bound by a common set of rules in their relations with one another, and share in the working of common institutions' (1977: 13). Bull's distinction has been challenged by James (1993), and this challenge has subsequently been endorsed by Wendt (1999: 254), because, to them, all but the most elementary forms of interaction would require rules so that there really is no clear demarcation between Bull's 'system' and 'society'. Still, it would seem reasonable to suppose that 'the element of international society', as defined by Bull, may become more, or less, pronounced in world politics.

In this line of thinking, 'international society' is not a society of states *out there* in the world, but rather an ideal-type to which any system of states may approximate to varying degrees. However, it must be noted that a group of states will approximate to 'international society' to the extent that they think of themselves as constituting a society of that kind, and that therefore, in Bull's thinking, as in Manning's earlier, 'international society' is not a concept external to the practice of states. In Bull's thinking, the element of international society is in competition with two other elements: that of international system and that of world society, the three ideal types corresponding roughly to the Realist, Rationalist and Revolutionist interpretations of world politics, respectively.[5]

What is noteworthy is that Manning and James, too, acknowledged that to depict the world as a society of sovereign states is not the only way to represent it. Manning noted that there is another layer to the world: 'Within, beneath, alongside, behind and transcending, the

---

[5] This reveals the extent of Wight's influence on Bull. As will be explained in Chapter 3, however, the equation of 'international system' in Bull's terminology with predominantly Realist conditions is only partially valid. But this need not detain us here.

notional society of states, there exists, and for some purposes fairly effectively, the nascent society of all mankind' (1975: 177). According to him, however, it was a concern, not of a 'formal-structure study', but of 'social dynamics proper' (1975: 201), to investigate this human universe, which, he acknowledged, was very complex as it contained many social organisms – 'the peoples, and the people, and the groups, the organisations, and the associations not yet articulated for effective action' (1975: 201).

Manning's distinction between the object of 'formal-structure' study and that of 'global social dynamics' corresponds to James' distinction between 'international society' of sovereign states and what he idiosyncratically called the 'international system', consisting of states and all kinds of non-state actors.[6] It is noteworthy that neither Manning nor James considered the object of 'global social dynamics' to consist of individual human persons. This might be contrasted with the case of Bull, for whom 'the great society of all mankind' (1977: 20) or 'human society as a whole' (1977: 22) consisted of 'individual human beings' (1977: 22). But when Bull talked in this way, he was partly following the classical natural law tradition, in which 'the great society of all mankind' functioned as a normative postulate (Bull, 1977: 20), and was also adding to it a modern assumption that the individuals were the ultimate units of society. Importantly, Bull (1977: 20–2, 276–81) also spoke of 'the global political system' (which he used interchangeably with 'the world political system'), by which he had in mind any historically specific political institutional arrangement that encompassed the whole of humanity. He maintained that this first appeared in the late nineteenth century and early twentieth century and took the form of a global system and society of states (1977: 20–1). But he contended that a new global political system was now emerging which could not be described exhaustively as simply a system or society of states – for other kinds of actors were involved in it (1977: 21; 276–81).[7]

---

[6] James used 'international system' in this sense in his first-year lectures on 'International Society' which he gave for a number of years at Keele University.

[7] Before the emergence of the *global* political system, various *regional* political systems coexisted. Bull conceded that the intermeshing of the various parts of the world was not simply the work of states: 'private individuals and groups played their part as explorers, traders, migrants and mercenaries, and the expansion of the states-system was part of a wider spread of social and economic exchange' (1977: 21). But, he argued, the *political* structure to which these developments gave rise was one simply of a global system and society of states (1977: 21). Bull initially used the two terms *'global* political system' and *'world* political system' interchangeably in a generic sense to denote *any* political

It is noteworthy, however, that while Manning recognized the importance of studying global social dynamics, he did not himself engage in it in any substantive manner, and James effectively dismissed it as too complex to pursue (1989: 223). As for Bull, he acknowledged the moral priority of the 'human society as a whole' to the 'society of states' when he argued that '[o]rder among mankind as a whole' is morally prior to 'order among states' (1977: 21–2). However, he did not make any direct enquiry into the structure or workings of the contemporary human universe as a whole, even though he (1977: 276–7; 2000a, 252) conceded that there is now a global political system of which the system/society of states is only part and that many of the issues that arise within this global political system cannot be satisfactorily dealt with in a framework that confined our attention to the relations of sovereign states alone.

This tendency common among Manning, James and Bull to avoid involving themselves in an empirical study of the human universe as a whole seems consonant with these three Rationalist writers' self-conscious distancing from Revolutionism. According to Wight's tripartite classification, Revolutionism, as we saw, is distinguished from the other two by its insistence that 'it was only at a superficial and transient level that international politics was about relations among states at all' (Wight, 1991: xii). As Bull explains:

> [According to this position] at a deeper level [international politics] was about relations among human beings of which states were composed. The ultimate reality was the community of mankind, which existed potentially, even if it did not exist actually, and was destined to sweep the system of states into limbo.   (Bull, 1991: xii)

---

arrangement governing the whole of mankind (1977: 20–1), but in the final part of *The Anarchical Society*, 'the world political system' is used in the more specific sense of 'the world-wide network of interaction that embraces not only states but also other political actors, both "above" the state and "below" it' (1977: 276). Still, Bull's key contention appears to be that the states-system has always been part of a wider social complex; that, nonetheless, when the states-system first came to cover the whole globe in the late nineteenth and early twentieth centuries, states were by far the most important political actors; but that more recently the global social complex has come to contain a wider variety of politically significant actors. Crucially, however, what is meant by 'political' remains unarticulated. In making sense of Bull's discussion, it is also important to bear in mind that there were normative and empirical aspects to it. The 'great society of all mankind' (which he unquestioningly assumed consisted of individual human persons) was the notion he used on the normative plane, whereas the 'world/global political system' (now, according to him, consisting of state and non-state political actors, though not earlier) related to his empirical concern.

While allowing for a possibility that some day there may be a true *Gemeinschaft* of all the human race, Manning (1972: 310; 1975: 71, 179) was sceptical of the scenario of the withering away of sovereign states. James (1972: 34) effectively discounted such a possibility. Bull (1977: ch. 11) took somewhat more seriously the idea that a new form of world political system (in particular, what he called a new medievalism) might emerge in the future, but he, too, remained persuaded that the sovereign states system continued to be functional and was here to stay.

The functional and historical dimensions of the institutional study of international relations will be dealt with below in turn. For the moment, it is sufficient to note that the writers examined here had a good deal of confidence in the continuing relevance of the existing institutional framework of world politics, structured as a system/society of sovereign states, and because of this their primary focus was on this structure itself. Nonetheless, they were broadly similar in their basic belief that, empirically, the system/society of states was always part of a wider social complex that included state and non-state actors.[8]

The functional study of international society

The English School writers' second objective has been to study how, and how satisfactorily, the institutional structure of the contemporary international society has functioned, and how this compares with other possible institutional structures. The question of how, and how satisfactorily, any kind of institutional structure functions within a particular realm is one that could not meaningfully be addressed without reference to some specific set of goals pertaining to that realm. 'Order' has been the chief preoccupation of the English School writers in this respect (James, 1973b; Manning, 1975: 10), and here Bull's contribution is by far the most far-reaching.

Bull on basic values

The starting point of Bull's argument is that security against violence, observance of agreements and stability of property, private or public, are the three primary goals of society. According to him, every society

---

[8] See Buzan (2004) for his painstaking effort to characterize, in his own way, the structure of this wider global social complex. He sees this complex as a combination of three ideal-type societies: inter-state, inter-human and transnational. These consist of states, individual human persons and transnational actors, respectively, and each is capable of being global or regional.

will be found to aim at satisfying these basic goals, and a society which does not satisfy these goals to some extent hardly deserves its name. To the extent that these goals are met within a given society, that society can be said to be 'orderly'; and, for Bull, 'order' in social life is thus 'a pattern of human activity that sustains' (1977: 5) such goals.

One may expect Bull to argue, by simple analogy, that international society, too, is found to aim, by a number of means, to satisfy the three basic goals, which, when transposed to international relations, will amount to security against inter-state violence, observance of international agreements and respect for sovereignty; and that this society deserves its name because these basic goals are satisfied to some extent. In substance, this is roughly what Bull maintains, but he prefers a more direct approach to analogical reasoning, and focuses on what the members of modern international society, particularly the major powers, have considered to be the goals of that society.[9]

According to Bull (1977: 16ff), there are six such goals: (i) the preservation of the system and society of states itself against challenges to create a universal empire or challenges by supra-state, sub-state and trans-state actors to undermine the position of sovereign states as the principal actors in world politics; (ii) the maintenance of the independence or external sovereignty of individual states; (iii) peace in the sense of the absence of war among member states of international society as the normal condition of their relationship, to be breached only in special circumstances and according to principles that are generally accepted; (iv) limitation of inter-state violence; (v) observance of international agreements; and (vi) the stability of what belongs to each state's sovereign jurisdiction. Of these, the last three are acknowledged to be international applications of the three basic goals of any society that Bull had identified. Looking at these goals enumerated by Bull, we may be struck by conceptually untidy overlaps between them.

Be that as it may, Bull had defined 'order' in social life as 'a pattern of human activity that sustains elementary, primary or universal goals of social life' (1977: 5), and 'international order', correspondingly, as 'a pattern of activity that sustains the elementary or primary goals of the

---

[9] It is consonant with this (usually unnoticed) historically contingent nature of Bull's 'goals of international society' that whereas he characterizes his three goals of *all* societies as elementary, primary and *universal* (1977: 5), he drops the last qualification, for the most part, in characterizing his 'goals of international society' (see 1977: 8, 18, 19; cf ibid.: 16).

society of states, or international society' (1977: 8). International order can therefore be said to exist to the extent that there is a pattern of activity that sustains the elementary or primary goals of international society, and now that these have been identified, Bull is able to ascertain that international order does exist to some extent (1977: ch. 2). Bull's next move is to ask how this degree of international order is sustained, and in this context he advances a complex argument summarized in the previous section – that it is through the combination of three kinds of rules and five institutions of international society that order among states has historically been maintained.

How these institutions function is a difficult question to answer in general terms. Still, Bull's overall assessment is that these institutions contribute considerably towards the maintenance of international order, and that this in turn contributes considerably towards the achievement of the elementary and primary goals of 'social life among mankind as a whole', consisting not of states, but of individual human persons. The idea of the elementary and primary goals of 'the great society of all mankind' (Bull, 1977: 20) is problematic in that it is unclear how they can be ascertained. It is easy to see that they have not been identified by an anthropological observation on a global scale. Rather it appears that they were *postulated* by Bull for the social life of the human race as a whole (Suganami, 1986). Uncharacteristically for a relatively careful thinker, Bull never seems to have confronted this question. He appears to have taken a simple line that the global society of all human individuals, inasmuch as it is seen as a society, must have as its elementary and primary goals those he has identified as the elementary and primary goals of *any* society, i.e. security against violence, observance of agreements and stability of property (Bull, 1977: 19–20).

It should be noted here that these are the sorts of goals that are cherished by those who are satisfied with the existing scheme of things. Plainly, those who are not satisfied with the status quo would not go so far as to suggest that such goals did not matter. But they would not be concerned about security against violence, observance of agreements, or stability of property *in the abstract*. Their primary concern would be with more concrete issues, such as whose lives were made more secure against what kind of violence, how agreements were reached with what kinds of content, and who benefited from the stability of property more than others. Only those who had no immediate concern with such concrete issues could sit back and talk in the abstract. This line of thinking shows that Bull's normative starting point is shaky. His point of departure appears to be one that has been abstracted from the position of the socially satisfied, and made plausible by an accompanying claim that even the socially underprivileged would not deny the elementary importance of the three basic goals *seen in the abstract*. Against this line of criticism, Bull will retort that he does not in fact subscribe to these goals *unconditionally* (see Bull, 1977: xiii, 77–98), but this aspect of his argument is underdeveloped.[10]

So far, Bull's argument has been summarized to reveal his basic moves. But it should be noted that he went far beyond other English School authors of his period in presenting a very detailed discussion on: (1) whether any particular kind of international legal norms are more likely to contribute effectively to the maintenance of international order than any other; and (2) whether, with respect to certain specific goals, international society based on the division of the world into sovereign states may function less well than other possible global institutional arrangements. Of these two themes, the first famously led Bull to draw a distinction between what he called 'pluralism' and 'solidarism'. Bull favoured 'pluralism' as conforming to what he considered to be the contingencies of the 1960s and 1970s, though it is sometimes noted that, later in his life, he began to be more open-minded about the beneficial impact of incorporating practices and institutions that are consonant with a version of solidarism. The second of the two themes was central to Part Three of *The Anarchical Society* which he wrote in the 1970s against the challenges of some globalist writers, especially those engaged in the World Order Models Project, led by Richard Falk and Saul Mendlowitz.

Pluralism and solidarism

On the first question of whether any particular kind of international norms is more likely to contribute effectively to the maintenance of international order than any other, Bull responded by juxtaposing two tendencies in international law – the nineteenth-century 'pluralist' tendency, the other, the twentieth-century 'solidarist' tendency. Bull found a paradigm of pluralism in the nineteenth-century system of positive international law as presented in Oppenheim's textbook (1905–6). Bull contrasted this with the twentieth-century trend,

---

[10] See Chapter 3 below on the English School's ambivalent attitude towards normative questions.

embodied in the Covenant of the League of Nations, the Kellogg-Briand Pact, the Charter of the United Nations, and the Charter of the International Military Tribunal at Nuremberg. However, he saw in these documents a reformulation of an older doctrine of 'solidarism', a classical statement of which he claimed to find in the writings of Grotius; hence his reference to the twentieth-century legal trend as neo-Grotian.[11]

The central difference between solidarism and pluralism is said by Bull to be that whereas, according to the former, there is solidarity or potential solidarity in international society sufficient to enable enforcement of the law against the law-breakers, according to the latter, 'states do not exhibit solidarity of this kind, but are capable of agreeing only for certain minimum purposes which fall short of that of the enforcement of the law' (Bull, 1966b: 52). So, in essence, what distinguishes the two positions is the difference in their respective *empirical* judgements about the world as it currently is, solidarism suggesting that there is much solidarity in the world already, and pluralism offering a more sceptical interpretation.

However, Bull goes on to argue that there are also three issues that divide the two positions *as embodied in the writings of Grotius and Oppenheim*: (i) the place of war in international society; (ii) the sources of the law by which member states of international society are bound; and (iii) the status in the society of states of individual human beings. Having defined 'solidarism' and 'pluralism' initially in terms of the presence or otherwise of solidarity or potential solidarity among states sufficient for the purpose of law enforcement, Bull now appears to have expanded the scope of the two doctrines considerably, influenced by what he took to be the two paradigmatic texts embodying solidarism and pluralism respectively. This move has to some extent obscured the meanings of the two terms in Bull's own usage, and allowed some later writers to contrast them in ways which are not fully consonant with their initially intended meanings. This makes it necessary to articulate the defensible core of the distinction when explicating Bull's line of thought structured around the two contrasting terms.

---

[11] Bull used the term 'Grotian' in two different senses: (i) to describe the broad doctrine that there is a society of states, and (ii) to describe the solidarist form of this doctrine against Vattelian pluralism. See Bull (1977: 322, n. 3). On the problematic nature of the view that the twentieth-century international law revives Grotian ideas, see, among others, Onuma (1993b: 97–8, n. 137).

As for the first area of disagreement, noted in the previous paragraph, which, according to Bull, separates Grotius from Oppenheim, Bull presents Oppenheim as advocating that international law had no role to play in distinguishing between legitimate and illegitimate grounds for resorting to war: the chief function of international law in this area was confined to the legal control of the ways in which states, as belligerents or neutrals, behave in time of war. In short, according to this position, *ius ad bellum* was not a concern of positive international law; only *ius in bello* was. By contrast, Grotius is presented as arguing that distinguishing between states which resort to war for rightful reasons and those which, without justice, start a war was an important function of law governing the relations of sovereign states.

Bull's evaluation of the two positions attributed to Oppenheim and Grotius respectively is quite detailed. But the upshot of his lengthy discussion, which in substance closely follows Vattel's defence of what he termed 'the voluntary law of nations' (Forsyth et al 1970: 89–125), is that whereas 'Oppenheim's system is free of the domestic analogy, the Grotian system makes important concessions to it' (1966b: 65). Bull explains this as follows:

> In international society as conceived by Oppenheim . . . the analogy [of war] with police action [on the one hand] and crime [on the other] is rejected. Since war is taken [by Oppenheim] to be a legitimate political act of states, the consideration which informs the rules governing its conduct is not that of ensuring the victory of a just party but that of limiting the dimensions of the conflict so that the international order is not destroyed by it. The duty to observe the laws of war, the right of neutrality, the obligation of alliances, the right of sovereignty and duty of non-intervention, the silence of international law concerning the private duty to bear arms, are devices for the limitation of conflict. (1966b: 65)

Grotius, too, recognized such institutions as the laws of war, neutrality, alliances and non-intervention, says Bull. But, according to Bull's reading, Grotius 'seeks to circumscribe their operation with qualifying clauses drawn from his doctrine of the just war' (1966b: 66). Thus, for example, Bull points out that nowhere does Grotius say that the privileged position afforded by natural law to the just party is overridden by the positive law of nations. That is to say, according to Bull's interpretation, while Grotius acknowledged that customary international law did not discriminate between just and unjust causes of war and therefore accorded the same rights and duties to all belligerent states in time of war, he nevertheless considered it right that the state resorting to war for just causes be permitted more legal rights and freedom than the unjust opponent (1966b: 60). Similarly, according to Bull, Grotius held the view that the status of neutrality 'does not oblige neutral states to adopt an attitude of impartiality but requires them instead to adopt a qualified discrimination in favour of the just party' (1966b: 61). Furthermore, Grotius, says Bull, held that 'the principle that war be fought only for a just cause must override the obligations of a treaty of alliance' (1966b: 62); that 'the right of a sovereign state to take up arms for a just cause applies to civil conflicts as well as international ones' (1966b: 63); and, finally, that 'if an individual subject believes the cause of the war in which he is ordered to bear arms to be unjust, he should refuse' (1966b: 64).

Bull considered that the Grotian stance, summarized in this way, embodied 'concessions to the domestic analogy' because to argue in this way is to assume that the standards of behaviour within and between states ought fundamentally to be similar, that what is right within the boundaries of states ought also to be pursued across them. And Bull held that the tendency on the part of Grotius to make concessions to the domestic analogy has a twentieth-century counterpart, 'neo-Grotianism', present in the League Covenant, the UN Charter, and the Charter of the International Military Tribunal at Nuremberg – even though Bull also recognized that there are some important differences between Grotius's prescriptions and those embodied in the twentieth-century neo-Grotian legal instruments (1966b: 66).

In short, what is contrasted by Bull here, under the rubrics of 'solidarism' and 'pluralism', and in the light of his reading of Grotius and Oppenheim, are two standard views concerning the ways international law should regulate states' recourse to war. According to the 'discriminatory' view, international law should recognize the difference between legitimate and illegitimate reasons for war and, once war begins, it should discriminate in favour of the legitimate against the illegitimate parties. This view entails a wide variety of positions, encompassing a relatively mild one of the sort Bull attributes to Grotius and a more radical one advocating the need for a collective security system or even an international police force. According to the 'non-discriminatory' view, by contrast, international law should not concern itself with the distinction between legitimate and illegitimate recourse to war, and in war, it should treat all parties equally. This was the prevailing view of the nineteenth century against the background of which Oppenheim wrote his textbook.

But, as was noted above, this is not the only way in which Bull contrasts 'solidarist Grotius' and 'pluralist Oppenheim'. For, according to Bull, the two writers also disagree on the issue of the sources of law: Grotius believed in natural law governing the relations of sovereigns and gave it a fundamental status, whereas Oppenheim, denying the existence of such a system of law, was concerned exclusively with positive international law arising from custom and treaty (Bull, 1966a: 66–7). According to Bull, Grotius's naturalism contributed to his solidarism – for Grotius believed that certain *a priori* principles of justice, contained in the law of nature, ought to apply to international relations and in so asserting, Grotius did not pay attention to the empirical question of whether there was a sufficient degree of solidarity in international society to make such principles effective. Oppenheim's positivism, which paid attention to historical events, contributed, in Bull's view, to his tendency to appreciate that states in international society were united only for certain minimum purposes (Bull, 1966b: 67). In short, Grotius's inclination for *a priori* reasoning led him to advance solidarism while Oppenheim's legal positivism and empiricist tendency made him lean towards pluralism.

This explanation is not implausible in the case of the two particular writers contrasted by Bull, but it should not be taken to suggest that *all* believers in natural law are necessarily solidarists. For instance, Vattel ([1758]1916), who inspired Bull's pluralism, still believed in natural law. Nor are legal positivists by nature pluralists. In fact this is demonstrated by the very case of Oppenheim. Though unnoticed by Bull, Oppenheim was an ardent supporter, prior to World War I, of the move to set up a permanent international court of justice (Oppenheim, [1911]1921), and, afterwards, of the League of Nations (Suganami, 1989: chs. 4 and 5). This means that Oppenheim in fact went far beyond Grotius in the concessions he made to the domestic analogy. Thus, although Bull does not sense this, the distinction between naturalism and positivism cannot serve as a defining condition for the solidarism/pluralism distinction.

A third difference between Grotius and Oppenheim, according to Bull, is that whereas in Oppenheim's conception states were the sole subjects of the rights and duties under international law, Grotius acknowledged the existence of the great community of mankind in which human beings were subjected to the law of nature. This, however, is an unfair comparison in that, unlike Grotius, Oppenheim, in writing his textbook, was concerned solely to present the then existing positive international law which, as a matter of fact, had nothing to say about the community of mankind. For all we know, Oppenheim himself, like Grotius earlier, may well have believed in moral norms to which human beings are subject *qua* members of the human race. What Oppenheim denied was that such moral principles, if present, formed part of the system of positive law accepted by the states of his time as governing their relations. In fact, there is no difference in this respect between the two writers because Grotius ([1646]1925), too, considered the positive 'law of nations' to be distinct from the 'law of nature' or universal moral principles. Still, Bull rightly noted, a society formed by states and sovereigns was secondary in Grotius's thinking to the universal community of mankind, and the legitimacy of the former was derivative of the latter (Bull, 1966b: 68).

The difference between an exclusive concern with the society of states and a position which sees this as just one layer of the world underneath which lies the moral community of mankind does not, of course, necessarily correspond to the difference between pluralism and solidarism. This is because, as the example of Vattel again demonstrates, the latter of these two views can yield a pluralistic stance by simply giving priority to the needs of states over moral imperatives of humanity. Still, Bull sees Grotius as a solidarist *because* Grotius gave priority to the moral community of mankind. Bull points out that Grotius's endorsement of conscientious objection and, more importantly perhaps, his argument in favour of humanitarian intervention (or what would nowadays be conceived of as such) were possible because Grotius took human beings to be the ultimate subjects of normative consideration regarding international relations (Bull, 1966b: 64, 68). By contrast, Bull took it to be an integral part of the pluralist doctrine, contained in the positive law of nations as exposed by Oppenheim, that sovereign states were held to have the duty not to intervene in one another's internal affairs (Bull, 1966b: 63).[12]

Here then is an important contrast between solidarism and pluralism; the former gives moral priority to individual human persons whereas the latter either neglects human persons altogether or

---

[12] Whether Oppenheim personally upheld such a normative position cannot be inferred from his exposition of positive international law of his time – a point that is neglected in Bull's exposition.

considers states to have moral priority. Here, however, emerges a curious, and not often noticed, conceptual incongruence in that Bull, too, argued for the moral priority of the goals of the society of mankind over those of the society of states (1977: 21–2), yet he was (by his own admission) not a solidarist. He was clearly a pluralist in the sense that between (1) the system of international law free of the domestic analogy, which he saw as exemplified in the nineteenth-century system portrayed by Oppenheim, and (2) the one which made concessions to it, which Bull found in the writings of Grotius, and in a number of key twentieth-century legal instruments, he considered the former to be superior. However, what must be noted here is that Bull saw the system presented by Oppenheim as superior *only in the empirical sense* that it was more in tune with what Bull took to be the twentieth-century reality of international society. It should be remembered that pluralism and solidarism, as initially defined by Bull, are in essence differing empirical judgements about the extent of solidarity or potential solidarity present in the existing international society.

Seen in this way, an apparent incongruence – that even though they both believe in the moral primacy of the community of mankind, Grotius, for Bull, is a solidarist and Bull presents himself as on the side of pluralism – disappears. What separated them was their respective assessments of the degree of solidarity present among sovereign states in their own times. Bull may explain this difference in terms of Grotius's tendency for *a priori* reasoning (in harmony with his naturalism) and Bull's own empiricism (consonant with his positivism). But the view that a legal positivist, being an empiricist, tends towards pluralism is plausible only in a world in which, empirically, pluralism is the more defensible view. Bull, of course, considered that he lived in such a world.[13]

On the basis of the foregoing discussion, 'solidarism' may be considered as an interpretation of the existing international society which sees a sufficient degree of solidarity or potential solidarity among states to make effective a relatively demanding system of international law. Such a system would typically incorporate the distinction between legal and illegal reasons for war, a mechanism of law enforcement

---

[13] It may be said of Bull that he was a pluralist in his empirical thinking but that in his normative orientation he was a solidarist. Wheeler and Dunne (1996: 106) suggest that Bull was a solidarist *because* 'the ultimate moral referent of his theory is the welfare of individual human beings'.

against those which illegally resort to war, and the principle of the international protection of human rights. A 'pluralist' is not necessarily or even primarily someone who rejects the values such legal principles aim to protect, but who nevertheless considers it on balance unprofitable to try to incorporate these principles into international law, given the present circumstances of international society marked by the lack of sufficient solidarity among states – unprofitable from the viewpoint of achieving the desired goals without sacrificing the minimum goal of the orderly coexistence of states.[14]

To the extent, however, that the degree of solidarity among states may be expected to vary from one set of states to another, or from one historical period to another, neither solidarism nor pluralism, understood in this way, should be treated as stating a universal or timeless truth about international society. It may therefore be that a generally pluralist international society – or one in which a pluralist interpretation prevails and which therefore is oriented more or less exclusively towards a minimalist goal of ensuring an orderly coexistence among sovereign states – has a solidarist core or pockets of solidarism – in which a solidarist interpretation is dominant and where therefore higher goals, such as international and cosmopolitan justice, are aimed at and to some extent realized. It may also be that a pluralist international society evolves over time into a more solidarist one.[15]

Bull, when he wrote 'Grotian Conception of International Society' (1966b), was clearly a pluralist, as was John Vincent, when he published *Nonintervention and International Order* (1974). In the later Bull (2000d), and also in the later Vincent (Vincent, 1986a; Vincent and Wilson, 1993), however, it is sometimes said that we find some signs of their willingness to move towards a somewhat more solidarist conception of international society (Wheeler, 1992; Alderson and Hurrell, 2000: 206). Thus, Bull, having earlier (1977: 152) suggested that the international protection of human rights was potentially subversive of the minimum goal of the orderly coexistence of sovereign states, now (1984a) acknowledged the importance of taking seriously the Third World countries' demands for a more equitable distribution of the world's wealth and resources, though it may also be noted that he

---

[14] A pluralist, however, need not be committed to the view that the present circumstances are transient; s/he may well consider that they are unlikely to change. See Jackson (2000: ch. 15).

[15] See Buzan (2004: esp. 231–40), for a detailed analysis.

continued to reject neo-Grotianism as 'at best premature' (1986a: 330) with respect to the legal control of the use of force by states. In a parallel fashion, Vincent, having earlier (1974) been determined to oppose legalizing any international use of force even against massive human rights violations by states, now (1986a: 125) acknowledged that the right to life (or right to security against violence and a right to subsistence) was an internationally recognized basic human right, and conceded that 'the principle of non-intervention no longer sums up the morality of states' (Vincent and Wilson, 1993: 129), although he still did not argue that humanitarian intervention by international organizations or states must be permitted when large-scale violations of human rights occur.[16]

There appears to be a number of inter-related reasons for this subtle shift in their positions. First of all, they took it to be the case that international society itself was evolving in the direction of increased solidarism, not only in its normative aspirations, but apparently also in the degree to which such aspirations were taken seriously by states (Vincent, 1986a: 129–30; Wheeler, 1992; Bull, 2000b: 146–7; 2000d: 221, 225). This was of course the background against which they shifted their focus from the issue of order to that of justice. *The Anarchical Society* (1977) was 'a study of order in world politics', whereas Bull's 1983 Hagey Lectures were on 'Justice in International Relations' (2000d); correspondingly, having written *Nonintervention and International Order* (1974), Vincent now wrote on *Human Rights and International Relations* (1986a).

This does not mean that they came to abandon their concern for the minimum goal of the orderly coexistence of states. Characteristically, Bull maintained that 'order in international relations is best preserved by meeting demands for justice, and that justice is best realized in a context of order' (Bull, 2000d: 227; see also ibid., 243). Similarly, Vincent argued that an international consensus that all states must respect universally acknowledged basic human rights was not inimical to the survival of international society, but, on the contrary, consolidated it (Vincent, 1986a: 150–1). Still, the two authors' shift of intellectual focus from 'what would be good for order in the world of states' to 'what ought morally to be done about injustices in the world of mankind'

---

[16] A similar view is expressed by Bull in his conclusion to his collected volume on intervention (Bull, 1984b: 181–95). Wheeler (1992) gives a comprehensive comparative account of the earlier and later views of Bull and Vincent on humanitarian intervention.

appears to have contributed to reducing their earlier tendency to dwell sceptically on what could not be achieved in world politics without upsetting the minimum goal of international order.

It is possible that there were some readjustments in the two authors' strengths of feeling about what ought urgently to be done to ameliorate the appalling conditions of life in the community of mankind, to which no doubt they came to be exposed with increased intensity. Of course, Bull in particular often proclaimed that academics ought to detach themselves from such feelings in their analysis of world politics (Bull, 1977: xv; 2000a: 261–2). Still, one's judgement about how much solidarity or, for that matter, potential solidarity there exists at present in the society of states is to a considerable extent speculative in nature, though, in order to make one's judgement persuasive, one would make a judicious use of empirical illustrations to support it. If one does not feel very strongly that, for instance, a massive human rights abuse in one country is a serious moral concern for the rest of humankind, one may tend to be relatively tolerant of an empirical suggestion that there is no sufficient solidarity in the world at present to make it on balance profitable to permit or legalize humanitarian intervention. By contrast, if one feels very strongly that such a situation constitutes a serious moral concern for the rest of mankind, one may come to be more receptive to the view that, unless there is an overwhelming empirical evidence that permitting or legalizing humanitarian intervention would have disastrous side-effects, states should be permitted to resort to it within certain constraints under such circumstances. One's empirical speculation (especially about what is possible in the circumstances one sees as prevailing) is difficult to separate from one's moral view and the strength with which one holds it – a subject to be revisited later in the discussion.

The relative efficacy of the sovereign states system

On the second question of whether international society based on the division of the world into sovereign states may function less well than some other global institutional arrangement with respect to certain specific goals, Bull no longer confined his attention to what he had earlier identified as the three basic goals of world society, but conducted his discussion with respect to the goals of: (i) peace and security, (ii) economic and social justice, and (iii) environmental protection. According to Bull's globalist opponents, such as Richard Falk, these were the values the human race needed to aim to protect with some urgency, and to that end the sovereign states system required a far-reaching structural alteration (Bull, 1977: ch. 12).

Against this, Bull took the view that there was no good reason to believe that an alternative kind of global organization, such as a world government or what he called a neo-medieval order, is more effective in managing the problems that the human race is faced with at the current phase of its history.[17] He acknowledged that the goals of economic and social justice, and of the efficient control of the global environment are hard to attain within the framework of the sovereign states system. However, in his judgement, even with respect to these goals, the states-system is an acceptable mode of organizing the world. According to him, peace and security between separate national communities are a prerequisite for any move towards economic and social justice, or towards an improved control of the global environment, and the sovereign states system is a reasonably efficient, and at present the most familiar, means for obtaining these preliminary goals. Moreover, in his view, the states-system does in fact make some, not inconsiderable, contribution towards the goals of justice and efficient environmental control. At any rate, there is no assurance that a world government or any other conceivable global institutional arrangement can render to mankind significant assistance in its pursuit of these goals. This is because, according to Bull (1977: ch. 12), economic and social injustices and environmental problems have much deeper causes than the political organization of the world.

But if the sovereign states system is to contribute to the goals of economic and social justice and of the efficient environmental control, in addition to the more basic goals of peace and security, Bull argued, the element of international society must be preserved and

---

[17] Bull wrote (1977: 255): 'We might imagine, for example, that the government of the United Kingdom had to share its authority on the one hand with authorities in Scotland, Wales, Wessex and elsewhere, and on the other hand with a European authority in Brussels and world authorities in New York and Geneva, to such an extent that the notion of its supremacy over the territory and people of the United Kingdom had no force. We might imagine that the authorities in Scotland and Wales, as well as those in Brussels, New York and Geneva enjoyed a standing as actors in world politics, recognised as having rights and duties in world law, conducting negotiations and perhaps able to command armed forces. We might imagine that the political loyalties of the inhabitants of, say, Glasgow, were so uncertain as between the authorities of Edinburgh, London, Brussels and New York that the government of the United Kingdom could not be assumed to enjoy any kind of primacy over the others, such as it possesses now. If such a state of affairs prevailed all over the globe, this is what we may call, for want of a better term, a neo-mediaeval order.'

strengthened. For this purpose, he maintained, 'a sense of common interests among the great powers, sufficient to enable them to collaborate in relation to goals of minimum world order' (1977: 315) would be essential. But he added: 'a consensus, founded upon the great powers alone, that does not take into account the demands of those Asian, African and Latin American countries cannot be expected to endure' (1977: 315). Further, Bull maintained that the future of international society is likely to depend on the preservation and extension of 'a cosmopolitan culture, embracing both common ideas and common values, and rooted in societies in general as well as in their elites' (1977: 317). He added:

> We have also to recognise that the nascent cosmopolitan culture of today, like the international society which it helps to sustain, is weighted in favour of the dominant cultures of the West. Like the world international society, the cosmopolitan culture on which it depends may need to absorb non-Western elements to a much greater degree if it is to be genuinely universal and provide a foundation for a universal international society.   (1977: 317)

In short, according to Bull, the existing formal structure of world politics, the sovereign states system, would be an efficacious means, at the global level, for achieving a variety of goals facing the human race, if the element of international society within it could be strengthened and the underlying cosmopolitan culture made more genuinely cosmopolitan.[18] This line of thinking reflects Bull's interest in the historical study of international society which the British Committee on the Theory of International Politics had placed on its research agenda. Before turning, in the third main section of this chapter, to the English School's contribution in that field, a few observations are in order concerning Nicholas Wheeler's recent book, *Saving Strangers* (2000). This book is an important landmark in the contemporary evolution of the English School's thinking in that Wheeler's approach goes beyond the School's more traditional concern, as represented in Bull (1977) and Vincent (1974), which had centrally to do with identifying the best institutional means to strengthen international order. Wheeler's chief aim is to demonstrate how certain injustices in world

---

[18] Bull's seemingly reasonable prescription here – that more genuinely cosmopolitan culture, which incorporates non-Western values, be cultivated and made to underpin the workings of international society – is, however, largely vacuous unless it is made clear what it means to do this and who has the power or responsibility to do it.

society may be rectified within the framework of international society, and how this can be done without seriously undermining the goals of international order. The degree of idealism that drives Wheeler is at odds with the prevalent image of the English School as a group of somewhat conservative, almost complacent, thinkers (Suganami, 1983; Wilson, 1989) – though, as was noted, later writings by Bull (2000d) and Vincent (1986a) had begun to show signs of change. Vincent (1986a), in particular, had moved clearly into the realm of ethical enquiry in his book on human rights, and argued that the right to subsistence, as well as freedom from violence, is the most basic of all human rights, entailing corresponding duties, on the part of the outside states, to protect such values. Wheeler's book is an extension of this normative turn in the English School's orientation.

Wheeler's solidarism

On the basis of a detailed study of the evolution of norms with respect to humanitarian intervention before and after the end of the Cold War, and driven by his strong compassion for the victims of human rights abuses and sense of responsibility as a citizen of a major liberal democratic power, Wheeler has offered a comprehensive solidarist package against realist and pluralist scepticism. It is well to note, however, that in Wheeler's usage, 'solidarism' and 'pluralism' are contrasted specifically with respect to the right of humanitarian intervention. Moreover, whereas Wheeler uses 'solidarism' partly to denote an empirical judgement about the solidarity or potential solidarity existing in international society, he also uses it to mean a substantive moral doctrine in favour of an international protection of human rights worldwide (2000: 38). Furthermore, Wheeler's 'pluralism' is extended to cover the (for him, unduly conservative) view that the UN Security Council can endorse military sanctions *only* against a disturber of inter-state peace and security as opposed to a violator of universal human rights norms (2000: 200, 289).

Given that the apparent absence of solidarity sufficient to make the UN's collective security system work against a disturber of inter-state peace and security was a key factor that had led Bull to support 'pluralism', Wheeler's inclusion of an effectively operating UN collective security system under the banner of 'pluralism' is extraordinary. What sustains Wheeler's version of the pluralist/solidarist distinction, however, is his supposition that pluralism is concerned solely with the minimum goal of inter-state coexistence, whereas solidarism is concerned with the higher goal of the welfare of individual human persons living in separate states.

This way of contrasting the two positions faces a problem when someone maintains that he is deeply concerned about the welfare of individual human persons living in separate states, but that in his judgement the only practical way to achieve this at the moment is to try to protect the minimal goal of inter-state coexistence. As we saw, Bull's support of pluralism followed this line. Jackson argues in a similar way even more explicitly (2000: 30, 291–2), although at times he also reveals himself to be thinking that pluralism, or what he calls 'the pluralist ethics' (2000: 14), is good in itself (2000: 181–2) and that solidarist interventionism amounts to morally objectionable paternalism (2000: 412).

Wheeler's use of 'solidarism' partly as an empirical doctrine and partly also as a normative stance would seem problematic in that it is advisable to avoid using the same label to refer to two logically distinct positions. Still, the substance of Wheeler's 'solidarist' position is a coherent one. In substance, Wheeler points out that humanitarian intervention, when backed by the UN Security Council, has come to be seen as legally acceptable by international society (2000: 8, 16, 168–9, 183, 200, 285, 295), and argues that unilateral humanitarian intervention (without the authorization of the UN) to respond to supreme humanitarian emergency, where legitimate in the light of a set of criteria derived from the just war doctrine (2000: 33–52), should be accepted by international society – because this would contribute to the cause of justice without seriously undermining the requirement of order (2000: 309). Here he is critical of the pluralist scepticism that permitting unilateral humanitarian intervention would issue a 'licence for intervention' (Vincent, 1986a: 152), and considers that the legitimacy or otherwise of particular interventions should be subjected to judgements in a 'global public sphere' (2000: 299). What is crucial, he maintains, is that 'even the most powerful states know that they will be required to answer before the society of states and what Henry Shue calls "the court of world public opinion"' (Wheeler, 2000: 296). In this connection, it is Wheeler's view that those working in human rights NGOs, universities and the media should mobilize public opinion into a new moral and practical commitment to the promotion and enforcement of human rights (2000: 310) and contribute significantly to the shaping of the policies of the (Western) governments when faced with humanitarian crises elsewhere (2000: 52).

Wheeler recognizes that such crises are often deeply rooted in the political, economic and social structures of the societies concerned, requiring that humanitarian intervention be accompanied by a long-term commitment to help reconstruct them. In this connection, Wheeler also argues for developing a new West-South consensus on the legitimacy of humanitarian intervention through a new dialogue, in which, in exchange for Southern governments' acceptance that cases will arise where the slaughter of civilians by their governments is so appalling as to legitimate the use of force to uphold minimum standards of humanity, the West will make genuine commitment to redistributive justice (2000: 307). But Wheeler acknowledges that 'at the beginning of the new century, there is little evidence that the global rich in the West are ready to end their position of power and privilege' (2000: 308). It may be recalled here that Vincent (1986a: 147), too, had argued, as one of the consequences of accepting the human right to subsistence as primary, that richer societies in the world need to take seriously the extent to which they are implicated in the deepening of the rich-poor divide in the world.

A close textual examination of Wheeler's book reveals that he engages in three kinds of activity in his book: (i) exposition of a recent normative trend with respect to humanitarian intervention (2000: 285–6); (ii) argumentation designed to demonstrate the presence of potential solidarity in the world sufficient to make effective a set of norms concerning humanitarian intervention supported by his moral convictions (2000: 295); and (iii) statement of his ultimate moral vision towards which, he believes, the world ought gradually to be transformed, even though there is, he acknowledges, no evidence that such a transition is likely to occur at present (2000: 303–10). In the course of his argument, he moves almost imperceptibly from (i), through (ii), towards (iii). Given this, it would be interesting to examine how far the strength of Wheeler's commitment to his moral vision has influenced his exposition under (i) or argument under (ii).

Here we may recall that one's speculation about how efficaciously a more demanding set of norms could operate in the international sphere is shaped to some extent by one's temperament, political ideology and the strength of one's feelings about how urgently the more demanding set of norms ought to be introduced to guide the interactions of sovereign states. The last item explains why atrocious behaviour on the part of sovereign states has tended to produce a solidarist reaction, as witnessed by Grotius's publication of his book during the Thirty Years War, and the 'neo-Grotian' reactions, in the twentieth century, against the atrocities of the two world wars. Wheeler's solidarist stance therefore should be studied in conjunction with pluralist counterarguments and realist scepticisms, but these claims must in turn be subjected to a close scrutiny.[19]

The historical study of international society

The English School's historical study of international society (and especially its comparative study of states-systems) developed slowly in response to certain key questions which Butterfield and Wight placed on the research agenda of the British Committee on the Theory of International Politics and towards which Wight gave some tentative answers (Wight, 1977: Introduction; Dunne, 1998: chs. 5–6).

Wight took a states-system to be a group of states that are sovereign, in the sense that they recognize no political superior, and have more or less permanent relations with one another, expressed in four institutions: messengers, conferences and congresses, a diplomatic language and trade. On this definition, he found only three reasonably clear historical examples of states-systems: the modern or Western states-system which, according to Wight, arose in Europe in the fifteenth century and now covers the whole world; the classical Hellenic-Hellenistic system; and the states-system that existed in China during the Period of Warring States. However, he also studied suzerain state-systems, or systems in which one political unit asserts suzerainty or paramountcy over the rest (e.g., the systems centring upon Imperial China, Byzantium, the Abbasid Caliphate and the British Raj in relation to the principalities of the Indian subcontinent), as well as secondary states-systems, or systems whose members are themselves systems of states (e.g., the relations of Rome and Persia, the relations of Egypt, the Hittites and Babylon, and the relations of Eastern Christendom, Western Christendom and Islam) (Wight, 1977: 16–17).

---

[19] Jackson (2000) presents a pluralist challenge, but his position strikes as being dogmatic. He writes: 'There is no such [thing as a global] community and pluralists would be dead set against creating one *even if it were feasible.*' (2000: 415; emphasis mine). See Chapter 4 below for a more detailed discussion, and also Suganami, 2003. The need to base any prescriptive scheme on a sound empirical basis is stressed by Wendt (2000). A good discussion of the contemporary literature on humanitarian intervention is found in Wheeler (2001); and Shinoda (2000) contains a sophisticated look at the Kosovo case.

There were several questions Wight raised about these cases, of which the following four deserve special attention. (1) Historically, states-systems arose against the background of cultural homogeneity, but what level of cultural unity was necessary for their effective operation (Wight, 1977: 33–4)? (2) Is there a case for saying that every states-system can only maintain its existence on the principle of the balance of power, that the balance of power is inherently unstable, and that sooner or later its tensions and conflicts will be resolved into a monopoly of power, culminating in the establishment of an empire (Wight, 1977: 43–4)? (3) What case is there for preferring a states-system to alternative forms of political organization of which, historically, there were many examples (Wight, 1977: 44)? (4) Is there a wide variation between the common code of one states-system and that of another, or do they all belong to the great pool of practices supposedly common to the human race (Wight, 1977: 34)?

The first of these questions was especially topical due to the unmistakably multicultural nature of contemporary global international society. What are the prospects for the institutions of international society, which have their origins in the European civilization, now that they have come to encompass the whole world, comprising a variety of cultures? This question was addressed by the British Committee in its final phase, culminating in the publication of *The Expansion of International Society* (1984). Its editors, Bull and Watson acknowledged that, compared with the European international society of the nineteenth century, the global international society of the latter part of the twentieth century lacked solidarity because of a number of factors, cultural heterogeneity amongst them. The main conclusion of this collaborative volume, however, was (1) that new entrants to international society have accepted its framework of rules and institutions, though they have sought to reshape existing ones to eliminate discriminations against them, (2) that they have had to do so because they could not do without them even in their mutual relations, and (3) that the leading elements of all contemporary societies have accepted a cosmopolitan culture of modernity upon which rests international legal, diplomatic and administrative institutions (Bull and Watson, 1984: 430–5).

Watson subsequently published his own book, *The Evolution of International Society* (1992). This is a comparative historical analysis of a large number of states-systems. He abandoned Wight's distinction between systems of independent states, suzerain systems and empires,

and included under the rubric of states-systems any system comprising a number of diverse communities of people, or political entities
(1992: 13). He subdivided his examples into ancient states-systems (of
which ten cases were investigated from Sumer to the Islamic system),
the European international society (starting from Medieval Europe
and ending in the nineteenth-century Concert of Europe), and the
global international society of the twentieth century. He noted that in
any given states-system there are tendencies – in pursuit of order – to
move away from multiple independences in the direction of hegemony, dominion and empire. This was the pattern that interested
Wight in connection with his second question noted above (Wight,
1977: 43–4; Watson, 1990: 105). But Watson also noticed that there are
counter-pressures towards greater autonomy that make empires and
dominions loosen and break up.

According to Watson, 'in the practical operation of the states
systems . . . the midpoint [where the two pressures balance each other]
tends to be a varying degree of autonomy or domestic independence,
ordered by a degree of external hegemony or authority, individual or
joint' (1990: 106; see also Watson, 1992: ch. 12). With this understanding, Watson speculated on the future of the international system in the
aftermath of the demise of the Soviet Union. What he considered likely
was the development of joint hegemony, or concert, with the Unite
States as the leader. Such an arrangement might be resented by some
states, but, Watson argued, it may strengthen international order especially 'if the major powers conduct an active diplomatic dialogue with
other states and respond to their needs' (1992: 323). This echoes Bull's
similar formulation in *The Anarchical Society*, noted earlier (1977: 315).

Watson's was an ambitious undertaking, but an even larger and
more systematic work, encompassing 60,000 years of human history,
has appeared recently. This is *International Systems in World History*
(2000) by Buzan and Little. This work arose from the authors' deep
dissatisfaction with the ahistoricity of Waltz's neo-realism and has
taken seriously some leading English School writers' conviction that
the study of history is indispensable to the understanding of the
present and the future of world politics.[20]

---

[20] What the English School writers meant when they held that the study of history is
indispensable to the understanding of the present and the future of world politics will
be explored in Chapter 3. Buzan and Little agreed with some leading English School
writers that generalizations about world politics must be based on extensive historical

Buzan and Little are critical of the existing IR discourse, derived nearly exclusively from the experience of the Westphalian inter-state system. One key move Buzan and Little make, in their effort to transcend the limitations of the Westphalia-based IR, is to define international systems as containing a wide range of arrangements: empires are included under the rubric as a 'hierarchical' international system; what they call 'pre-international systems' comprise 'bands, tribes, clans, and perhaps chiefdoms'; 'economic international systems' typically involve 'tribes, empires, city-states, clans, and early forms of firms'; and 'full international systems', encompassing military-political, economic and socio-cultural exchange, may consist of like units, such as city-states or national states, or unlike units, such as empires, city-states and barbarian tribes (see Buzan and Little, 2000: 6, 96, 101, 102).

The story that emerges is about how the geographical size of socio-cultural, economic and military-political systems gradually expanded, causing the progressive merging of what had been distinct regional systems, and resulting in the formation of the contemporary global system (Buzan and Little, 2000: 109–11). As to the present and the future, however, their story is a familiar one: they point to the possibility of a fundamental transformation in the developed part of the world in which great power wars have become effectively obsolete, the interactions between the units are shaped dominantly by economic factors, and the rapidly increasing capacity of mass communication might undermine the territorial basis of politics and culture.[21]

The third question, noted above, concerns the relative merits of states-systems, or systems of independent states, exemplified by the modern international society, as against alternative forms of political organization. The final part of Bull's book (1977) contains the most detailed discussion of this issue, and defence of the states-system, presented by the English School, which we already saw. An argument

knowledge and were clearly impressed by the scale of their historical knowledge claims. Still, apart from their historical orientation and also their discussion of legitimacy (2000: 332–3), inspired by the work of Wight (1977) and Watson (1992), there is little that is distinctively English-School-like in their book's contents. It is more in the nature of a corrective to Waltz's neo-realism, incorporating some leading English School writers' injunction to accumulate historical knowledge before generalizing. For a full-length treatment of 'legitimacy' in international society, see Clark, 2005.

[21] See Buzan and Little (2000: ch. 16). A similar view, invoking Bull's neo-medievalism, is found in Tanaka (2002). See also Cooper (1996), cited in Buzan and Little (2000: 359); Tanaka (2002: 155), too, refers to Cooper's ideas.

in favour of an alternative form of political organization, however, has been advanced from a political-theoretical perspective by Andrew Linklater (1996b, 1998), who, while coming from outside of the English School tradition, has appreciated the presence of valuable insights and scholarship in some of its foundational texts. He sees in Bull's own notion of neo-medieval order a more satisfactory institutional expression, than the sovereign states system, for the 'politics of inclusion' to which he is committed, although he is also aware that this alternative structure can at present become operative only in the (mainly European) solidarist core of the global international society.

The fourth question, noted above, concerns the historical variability of the norms governing different international systems. Do they show a wide divergence, or do they converge on some common set of principles? To the extent that the prevailing norms diverge, is there any discernible pattern, and what explains the divergence? These are among the questions which are currently animating a number of scholars in Britain and elsewhere. Linklater (2002a) has turned his attention to studying the historical sociology of states-systems, focusing on how 'harm' has been defined and regulated in various systems. But the idea that the norms and institutions governing different states-systems either in Wight's narrower sense or Watson's broader sense may or must have varied historically because, after all, these things are not naturally given but socially produced, is by no means a uniquely English School view. Historical sociologists, constructivists and genealogists who do not consider themselves as necessarily linked with the English School are now producing important works in this area, though at least in some cases the works of the English School, particularly those of Wight, Bull and Watson, seem to have provided a point of departure for their investigations (Der Derian, 1987; Reus-Smit, 1999).

Conclusion

In this chapter, substantive contentions of the English School were summarized in terms of the three dimensions of their main subject-matter – structural, functional and historical. With respect to each, the English School has made some significant contributions.

As for the formal structure study of contemporary global international society, much has already been done by Manning, James and Bull to identify its age-old features.[22] There is of course a continued need to know 'what the law is' on all aspects of international relations, and there is also a need to identify principles of political legitimacy in contemporary international society. At the regional level, the extent to which the European Union has succeeded in altering the traditional institutional structure of the European international society will continue to be debated, and Bull's idea of a neo-medieval order will be tested against this and other regions, as well as at the global level. To unravel the authority structure of contemporary world politics, in which state and non-state authorities appear increasingly to co-act in its governance, a more detailed analysis is needed than has been conducted so far by English School writers with respect to the institutional structure specifically of the society of sovereign states (see, for example, Hall and Biersteker, 2002).

As for the functional study of international society, it must be acknowledged that the English School's questions have been rather large and general ones – 'how does the institution of the balance of power contribute to the maintenance of international order?'; 'is the nineteenth-century system of international law better suited to the contemporary reality than the twentieth-century one in the area of the legal control of the use of force by states?'; etc. In dealing with such broad questions, the English School have tended to structure their discussion in terms of the contest between two opposing positions, pluralism and solidarism.

In this chapter, Bull's distinction between these two contrasting positions was scrutinized, and Wheeler's more recent advocacy of solidarism was examined. To the extent that pluralism and solidarism are opposing judgements about what legal rules will be more, or less, effective as a means of securing desired ends, it is not possible to eschew a detailed empirical inquiry to reach plausible conclusions, and here work done by some regime theorists might perhaps supply helpful insights (Rittberger, 1993; Haas, Keohane and Levy, 1994; Hasenclever, Mayer and Rittberger, 1997).

It may, however, be that the opposition between pluralists and solidarists is attributable to the influence of their respective normative attitudes or, for that matter, that the two positions are themselves

---

[22] English School writers have, however, been neglectful of what Manning had acknowledged to be complex, difficult, but necessary to study – the 'social dynamics' (1975: 201) of the world, or 'the multi-dimensional interplay of social forces' (1975: 34).

contending normative positions. In either event, the parties concerned should scrutinize the grounds on which their respective commitments might be justified. This last point applies more generally to the works of the English School. They are unanimously in favour of the division of the world into sovereign states, but even Bull – the most articulate thinker in this area within the English School – is less than adequate in his defence of what he calls the elementary, primary and universal goals of every society, including human society as a whole, on which his endorsement of the sovereign states system is ultimately based (Suganami, 1986; 2001b: 207).[23]

As for the historical study of international society, there is much more to be done. But any historical study must be underpinned by metahistorical considerations regarding what history is for. The English School's attitudes towards history are in fact quite complex, as will be discussed in the next chapter. On the whole, the School has tended to regard a historical study as an intellectually richer alternative to a more abstract social science (Bull, 2000a), but the two are complementary. One important function of historical study is a 'critical subversion of established discourses' (Alderson and Hurrell, 2000: 35), but the English School's positive assessment of the modern Western statessystem, which now covers the entire world, has meant that their historical works have not been directed to that end.

This chapter has revealed close similarities and intricate interconnections in the English School authors' substantive arguments about their subject-matter. There are very many things they say which together form a piece of intellectual tapestry; and there are many things they leave out in common. In the next chapter, we move on to examine the methodological and epistemological parameters within which their substantive works on international relations have been produced – to see whether, in this area too, there may be some unity in the School's thinking.

---

[23] A need for a more careful meta-ethical reflection will be noted in Chapter 3.

3 The English School on 'International Relations as an intellectual pursuit'

In a brief but perceptive discussion paper, 'Exporting the English School?', Martha Finnemore has made a few critical observations about the School's approach to the study of international relations, and offered some friendly advice to followers of this approach about how to make the School products more exportable to the US market. According to her (2001: 509), '[g]iving the English School more salience in American IR debates . . . would be a real improvement' – for 'American scholarship would be enriched by incorporation of the historical and normative orientations the English School brings'. There is, in her judgement, 'an eager audience for the theoretical frameworks that provide traction on such issues', but hitherto 'the School's lack of clarity about both method and theoretical claims has made it difficult for American scholars to incorporate it into their research' (2001: 509). Therefore, 'addressing these issues might make the English School more useful to more US researchers' and it 'might also have the converse effect of sharpening work within the English School' (2001: 509).

While acknowledging that the orientations of the English School are 'historical and normative' and suggesting that the School may perhaps have a valuable 'theoretical framework' to offer, Finnemore complains that the School has not explained clearly what its 'method and theoretical claims' are. '[F]or many American scholars, simply figuring out what its methods *are* is a challenge' (2001: 509; emphasis Finnemore's) for 'English School authors . . . almost never provide systematic discussions about rules of evidence' (2001: 509) – so that it is difficult to know, for example, when we can claim that there is an international society, as opposed to merely a system. Also, where they present historical generalizations, it is not always clear why certain cases are included and others omitted from their samples (2001: 510). Finnemore adds that they do not clarify 'exactly what kind of enterprise theirs is, theoretically, and what its contribution is, exactly, within the larger world of IR scholarship' (2001: 511).

Given some prominent English School authors' effective self-identification as contemporary contributors to the Grotian Rationalist tradition, defined in contradistinction to Hobbesian and Kantian traditions of international theory, Finnemore's criticism that they lack theoretical self-reflection may appear quite unwarranted. What she has in mind, however, is that English School authors have not explicitly stated how their substantive arguments about international relations relate to those of other approaches, in particular, neo-realism, liberal institutionalism and constructivism, which have been dominant in the American study of international relations since the dawn of the 1980s.

Of course, the first significant wave of English School writings, produced in the 1960s and 1970s, predated much of these more recent debates in IR. These writings, formative of the English School's identity, initially indicated some of their leading authors' strong opposition to the rising tide of behaviouralism (Manning, 1975: 6, ch. 16) and 'scientism' (Bull, 1969) in American IR. No comparable self-assertions, by English School authors, have taken place, however, in subsequent disciplinary debates. Indeed, the English School's international society perspective itself was relatively marginalized in the 1980s and early 1990s under the sway of Waltzian neo-realism and critical debates that came to surround it (Hurrell, 2002: ix) – although there were, in the 1990s, occasional reflections and commentaries on some of the main characteristics of the leading English School authors' approaches and how they may relate to those emanating mainly from the United States (Evans and Wilson, 1992; Buzan, 1993; Dunne, 1995a, 1995b).

Given, however, the extraordinary extent to which, particularly in the American and American-inspired study of international relations, differences and similarities between neo-realism and neo-liberal institutionalism have been expounded as a core knowledge of the discipline of International Relations (Lamy, 2001), and now, with added zeal, the differences and similarities between these two positions (bracketed together as 'rationalism'), on the one hand, and constructivism, on the other, are in turn explicated (Wendt, 1999; see, however, Suganami, 2002), it is understandable that Finnemore – herself an American constructivist (Finnemore, 1996; 2001: 509) – should think that English School authors' lack of detailed reflection on their identity within this particular intellectual mapping constitutes a barrier against their importation into the American IR world.[1]

Finnemore concludes her paper by stating that she is in fact 'an admirer of the School *as it stands* and [has] no particular quarrel with it *in its current form*' (2001: 513; emphasis added) and that her suggestions have been prompted solely in response to the 'concern that English School work should be more widely read and more influential' (2001: 513). It would not do, however, to pretend that there were no problems with English School works – for, as we saw, it is also Finnemore's view that English School authors' empirical claims are methodologically opaque and therefore, we may surmise her to be thinking, quite shaky. Further, her advice for theoretical self-reflection – or product specification – is not just for the sake of trans-Atlantic salespersonship; she thinks this will help followers of the English School tradition formulate their distinctive research agenda which some of them feel they should do at the present juncture to build on its past achievements (Finnemore, 2001: 513; Buzan, 2001).

Finnemore's overall gentleness towards the School may be due to the affinity she perhaps perceives between the general orientation of the School's leading works and her own approach. Indeed, one of her earlier works (1996), on the emergence of humanitarian norms in international relations, is strikingly English-School-like both in her choice of subject and the way in which she discusses it, which is basically historical and interpretative – apart from her very self-conscious

---

[1] This, however, has now been rectified by Alderson and Hurrell (2000: ch. 2), Hurrell's Foreword to the third edition (2002) of *The Anarchical Society*, and Reus-Smit (2002). Buzan (2004: 161–2) also rehearses the now familiar list of differences between the English School's approach to institutions and that of the regime theory. Of these, Hurrell's Foreword to the third edition of *The Anarchical Society* is especially helpful in making the reader appreciate succinctly the similarities and differences between the English School's approach, on the one hand, and realism, neo-realism, neo-liberal institutionalism and constructivism, on the other (Bull, 2002: vii–xv). According to Hurrell, Bull's approach (which can be taken to be central to the English School's approach as a whole) resembles these various strands of thought in a number of ways. But it differs from realism and neo-realism mainly in drawing special attention to the relevance of rules, norms, common understandings and mutual expectations in understanding international politics; it differs from neo-liberal institutionalism in stressing the importance, to the growth of international cooperation, of the historically evolved sense of community among states; and it differs from constructivism in its interest in the actual historical evolution of the institutions of international society, the special importance it attaches to international law as a concrete historical practice, and the extent to which it draws attention to the brute material facts as constraints on practice as well as its analysis.

targeting of neo-realism and neo-liberal institutionalism as approaches she feels the need to transcend. Still, her criticisms of the English School are quite pertinent and should not be brushed aside; there is indeed a certain lack of clarity about what it is that English School writers are doing, or advocating should be done, in their study of international relations.

This chapter therefore examines three basic areas in which this is particularly noteworthy. A first area concerns their attitudes towards history; a second relates to what kinds of knowledge they think they are, or should be, seeking, given their well-known scepticism towards scientific approaches in International Relations; and a third relates to their attitudes towards norms and values. There is a considerable lack of clarity, unsettledness and even contradictions in their collective and individual thinking in these deeper areas – even though they are united outwardly in their belief that, despite its formally anarchical structure, there is, in contemporary international society, a considerable degree of order enjoyed by sovereign states. It may be tempting in this context to say that their methodology is characterized by *pluralism*. This, however, obscures the fact that their pluralism, which a couple of commentators (Little, 2000; Buzan, 2001) consider as the School's distinctive and commendable feature, is not a result of any self-conscious methodological decision taken collectively or individually by its leading figures. Admittedly, the English School is quite a broad church, but a detailed articulation of their deeper thoughts may still yield some common parameters and tendencies which it is the purpose of this chapter to explore.

History, historical knowledge and IR

One common thread that unites the English School is its acknowledgement of the importance of history or historical knowledge to the study of international relations. This does not mean that everyone associated with the English School has written historical works or made an extensive use of historical knowledge in their discussion of international relations. Manning, for instance, did neither. Nor does it mean, of course, that scholars not associated with the English School have not done either of those things. Hans Morgenthau readily comes to mind, who, incidentally, is reported by Watson to have agreed with him 'about the relevance of past experience to the understanding of current international affairs' (1992: 9). But, even for Manning, there is 'no point in denying the linkage between International Relations and International History' (Manning 1951a: 17) and 'international history is, for the student of international relations, essential underpinner number one' (Manning, 1954: 44).

But to say that historical knowledge (or, in the present case, International History or World History) is vitally important to the study of international relations (or International Relations) is at the same time to acknowledge that they are *not* identical in nature or scope. Therefore, what sort of relationship English School writers have assumed to exist between the two kinds of knowledge is an interesting issue to explore. But, as we shall see, we encounter a number of deep uncertainties in this area.

This section will first outline what these uncertainties are with reference to the writings of Bull and Watson. This is followed by a revelation that, according to Bull as well as Wight, historical knowledge does not necessarily supply the best guide for political action, although, it will be argued, this is not the same as saying that, in their judgement, historical knowledge is irrelevant to the study of contemporary international relations. The discussion will move to the key English School authors' interpretations of history (as recursive or progressive) and to their important realization – which, however, they do not develop – that historical interpretations are intrinsically theoretical. An attempt is made at the end of this section to summarize the leading English School authors' wide-ranging and at times contradictory views on history, historical knowledge and the study of international relations.

A good starting point for our discussion here perhaps is a remark by Buzan and Little (2000: 29) that '[i]n contrast to mainstream American IR, the English School were simply not constrained by the notion that the study of history and the development of theory are incompatible'. But on what grounds, it may well be asked especially by those who are closer to the English School way of seeing things, could the two goals be deemed ever to be actually *incompatible*? Buzan and Little do not explain this, but underlying the view that they attribute to American IR is, undoubtedly, the well-known distinction between idiographic and nomothetic approaches. The former seeks to establish knowledge about past events under descriptions unique to themselves, while the latter is interested solely in the knowledge of regular patterns under which particular events can be subsumed. Waltz's well-known distinction (1959) between explaining the occurrence of particular wars and the recurrence of war is based on the distinction between the two approaches, as is his later claim (1979) that his theory is concerned solely to explain recurrent features of international politics, and not particular events occurring in that realm.

The standard distinction in the American study of international relations between IR, which as a branch of social or political science stands for the nomothetic concern, and International or Diplomatic History, which is supposed to be idiographic in orientation, has at least one merit. It is clear. Perhaps because of this, the distinction is accepted widely by IR scholars whether or not they are American or American-inspired (Hollis and Smith, 1990; Elman and Elman, 2001). English School authors form an exception to this general rule in that they do not entirely accept the standard formula, 'International Relations: International History = nomothetic: idiographic'. However, they do not entirely reject it either, and this produces a first area of uncertainty or ambiguity in their thinking about History and its relation to International Relations: *how far, according to them, is IR to be idiographic and how far is it to be nomothetic?*

A good illustration of this ambiguity is found in Bull's 1972 piece on the nature of International Relations as an academic pursuit. In this remarkably candid statement of his views about the intellectual status of IR, he reveals considerable uncertainty, on his part, about the precise nature of historical knowledge. In particular, he declares his adherence to the covering law model of explanation[2] and wonders how this position could be reconciled with his belief that the importance of historical knowledge – whether for Historians or IR scholars – lies in its ability to familiarize the student with the unique qualities of singular actors. He explains:

> [H]istory is the vehicle through which we can acquire feeling or grasp of the singular (singular, not particular) actors which dominate world politics. The United States of America is the United States of America: to consider it a special case of the category of great powers, or nuclear powers, or multicultural countries, or countries of

---

[2] The covering law model of explanation, or the deductive-nomological model, asserts that to explain the occurrence of a particular event involves the following three moves: (1) to show that there is a well-substantiated general pattern, or law, that under a certain type of circumstances, the type of event in question always occurs; (2) to show that the type of circumstances existed; and (3) to demonstrate that, given (1) and (2), the conclusion that the type of event occurred is logically necessary. See Dray (1957); Suganami (1996: ch. 4).

settlement, is helpful but it does not tell us enough. To understand how it acts we have to acquire a sense of its singularity that is best imparted by historical knowledge. (2000a: 253)[3]

An endnote Bull attaches to the last sentence is worthy of attention:

> This passage will cause pain to students of the logic of the late Professor John Anderson. We explain events by showing that they are instances of something wider, i.e., by denying their singularity. To assert the singularity of the United States of America is to deny the possibility of fully explaining it. Here I simply note this paradox, without attempting to find a solution to it. (2000a: 264, note 8)

A solution to this apparent paradox is readily found in noticing the inadequacy of the covering law model of explanation itself, but this need not detain us here.[4] What is important to note in the present context is that, in Bull's judgement, historical generalizations are *not enough*. But this is to say that they *do* after all constitute some significant knowledge about the world, but that they need to be supplemented by idiographical historical knowledge. International Relations, therefore, should be partly nomothetic and partly idiographic, but how far it should be one way or the other remains uncertain in Bull's essay and in the writings of the English School more generally.

This complicates the issue somewhat because the distinction between International Relations and International History is no longer very clear-cut, unlike when the distinction is based on the nomothetic/idiographic divide. Bull's solution to this, however, is very simple and straightforward: the former studies the past to 'throw light on contemporary interstate politics' whereas the study of the past *in its own right* 'properly belongs to the Department of International History' (2000a: 249). Now, the view that a study of the past can throw light on contemporary inter-state politics is widely shared by English School authors as well as by others, but precisely how this is so is not explained fully by the English School. This constitutes a second area

---

[3] 'Singularity' here means 'uniqueness'. A singular/unique item is not deemed to be a 'particular' instance of a general catetory. But here Bull fails to note that any item can be 'unique' or 'particular' depeding on how that item is described.

[4] Demonstrating, in accordance with the model, that a particular sequence of events is an instance of a well-known general pattern, is insufficient to explain how it is that the connection holds. See Suganami (1996), (1997), (1999); Wendt (1999). In rejecting the covering law model of explanation, Suganami argues for the centrality of the narrative mode of explanation in history, social science and natural science. His current research project concerns the role of narrative explanation in world politics.

of uncertainty: *how is it that, according to them, historical knowledge sheds light on the present?*

A study of the past can throw light on contemporary inter-state politics most obviously by providing historical background in the context of which current inter-state politics are conducted: the current phase in the relations between Israel and the Palestinians, for instance, could not be understood fully without the background knowledge of their past. Bull acknowledges that this is one reason why the study of history is vital to IR (2000a: 249). It should be noted in this connection, however, that Bull does not ask if this kind of historical study properly belongs to International Relations or to International History. A likely answer is 'both', and with it disappears a sharp demarcation between the two branches of knowledge. Indeed, according to Bull (2000a: 252–3), International Relations has a distinctive subject-matter, but it is not, in the full sense, a subject: 'We cannot say, as we can say of mathematics or history or philosophy or economics, that it not only has its own distinctive field of enquiry, but also has its own recognizable methods and techniques. Like political studies generally, of which international relations or world politics forms a part, it is the scene of contending approaches and techniques.' There is nothing to prevent a student of International Relations from seeking to make sense of the current Israeli-Palestinian conflict in the light of its historical background, and likewise there is nothing that prevents a student of International History from using the knowledge of the historical background to shed light on the present situation. The two cannot be distinguished.

Understanding the historical background of contemporary world affairs, indispensable though it is, is unlikely, however, to be the sole reason for engaging with the past, according to the English School's way of thinking. In fact, this is quite unlikely to be the sort of thing Bull had in mind, when he held that it was 'in order to throw light on contemporary interstate politics' (2000a: 249) that he and others, in the British Committee, were conducting a comparative study of the contemporary international system with past international systems – including those of 'the Hittites, the Chinese "period of warring states", classical Greece, the post-Alexandrine Hellenistic world and the Dark Ages': most of these are far too distant to be meaningfully treated as a historical background to the present. What appears to be in the back of Bull's mind here is that somehow *comparative* knowledge helps deepen our understanding of particular instances. Of course, his apparent subscription to the covering law model of explanation should have led him to express a stronger view – that it is only in the light of well-substantiated generalizations, based on comparative methods, that we could hope to understand particular cases, including the present one. In any case, it is clear from Bull's own statement that at least one reason why historical study is an essential companion to theoretical study in IR, in his view, is that the former provides cases against which empirical generalizations can be tested (2000a: 254).

But this essentially nomothetic orientation, regarding the importance of historical knowledge to the understanding of the present, does not sit comfortably with Bull's notably historicist claim. According to this view, international politics has to be 'understood as a temporal sequence of events' and theoretical approaches are inadequate to the extent that they 'employ a timeless language of definitions and axioms, logical extrapolations or assertions of causal connection or general law, and do not by themselves convey a sense of time and change' (2000a: 253; see also Butterfield, 1972: 338; Wight, 1977: 16).[5] Bull's stress on the historicity of events makes him go on even to remark that history is important for theory 'also because theory itself has a history, and understanding of the theorist's historical position is essential to criticism of him and self-criticism by him' (2000a: 254). This reveals a third area of uncertainty. *It is unclear how the seemingly nomothetic defence of the relevance of historical knowledge to the understanding of the present squares with the historicist defence of the importance of historical knowledge.*

To summarize: already in a single essay, written by a leading theorist of the English School, a few deep uncertainties, inter-related and unresolved, are found concerning the place of historical knowledge in International Relations. They relate to: (1) how far, according to Bull (or, more generally, the English School) IR should be nomothetic and how far it should be idiographic; (2) precisely how it is that, according to him (or, more generally, the English School), historical knowledge is important to the study of contemporary international relations; and (3) how his or the School's apparently nomothetic defence of the relevance of historical knowledge relates to his or the School's historicist stress on temporality of events in international politics and on the contextuality of any theorizing about international relations. In the

---

[5] Quoting Maurice Mandelbaum (1971), Hayden White (1975: 98, n. 1) explains 'historicism' as a demand that 'we reject the view that historical events have an individual character which can be grasped apart from viewing them as embedded within a pattern of development'.

absence of some further efforts to address these questions on the part of Bull or other English School writers, it is difficult to know exactly what his or their position is on the place of historical knowledge in International Relations – other than that it is important.

Similar uncertainties are found in the writings of Adam Watson. Compare the following passages from his *The Evolution of International Society*:

1. 'An understanding of how the contemporary society of states came to be what it is, and how it may develop in the future, requires a sense of how other societies operated and developed in the past. But we will not gain much understanding if we merely trace our present arrangements back in time. We need to examine the different patterns of relations between states in their own individuality and on their own merits; and then compare them' (Watson, 1992: 1).
2. 'A realistic understanding is very difficult to obtain if we remain imprisoned in the conventional legitimacies and half-conscious assumptions of our own time. We need a broader base of comparison. As the natural sciences and medicine look for many examples of a phenomenon in order to understand it well enough to modify it, so history can enable us to distinguish the area of necessity from the area of choice' (Watson, 1992: 319).
3. 'The experience of the past is only one guide to the options for the future, but I believe it is an indispensable one. Whatever arrangements our system of communities may develop, it will remain substantially the heir to its own past' (Watson, 1992: 325).

The first passage shows that Watson thinks it important, or not unimportant, to study how the contemporary society of states and its institutions evolved from its predecessors.[6] However, he is also suggesting that the past is not just an underdeveloped form of the present or the future.[7] We must therefore treat the past in its individuality – yet, ultimately, we need to compare. The second passage suggests that the comparative study of states-systems should investigate as many examples as possible so that we may obtain more secure

---

[6] 'The Greek ideal of the city state was imported by the Renaissance into the European system, and the legitimacy of untrammelled independence remains a strong commitment of our international society today' (Watson, 1992: 49). 'Looking back to its predecessors, we shall note how the European society was the heir not only of its medieval past but also of the Greek, the Macedonian and the Roman societies: both historically, and by conscious European adaptation of classical models' (Watson, 1992: 135). Clearly, Watson took historical origins of the present system to be a worthy subject of enquiry.

[7] See Butterfield (1951c). Watson (1992: 5) acknowledges his deep indebtedness to Butterfield.

generalizations about what seems inevitable and what seems not in any states-system.[8] Given this, the third passage might be interpreted to suggest this: that whatever the arrangements may be that our system develops in the future on the basis of the present arrangements, the process of evolution is subject to the same kind of objective forces (or tendencies largely beyond human control) that had governed other systems; and what freedom we have in altering the present system is likely also to be similar to what was experienced in the past systems. But, then, Watson clearly thinks that there are differences as well as similarities among states-systems, and he is therefore somewhat unlikely to be supposing that the area of necessity and the area of choice do not alter from one system to another.[9]

We are therefore left wondering precisely how it is that historical knowledge is important to the study of contemporary international relations. Is it because the future, which will not be the same as the past, will still have to start from the present, which in turn is rooted in the past, so that the present and the future can only be made sense of as part of a story slowly unfolding from the time past? Is it rather because the present and the future are essentially similar to the past, all subject to similar kinds of impersonal forces? And does Watson really think this to be the case? Here again, as in Bull, we sense an unresolved tension between the historicist and nomothetic outlooks with a small degree of concession also made to the idiographic approach.

However, this may be to miss Watson's point altogether. It may be that he is not thinking of historical knowledge primarily as having some limited use in *predicting* the future, but rather in supplying us with an indispensable tool for *speculating about our future options*. The two are quite distinct. The idea that historical knowledge may be useful in guiding our speculations about alternative structures of the future world is also clearly present in Bull's writing. Thus, in chapter 10 of *The Anarchical Society*, Bull considers where the present

---

[8] It was precisely this concern that has led Buzan and Little (2000) to study 60,000 years of world history – mainly to refute Waltz's historically unsubstantiated claim (1979: 66) that anarchical international relations have shown remarkable sameness over the millennia.

[9] According to Watson's interpretation, there are impersonal forces in operation in any states-system which tend to make the system settle somewhere between autonomy and hegemony (1992: 122), but the process is also influenced by the prevailing notion of legitimacy about the proper way of structuring the world and the balance of material advantage both for the rulers and the ruled (1992: 131). It is unclear what constitutes the impersonal forces in addition to such things as legitimacy and advantages.

international society may be moving towards, and suggests that if it were to be transforming itself into a structure other than a society of states, then it might be one of the four historically precedented alternatives: 'a system but not a society', 'states but not a system', 'world government' and 'a new mediaevalism' (1977: 248ff).

But, significantly, Bull ends the chapter with a brief section on non-historical alternatives, in which he asserts: (i) that the range of possible alternatives cannot be listed exhaustively; (ii) that the actual form of the future universal political organization cannot be predicted; (iii) that we cannot take seriously the attempts to spell out the laws of transformation from one kind of universal political system to another; (iii) that attempts to present non-historical alternatives in fact rely on historical experience; and (iv) that, in thinking about the future,we should bear in mind that our imagination is so limited that we cannot in fact transcend our past experience (1977: 255–6). Bull is therefore not only rejecting the view that the long-term future is predictable, but he is also asserting that the future is greater than what history can teach us, and almost lamenting that our imagination is delimited by our historical knowledge and experience. History may be an indispensable guide to our speculation, but our speculation may fail precisely because it has to be guided by history, Bull seems to be saying.

Here we are beginning to see in Bull a rather complex position on the relevance of historical knowledge to the study of international relations: *history does not enable us to predict the future, but it is indispensable in our speculations about our future options; still, our speculations may be misguided precisely because they are historically based.* A parallel view is expressed by Wight in an unexpected passage:

> Historical precedents, even if they can be reduced to serviceable order, shed only an indirect light on present circumstances. To estimate the prospects of the Russo-Sino-American triangle, we must make political judgements, measuring the visible task against the visible resources. This is what Thucydides meant when he singled out, as supremely worthy of admiration in Themistocles, the grasp of *ta deonta* – the things necessary, the proper expedient, the decisive elements in the situation. And he linked it not with a sense of the past but with a sense of the future: a power of divination, an insight into how things would work out, 'Wisdom to foresee clearly the issue for better or worse that lay in the still dim future'.
>
> It is possible that, as the world has gone on since those days, politicians (and others) have increasingly acquired an historical

perspective; and if a man has an historical perspective it will of course colour his notion of the 'task' or 'need' of the current generation. The strong historical consciousness of Churchill and Kennedy has led Dr Rowse and others to argue that statesmanship is founded upon a sense of history. It might be easier to maintain the converse, that the majority of successful politicians and reformers have done without an historical sense. Cicero had a richer understanding of Roman history than Caesar; it was one reason why he was a less competent politician. Of French statesmen, the most conspicuously endowed with historical culture is Guizot, a sublime failure; the least so, Richelieu, who made history. The opposition to Wilberforce over the slave trade (as to most reformers) was largely grounded upon arguments of historical stability. King Frederick William IV, if we may stoop so low, had livelier and more colourful thoughts about history than his representative at the Federal Diet, Count von Bismarck. In the past century, the influence of historicist ideologies on politics offers warnings of self-deception rather than examples of sagacity.   (Wight, 1977: 191–2)

So, according to Wight the historian, historical knowledge does not necessarily supply a good guide to political action; good political judgement does. And good historians are not always good politicians – because the knowledge of history may mislead.

But, of course, this is not to say that historical knowledge is not important for students of international relations. After all, it was precisely Wight's historical knowledge that enabled him to write so eruditely as in the above passage on the relationship between historical knowledge and political wisdom. In any case, Wight is quite explicit about the importance of historical knowledge to the students of contemporary international relations. He wrote:

> One of the main purposes of university education is to escape from the *Zeitgeist*, from the mean, narrow, provincial spirit which is constantly assuring us that we are at the peak of human achievement, that we stand on the edge of unprecedented prosperity or an unparalleled catastrophe; that the next summit conference is going to be the most fateful in history or that the leader is either the greatest, or the most disastrous, of all time. It is a liberation of the spirit to acquire perspective, to recognize that every generation is confronted by problems of the utmost subjective urgency, but that an objective grading is probably impossible; to learn that the same moral predicaments and the same ideas have been explored before. One need read very little in political theory to become aware of recurrences and repetitions. Thus, if one turns to E. H. Carr's *The Twenty Years' Crisis* after Hobbes' *Leviathan*, one cannot fail to note

that the basic arguments are the same. To read about the Wars of Religion, and the theories of the Huguenots, Calvinists, and Jesuits, is at once to be struck by the parallel with modern totalitarianism, especially Communism. (1991: 6)

Wight's 'international theory' was built on this key assumption – that the positions the human race has taken concerning the nature of international relations are reducible to a few ideal-types and that there is nothing fundamentally new in our thinking about international relations. 'International politics is the realm of recurrence and repetition; it is the field in which political action is most regularly necessitous' (Wight 1966a: 26), and this, in Wight's thinking, applied also to the realm of international thought.

Wight's emphasis on 'recurrence and repetition' as a distinctive characteristic of the international political realm is anti-progressivist, and it is uncertain how unreservedly Bull or Watson accepted this line of thinking. Bull, at any rate, betrays his progressivist leaning from time to time. Three examples may be noted.

A first illustration has to do with his view that, quite commonly, a rule may emerge in inter-state interactions initially as an operational rule, then become established practice, then attain the status of a moral principle, and finally come to be incorporated in a legal convention. He observes that this appears to have been the genesis of many of the rules now embodied in multilateral treaties or conventions concerning the laws of war, diplomatic and consular status, and the law of the sea (1977: 67). Implicit in this line of thinking is Bull's view that when there is a felt need to manage certain aspects of international relations, international society's response tends to become progressively more formal, technical and rational. This relates to a second illustration, in which Bull reveals his progressivist view of modern world history. He wrote:

> [I]n a longer historical perspective part of what I have been describing as the revolt against the Western dominance [in international society in the twentieth century] is best seen . . . as the working-out within Asian, African and Latin American countries of historical processes that are not unique to them but are universal: the emergence of sovereign states, the rise of national consciousness on a mass scale, the adaptation of society to modern science and technology, the development of a modern economy, and the attempt to preserve cultural identity and some element of continuity with traditional modes of life against the inroads made upon them by these changes. These are processes in which all peoples today are

involved, in one way or another, not just those of the Third World. To the extent that in one group of peoples today these processes have long been at work and have gone further, while in another group of peoples the same process began more recently and have gone a shorter distance, the idea of a division of the society of nations into 'developed' and 'developing' countries has some meaning.

(2000d: 232–3)

And, thirdly, according to Bull, in this worldwide process of evolution, what he called 'the revolt against the West' represents at least in their broad direction a forward movement in human affairs and a step towards greater justice in international relations (2000d: 244).

It should at this juncture be noted that anti-progressivist and pro-gressivist interpretations of world history – both of which are *prima facie* plausible, though not necessarily to the same degree to everyone – are attempts to make sense of the world, and that the same can be said of international relations theory. It is here that Wight's tentative equation of theoretical understanding of international politics with historical interpretation (Wight, 1966a: 33) begins to make some sense. Bull, while not accepting this equation (Bull, 2000a: 253), rightly observes that '[a]ny historical study, even one of a purely narrative kind, has its own intellectual structure of hypothesis and argument, and putting together conclusions of two or more historical studies is not a matter of assembling "data" but of uncovering the intellectual structure of each study and marrying it with that of the other' (2000a: 254). He might have added that the intellectual structures of two or more historical studies, when uncovered, might turn out to be very different, even irreconcilable, such that their conclusions could not easily be put together. What is implicit in this line of thinking, which is not fully spelled out by Wight or Bull, is that reading histories of international relations and grasping theories of international relations go hand in hand, not in the sense that, as suggested by some (including Wight and Bull), history substantiates or refutes theoretical generalizations, but in the sense that theory is integral to history: to have an understanding of the history of international politics is to have a theoretical grasp of the subject.

It is difficult to say, on the basis of the above survey, which of the many views about historical knowledge and its relation to IR (and also to the practice of international politics) truly represents the English School. English School authors make a number of points which do not appear necessarily to form a clear and coherent set. However, at a risk of overgeneralization, we may say that the following positions effectively sum up their central tenets in this area:

1. The subject-matter of International Relations is intrinsically historical, and therefore atemporal approaches to the study of international relations must be considered inadequate.
2. In any empirical study of international relations, by historians and IR specialists alike, an idiographical dimension cannot be neglected.
3. Therefore, the standard formula, 'International Relations: International History = nomothetic: idiographic', cannot be accepted.
4. It is not intellectually unworthy, however, to search for historical generalizations, but we should bear in mind that there may be differences, as well as similarities, in the cases compared, when the scope of investigation is large, as it should be.
5. Historical knowledge not only enables, but also delimits, our speculations about future options, and does not necessarily supply a good guide to political action.
6. In our own thinking about international relations, we should be reflective about two possibilities – one, that our ideas about international relations may be historically bound, and the other, that there is likely to be little or nothing radically new in human thinking about the subject (Bull, 1969: 37).
7. History of international politics can plausibly be written as a story of recurrence and repetition, but in writing a history of modern international society, it is possible to draw attention to some signs of progress towards a more rational world.
8. Historical narratives about world politics are intertwined with the theories (or interpretations) of the fundamental characteristics of world politics. An important implication of this last point, not fully realised by English School authors, is that one of the key functions of doing history is to enable us to engage critically with dominant interpretations of world politics underlying current practices.

Martha Finnemore is entirely right to draw attention to the historical orientation of the English School's scholarship, but she does not spell out what is embodied in the School's historically oriented approach to the study of international relations. Followers of the English School, especially those of Wight, Watson and Bull, would, it is submitted, tend to exhibit, in their approach to the study of international relations, attitudes towards history which embrace some of the eight elements, which have been distilled above from these authors' pronouncements and incidental remarks.

Science, Sociology and International Relations

Another common thread that unites the English School is its firm belief that attempts to formulate scientific laws and, in the light of these laws, to predict or explain international outcomes are unlikely to succeed. 'Those at any rate', Manning had remarked, 'who see the similarities between Diplomatics [or study of international relations] and, for instance, cricket may need a lot of convincing that the outcome of an impending "Berlin" showdown ought by scientific methods to be already even only approximately predictable, when the summit season is still only about to begin' (1975: 213). And, according to Bull, there is very little of significance that can be said about international relations if it is insisted that we must first find laws that meet the strict scientific standards of 'verification and proof' (1969: 20). Of course, the English School position is not that, therefore, there is very little of significance that can be said about international relations, but rather that there is much of significance that can be said about this subject-matter which derives from 'a scientifically imperfect process of perception and intuition' and relies on 'exercise of judgement' (Bull, 1969: 20).

There is much that is reasonable in this line of thinking, but unless its details are spelled out, the sensible core of the English School thinking is obscured, leading Finnemore to remark, as we saw, that 'simply figuring out what its methods *are* is a challenge' (2001: 509; emphasis Finnemore's). In understanding the basic position of the English School that International Relations is not a science, the following three points need to be taken into account.

First, although English School authors are deeply sceptical about ever finding scientific laws pertaining to international relations (and they are likely to be thinking that this is because there are no such laws after all), they are not, as we saw, averse to studying history with a view to drawing some broad generalizations. Their view is that history of international relations can plausibly be written so as to highlight some general tendencies in the workings of international politics, but that patterns thereby discerned in international phenomena are no more than inexactly expressed empirical generalizations, not comparable to laws formulated by natural scientists.[10]

Second, English School authors would not hesitate to say that, despite our ignorance of, or even the absence of, laws governing international phenomena, it is nevertheless possible to give an account of some significant aspects of international relations. But it will be recalled that Bull had himself expressed his anxiety about this position, acknowledging that this poses a paradox to those, including himself, who in principle subscribe to the covering law model of explanation (Bull, 2000a: 264). Now, of course, most IR specialists who accept this model in their field of study would not insist that, in order to be able to explain an international outcome at all, we need to have identified a law, stating exactly under what type of condition the type of outcome in question would always follow. Faced with an inability to produce such exact laws, they would dilute the requirement considerably. The following remark supplies a typical illustration:

> An 'explanation' is a statement (or a set of statements) that demonstrate that the outcome of a particular event is merely an example of an established pattern. If the historian is going to convince me that internal unrest led to a war initiation by Anatolia against Catalonia in 1859, he or she must demonstrate to me that internal unrest *generally* does increase the probability of war initiation among a class of states to which Anatolia belongs.
>
> (Ray, 1995: 138; emphasis Ray's)

Given (1) the taken-for-granted attitude on the part of many IR specialists, especially in the United States, that this is the procedure we are required to follow in explaining international phenomena, given also (2) the philosophical anxiety about this issue on the part of Bull, the English School's leading theorist, and given in any case (3) the School's own willingness, in principle, to seek general patterns in international history, it will not be unreasonable to demand that the School and its followers clarify the sense in which their accounts of international relations *explain* their subject matter.

It should be noted in this connection that it is quite misleading for them to suggest that only if 'strict standards of verification and proof' were abandoned would it be possible to make significant remarks

---

[10] See Bull (1966/1969: 30) for his view that the difficulties the scientific theory has encountered in the study of international relations is due to *the inherent nature* of the subject matter.

about international relations; this would make it sound as though accounts of international relations, *not* invoking scientific laws, were, by virtue of that very fact, no longer subject to empirical substantiation. It would be implausible of course to suggest that English School authors did not care about evidence. Yet their weariness towards scientific methodology with its 'strict standards of verification and proof' has gone hand in hand with their inclination to offer empirical statements about international relations without providing 'systematic discussions about rules of evidence', as Finnemore (2001: 509) has rightly complained. However, weakness on the part of English School writers is quite independent of their otherwise sensible claim that significant aspects of international relations can be accounted for without the knowledge of (or despite the absence of) laws governing that realm, and there remains the need therefore to clarify the epistemological character of their accounts of international relations.

Third, when English School authors stress the importance of judgement and intuition in our intellectual engagement with international affairs, it is worth noting that the scope of questions which they consider to be central to the study of international relations is very wide. It is broad enough in fact to encompass those for which there are, by their own admission, no objective criteria for valid answers (Bull, 1969: 26; Manning, 1975: 124ff). Therefore, their idea of what is intellectually worthy or legitimate in the study of international relations is different from that of those, in particular, for whom only those questions are intellectually worthy for which there are definite criteria for valid answers. Given this, it is especially noteworthy that the School shows an ambiguous attitude towards the issue of whether it is appropriate, in the academic study of International Relations, to raise substantive moral questions, which arguably are a primary example of problems requiring judgement and intuition. While stressing the need to exercise judgement and intuition, they appear, at least in some cases, to shy away from engaging forthrightly in one area where they are most pertinent.

Of the three points noted above, there is not much to add to the first, except in its relation to the second. And the third point is best discussed in connection with the English School's treatment of norms and values, which is the topic of the next section. This section therefore offers a few further observations on the second issue – the epistemological nature of the English School's accounts of international relations.

On this subject, Manning, who had reflected on it more than any other English School writers, had earlier suggested that International Relations was a branch of Sociology though, he added, it was also much akin to history (Manning, 1951b: 53, 73; Manning, 1954: 65). But, clearly, in making the first half of this observation, he was not thinking of a Durkheimian positivist sociology, which was later to inspire Waltz's theory of international politics (Waltz, 1979) – for such an approach would have led Manning to argue for formulating a theory aimed at explaining recurrent features of international relations, which he did not. What Manning had in mind, as we saw in Chapter 2, was the approach to the study of society which attempts to give an account of what goes on inside it 'in the light of premises and preconceptions' (Manning, 1975: 211) that prevail within its boundaries. Social Anthropology or Ethnography may have been a more appropriate label than Sociology, and his admiration for Malinowski is therefore fitting in this context (Manning, 1975: 204ff). Manning wrote:

> Let the student of International Relations think then of the international society as Malinowski did of his Trobrianders, and be content with nothing other than whatever may prove to be the nearest practicable approach to a personal participation – in the role, as it were, of sovereign state – in the life of the international family.
>
> (1975: 204–5)

For Manning, the aim of International Relations as a university undergraduate subject is to enable students to achieve 'a progressively deeper insight into the nature of international relationships' and 'an ever improving aptitude for appreciating an international situation as it presents itself to the experienced statesman's eye' (Manning, 1951a: 14). He praised Alfred Zimmern as a great teacher of International Relations because he was able to convey to his students what life was like as lived by the states of his day in their interrelations – just as Malinowski was able to teach his pupils about the life of the Trobriand Islanders. Manning added: 'What fortune for those generations of grateful young men that it seems never to have occurred to him [Zimmern] to try to make his subject look like economic theory' (1975: 206). Echoing Manning, Bull was later to remark: 'The student whose study of international politics consists solely of an introduction to the techniques of systems theory, game theory, simulation, or content analysis is simply to shut off from contact with the subject, and is unable to develop any feeling either for the play of international politics or for the moral dilemma to which it gives rise' (1969: 28).

In their relatively early discussion of epistemological issues surrounding IR, therefore, what those English School writers who contributed to this subject drew special attention to was the centrality of *Verstehen*, or explanation of what goes on in a social field, by penetrating the minds, and uncovering the assumptions and motives, of its relevant actors, and imparting the knowledge or understanding thereby gained to those who are seeking to make sense of the situation. It is no surprise then that International Relations is akin in their view to History, Sociology and Social Anthropology for all these subjects at least in part engage in this mode of account-giving.

This does not mean, however, that English School writers do not engage in causal analysis, which is often juxtaposed to *Verstehen*.[11] A very explicit claim to do so is found in *The Anarchical Society*. In it, Bull declares as follows:

> A central theme in this study is that the rules and institutions to which reference has been made carry out positive functions or roles in relation to international order. In this study what is meant by statements of this kind is simply that these rules and institutions are part of the efficient causation of international order, that they are among the necessary and sufficient conditions of its occurrence.
>
> (1977: 74–5)

Since Bull stresses elsewhere in the same volume (1977: 6, 54, 65) that order is in fact possible *without* the rules or institutions, he is clearly contradicting himself in suggesting at the same time that these are among the *necessary* conditions of international order. And to say that these are part of the *efficient causation* of international order and *sufficient conditions* of its occurrence would seem to be a confusing way of putting simply that they *contribute to* order among states. Nonetheless, what is important to notice here is that, in Bull's thinking, the rules and institutions he has identified not only form part of shared 'premises and presuppositions' in the light of which international interactions are carried on (and in the light of which, therefore, we can make sense of what goes on internationally), but also contribute causally to the achievement of 'the elementary or primary goals of the society of states' (Bull, 1977: 8).

---

[11] See, in particular, Hollis and Smith (1990). Compare, however, Suganami (1997), which deconstructs the simplistic explanation/understanding dichotomy underlying Hollis and Smith's contention that there are always two kinds of story to tell about social phenomena.

But precisely what kind of causal claim is this, and on what grounds is it defended? Those who are puzzled about the epistemological status and methodological principles of the arguments emanating from the English School may well raise this question.

It is important to recall here that, in Bull's structure of thought, what he calls the rules and institutions of international society are an instrument through the efficacious operation of which the elementary or primary goals of the society of states (or goals of international order) are maintained. Thus, to say that these rules and institutions contribute causally to the achievement of these goals is the same as saying that these rules and institutions are operative and efficacious to some significant extent. But, of course, Bull would not have subscribed to the view that it was possible to make sense of international interactions in the light of these rules and institutions if he had not judged that these rules and institutions were operative and efficacious to some significant extent. It turns out, therefore, that Bull's causal thesis, said to be central to his main book, is a corollary of his key judgement that what goes on internationally can be understood in the light of the rules and institutions of international society.

An analogy may help clarify this point. It is reasonable to suggest that the traffic regulations of our community contribute to its road safety. It is easy to see, however, that this is concomitant with a judgement that we can make sense of what goes on on our roads partly in the light of the relevant traffic regulations. Bull's causal thesis, then, is not significantly different in quality from a plausible commonsense view that our community's traffic regulations contribute to its road safety.

But there is one further observation to add to this: the plausibility of such a view – that traffic regulations contribute to road safety – appears to result from the sheer implausibility of a contrary view – that they make *no* difference. Similarly, the plausibility of Bull's causal thesis appears to derive from the sheer implausibility of a contrary judgement that rules and institutions of modern international society have made no difference whatsoever to the quality of life internationally. Surely, it may therefore be objected, it is true but rather trivial to say that these things contribute to international order by their presence, more than by their absence. Nonetheless, given the formally anarchical structure of international society and a relatively common expectation that there will consequently be little or no international order to speak of, it is reasonable for Bull to have felt it worthwhile to spell out the view, which he shared with other English School writers, that a degree of order found in international society – which, given anarchy, is perhaps quite remarkable – is to some extent attributable to its historically evolving rules and institutions.

One other thing that some English School writers have done in their investigation into international relations is to make use of ideal-types, as was rightly noticed by Finnemore. 'My own sense of the English School's theoretical contribution', she remarked, 'is that it offers something like a set of Weberian ideal-types about international social structures' (2001: 512). Indeed, Bull's concepts of 'international system', 'international society' and 'the great society of all mankind' are best construed as ideal-types in the light of which a given world political structure can be depicted. In Bull's account, each of these becomes an element contained in the global political structure to varying degrees over time, and the contemporary world can be understood as combining all three. This suggests that, in Bull's thinking, the contemporary global political structure is never entirely an international system, an international society or a great society of all mankind. It is because of this that it makes sense for him to say, for instance, that *the element of* international society should be extended in order to ensure a more orderly coexistence of states (Bull, 1977: 315).

Finnemore, however, asks, '[H]ow do you know an international society (or international system or world society) if you see one?' and criticizes English School authors for only giving definitions for analytic categories and almost never providing systematic discussions about rules of evidence (2001: 509). Bull's response to this will be that 'international society', 'international system' and 'world society' *are* analytic categories, to which he has given his definitions, and international society, for instance, is not something you see, but an idea in light of which we can make sense of an aspect of contemporary international relations.[12]

One observation to enter here is that Finnemore's question 'how do you know an international society . . . if you see one?' would have struck someone like Wight as ahistorical. Wight drew attention to what

---

[12] It should, however, be noted that English School writers, including Bull himself, at times also use 'states-system' as a general label for the basic political structure of the world consisting of states, and 'international society' as a label for the contemporary world, going back at least to the Westphalian system. Hence, for example, the title, *The Expansion of International Society*.

he called 'the internal marks' of the states-system that originated in Western Europe, which, according to him, were sovereign states, their mutual recognition, their accepted hierarchy, their means of regular communication, their framework of law and their means of defending their common interests (or the balance of power). Here he was not so much defining the concept of the international system as portraying the characteristics of modern states-systems 'which have become clearer during those three centuries [between the time of the Council of Constance, 1414–18 and that of the Congress of Utrecht, 1712–13]' (Wight, 1977: 129). It remains the case, however, that Bull drew attention to such historically evolved internal marks of Western states-systems as a quality pointing to its 'societal' (as opposed to merely 'systemic') status, thereby using 'system' and 'society' as analytical concepts in the light of which historically evolving structures of the world could be made sense of.

Finnemore, however, is right to point out that English School authors have not elaborated on 'mechanisms for change' between the three ideal-typical structures. How is it exactly, she asks, that politics moves from an international system, or a situation which is dominantly systemic, to an international society, or where the societal element is dominant, or from there to a world society, or where that element is supreme (2001: 513)? Given the English School's self-image as following partly historical and partly sociological lines of investigation, it is unsurprising for others to be curious about this apparent lacuna.

There are a number of reasons for this apparent neglect. First of all, to the extent that they are interested in the transformation of a more systemic relationship to a societal one, their approach will be circumscribed by their idiographical orientation – as can be seen in Bull and Watson's *The Expansion of International Society* (1984). Even though in their historical reconstruction they may pay attention to mechanistic elements which appear to have operated in the particular historical process under investigation (see Suganami, 1984), it does not come very naturally to them to try to make a systematic list of causal mechanisms for change in the way Alexander Wendt (1999: ch. 7), for instance, has done, let alone to search for a general theory of social transformation, which they would dismiss as an ahistorical scientism.

In this connection, it is also important to note that the cases of system-to-society transformation, examined in *The Expansion of*

International Society, fall into a relatively narrow range when compared with Wendt's ambitious concern to cover the phenomena of the political transformation of inter-state relations more comprehensively. This point requires a further explanation.

By an international society, as is often repeated, Bull and Watson 'mean a group of states (or, more generally, a group of independent political communities) which not merely form a system, in the sense that the behaviour of each is a necessary factor in the calculations of the others, but also have established by dialogue and consent common rules and institutions for the conduct of their relations, and recognize their common interest in maintaining these arrangements' (Bull and Watson, 1984: 1). Because international society, defined in this way, is associated with the Grotian tradition, in Wight's tripartite scheme of Hobbesian, Grotian and Kantian views, there has been a tendency to associate the English School idea of 'international system' with the Hobbesian one. This is not in fact an implausible interpretation, especially given Bull's (and, following him, Watson's) reference, as a distinctive feature of a system, to the behaviour of each being 'a necessary factor in the *calculations* of the others' – a formulation which tends to conjure up a realist imagery of international politics.

Such a grouping of states may, of course, find themselves in that kind of situation because intense international interactions which developed there have, for some contingent reasons, deeply ingrained in them the Hobbesian international political culture of enmity. Call this 'Scenario A'. But a group of states may only form a system in Bull's sense simply because interactions which have taken place there have so far not been very intense at all – such that although the states, in making decisions, do take into account what the others do, the system has not yet developed either any complex societal arrangements or even a deeply internalized Hobbesian international culture of enmity. Call this 'Scenario B'. In such a case, the depth of socialization is simply not very advanced, rather than it being the case that they are socialized deeply into the Hobbesian culture of enmity and thereby lack the Grotian societal elements of dialogue, consent, common rules, and so on.

The Expansion of International Society, the English School's key text in this subfield, is focused on the entry of states outside, or on the fringe, of Western international society into that society, and thus it is about the socialization process of the outsiders in which the insider/outsider interactions were not intense initially. Its focus, therefore, is not on

Scenario A, but on Scenario B. English School authors have not in fact addressed the issue of what causal mechanisms may operate to get the states out of the Hobbesian international state of nature towards a more cooperative one.

The reason for this seems to be the view that, *historically*, states or political communities have not found themselves in the Hobbesian state of nature. Here is Watson's resounding conclusion based on his study of international societies since Sumerian times:

> We may conclude that regulatory arrangements always come into being between civilized polities when the volume of contacts becomes worth regulating. Anything more intimate, a society that goes beyond rules and institutions to shared values and assumptions, has hitherto always developed within a cultural framework, even if some of the values and assumptions are later adopted by communities outside the culture. (1992: 318)

English School authors have not worked on causal mechanisms that explain a transition from a Hobbesian 'system' to a Grotian 'society' because, to them, the latter is the more natural state, and what underlies this, as succinctly captured in Manning's phrase, is 'a situationally generated pragmatic inevitability' (1972: 328) – a concept he shared with H. L. A. Hart (1961: 189–95).[13]

There are two problems, however. Watson does not define 'civilized polities', and therefore, the tremendous range of cases covered in his volume notwithstanding, it is uncertain, as Finnemore complains (2001: 510), whether all the relevant instances have been covered as a basis of his general pronouncement. There will also be some objection to the plainly rationalistic and voluntaristic view that underlies Watson's interpretation of the origins of social institutions, and we can certainly demand, from his followers, a more detailed empirical study of the historical evolution of social arrangements in inter-societal relationships.

---

[13] Wendt, whose argument about transformation of international political culture has the merit of taking into account an important factor of the depth of socialization, or the degree of internalization of the prevailing culture (1999: 255), stresses the difficulty of leaving the Hobbesian system if the culture is deeply set. He does not in fact spell out the mechanism of transformation which can operate specifically from the Hobbesian starting point to the more cooperative world; instead, his focus is on how a somewhat more cooperative (in his terminology, 'Lockean') system of 'rivalry' moves towards an even more cooperative ('Kantian') one of 'friendship'. Interestingly, his implicit justification for this is that, historically, the Western international system has found itself already in the Lockean state (Wendt 1999: 339).

There are a few other reasons for English School authors' relative lack of interest in investigating the causal mechanisms for progressive transformation. For example, especially in their earlier works, English School authors were on the whole more concerned about the possible deterioration of international order, and how to prevent it, rather than in speculating on causal mechanisms that might bring about a more cooperative international environment or, for that matter, one in which the element of world society comes to dominate.[14] This is not surprising given that they were writing against the historical background of two world wars in one generation, followed by the outbreak of the Cold War accompanied by the 'revolt against the West'. There were of course signs of progressive political transformation, but the most conspicuous one was taking place in Europe, and English School writers tended to see this as a regional phenomenon, not altering the global political structure (Manning, 1975: 180; Bull, 1977: 266; see further Suganami, 2001d: 414–16).

One final observation to add here is that English School authors tend to think more about what states or governments could and should do to protect and enhance the quality of life internationally (which includes the question of what rules and institutions states should prefer to live under) than about what objective social forces may contribute to change in this (or any other) direction. In this sense, their approach is agent-centred and normative. The idea that international society is a cultural achievement that needs to be kept alive and extended by a concerted effort, especially from its leading member states, runs through the writings of the English School. However, as we saw, there is also a tendency among some of them to suppose that there are forces in operation that incline the world towards somewhere in the direction of a society of states (Manning, 1975: preface to reissue; Bull, 1977: 315–17; Watson, 1992: 311–25; see also Butterfield, 1966a: 147).

The following points summarize the main arguments of this section:

1. At the centre of the English School's approach to the study of international relations is its stress on explaining what goes on internationally by penetrating the minds, and uncovering the assumptions and motives, of its key actors.

---

[14] The latter is also beyond the concern of Wendt's analysis. His Kantian international culture is a culture of inter-state friendship (1999: 297ff), and does not correspond to the English School's Kantianism or world society perspective.

2. Causal analysis is not excluded from the repertoire of the English School, but this tends to be done as part of their historical analysis. Bull's claim to engage in causal analysis in his main work is legitimate, but, as a causal argument, his is quite underdeveloped.

3. English School authors also use some ideal-types as a means of describing international relations, such as, most notably, international system, international society and the great society of all mankind.

4. For a number of reasons, they have not done much work on mechanisms of political change. A more detailed empirical study of the historical evolution of social arrangements in inter-societal relationships is what we may reasonably expect of the followers of the English School tradition, given its deployment of historical and sociological approaches and its interest in the normative framework of inter-societal relations.[15]

Norms, values and International Relations

While discounting the possibility of developing a rigorously scientific theory of international relations, English School authors are not opposed to approaching their subject-matter 'in the spirit . . . of science' (Manning, 1954: 46). Bull has thus remarked that '[i]nsofar as the scientific approach is a protest against slipshod thinking and dogmatism, or against a residual providentialism, there is everything to be said for it' (Bull, 1969: 36).

Still, it was Manning's view that International Relations was 'also the exercise of an art, training in an art' (1951b: 53) and that 'trained intuition' was an important aspect of IR as an undergraduate subject (1951b: 49). Likewise, Bull stressed the need for judgement and intuition in International Relations against the charge that non-scientific works in IR are mere 'intuitive guesswork' or 'wisdom literature' (2000a: 256). The readiness of these leading English School authors to discard strict scientific standards of 'verification and proof' in favour of judgement and intuition, while remaining firmly opposed to slipshod thinking, dogmatism and providentialism, is intelligible when it is realized that the range of questions they consider intellectually worthwhile goes beyond what can be answered by *scientific* methods alone.

---

[15] This theme will be dealt with more extensively in the following chapters of this volume.

We have already seen that learning to appreciate 'an international situation as it presents itself to the experienced statesman's eye' was, for Manning, a key aim of education in IR (Manning, 1951a: 14), and that Bull likewise stressed the importance of developing a feel for the play of international politics and for the moral dilemma to which it gave rise (Bull, 1969: 28). Such things require empathetic understanding of international politics and disciplined interpretative skills, which may be partly what Manning and Bull had in mind when they spoke of the need for judgement and intuition, even though, because of the multi-interpretability of international actions, 'any answer we provide . . . will leave some things unsaid' and may even 'be no more than an item in a conversation that has yet to be concluded' (Bull, 1969: 26).

It would seem quite reasonable, however, to suggest that one area in which judicious judgement and trained intuition are as clearly necessary as scientific methods are redundant is where substantive moral questions are asked about international relations. We might therefore expect English School writers to show the same kind of open readiness in stating that such questions are central to IR as the readiness with which they have discarded strict scientific methods from the study of international relations. Indeed, according to Bull's defence of the classical approach, central questions in the theory of international relations are at least in part moral questions, and this, he says, is precisely the reason why we have to rely upon our capacity of judgement (1969: 26). Nevertheless, it is far from the case that English School authors are openly and unreservedly committed to treating substantive moral questions as central aspects of International Relations. If anything, they have tended on the whole to be rather hesitant to be involved, or be seen to be involved, in normative argumentation, aimed to arrive at prescriptive conclusions – although more recent writers have not shied away from stating their normative views more explicitly (Vincent, 1986a; Wheeler, 2000). If there is any lack of clarity in their positions, this, arguably, is the most conspicuous.

In explicating the English School's attitudes towards 'normative' questions, we should bear in mind that English School authors see no problem with attempts to identify the existing normative framework of international relations. They are positivistic in the sense in which legal positivists are so. Perhaps they should be more conscious of a methodological problem here in that what counts as evidence for an assertion that such and such is a normative principle accepted in contemporary international relations, or for that matter, such and such is an *institution* of the existing international society is a question requiring a careful reflection. But the point here is that English School authors do not see any fundamental epistemological trouble in the activity of stating – from a positivistic, anthropological, external standpoint – what the rules, norms and institutions are of a given society. This extends to the question of values, so that they do not see it as epistemologically problematic simply to offer what they see as essentially a factual statement – that such and such is held to be an important value in a given society, international or otherwise. A primary example of this is Bull's treatment (1977: 8–20) of the elementary goals of modern international society which are a set of values that, in his interpretation, the modern society of states itself and especially its dominant members have treated as vital. Also noteworthy here is Manning's advice, when making a normative statement, to preface it with: 'to my way of thinking' (1975: 126). He claims that this qualifying phrase transforms a normative statement into a factual one – from 'X ought to be done' to '*I as a matter of fact hold the view that* X ought to be done.'

Moreover, English School authors do not see any serious epistemological problem with offering *instrumental* advice of the form: 'if X is your goal, then Y is the way to achieve it'. Manning has remarked in passing, 'Without . . . formally presenting itself as a policy science, social cosmology [or IR] may, in passing, animadvert upon the technical adequacy of given nostrums' (1975: 211). A more substantive illustration is Bull's insistence that his defence of the states-system and of the institutions of international society that he has identified is delimited by his book's aim to work out what is (technically or instrumentally) the best means of achieving 'order' – which, by his own admission, is 'not the only value in relation to which international conduct may be shaped' (1977: xii). He added: 'A study of justice in world politics, which may be envisaged as a companion volume to the present one, might yield some very different perspectives from those that are expressed here. But this is a study of order in world politics' (1977: xiii).

Judicious judgement and trained intuition might be called for when working out an instrumental advice – in the form of hypothetical imperatives – which we are invited to read in Bull, and they may also be necessary in putting forward a plausible interpretation of what rules, norms or institutions can be said to exist in international society. But these qualities, arguably, are even more crucial in dealing with substantive moral questions, and given English School authors' apparent hesitancy in tackling such questions, we should ask what is the position of the English School (and if there is no unity here, what are the positions of its leading figures) on the place of moral questions and deliberations in International Relations as an intellectual pursuit.

A very clear-cut answer is found in the case of Alan James, for whom such questions are entirely unworthy of intellectual pursuit within IR as an academic discipline. He believes there is no way of responding to these questions objectively. There is also a strong element of moral scepticism in Bull's writings, in which we find him state categorically that moral questions 'cannot by their very nature be given any sort of objective answer' (1969: 26), and further that '[t]here is no such thing as "rational action" in the sense of action dictated by "reason" as against "the passion", a faculty present in all men and enjoining them to act in the same way' (1977: 126). He suggests that such a faculty is some eighteenth-century philosophers' illusion (2000a: 259). It is understandable, therefore, to find Bull insisting that his main book, *The Anarchical Society*, was only dealing with hypothetical imperatives, not substantive moral questions, for which, by his own admission, no objectively defensible answers could be given. But, according to him, substantive moral questions *are* an integral part of the theory of international relations, to which it would be disingenuous to suggest his book was not intended as a serious contribution. If the political framework of world politics, organized as a society of sovereign states, is argued to be the best practically available alternative for the achievement, not of any goals, but specifically of those which are presented as having the status of the elementary, primary and universal goals of all social life, it is difficult to see that such an argument is not actually a moral one. Besides, in the third part of *The Anarchical Society*, Bull does not hesitate to defend the society of sovereign states as currently the most suitable institutional structure for the achievement not only of peace and security, but also of economic and social *justice* (1977: ch. 12; see also Chapter 7).

A main source of this ambivalence on Bull's part is found in the combination of his desire to avoid dogmatism in intellectual pursuit (1969: 36) and his conviction that moral questions, which are important in the practice of international relations, can still be 'subjected to rational investigation' (2000e: 167) and 'probed, clarified, reformulated, and tentatively answered' – although, ultimately, from 'some arbitrary standpoint' (1969: 26). To the extent that answering substantive moral questions would require him to adopt some arbitrary standpoint,

Bull's disapproval of dogmatism and his desire not to be seen to be dogmatic, would work against his involvement with such questions. To the extent, however, that he considered it possible – 'according to the method of philosophy' – to probe, clarify, reformulate and tentatively answer such questions, it was natural for him to have considered them as worthy of serious intellectual attention (1969: 26). Thus, it was possible, in his view, to reflect critically on the moral system to which one tentatively subscribes, in comparison with others, and to study the implications of one's fundamental moral beliefs to the important issues of contemporary world politics. Bull's 1983 Hagey Lectures, 'Justice in International Relations' (2000d), were written, at least in part, from this angle, and in them we find him considering moral implications of liberalism for contemporary global issues.

Manning, too, had considered substantive moral questions worthy of intellectual engagement, characterizing them as 'deliberative' questions, for which, in contradistinction to the 'inquisitive' variety, there are no definite objective answers to offer, but merely more or less persuasive arguments (1975: 124ff), involving '[t]he probing of presuppositions, the evaluating of ends, the weighing of issues, the elucidating of concepts – all philosophical rather than restrictively scientific undertakings' (1975: 211). Besides, Bull was a traditionalist under Wight's influence. Normative questions were central to the theory of international relations, understood as traditions of speculations about inter-state relations. Earlier contributors to the traditions – some of them eighteenth-century philosophers – have collectively bequeathed upon us a variety of perspectives on these questions, which Bull, like Wight, felt we were somewhat unlikely to be able to transcend. Nothing captures Bull's ambivalence towards normative engagement with international relations so strikingly as his criticism of Brian Midgley's work on natural law as 'dogmatic' (2001e: 169) which is combined with what Midgley has rightly characterized as Bull's 'nostalgia' for natural law (Midgley 1979: 262).

One observation that should be added here is that none of the leading English School writers, such as Bull and Manning in particular, who had addressed the issue of how IR as an intellectual pursuit should deal with substantive moral questions, was able to base their discussion on deep meta-ethical reflections (see Manning, 1975: 126–7; Bull, 1977: 78). Bull apparently took the line that social values are of two kinds: objective values that come under the rubric of 'order' and subjective ones subsumed under the rubric of 'justice' (1977: 78). This crude dichotomy, and his assertion that 'life, truth and property' are values of the first kind, is strikingly arbitrary.

Here it is pertinent to take a brief look at John Vincent's work, *Human Rights and International Relations* (1986a), which is more explicitly normative than any preceding English School texts. According to him:

> Human rights now play a part in the decision about the legitimacy of a state (and of other actors and institutions) in international society, about whether what it is or what it does is sanctioned or authorized by law or right. It is not now enough for a state to be, and to be recognized as, sovereign. Nor is it enough for it to be a nation-state in accordance with the principle of self-determination. It must also act domestically in such a way as not to offend against the basic rights of individuals and groups within its territory. The question of what these basic rights are may not be resolved in international law . . ., but the argument here is that the right to life is basic if there are such things as basic rights. (1986a: 130)

However, Vincent's 'argument here' is simply that no one can enjoy human rights unless she or he is alive, therefore the right to life is the most basic of all human rights. He added that 'the right to life is a nonsense unless it demands sustenance against deprivation as well as protection against violence' (1986a: 145). Of the various kinds of duty that may correlate with this right, he argued that the duty to aid those incapable for providing for their own subsistence was the most elementary (1986a: 146).

That may well be so. What is problematic is the mode of his reasoning. The truism that in order for anyone to enjoy human rights, she or he must first be alive points basically to the precondition of a particular person's ability to enjoy her or his human rights. It is not certain that this solves the moral-political question of which, among the total set of human rights, is the most primary, or which class of rights is more important than others. It is not implausible to suggest that some individuals may have to sacrifice their lives (and thereby forgo the enjoyment of any human right) in order that some very fundamental human rights are protected. This does not show, of course, that the right to life is *not* the most fundamental. But it does seem to show that an analysis of the precondition for a particular individual person's ability to enjoy human rights is not identical with an analysis of the priority of some human rights over others. In any case, more detailed examination would seem to be required regarding the methodology of moral argumentation than is exhibited in Vincent's argument.

English School research projects

The English School's approach to the study of international relations has historical, sociological and normative dimensions. This chapter has discussed each of these dimensions in turn and attempted to clarify exactly what it is that they are doing, or think should be done, in International Relations as an intellectual pursuit. The discussion of this chapter has been conducted against a reasonable complaint, represented by Finnemore, that the epistemological status and methodological principles of English School arguments are left rather obscure.

As for the historical dimension, it is widely held by English School writers that the subject-matter of International Relations is intrinsically historical, and that therefore atemporal approaches to the study of international relations are inadequate. English School writers stress that, in any empirical study of international relations, by historians and IR specialists alike, an idiographical dimension cannot be neglected. They do not therefore accept a standard formula, 'International Relations: International History = nomothetic: idiographic'. In their view, however, it is not intellectually unworthy to search for historical generalizations. But, when doing so, they suggest, our scope of investigation should be wide, and we should bear in mind that there may be differences, as well as similarities, in the cases compared. Further, according to them, historical knowledge not only enables, but also delimits, our speculations about future options, and does not necessarily supply a good guide to political action. In our own thinking about international relations, they stress, we should be reflective about two seemingly contradictory possibilities, one, that our ideas about international relations may be historically bound, and the other, that there is likely to be little or nothing radically new in human thinking about the subject (Bull 1969: 37). History of international politics may plausibly be written as a story of recurrence and repetition, they accept, but some English School writers also draw attention to some signs of progress in the modern international society towards a more rational world. There is also an awareness on the part of some of its leading authors that historical interpretations and theoretical insights concerning international relations are closely intertwined in the specific sense that even plain historical narratives have intellectual structures of hypotheses and arguments embodied in them.

As for the sociological dimension, the English School's approach to the study of international relations is characterized by its stress on explaining what goes on internationally by penetrating the minds, and uncovering the assumptions and motives, of its key actors. Causal analysis is not excluded from the repertoire of the English School, but it tends to be done as part of their historical analysis. English School authors also use some ideal-types as a means of describing international relations, such as international system, international society and world society. For a number of reasons, however, they have done little on mechanisms of political change. A more detailed empirical study of the historical evolution of social arrangements in inter-societal relationships is what we may reasonably expect of the followers of the English School tradition, given its deployment of historical and sociological approaches and its interest in the normative framework of inter-societal relations.

As for the normative dimension, ascertaining the institutional framework of historical and existing international societies is the English School's forte, and they also consider it epistemologically unproblematic to offer instrumental advice on what sorts of rules, norms or institutions are especially suited to the achievement of some given goals. However, although they have eschewed deep meta-ethical considerations about the status of our moral claims, the School's key contributors have expressed their firm view that substantive moral questions cannot be given answers which do not begin at some arbitrary starting points. Their hesitance to get involved in substantive moral questions is therefore quite understandable. Nevertheless, there is willingness, on the part of some leading English School authors, to consider substantive moral questions as integral to the study of international relations. They consider them to be so partly because earlier contributors to the 'classical' study of international relations were preoccupied with these questions, which now helps us explore and reflect on our own positions, and partly also because the process of probing, clarifying, reformulating and tentatively answering moral questions is, to them, fundamentally an intellectual exercise, which Manning and Bull characterized as 'philosophical'.

It would not be meaningful to talk of the 'English School research projects' if this were taken to mean that there was a range of projects belonging intrinsically to the School clearly distinguishable from the rest. However, any study of international relations that self-consciously operates more or less within the parameters outlined in the foregoing discussion of the English School's approach – with an awareness that these parameters are those of the English School – will be seen broadly to belong to that School's tradition. But, of course, doing what the key English School writers have not so far done much of, or deliberately going beyond their common parameters is also a way of engaging with their work. A detailed empirical study of the historical evolution of social arrangements in inter-societal relationships has already been noted as one of the areas in which progress may be made. Other possibilities, recognizably English-School-like, may include, for instance, a comparative and critical study of leading works on world history in the light of the theoretical assumptions about international relations that underpin them, or a normative theory of international relations which is more reflective of its meta-ethical foundations. There is, in any case, nothing inappropriate in a desire to use the achievements of English School writers as a point of departure for furthering the study of international relations, and much to be gained by taking note of their contributions and potentialities, as the following chapters try to demonstrate.

4 Progress and its limits: system, society and community in world politics

The English School has been centrally concerned with the study of 'progress and its limits' (Mayall, 2000c) and repeated references to the three great traditions of international thought reflect this important fact. The Hobbesian or Machiavellian perspective represents the anti-progressivist approach to international relations which contends that states belong to an international *system* in which there is seldom relief from competition and conflict. States in this condition are principally orientated towards strategic action – to containing, outmanoeuvring or incapacitating actual or potential adversaries. Most are concerned with maximizing the 'power to hurt' and with protecting themselves from the harm opponents can cause (Schelling, 1966). Social learning occurs in the strategic domain most obviously through the accumulation of ever more powerful instruments of violence and the parallel evolution of doctrines about their most effective use. The Kantian tradition represents the progressivist tendency in international thought since its members believe in the existence of a latent *community* of humankind and are confident that all political actors have the capacity to replace strategic orientations with cosmopolitan political arrangements which are governed by dialogue and consent rather than power and force. Social learning is not restricted to the strategic domain but can unfold in the moral sphere as separate political communities come to identify more strongly with humanity as a whole and weave cosmopolitan principles into the conduct of their external affairs.

The Grotian tradition occupies the intermediate position since it believes there has been qualified progress in world politics as exemplified by the existence of a *society* of states which places constraints on the state's power to hurt and facilitates international cooperation. States in this condition are orientated towards communicative action

– to participating in diplomatic dialogues in which they advance claims and counterclaims with a view to establishing global standards of legitimacy which distinguish between permissible and proscribed behaviour.[1] Social learning takes place as states develop conventions and understandings – a global constitution in short – for preserving international order.[2] In *The Anarchical Society*, Bull distinguished this position from the Kantian perspective on the grounds that states do not have the ability to undergo a process of moral learning which culminates in agreed notions of cosmopolitan justice – but it must immediately be added that the English School and the broader Grotian tradition do not have a settled position on the possibility of moral progress in world politics.[3]

Bull's claim that each of these traditions of international thought is relevant to the development of the contemporary society of states, and Wight's observation that tensions between them may have appeared in earlier states-systems, lead to two further points (Wight, 1977: ch. 1; Bull, 2002: 39). The first is that the interplay between systemic forces, societal principles and visions of human community may have shaped the evolution of all known international societies. The relative importance of each of these phenomena may have changed over time but the societal element has never been totally eclipsed even in the darkest hours when international society has been engulfed in major war. The second point is that the several 'theatres of operation' which exist in the modern society of states (Bull, 2002: 39) – and which may have

[1] On the distinction between strategic and communicative action, see Habermas (1984). For a more recent discussion, see Lynch (2002).

[2] It should be stressed that the members of the English School do not use the notion of social learning to explain the development of international society. The term was first used in International Relations by students of security communities and regional integration.

[3] The Grotian tradition is divided over the extent to which social learning in the Kantian sense (i.e. learning in the form of reaching an agreement about universal moral principles which are present in human reason) can occur in relations between states. Solidarists such as Kant believe that social learning of this kind takes place, whereas pluralists such as Vattel do not because societies are fundamentally divided over questions of justice. Writers such as Bull are generally closer to Vattel on this point, while Vincent and Wheeler are somewhat closer to Kant. The debate between pluralism and solidarism is principally an empirical debate about the level of 'solidarity, or potential solidarity, of the states comprising international society'. But Bull also notes that pluralists and solidarists are divided over the basic members of international society, with the former claiming it is states, and the latter claiming it is individuals that are the fundamental units. Solidarism therefore introduces the normative claim that the society of states 'is secondary to that of the universal community of humankind, and its legitimacy derivative from it' (Bull, 1966b: 68). See above, pp. 59ff.

existed in earlier international societies – display very different patterns of political development. The Hobbesian interpretation of international relations, for example, may be validated in some theatres but
the Grotian, and to some extent the Kantian, approaches may capture
the principal dynamics elsewhere (for further discussion, see below,
pp. 195–6).

It has been argued that the English School is committed to methodological pluralism and does not privilege any single dimension of world
politics (Little, 2000). This is a useful reminder that its members do not
believe order and society in international relations can be understood
in isolation from geopolitical rivalries and cosmopolitan attachments.
But the difficulty with this interpretation is that it suggests that international society is only one of three dimensions of world politics that
interest the English School (see above, pp. 29ff). The interpretation
which has been proposed here is that explaining international society
is its central purpose, and its observations about the dimensions
of world politics which are central to the Hobbesian and Kantian
approaches must be viewed in this light.[4]

In his analysis of international society, Wight came close to realism
by stressing that the struggle to tame geopolitical competition has
always failed in the past, the result being the violent destruction of
previous states-systems. Others, such as Vincent and Wheeler, are
closer to the Kantian tradition because they believe there is evidence
of global normative development at least in the modern society of
states. Both standpoints are chiefly concerned with understanding
international society; their comments about geopolitical rivalry and
cosmopolitan moral sentiments are intended to highlight different
pressures and tendencies in this unusual form of world political organization. Following Wight (1991: 14), it is best to regard the English
School as sloping 'upwards' on one side 'towards the crags and preci-
pices of revolutionism, whether Christian or secular' and sloping
'downwards' on the other 'towards the marshes and swamps of realism' (but as ultimately rejecting both points of view). Wight's observation that the Grotian tradition is the *via media* between the Hobbesian

---

[4] Butterfield and Wight (1966: 12) maintained 'the frame of reference' of the British
Committee was 'the diplomatic community itself, international society, the states-
system. The Committee found themselves investigating the nature and distinguishing
marks of the diplomatic community, the way it functions, the obligations of its
members, its tested and established principles of political intercourse.'

and Kantian traditions remains the most useful summation of its distinctive approach to the question of how much progress in world politics is possible (ibid.: 15; Wight, 1966b: 91).

As mentioned earlier, realist pessimism is incorporated in Wight's belief that states-systems seem prone to self-destruction, but a rather different emphasis is found in Watson's contention that a 'strong case can be made out, on the evidence of past systems as well as the present one, that the regulatory rules and institutions of a system usually, and perhaps inexorably, develop to the point where the members become conscious of common values and the system becomes an international society' (Watson, 1987: 151).[5] Watson's seemingly progressivist – even teleological – comment is not incompatible with the belief that the fate of states-systems is to be destroyed by force, but it suggests that normative tendencies can check centrifugal tendencies and at least defer the moment when war finally destroys the states-system (see below, p. 195). Watson's additional observation that modern states may be 'consciously working out, for the first time, a set of transcultural values and ethical standards' suggests that such countervailing moral forces may now be so strong that modern states can develop the global moral consensus which eluded states-systems in the past (Watson 1987: 152).[6] It would be wrong to conclude that this optimistic observation about the modern states-system assumes that future global progress is guaranteed and that dramatic reversals can be firmly ruled out. Even so, Watson's claim about emerging transcultural moral principles raised the intriguing question of whether the modern society of states has an unprecedented capacity not only to avoid

---

[5] Bull's distinction between a system of states in which each state must take account of the others' geopolitical intentions (and in which there is an ever-present possibility of generalized war) and a society of states which collaborates to preserve the common rules and institutions informs Watson's formulation. See the earlier discussion on pp. 52ff.

[6] Watson (ibid.) adds that 'Bull and I inclined towards this optimistic view, but uncertainly'. Vincent's analysis of global potentials for developing a more just universal human rights culture exemplifies the claim that modern states have the capacity to develop transcultural moral standards (Vincent, 1986a). His study of human rights came closer than any other work of the English School from that period to the spirit of communicative ethics which maintains that principles of morality and justice cannot be imposed on one section of international society on all others but must emerge from a genuine dialogue from which no single persuasion is excluded. See also Vincent (1992) and Linklater (1998: ch. 3) on communicative ethics. Watson and Vincent's stress on transcultural moral principles which do not ride roughshod over cultural differences sought to identify prospects for enlarging the global moral consensus within modern international society.

regressing to a highly conflictual international *system* but to evolve in unique ways because of powerful visions of universal solidarity.[7]

Analysing the significance of system, society and community in world politics can help explain three phenomena: the dominant forms of learning across the society of states as a whole and in particular 'theatres of operation', the destructive tendencies that may undermine international society and weaken global loyalties, and the potentials for further advances in controlling violence and institutionalizing cosmopolitan ethical commitments. The uniqueness of the English School can be found in its focus on how sovereign states learn to control violent tendencies by agreeing on some universal moral and legal principles which bind them loosely together in an international society; it is also to be found in its reflections on the prospects for, and constraints on, the development of transcultural principles which can strengthen global ties. On this interpretation, the English School's contribution to the study of international relations runs parallel to Elias's contribution to Sociology which analysed the 'civilising process' in which individuals learn how to control aggressive inclinations and adjust their thoughts and actions in response to the legitimate needs of other members of society.[8] The notion of civility which features in Jackson's recent account of international society, and earlier

.

___

[7] It is also worth noting that the modern society of states is different from its predecessors because there is no external power with the capacity to absorb its members within a universal empire. The unilateralist stance in recent American foreign policy is fascinating because the question of which trend will prove stronger in the long term (the 'Hobbesian' or the 'Grotian' or 'Kantian') would seem to be 'in the balance'. For further discussion, see Dunne (2003).

[8] It is important to add that Elias (1996) was also concerned with understanding 'decivilising processes' which undermine earlier achievements in pacifying social relations and extending emotional identification between members of the same community. He argued that 'civilising processes are always accompanied by decivilising processes: the question is which one is the more important at any stage of social development' (Fletcher, 1997: 82ff). This could almost serve as a summary of the English School's analysis of international relations, and as the 'team motto'. This is not the place to enter into a detailed analysis of Elias's study of the civilizing process and its relevance for the study of international relations – only to stress an especially promising line of future research. It should be emphasized, however, that Elias was mostly interested in how individuals learn to internalize restraints on force within stable monopolies of power – specifically modern states – whereas the English School has been concerned with how restraints are internalized in an 'anarchical society' where there is no monopoly of force, but a balance of power and/or hierarchies of power which may have some of the same consequences. For further discussion, see Van Benthem van den Bergh (1992). A brief summary of the relevance of Elias's work for the sociology of states-systems is considered in Chapter 6.

in the writings of Butterfield, Watson and Wight, is the neglected link between the two perspectives.[9]

Civility or the 'civilising process' are useful tools for thinking further about Watson's observations about the transformation of international systems into international societies and about the evolution of global ethical standards in the modern states-system – not least because important questions arise about how such developments take place and whether the English School can satisfactorily explain them (see Finnemore, 2001: 513). This chapter considers such questions in four parts. Part One analyses the English School's brief reflections on how states have made – and can make – the most elementary forms of progress beyond involvement in an international system. States in the intermediate condition between participation in a states-system and membership of an international society, which will be described below, have a common interest in controlling violence and in restraining foreign policy behaviour, but they lack the level of trust and the capacity for close cooperation which makes a pluralist international society possible. In this context, Keal's analysis of the role of 'unspoken rules' in relations between the superpowers at the end of World War II will be used to suggest ways in which the English School can develop a general account of how states-systems can be transformed into international societies.[10] Parts Two and Three discuss the English School's

---

[9] On the uses of the concept of civility for this task, see Jackson (2000: 408) and Burke et al (2000). The final sentence of Wight's lectures in which he claims rationalism has been 'a civilizing factor' in world politics is also worth noting (Wight, 1991: 268). Butterfield (1953: ch. 7) maintains that the existence of international stability as against a state of war needs to be seen in conjunction with 'the whole civilizing process [which] lies in the development of an international order'. For further discussion, see Sharp (2003). Curbing aggressive impulses and egotistical behaviour are its crucial constituent parts. The following claim in Watson (1982: 20) is also worth noting: 'The diplomatic dialogue is . . . the instrument of international society: a civilized process based on awareness and respect for other people's point of view; and a civilizing one also, because the continuous exchange of ideas, and the attempts to find mutually acceptable solutions to conflicts of interest, increase that awareness and respect.' Manning referred to similar themes in his claim that coexistence between states requires 'a kind of formal correctitude, a degree of mutual self-respect, a growth of gentle manners' as well as a 'measure of understanding, born of an appreciation of individuality, each seeing the other as significantly unique' (see Suganami, 2001a: 103).

[10] Whether Watson is right to argue that 'the regulatory rules and institutions of a system usually and perhaps inexorably' lead to the development of society is left to one side in this discussion. The English School has not provided a comparative analysis of states-systems which tests this intriguing suggestion. Watson's claim is counter-intuitive since there seems no obvious reason why the members of a system could not remain in a pure state of war or engage in mutual destruction. The point of the present analysis is

more central aim of analysing the foundations of pluralist and solidarist international orders. These sections consider its observations about the extent to which such global arrangements frustrate or encourage efforts to remake international society in accordance with visions of a community of humankind; each section therefore seeks to clarify its position on the extent to which global political progress is possible. Part Four considers the significance of the English School's study of the expansion of international society for an inquiry into the prospects for the growth of 'transcultural values and ethical standards' in world politics. The main question in this final part is whether Watson's comments about the development of transcultural moral values in the contemporary society of states suggest ways of moving beyond traditional English School scepticism about the Kantian proposition that independent political communities can make significant progress in using cosmopolitan moral principles to transform global social and political relations.

One last comment is in order. The main purpose of this chapter is to consider the English School's analysis of progressive possibilities in world politics, but it is important to remember its conviction that societies of states seem to be incapable of eliminating violent tendencies which threaten international order and frustrate the development of universal solidarities.[11] An analysis of the role that the concepts of system, society and community play in English School writings is important to explain its distinctive approach to some of the oldest and most important debates in the study of international relations – debates about the extent to which progress in world politics is possible (see also Suganami (1984, 2002) and Brown (1995)).

Beyond strategic relations

The distinction between an international system and an international society is central to Bull's study of international order. This is an analytical distinction serving to identify ideal types, and Bull (2002: 15) was quick to emphasize that between systems and societies one can

therefore to consider in outline the reasons that can lead states to *progress* from an international system to an international society.

[11] It should be stressed that this interest in the comparative sociology of societies of states was largely confined to the work of the British Committee in the 1960s. For an analysis, see Dunne (1998: 124ff).

find 'cases where a sense of common interests is tentative and incho-ate'.[12] The important conceptual question is where one should locate the point at which states can be said to pass from involvement in an international system to membership of an international society (Stivachtis, 1998).[13] The important empirical question suggested by Bull's remarks is how any examples of past transitions from inter-national systems to international societies are best explained.

This is not an area the English School has investigated in any detail.[14] There is no counterpart in the English School to Keohane's analysis of how rational egotists can learn how to cooperate in the inhospitable context of anarchy (Keohane, 1984) – and no sympathy for the view that such an account can be constructed in game-theoretical terms. Were the English School to set out to create a general theory of the transformation of past systems of states into societies of states, it would start with historical inquiry.[15] In the absence of this mode of analysis, it is necessary to look to English School analyses of specific historical episodes for clues as to how it might construct a more general account of the emergence of international societies.

Some of the elements of such an account can be derived from Keal's analysis of how unspoken rules contributed to order between the superpowers at the end of World War II. Keal focuses on how the

[12] Relations between Greece and Persia provide an interesting illustration of this claim. For further reflections on the extent to which they become participants in a society as opposed to a system, see Wight (1977: ch. 3). See in particular his comments about Persia's ambiguous relationship within Hellenic international society and his observa-tions about parallels with relations between European international society and the Ottoman Empire (Wight, 1977: 89–90, 105). A more detailed discussion of the Ottoman Empire can be found in Naff (1984).

[13] Shaw (1994: 127–8) argues that the distinction between system and society is 'suspect' if society is understood not in terms of a normative consensus but as a set of 'relationships involving mutual expectations and understandings, with the possibility of mutually orientated actions'. See also Halliday (1994: 101–3) on problems with the English School notion of society. On a related issue, Dunne (2001: 70) argues for the need to 'think about variations *within* international society rather than to cling on to a narrow and restrictive notion of international society as an "in-between", that which is not part of the international system or part of world society'.

[14] Bull and Watson (1984) consider how several regional international systems became part of the first ever universal society of states. But as the title of their famous work indicates, they were concerned with the globalization of the European society of states rather than with how an international system turned into an international society.

[15] An interesting question is whether, Watson aside, members of the English School believe there are many (or any) historical examples of systems of states which were gradually transformed into international societies. Wight's claim that trade has often preceded diplomacy in creating the elements of civility does seem to imply that it is meaningful to ask how past international systems were transformed in this way.

element of society survived in this period in the face of powerful systemic pressures – his is not an account then of how an international system became an international society – but his analysis invites broader reflections on how elementary progress beyond purely strategic relations is possible.[16] The argument is that the United States and the Soviet Union came to an implicit understanding about the boundaries of their respective spheres of influence through a process of 'non-verbal symbolic action' rather than through public dialogue. Indeed, diplomatic efforts to formalize the existence of spheres of influence could easily have ended in profound disagreements because of high levels of distrust (Keal, 1983: 51). Tacit understandings which developed gradually from precedent-setting actions and reactions formed one of the keystones of the post-World War II international order.

This analysis of the Cold War years invites certain hypotheses about how international systems may have developed into international societies in earlier times – and about how such development is possible (see also Bull, 2002: 214; see also pp. 64–5). The most obvious, of course, is that adversaries make the most basic transition beyond purely systemic relations because of a fear of destructive war. The creation of the post-World War II order is an example of a more general point, which is that restraints on the use of force are the core elements of a global civilizing process which replaces a condition in which systemic pressures are absolutely dominant. No less important is moderation in foreign policy, given that behaviour which may not be designed to intimidate can seem threatening to others and generate fear and hostility – as explained by analyses of the security dilemma. Regard for reciprocity – specifically the realization that claiming more for one's own state than one is prepared to grant others invariably breeds resentment – is also a fundamental part of the most basic forms of civility in international relations.[17] It is difficult for confidence and

---

[16] It might be argued that the United States and the Soviet Union formed a society rather than a system in this period although this has been a matter of dispute (see Miller, 1990: 77–80). Wight (1991: 50) suggests that it was 'reasonable' to see world politics immediately after 1945 as 'divided into two international societies' which were 'overlapping' in certain respects. See Bull (2002: 40–1) for a related point. The main issue for the present discussion is that Keal's reflections on this period reveal how states can become involved in a civilizing process which checks systemic forces while falling well short of the civil order intrinsic to a pluralist society of states.

[17] On the importance of reciprocity in social life, see Gouldner (1960). On its importance for relations between the superpowers at the close of World War II, see Keal (1983: 61, 92 and 151ff). On its more general significance for world politics, see Keohane (1986b).

trust to develop between past or potential adversaries, or for the transition from system to society to occur, in the absence of elementary forms of empathy which include the ability to see the world from the other's point of view. Bull maintained that states have demonstrated their ability to create orderly relations, but invariably encounter great difficulties in agreeing on the meaning of justice although he added that 'commutative' or 'reciprocal' justice is integral to international order.[18] An analysis of the evolution of such orientations to action is important for understanding progress beyond a condition in which states are concerned exclusively with outmanoeuvring, dominating or coercing one another, and in which learning occurs only in the strategic sphere, to one in which adversaries introduce civility into their transactions. Relations between states in the circumstances just described are no longer purely systemic but they cannot be said to signify the existence of an international society because common interests remain 'tentative and inchoate'. Perhaps one should not search for the precise point when a system of states has turned unambiguously into a society of states; in the course of such a transition, a lack of certainty about such matters is to be expected. There is a strong case, however, for accepting the argument that progression to international society occurs when states recognize not just the empirical reality but the legitimacy of each other's separate existence (Buzan, 1993: 330; Stivachtis, 1998).

Unspoken rules can leave the boundaries of spheres of influence vague and uncertain and, as the Cuban missile crisis revealed, they do not necessarily rule out manoeuvres to test the other's will to assert its influence in strategically important areas. Explicit understandings about what is permissible and what is proscribed in the relations

---

[18] Bull (2002: ch. 4) stresses the tension between order and justice in international relations but his distinction between 'commutative' or 'reciprocal' and 'distributive justice' should be kept in mind in this context. Commutative justice, according to Bull (2002: 77–8), revolves around a 'process of exchange or bargaining, whereby one individual or group recognizes the rights of others in return for their recognition of his or its own'; distributive justice revolves principally around notions of fairness in the distribution of resources. Bull (ibid.) argues that international politics is 'the domain pre-eminently of ideas of "commutative" as opposed to "distributive" justice'. One might add that commutative justice is essential for the existence of any social order, domestic or international. Important here is Keohane (1986b: 21), which relies on Gouldner's claim that reciprocity prescribes that people should not harm others except in retaliation for harm already received and requires that individuals should 'help those who have helped them'. Later chapters consider the relevance of the harm principle for the development of 'radicalised rationalism'.

between great powers may be preferable to unspoken rules for that very reason. The question is whether express agreements can be negotiated.[19] Formalizing such agreements in the early stages of the movement beyond an international system may be impossible because of mutual suspicion. Regarding the post-World War II order, Keal (1983: ch. 7) argues that joint efforts to formalize the existence of *de facto* spheres of influence would have been condemned for manifestly violating the principle of sovereign equality. Although they might have strengthened international order, such agreements would have been widely regarded as 'intrinsically unjust' by virtue of frustrating popular aspirations for national self-determination (Keal, 1983: 203–4). Bull's observations about the tension between order and justice in international politics are illustrated by the fact that spheres of influence are not freely entered into by all the involved parties but usually survive because the great powers have no compunction in crushing efforts to secede from them (Bull, 2002: ch. 4). Keal's point that it would have been difficult for the superpowers to formalize agreements about spheres of influence is a reminder that the United States and the Soviet Union could not completely ignore the principle of equal sovereignty. The more general point as far as transitions from international systems to international societies are concerned is that the growth of elementary forms of civility in relations between great power adversaries is perfectly compatible with the brutal suppression of weaker powers and violent efforts to subdue non-compliant populations. Two questions are raised therefore by the first stages in the transition from an international system to an international society: the first is how great power adversaries can build on elementary forms of civility and further reduce the possibility of becoming embroiled in major war (the question here is how they can move beyond the condition in which common interests are 'tentative and inchoate' to one in which all are committed to preserving an international society which recognizes rights to a separate existence); the second question is how far they

---

[19] The following point is crucial to developing an account of how international systems can develop into international societies, and how the element of society can survive in the face of powerful systemic pressures: 'It is not uncommon for a rule to emerge first as an operational rule, then to become established practice, then to attain the status of a moral principle and finally to be incorporated in a legal convention; this appears to have been the genesis, for example, of many of the rules now embodied in multilateral treaties or conventions concerning the laws of war, diplomatic and consular status, and the law of the sea.' See Bull (2002: 64–5).

can make progress in overcoming the tension between order and justice mentioned above. These are central preoccupations of the English School to which the discussion now turns.

The strengths and weaknesses of pluralist international society

An account of the simplest form of progress beyond purely strategic orientations invites the question of how political communities can advance still further by agreeing on the principles of a pluralist society of states. A related issue is how far progress in this direction has its own distinctive limits. At this point in the discussion it is essential to consider Wight and Bull's different approaches to the origins of international societies. Wight (1977: 33) argued that every known society of states has emerged in a region with its distinctive culture or civilization. Bull (2002: ch. 1) rejected the claim that a shared culture is a necessary condition for the emergence of a society of states while recognizing that in practice, the main 'historical international societies . . . were all founded upon a common culture or civilisation' (Bull, 2002: 15). His account of the formation of societies of states began with a discussion of primary goals which are common to all social systems. Bull's analysis of those goals was mainly concerned with explaining order in the modern society of states, but it lends itself to another purpose, which is explaining how states that have moved beyond purely strategic orientations have made – and can make – further progress by associating together in an international society. It is unclear whether Bull agreed with Watson that there is a strong case for believing that systems of states may have evolved 'inexorably' into societies of states, but there is no doubt he thought that Wight was incorrect in thinking that international societies can only emerge when the constituent parts are already united by a common culture.

Bull's explanation of the possibility of a society of states relies on a conception of reason which is derived from Hume (Bull, 2002: 120–1). His main argument is that reason is powerless to determine the ends which all human beings should ideally pursue. This does not only place Bull at odds with the Kantian approach to world politics which maintains that humanity can come to understand the moral necessity of perpetual peace by consulting reason – it also separates him from Grotius's explanation of international society which rests explicitly on a natural law doctrine.[20] Drawing on the writings of Hume and Hart, Bull (2002: 6) defended the 'empirical equivalent' of natural law which begins with the sociological fact that the members of human collectivities have some basic primary goals or fundamental interests in common. For Bull, as for Hume and Hart, reason is an instrument that enables human beings to learn how to create 'practical associations' which protect primary goals.[21] According to Bull it is the existence of these primary goals – rather than some idea of rationality which assumes all human beings have access to universal moral truths – that makes an international society possible.[22]

As explained in Chapter 2, Bull argued that all separate societies are arrangements for securing primary goals of avoiding violence, preserving property rules, and ensuring promises are kept. These goals are constitutive of bounded communities in all times and places – they also underpin international society. As with the individual members of separate societies, so with states – they too have found it prudent to agree that the use of force should be controlled, property rights (sovereignty) should be respected, and agreements (treaties) should be kept. On this foundation the modern society of states has erected three further primary goals (see above, pp. 56ff, p. 129). The result is an 'anarchical society' because there is no legal and political authority to which independent political communities are morally or legally obliged to submit; states retain control of the instruments of violence whereas most national governments have disarmed their populations in whole or in part; unlike citizens of separate states, sovereign communities do not only make the law but monopolize the right to interpret and enforce it. Bull rests his account of the modern European, now universal, society of states on these foundations, and he does not claim to have developed a general theory of how all past international societies have come into existence. However, his analysis of primary goals can be used for exactly that purpose. It can provide a more

---

[20] For Bull's standpoint on natural law, see Bull (2000e).

[21] Following Oakeshott (1974), Nardin (1983) distinguishes practical associations which seek to ensure coexistence between their members from purposive associations which are concerned with realizing shared ideals or common objectives.

[22] This is a major break with Grotius's account of the society of states in one crucial respect. For Grotius, order is made possible by the law of reason which is everywhere the same. Voluntary agreements have a distinctly secondary role: they validate the truths of the natural law, but they do not create them (Bull, 1990: 78). Bull (ibid.: 90) notes that Grotius made very few references to 'the law of embassies or [sought] to treat the diplomatic system as evidence of the existence of an international society'.

general explanation of how international systems in which strategic orientations dominate can evolve into international societies in which the constituent parts have common interests, recognize common rules and cooperate to preserve order-enhancing institutions.

Earlier in this chapter, it was claimed that the movement beyond a system of states involves the growth of civility and demonstrates the existence of a global civilizing process. The pluralist conception of international society takes this process further and marks the point at which a system of states is transformed unambiguously into a society of states. In an international system, according to Bull's definition of this ideal-type, states accept the empirical reality of each other's existence; in a pluralist international society they take the additional step of respecting one another's right to sovereign independence. Participants in an international system may strive to balance each other's military power, but equilibrium is 'fortuitous' rather than designed; in an international society the balance of power is 'contrived' because the member states believe that order will not survive without close cooperation to prevent any single state from acquiring preponderant power (Bull, 2002: 100–1). In an international system, decisions not to use force largely depend on the deterrent effect of the balance of power, and there is no guarantee that restrictions on violence will survive if one state believes it has a decisive military advantage. In an international society, most great powers or the majority of states abandon the goal of universal domination and they are vigilant in preserving the balance of power, knowing that a state may try to convert the society of states into an empire at some point in the future. In an international system, adversaries endeavour to think from the standpoint of others in order to reduce danger or damage to themselves; in an international society, states need to think about what is best for international society as a whole since they cannot easily disentangle their own welfare from the interests of the larger association. Finally, in an international system, and in the early stages of progress towards global civility as described earlier, some rules and understandings may be unspoken or tacit; in a society of states, the main rights and duties which states have, and the core principles which regulate their interaction, are the product of a collective commitment to diplomatic dialogue.

The growth of civility that marks the appearance of an international society is evidence of social learning. It is the outcome of the ability to organize international relations around principles of responsibility and accountability which are inevitably undeveloped when common interests are no more than 'tentative and inchoate'. The modern European society of states appears to be unusual in having developed sophisticated institutions such as resident embassies and the principle of diplomatic immunity for the purpose of exploring the possibilities for agreement, and it seems unique in having introduced the institution of international law as a means of establishing binding rules. At times, Bull and Wight seem to believe that the modern world has progressed beyond earlier societies of states by virtue of having acquired these sophisticated instruments for maintaining international order; this is to suggest that societies of states display different levels of institutional development and organizational complexity.

The existence of a pluralist society of states supports a qualified progressivist interpretation of international relations which is a distinctive feature of the English School's approach to world politics. A pluralist framework places constraints on violence, but it does not outlaw the use of force and is, in any case, powerless to eradicate it. Although the English School recognizes that force is often the instrument that states use to promote selfish interests, it also sees war as one of the key institutions of international society. War is not only an instrument of realist foreign policy but is also a crucial mechanism for resisting challenges to the balance of power and violent assaults on international society (Bull, 2002: ch. 8). The contention that war has the function of preserving international society reveals not only progress beyond an international system in curbing aggressive impulses but close cooperation to check actual or potential threats to the global political order. These developments can be regarded as progressive since they involve the attainment of levels of civility which are not found in systems of states or in the transitional condition between 'system' and 'society' described earlier. However, progress in the shape of pluralist arrangements has definite limits, and three of them warrant brief consideration. Each highlights the presence of serious moral deficits in international society which have given rise to political efforts to create improved global arrangements.

Bull described the first of them in his analysis of the recurrent tension between primary goals in modern international society. He pointed to a recurrent tension between the goal of preserving the society of states – which requires measures to preserve the balance of power – and the principle of sovereign equality (Bull, 2002: 16–18, 87–8). To illustrate the theme, Bull observed that the partition of

Poland by Austria, Russia and Prussia took place in 1772 in order to maintain the balance of power between the dominant states.[23] Here was one of the clearest examples of the tension between order and justice in international relations. The point can be put differently by arguing that the decision to sacrifice the sovereignty of a small state on the altar of great power equilibrium reveals the limits of civility in the history of modern international society.[24]

The absence of global mechanisms for protecting individual human rights is a second moral deficit of pluralist international society. Its constitutive principles are designed to promote coexistence between major powers which have rival conceptions of human dignity or human rights as well as divergent security interests. Order between the great powers depends on an implicit or explicit contract to regard human rights issues as sovereign matters in which the wider association of states has no legitimate interest. The idea of territorial sovereignty – the cardinal principle of pluralist international society – creates the obligation to refrain from intervening in others' internal affairs: what any one state regards as a serious violation of human rights must therefore go unpunished. In recent times it has been argued that an exception arises when human rights atrocities in one state endanger the security of neighbours, for example through the forced expulsion of considerable numbers of refugees. This raises complex issues about when one or more of the members of a pluralist society can use force against a regime that has what Vattel called 'a mischievous disposition' which is taken here to mean the willingness to harm other states by threatening them with the mass influx of refugees. Vattel's version of pluralism permitted collective action to put such a regime 'out of its power to injure them'.[25] Bull (1984b: 181ff) suggested that the modern society of states has moved in the direction of solidarism by deciding that it is morally and legally entitled to take action to prevent human rights violations while stopping short of embracing new principles of humanitarian intervention. The absence

---

[23] Bull (2002: 103). More recently, Jackson (2000: 273) has argued that Bosnia's 'inherent right of self-defence' was limited in the name of the supposedly higher goal of regional order.

[24] This can also be regarded as illustrating Elias's point that civilizing and decivilizing processes invariably develop in tandem (see p. 121, note 8).

[25] 'If there is any where a Nation of reckless and mischievous disposition, always ready to injure others, to traverse their designs, and to raise domestic troubles, it is not to be doubted that all have a right to join in order to repress, chastise, and put it ever after out of its power to injure them' (quoted by Welsh, 1996: 189–90; see also Vattel, 1970: 120).

of a global consensus about what counts as an intolerable abuse of human rights has been a crucial factor here.[26] In addition, most states have been fearful that relaxing the prohibition against intervention will only make it easier for great powers to breach territorial sovereignty, ostensibly for humanitarian reasons but in reality to promote their own interests. The consolidation of the universal human rights culture has presented the contemporary pluralist order with the awkward question of whether it can incorporate solidarist principles into international society without weakening general respect for the principle of non-intervention.[27]

A third limitation is inherent in the notion of civility which has often been associated with the belief that civilized societies have advanced beyond the allegedly savage or barbarous parts of the world. Wight (1977: 34) maintained that every society of states has marked itself off from the less civilized regions of the world, and shared perceptions of separateness (or external 'cultural differentiation') had fostered solidarity between its component parts. The predictable corollary has been

---

[26] Bull (1982: 266) maintained the modern society of states was united on the need to eradicate apartheid but that was as far as the global moral consensus extended.

[27] Stated in these terms, pluralism and solidarism appear to be opposites. Buzan (2004: 45–62) defends the case for regarding them as different points on a spectrum, with pluralism referring to relatively thin and solidarism to relatively thick levels of agreed values. He argues that solidarism should not be reduced to an agreement about human rights which international society should be prepared to defend by force. It can be grounded instead in a consensus with respect to trade matters which does not necessarily involve the collective enforcement of the law against any non-complying state. This indicates that a solidarist international society could be based on a foundation other than the concern for human rights. Whether it can exist without some form of collective enforcement is, in Buzan's view, 'unclear'. Solidarism in Bull's original sense comes with no such ambiguities. Collective enforcement is an essential part of the concept, and understandably in connection with human rights given the question of whether sovereignty must take priority over human rights or whether states might be forced to respect them by international society as a whole. Vincent's discussion of the right to starvation offers a vision of solidarism in which shared values regarding the rights of individuals is the pre-eminent consideration; collective enforcement plays no part in this approach to solidarism; and the growth of shared values may consolidate sovereignty rather than undercut it (see Gonzalez-Pelaez and Buzan, 2003). On one level, this supports Buzan's claim that solidarism need not be reduced to the collective enforcement of human rights, but whether it can be conceived of independently of human rights or human dignity or some such concept is another matter. Buzan's use of solidarism to describe a condition in which states agree that each has a right and duty 'to foster its own distinctive national culture insulated from the others' is too broad (see Buzan, 2004: 142). Solidarism is a term which has been used to describe the potentiality for an agreement about matters of human well-being which were not part of the traditional diplomatic agenda (and also to offer a moral defence of movement in that direction). There is much to be said for preserving this conventional meaning.

that states have claimed rights against 'uncivilized' peoples which were regarded as unacceptable in their relations with each other. This is abundantly clear from Vattel's distinction between civilized peoples organized into sovereign states and uncivilized peoples who, lacking the institutions typical of a genuinely civil order, suffered a proportionate diminution of entitlements and rights. Vattel argued that settlers could not be accused of departing 'from the intentions of nature when [restricting] the savages within narrower bounds' since the latter had 'more land than they [had] need of or [could] inhabit and cultivate' (quoted in Williams, 1986: 128). It was a short step from here to 'the standard of civilisation' which was used in the nineteenth century to justify European domination of non-European peoples (see Gong, 1984), and a short step to the notion that advanced peoples had the right or duty to bring civilization to peoples deemed to lag behind.

Vattel's pluralism should not be equated with the racial doctrines which the European colonial powers used to justify absolute rights over conquered peoples, including the right to destroy them and to eradicate their forms of life – the main point is that there is nothing in a pluralist society of sovereign states which requires them to show stateless peoples the respect and recognition they demand of each other. To put the point another way, the rules and principles which maintained international order pertained only to relations between Western societies and were compatible with the domination and exploitation of 'backward peoples' (Keal, 1995). The history of the European international society illustrates this tragic point but, in recent years, the struggle for recognition on the part of indigenous peoples has been undertaken in order to achieve moral standing in the global order (Thornberry, 2002). Of course, it is important not to overlook the various critics of European imperialism who condemned cruel behaviour towards subordinated peoples. In the case of the conquest of the Americas, Las Casas, Vitoria and others defended the rights of the 'newly discovered Indians' and drew on religious conceptions of the unity of humankind to confer junior status on backward societies which remained ignorant of the truths of the Christian religion (see Donelan, 1984). The idea of civility in the writings of Vitoria as well as Vattel was employed to urge self-restraint on the part of the imperial overlords. But those who urged moderation almost always claimed that indigenous peoples were not sufficiently advanced to determine their social and political development.

Pluralist international society represents progress in developing civility in relations between separate political communities, but the denial of the rights of small nations and indigenous peoples, and the absence of means of protecting individuals from human rights abuses, are among its principal deficiencies. These moral deficits have prompted forms of political action and protest designed to reduce or overcome tensions between civility and uncivility; contradictions between current realities and future possibilities have led to demands for improved global arrangements. New forms of world political organization which eradicate these global deficiencies are in principle possible, although those who defend pluralism are inclined to argue that the quest for such arrangements might prove to be a distraction from the endlessly troubled task of preserving order in the context of anarchy. The interesting question, then, which the English School has discussed at length, is whether visions of global political progress which look beyond the pluralist framework can be realized in practice.

Towards solidarism in International Relations

The argument thus far has been inspired by Watson's observation that international systems have tended to evolve into international societies. We have seen how the English School can account for the movement from a system of states to a pluralist international society; and we have seen how a qualified progressivist interpretation of world politics can be built around the notion that pluralist arrangements develop forms of civility that are latent within the idealized condition described earlier in which states move beyond purely strategic forms of interaction. Watson's claim that the modern states-system has been the setting for unusual agreements at the level of transcultural values informs the remaining parts of this chapter. His observation raises the question of whether the modern pluralist order is evolving in a solidarist direction which overcomes some of the moral deficits described in the last section. Related issues are whether such a movement can be regarded as progressive in nature, and whether it contains defects and dangers which require more radical efforts to create an ethical international society.

Members of the English School have not provided evidence of any significant shift from pluralism to solidarism in earlier systems of states. For the most part, their analysis has concentrated on the ingredients of order between independent political communities and on possible tensions between realist, rationalist and revolutionist themes in all international societies (Wight, 1977: ch. 1). Wight's observation that societies of states seem destined to end in violence strongly implies that solidarism can be little more than aspirational. But if revolutionist tendencies have existed in all societies of states, then solidarist potentials were present to some extent and the movement from a pluralist to a solidarist international society was, in principle, possible in other times. The English School's analysis of solidarism has been especially concerned with the role of the human rights discourse in recent international history but this inquiry raises the issue of whether contemporary international society is profoundly different from its predecessors in that solidarist commitments are not only firmly embedded in its constitution but may yet come to have greater influence on its future course of development (for further discussion, see Chapter 6).

Wight's claim that all societies of states have appeared within culturally unified regions is worth recalling at this stage for two reasons: first, Wight's implicit position is that the existence of a common culture is necessary for the emergence of the most basic pluralist rules of coexistence; second, the apparent implication of this standpoint is that this also holds for the growth of solidarist commitments. We have seen that Bull rejected Wight's claim that some degree of cultural unity is a necessary condition for the development of an international society (although he maintained that cultural similarities are desirable since they undoubtedly increase the likelihood that its institutions will function smoothly).[28] Bull stressed that the solidarist tendencies which exist in the contemporary world are derived from the transnational moral and religious culture which characterized medieval international society. We consider the implications of this claim first before turning in the next section to the question which shapes Bull and Watson's analysis of the expansion of international society – whether the absence of a common culture in the modern universal society of states, and the strength of support for pluralist principles in many regions of the world, have reduced the prospects for greater solidarism.

[28] Bull's argument was that a common 'international political culture' can strengthen the 'diplomatic culture' which unites the professional corps responsible for the conduct of foreign policy. He noted that the expansion of international society entailed a contraction of the former, though not of the latter, phenomenon. The emergence of a 'cosmopolitan culture of modernity', which he regarded as largely confined to elites, contained the promise that some features of the solidarity which existed in the old European states-system could be recovered in the post-European order. For the more detailed analysis, see Bull (2002: 304–5) and Bull and Watson (1984: 434–5).

Bull observed that the early modern European architects of the pluralist order borrowed heavily from medieval political culture.[29] Earlier Wight (1966b: 90–1; 1991: 128–9; see also Linklater, 1993) maintained that 'the political philosophy of constitutional government' which developed during the Middle Ages had been a major influence on the constitution of the emergent modern European system of states.[30] Medieval conceptions of universal justice which stressed the dignity of the individual were quickly subordinated to the task of preserving order between sovereign states.[31] The notion of human dignity in the shape of the human rights discourse 'survived' but only 'underground' because of the dominant ideology which maintained that sovereign states are the ultimate members of international society and the sole subjects of international law.[32] The fact it survived at all is why the modern pluralist society of states has long contained distinctive and possibly unique solidarist potentialities.

To develop this point further, it is important to consider the implication of Wight's remarks about the impact of 'the political philosophy of constitutional government' on the society of states. Constitutionalism is the antithesis of absolutism – it is the doctrine that defends the need for legal constraints on the exercise of political power. No society of states can survive unless its members accept the necessity for constraints on the exercise of military power, but the modern states-system is unique in having drawn explicitly on a constitutional tradition to develop its moral and legal foundations. 'Rationalist constitutionalism', Wight argued, combined negative obligations to avoid causing unnecessary harm to others with positive obligations to collaborate to preserve the balance of power (1991: 130). In *The Anarchical Society*, Bull makes it clear that states can be signatories to

[29] Certain 'ideas of human justice historically preceded the development of ideas of interstate or international justice and provided perhaps the principal intellectual foundation upon which these latter ideas at first rested' (Bull, 2002: 82). The reference is to the medieval 'doctrine of natural law'.
[30] Significantly Wight (1973: 111) described the multiple balance of power as the 'international counterpart' of 'liberal constitutionalism'. In the lectures on international theory, Wight (1991: 130) referred to 'Rationalist constitutionalism' which 'fears and suspects power' and which has 'a presumption in favour of small powers'. For further discussion, see below, p. 241.
[31] In short, the rights of individuals were translated into the exclusive rights of states. See Bull (2002: 79–80).
[32] It is as if a 'conspiracy of silence' has existed between governments 'about the rights and duties of their respective citizens'. Bull (2002: 80) goes on to explain how this conspiracy has been partially 'mitigated' by the development of cosmopolitan law.

agreements of this kind without subscribing to any particular system of government – significantly, constitutionalism can exist internationally even though some states do not respect constitutionalist principles in the domestic sphere. But in the history of modern international society, many liberal states have argued that the constitutionalism of the whole is inextricably connected with the constitutionalism of the parts. The question for them is whether states have the right to expect others not only to preserve the balance of power but to organize their internal affairs in accordance with the principles of constitutional rule.[33]

Vattel's pluralism maintained that states have the right to defend themselves from regimes that demonstrate malicious intent, but they are not entitled to impose any single form of government on other societies. This is not a position that all advocates of constitutional authority have been keen to defend. Those who think international order is best served by the existence of constitutional government in all member states may wish to encourage the demise of governments that fall short of this ideal, as we have seen in recent discussions of 'regime change'.[34] One of the most difficult questions in modern international society is how constitutional states should behave towards governments which violate constitutional norms by waging war on sections of their own populations. For the members of a pluralist international society, the problem is how to incorporate solidarist principles into their arrangements; more specifically, it is whether there are any

---

[33] Wight (1977: 41) maintained that the modern society of states seems to differ from its predecessors by making the legitimacy or illegitimacy of particular forms of government a matter of global concern. That said, it is worth noting that Wight and Bull's remarks on the relationship between domestic and international constitutionalism differ from neorealism with its preference for systemic as against reductionist explanation. Bull and Wight's observation that a transnational culture committed to constitutionalism paved the way for the development of a modern international society of states draws attention to linkages between the 'inside' and the 'outside' which are omitted from Waltz's parsimonious theory of international politics (see Linklater, 1990a: ch. 1). The best illustration of this point is to be found in Wight's claim that principles of international legitimacy 'mark the region of approximation between international and domestic politics. They are the principles that prevail (or at least proclaimed) within a *majority* of the states that form international society, as well as in the relations *between* them' (Wight, 1977: 153).

[34] Wight (1991: 41ff) described this as a form of revolutionism committed to the notion of 'doctrinal uniformity'. Arguments in support of regime change in Iraq fused this language with concerns about supposed weapons of mass destruction. Significantly, the argument is that international legitimacy depends not just on constitutional rule, but on a commitment to national democracy.

circumstances in which the state's use of force against its own population is so severe as to justify even a temporary departure from the global norm that prohibits intervention.

The convention for more than three-and-a-half centuries has been that states should respect each other's sovereign independence however much they may disapprove of their domestic practices. It is only in recent years that the belief that constitutionalism should not be confined to relations between sovereign units but should be promoted within their respective territories has made sizeable inroads into the dominant state-centric view of international society. As Vincent (1990a: 252–3) argued, the rise of the sovereign state as a 'special actor in world society [led] in the nineteenth century to the submergence of the individual and his or her rights', but the dominant trend in the twentieth century has led to the 'rediscovery of individual rights in the passage back from international society to world society (and the search for a doctrine of humanitarian intervention)'.[35] In particular, the democratic celebration of the rights of men and women has forced states to recognize that if human rights are 'to mean anything at all', then it is essential to 'reduce the domain defended by non-intervention' (Vincent, 1990a: 254–5). As for Bull, given his ethical claim that international order should be judged ultimately by the extent to which it contributes to world order, it is unsurprising that he should have sympathized with this solidarist turn in international society;[36] but given his belief that the principle of sovereignty remained the key to contemporary international order, it is no less surprising that he shared Vincent's fears about the dangers of any general undermining of the principle of non-intervention (Bull, 1984b: 195; Roberts, 1993).

Bull and Vincent highlighted one of the great moral dilemmas which has dominated public debate since the passing of the bipolar era, and not least because of the evidence that casualties in civil wars now greatly outnumber casualties in traditional inter-state wars (Tilly,

---

[35] Vincent (1990a: 242), but see also Bull (1990: 86), claimed that the period in which Grotius lived 'marked the transition from a great society of humankind to a society of states, whereas now some see a movement in the opposite direction, from international society to a more inclusive world society'. With regard to apartheid and to other abuses of human rights, the 'practice of the United Nations since the 1950s has been to shrink the area reserved to domestic jurisdiction'. See Vincent (1990a: 250). For a critical interpretation and development of English School conceptions of world society, see Buzan (2004).
[36] The relationship between international order and world order in Bull's thought was discussed on pp. 53ff above.

1992: 201–2). The nature of the dilemma is well known: to maintain that sovereignty should never be breached is to abandon the victims of human rights to their fate; to argue that a state forfeits its sovereignty when it commits serious violations of human rights may open the floodgates to intervention whenever any state concludes the threshold between acceptable and unacceptable behaviour has been crossed. There has been no better illustration in recent times of Bull's observation about the 'terrible choices' which often confront foreign policy makers (Bull, 2000d: 227), and no better example of the great complexities involved in making the transition to more solidarist arrangements. The central issue for Bull was whether the great powers can agree on the conditions that justify humanitarian intervention: 'It is clear . . . that even when there is not consent by all the parties affected, but there is overwhelming evidence of a consensus in international society as a whole in favour of a change held to be just, especially if the consensus embraces all the great powers, the change may take place without causing other than a local or temporary disorder, after which the international order . . . may emerge unscathed or even appear in a stronger position than before' (Bull, 2002: 91). Bull (ibid.) added that it 'can scarcely be doubted that an international society that has reached a consensus not merely about order, but about a wider range of notions of international, human and perhaps world justice, is likely to be in a stronger position to maintain the framework of minimum order or coexistence than one that has not'. Conversely, an international society in which the great powers are divided over questions of justice and are unable to agree on rules governing humanitarian intervention is one whose members breach the principle of territorial sovereignty at their peril because the short-term benefits to the victims of human rights abuses are likely to be outweighed by the long-term damage to international order. However, Bull – and Vincent in his later writings – were unwilling to settle for a form of 'rule consequentialism' which rendered the society of states totally inactive when faced with the most terrible violations of human rights.[37]

Bull was undoubtedly correct that the movement from pluralist to solidarist global arrangements would not occur as long as the superpowers disagreed fundamentally about the meaning of justice. But since the end of bipolarity, the creation of international tribunals for

---

[37] Wheeler (2000: 29) stresses the rule-consequentialist character of Bull and Vincent's basic position. Vincent (1974) is clearly committed to that ethical standpoint.

investigating war crimes in Rwanda and in the former Yugoslavia, and the establishment of the International Criminal Court, have greatly strengthened the solidarist vision of the universal culture of human rights. Genocide in Rwanda and human rights violations in the former Yugoslavia have reopened the question of whether the society of states should be prepared to breach national sovereignty in the case of 'supreme humanitarian emergencies' (Wheeler, 2000: 13), and whether it could so in the post-bipolar world without lasting damage to international order. NATO's war against Serbia over Kosovo raised the intriguing issue of whether a self-appointed section of international society should assume responsibility for preserving civility within a sovereign state even in the absence of explicit United Nations support. These developments raised the question of whether the modern society of states is poised to make unusual progress in realizing solidarist principles and practices, and whether the English School should give this process, which includes a central role for humanitarian intervention, explicit moral support. For many, the recent wars against the Taliban and Iraq have demonstrated that international society (and the Bush Administration in particular) has returned to more traditional strategic considerations which are a major setback to such ambitions (see Dunne, 2003); for pluralists in particular, Bull's claim that the solidarist vision is 'premature' is as true now as it was when he first advanced it in the 1970s (Bull, 2002: 232). However, the strength of the universal human rights culture indicates that foreign policy makers will continue to face agonizing choices about whether or not to intervene to end supreme humanitarian emergencies, and for this reason it is important to consider recent reflections on intervention by members of the English School.

The first point to make is that an earlier consensus about the dangers of intervention has been replaced by substantial disagreements about the virtues of solidarism. Jackson (2000) responds to recent developments in world politics by going beyond Bull's empirical argument that pluralism is simply well suited to current political circumstances rather than the highest point in the history of world political organization. Jackson's work turns pluralism into a form of international political theory which makes precisely this claim.[38] On such foundations,

---

[38] The pluralist conception of international society 'is the most basic and at the same time the most articulate institutional arrangement that humans have yet come up with in response to their common recognition that they must find a settled and predictable

Jackson (2000: 42) proceeds to reject 'paternalism' in world politics in which he includes the idea of a moral right to intervene to rescue oppressed peoples but in an important argument, he maintains that pluralism and support for human rights are perfectly compatible on two separate scores. First, since many of the worst violations of human rights occur in war, the principle of sovereign equality should be defended for constraining force rather than condemned for its incompatibility with humanitarian responsibilities (Jackson, 2000: 291). Second, various sanctions which fall short of the use of force are available to states which wish to protect citizens from despotic regimes; the danger of military intervention is that it will undermine international order which is a value in itself, and not self-evidently less important than support for human rights. In connection with policy towards the former Yugoslavia, Jackson maintains that

> states who are in a position to pursue and preserve international justice have a responsibility to do that whenever and wherever possible. But they have a fundamental responsibility not to sacrifice or even jeopardize other fundamental values in the attempt. International order and stability, international peace and security, are such values . . . [and] . . . the stability of international society, especially the unity of the great powers, is more important . . . than . . . minority rights and humanitarian protections in Yugoslavia or another country – if we have to choose between those two sets of values.   (Jackson 2000: 291, 314)[39]

The key point is that efforts to preserve civility or constitutionalism in the relations between states, and especially in relations between the great powers, must generally take precedence over efforts to ensure civility or constitutionalism within national borders. Moreover, pluralists should not be belittled on the spurious grounds that they are less committed than solidarists to human well-being. The fear that the West will 'place itself above international society' leads Jackson (2000: 314)

---

way to live side by side on a finite planetary space without falling into mutual hostility, conflict, war oppression, subjugation, slavery, etc'. See Jackson (2000: 181).

[39] Jackson (2000: 310) adds that humanitarian intervention cannot solve deep structural problems in societies consumed by civil war, and intervening parties are usually unprepared to make commitments to social reconstruction that might take decades. See also Mayall (2000c: 36). Moreover, as in the case of NATO's war against Serbia, the intervening powers undermined their own moral position by tolerating a high level of collateral damage to civilians in order to keep their military personnel out of harm's way. See Jackson (2000: 289). The ethical problems here are also a central feature of Wheeler's solidarist position (see Wheeler, 2001a, 2001b).

to retreat from Bull and Vincent's heavily qualified position that collective humanitarian intervention might be justifiable in exceptional circumstances (Bull, 1984b; Vincent and Wilson, 1993: 128–9). Some may think this fear is clearly justified given the decision to use force against Iraq in 2003 without the support of the United Nations Security Council. Solidarists who defend the breach of national sovereignty have to recognize the risks involved in relaxing prohibitions against the use of force, and the dangerous precedents which may be set by condoning intervention. The weakness of Jackson's version of pluralism is that it does not explain how the victims of gross human rights abuses are to be helped if not by armed intervention when all other measures have been exhausted. It might also be suggested that his defence of pluralism does not address the question of how the potential for a more ethical international society can be released, although it should immediately be added that this is to support a critical approach to immanent global possibilities which Jackson (2000: 415–16) emphatically rejects.

Wheeler (2000: 27ff) approaches the growing tension between pluralist and solidarist norms which so interested Vincent and Bull by arguing that the end of bipolarity gave the society of states an unusual opportunity to introduce new principles of humanitarian intervention. Indeed, in a stronger argument, he contends that India, Vietnam and Tanzania could have invoked a right of humanitarian intervention in their respective engagements in Bangladesh, Cambodia and Uganda, and adds that other states could have endorsed their acts of intervention even though impure motives were involved, as in the case of Vietnam's war to overthrow Pol Pot (Wheeler, 2000: ch. 3). Wheeler is partly interested in advancing an ethical defence of humanitarian intervention, but this is connected with a sociological narrative about how the transition to a more solidarist world could occur. The key point of the narrative is that intervening powers can act as 'norm entrepreneurs' which invite other members of the society of states to take part in a diplomatic dialogue to rethink the classical prohibition of humanitarian intervention (Dunne and Wheeler, 2001: 177).[40] No less than Jackson, Wheeler is aware of the dangers involved in relaxing this prohibition, and the key issue for him is whether norm entrepreneurs can initiate a global debate about a category of human rights violations

---

[40] On norm entrepreneurs, see Finnemore and Sikkink (1998).

which are so severe as to justify a temporary departure from the principle of non-intervention which follows agreed and clearly defined rules. For Wheeler, NATO's war against Serbia had to be judged, not only by how far it achieved its immediate goals in Kosovo but also by the extent to which it initiated a global debate to draw up precise principles about such matters (Wheeler, 2001b: 160ff; see also Crawford 2002). In this stress on the need for tightly defined rules and for the importance of working with established diplomatic procedures, Wheeler is clearly mindful of the dangers involved in making the transition to a more solidarist international society.

Wheeler has been cautiously optimistic in some of his writings about the possibilities for a consensus about new principles of humanitarian intervention. Interesting ethical issues are raised by this approach, notwithstanding the fact that agreement may be increasingly unlikely in the aftermath of the war against the Taliban and regime change in Iraq. Arguably, the most important issue of all is how proponents of changes in international law should react if, as now seems inevitable, a majority of states decided to bring reinforced arguments in support of pluralist principles to a diplomatic dialogue about the rights or wrongs of humanitarian intervention. The question is whether states which are committed to supporting moving international law in a solidarist direction should abide by the majority view or reserve the right to act alone.[41] Wheeler may have been optimistic in the months surrounding the Kosovo conflict that 'norm entrepreneurs' could have succeeded in changing international law. Arguably, the logic of his argument that due process is necessary to legitimate change, is that the advocates of humanitarian war should accept the majority view even if that is to uphold the old conventions regarding the principle of non-intervention.

Despite important differences between them, Jackson and Wheeler are agreed that efforts to promote solidarism could further entrench dominant Western moral preferences and consolidate the West's economic and political power over international society as a whole. Bull (2000d: 221) addressed this danger in his remarks on the recent 'growth of . . . cosmopolitan moral awareness' and the appearance of a 'major change in our sensibilities' which includes greater regard for universal human rights and 'moral concern with welfare on a world

---

[41] For further discussion, see Chapter 7.

scale'. The upshot of these developments was that 'the idea of sovereign rights existing apart from the rules laid down by international society itself and enjoyed without qualification has to be rejected in principle' (Bull, 2000d: 220). But Bull was always quick to remind Western liberals that their conceptions of human rights do not always command the support of other peoples (Bull, 1979a). The 'nascent cosmopolitan culture' was heavily biased 'in favour of the dominant cultures of the West' (Bull, 2002: 305), and that was why many of the strongest advocates of sovereignty are to be found in the Third World. Addressing an issue which has since come to the forefront of world politics, he argued that 'the idea of the trial and punishment of war criminals by international procedure' may be 'just and wise' but it invariably 'operates in a selective way' and reflects the operation of 'power politics' (Bull, 2002: 85–6).[42] The import of these observations is that the passing of the bipolar era may have removed some constraints on the development of a solidarist world order, but one clear consequence is the dominance of Western liberal political and economic ideals in an era of American hegemony when the decision to wage 'preventive war', and to sideline the United Nations in the process, has effectively contracted the boundaries of international society (Dunne, 2003).[43]

As a bridge to the next section, it is useful to connect Bull's observations about Western dominance with Doyle's reflections on the democratic peace which argue that liberals may not be assiduous in observing the international law of war in conflicts with illiberal states (Doyle, 1983).[44] The related fear is that solidarist visions can be used to defend a homogeneous international society and to stigmatize those

---

[42] After World War II, the world 'witnessed the trial and punishment of German and Japanese leaders and soldiers for war crimes and crimes against the peace. It did not witness the trial and punishment of American, British and Soviet leaders and soldiers who *prima facie* might have been as much or as little guilty of disregarding their human obligations as Goering, Yamamoto and the rest . . . That these men and not others were brought to trial by the victors was an accident of power politics' (Bull, 2002: 85–6).

[43] One might nevertheless hesitate to leave the matter there because, as Hurrell (2002: 202) argued prior to the war against Iraq, the war against terrorism has simultaneously led to a major extension of global power and brought 'into sharper focus the already visible limits to an order based on imposition'. United States policy has not encouraged the development of an anti-hegemonic coalition to balance American power, but has led many states and civil society actors to use liberal principles, which are widely accepted in the United States, in defence of greater internationalism. For further discussion, see Glaser (2003).

[44] Butterfield (1953: ch. 7) argues that liberal states may not be exceptional in that they too can succumb to the temptation to act aggressively.

who fail to observe liberal principles of legitimacy. Non-liberal states then face the risk of external and unwarranted intervention in their internal affairs (Jackson, 2000: 360; Clark 2005: ch. 7). Burke's defence of a homogeneous international society at the time of the French Revolution is a reminder of the current dangers involved in seeking to transform the society of states in accordance with a solidarist vision.

For Burke, the survival of the European political order depended on commitments to dynastic principles of government in the constituent national parts. Applying the Roman law of vicinity and neighbourhood to international politics, he argued that a society which is a nuisance to its neighbours deserves to be punished, just as civil action is appropriate in response to a 'dangerous nuisance' in domestic society. Overthrowing the dynastic system of government constituted an international nuisance for Burke.[45] The question which arises in the contemporary world is whether some dominant forms of liberalism or neo-conservatism resemble the Burkeian view of international society by dividing the world between the elect and the damned and by unleashing decivilizing processes such as the erosion of respect for constraints on force and the selective regard for international law. In their writings on NATO's action against Serbia and on the war against Al Qaeda and the Taliban, the more solidarist members of the English School have registered their concern that the project of promoting liberal concepts of civility within other societies may have the paradoxical effect of corroding respect for civility in relations between independent political communities (Wheeler, 2002). These concerns can only be intensified by the decision to sideline the United Nations during the war against Iraq – not only because of increasing hostility in Muslim societies to the United States and Great Britain but also because of more general cynicism about the benefits of a Western-dominated international order. After the cautious optimism of recent years, which is evident in Wheeler (2000), it may be that the dominant tendency in the English School will emphasize the scale of the obstacles to the creation of a solidarist international society (see Dunne, 2003). An alternative response is to redouble efforts to construct visions of solidarism which do not assume that unity can only be achieved through the development of a homogeneous international society.

---

[45] An 'evil in the heart of Europe [had to be] extirpated from that center' because 'no part of the circumference can be free from the mischief which radiates from it' (Burke, quoted in Welsh, 1996: 178).

The expansion of international society

The constraints on the transition from a pluralist to solidarist international society are compounded by the coexistence of different
'theatres of operation', some uncompromising in their defence of pluralism, others keen to promote solidarism – or their version of it – in
their theatre of operation and beyond. Bull (1979b; 2002: 245ff, 266–7)
argued that neo-medieval arrangements might be developing in
Western Europe although he did not regard that as necessarily progressive.[46] His references to growing divisions between Western liberal-democratic and non-liberal societies would seem to represent a
challenge to Watson's prediction about the slow emergence of transcultural moral standards. The issue is whether agreement on such
values might be increasing in liberal-democratic areas but decreasing
in the wider world because of the phenomenon which Bull and Watson
analysed in the 1980s, namely the expansion of international society.
We can put this differently by asking how far progress towards solidarism is possible in a universal international society which lacks a
common culture but which can point to the achievement of sustaining
pluralist principles of coexistence (Bull and Watson, 1984).

The expansion of international society involved the dismantlement
of systems of exclusion which limited membership to the allegedly
more civilized sections of the human race. The process of expansion
has posed the problem of whether the founding members of international society and those that have recently joined their ranks can
agree on transcultural moral principles. Some of the constraints are
immense because perceptions of cultural or racial superiority amongst
the original members of international society have not entirely disap-
peared with the admission of new members. These perceptions have
deep roots in Europe's past, having been at the heart of relations
between Christian and non-Christian world peoples. In recognition
of this, some English School accounts of the origins and development
of Western attitudes to non-Western peoples have highlighted 'the
doctrine of Hostiensis that non-Christian communities had been deprived of their rights of political existence with the coming of Christ';
they have also emphasized the thinking of Spanish colonizers of the

---

[46] Little will be said about Bull's comments on neo-medievalism since this has been
considered elsewhere (Linklater, 1998: ch. 6). Some comments about neo-medievalism
and good international citizenship are offered on pp. 245ff.

'newly discovered peoples' who were no less certain of their right to judge the value of non-Christian forms of life and to convert them to Christianity while condemning the brutality of the conquistadores (Bull, 1984a: 120).[47] Significantly, their claims were cast in universalistic terms which stressed the rights and duties that all human beings had in an emergent world society.[48] Universal norms were assumed to give the Spaniards the moral right to wage a just war if efforts to preach Christianity were rejected, and also the right to intervene to prevent violations of the natural law such as cannibalism and sodomy. This is not the occasion to trace the development of Western theories of trusteeship and empire.[49] Suffice it to add that a secularized version of this egocentric world view was embodied in the 'standard of civilisation' which was used in the nineteenth century to justify excluding non-European peoples from the society of states and to define the level of political development they would need to attain before their admission could be contemplated. The standard of civilization later found expression in the League of Nations mandates system and the United Nations trusteeship system which established the duty to prepare colonial peoples for sovereign independence and to surrender power when the imperial overlords were convinced of their capacity for good government. Echoes of this standpoint can be seen in the contemporary universal human rights culture (Donnelly, 1998).

Bull and Watson (1984) remains the authoritative study of Western conceptions of superiority to other peoples, of the revolt by non-Western peoples against Western dominance, and of subsequent efforts to redraft the constitution of international society. The details of the revolt against the West need not detain us;[50] attention can turn instead

---

[47] Bull (ibid.) contrasts this with the argument of Paulus Vladimiri who defended the rights of the pagan Lithuanians against this view.

[48] The Spanish clergy claimed 'the right to travel and dwell in those countries' in order to attract converts to Christianity. To prevent the exercise of that right was to violate the conventions of the *naturalis societatis et commmunicationis* (the natural community of humankind). For a discussion of these points, see Ortega (1996: 102ff).

[49] For an account of theories of trusteeship, see Bain (2003).

[50] Bull (1984a: 220–3) identified five main components of 'the revolt against the West'. The first was 'the struggle for equal sovereignty' undertaken by societies such as China and Japan which had 'retained their formal independence' but were thought 'inferior' to the Western powers. These societies were governed by unequal treaties 'concluded under duress'. Because of the principle of extraterritoriality, they were denied the right to settle disputes involving foreigners according to domestic law. As a consequence of the legal revolt against the West, Japan joined the society of states in 1900, Turkey in 1923, Egypt in 1936 and China in 1943. The political revolt against the West was a second

to Bull's argument about the significance of the expansion of international society for the relationship between order and justice. As noted earlier, Bull (2002: ch. 4) stressed the tension between order and justice, and argued that progress towards greater justice could not occur in the absence of international order. The Hagey Lectures restated the theme that 'justice is best realised in a context of order' (Bull, 2000d: 227) but they also underlined the point that the 'measures . . . necessary to achieve justice for peoples of the Third World are the same measures that will maximise the prospects of international order or stability, at least in the long run'.[51] The contention was that order must seem legitimate in the eyes of the great majority of the world's population who live in abject poverty in its most impoverished regions, and not merely advantageous to the regimes that claim to represent them (Bull, 1983b).[52] This theme has lost none of its importance in recent years with growing global economic inequalities, and it has played an important part in public debates about the most appropriate long-term responses to the terrorist attacks on the United States in 2001 which are part of the continuing revolt against the West (Linklater, 2002b).

Bull's analysis of the importance of justice for order identified one reason why the comfortable powers might wish to promote new

and related part of this process. In this case, the former colonies which had lost their former independence demanded freedom from imperial domination. The racial revolt which included the struggle to abolish slavery and the slave trade as well as all forms of white supremacism was the third element. The fourth was the economic revolt against the forms of inequality and exploitation associated with a Western-dominated global commercial and financial system. The fifth revolt, the cultural revolt, was a protest against all forms of Western cultural imperialism including assumptions about how other peoples should live and efforts to universalize liberal-individualistic ideas about human rights. The religious revolt against Western ways of life (which is connected with opposition to American policy in the Middle East) has taken the cultural revolt further, most obviously by Al Qaeda.

[51] Bull here stresses the extrinsic value of justice, i.e. its capacity to contribute to international order. This is not to suggest he denied that justice had intrinsic value, but the logic of his argument is that, as a general rule, states will not defend justice for its own sake.

[52] Bull (ibid.) makes it clear that this is not primarily a moral argument but a political one since what is at stake is the survival of international order. Wight (1966b: 108) anticipated the general argument when he said of world politics since 1945 that it now seems as if 'there is a direct and positive relation between national justice and the maintenance of order: that if the Western Powers could not free their colonies quickly enough the colonies would secede morally to the opposing camp, that the West must run at top speed in order to remain in its existing position, that peaceful change is no longer the antithesis of security, but its condition. Order now requires justice.'

normative developments in international society, but he expressed serious doubts about the superpowers' ability to acquire the moral vision and political will which was needed to solve a mounting legitimation problem in world politics. We have seen that he believed the international society of states had made some progress in recognizing the need for stronger moral commitments to welfare internationalism but this, he suggested, had to be combined with vigorous efforts to promote greater justice between the world's different cultural standpoints. Bull was evidently concerned that affluent Western societies would be as slow to appreciate the global significance of increasing cultural differences as they have been to address global economic inequalities.[53] For his part, Vincent (1986a) believed that different standpoints could find common ground in joint efforts to secure freedom from starvation and malnutrition for all members of the human race. Reflecting Bull's concern that liberal values do not always resonate with people everywhere, Vincent argued that no single state or group of states could claim that certain human rights were self-evidently binding on the whole of humanity. On this view, progress in creating transcultural values and ethical standards could only occur through a process of diplomatic dialogue in which all cultural standpoints enjoyed equal respect. As an ethical statement, this position runs parallel to many approaches to dialogue, discourse and conversation in recent international political theory. Vincent's position was that dialogue between the more and less affluent societies would lead to progress in creating 'genuinely universal' principles such as the universal human right to be free from starvation and malnutrition, as opposed to spurious universals which satisfied the interests of the dominant powers. As Buzan (2004: 39–43) has noted, Vincent believed

---

[53] Bull's stress on growing cultural differences is clear from the following comments. He argued that it is important 'to remember that when . . . demands for justice were first put forward, the leaders of Third World peoples spoke as suppliants in a world in which the Western powers were still in a dominant position . . . the moral appeal had to be cast in terms that would have most resonance in Western societies. But as . . . non-Western peoples have become stronger . . . Third World spokesmen have become freer to adopt a different rhetoric that sets Western values aside, or . . . places different interpretations upon them. Today there is legitimate doubt as to how far the demands emanating from the Third World coalition are compatible with the moral ideas of the West' (Bull, 1984a: 213). Earlier, he had stressed that 'like the world international society, the cosmopolitan culture on which it depends may need to absorb non-Western elements to a much greater degree if it is to be genuinely universal and provide a foundation for a universal international society' (Bull, 2002: 305). Bull did not elaborate on the form this process of absorption should take.

that the idea of a right to be free of starvation provided the basis for progressing from a pluralist international society, which had largely neglected such ethical concerns, towards a world society based on cosmopolitan principles. Crucially, Vincent was less concerned with the relationship between the individual and the state, and with the extent to which international society should protect peoples from their own governments, than with the relationship between peoples and the world economy, and with the need for states to manage this relationship in 'a humane fashion' (see also Gonzalez-Pelaez and Buzan 2003: 324–5).

Bull and Vincent believed that the revolt against the West did not rule out a global normative consensus on the imperative of promoting welfare internationalism. They thought that cultural differences would prevent a broader agreement on substantive moral principles but they did not regard that as the decisive test of the extent to which international society is making progress towards cosmopolitanism. Non-Western powers had submitted their demands for political, economic and cultural justice before international society, and the extent to which the affluent powers met their legitimate demands was the true measure of the extent to which international society was making cosmopolitan progress. There is a latent vision here of what it would mean for the human species to create a more ethical society of states whose members agree that their legitimate loyalties to bounded communities should be combined with duties to alleviate the suffering of the poorest members of humankind, and with equally strong obligations to engage the less advantaged in a diplomatic dialogue about how their concerns could be satisfied with an improved international society.

There are very clear parallels between this standpoint and contemporary critical theory but, of course, Bull and Vincent did not advocate any of the versions of universal dialogue which have appeared in recent 'post-positivist' theories of world politics, or endorse notions of moral learning as found in Habermas's writings.[54] They were centrally concerned with the preservation of international order and society in the context of unparalleled economic inequalities and cultural diversity, and their defence of global justice must be seen in this light although it is important not to underestimate the depth of their conviction that the duty to create a world community is an end in itself. It is arguable that critical approaches to social learning provide

[54] See Linklater (1998) for further discussion.

useful resources for developing their ethical commitments to global change while steering clear of utopianism. Just as states can learn how to build a society of states, so can they learn to develop higher standards of legitimacy to judge the adequacy of global arrangements and foreign policy perspectives and specific decisions. Whether the evolution of such higher standards is the result of pragmatic reasoning about how to preserve international order or stems from some independent moral compulsion to create a more just world order which reduces human misery is not the crucial point. What is crucial is that the process of learning how to develop elementary forms of civility, and how to build and maintain pluralist or solidarist arrangements, can be extended further – as Bull and Vincent argued – in response to criticisms that international society fails to address the legitimate concerns of the most disadvantaged parts of the world. They capture this standpoint in their belief that international society is more likely to survive and flourish if it commands the consent of the world's population whose majority lives outside the economically affluent and politically stable West. This is the central ethical theme captured in the critical-theoretical position that all human beings should have an equal right in international society to give expression to their concerns about injury, vulnerability and suffering.

The expansion of international society can be regarded as the main reason why a transcultural moral consensus is possibly more elusive than it was when the society of states was confined to the continent of Europe (Brown, 1988). Solidarism based on Western liberal conceptions of the most fundamental individual rights does not seem poised to develop significantly beyond the liberal democracies. But the expansion of international society can also be regarded as one reason why the modern international system is subject to a more searching moral examination than its predecessors were. Demands to take account of the interests of the most vulnerable members of the human race have not been the norm in the history of international relations; pleas to reduce human suffering have rarely been heard or heeded; invitations to secure justice for moral and cultural differences have not made regular appearances; calls for a dialogue between the world's peoples and civilizations have been the historical exception rather than the general rule.[55] The belief that the legitimacy of the global political

---

[55] On the dialogue of civilizations, see Lynch (2000).

and economic order depends on progress in promoting 'universal solidarity' and sympathy that cuts across 'cultural divides' (Shapcott, 2000: 160–1) may yet prove to be the main reason why Watson is correct to argue that modern states are 'consciously working out, for the first time, a set of transcultural values and ethical standards' – but crucially, a set of values and standards which do not require conformity with some vision of the good life which may be preferred in the most powerful society or societies, and a set of values which reveal that very different societies can agree on forms of human solidarity in the context of radical cultural and religious differences. Therein lies the possibility of progress towards a universal community which reduces, even though it is unlikely ever to eliminate, the moral deficiencies and political dangers which were noted in the forms of world political organization considered in the earlier parts of this chapter.

Conclusion

An analysis of system, society and community in the writings of the English School casts light on its distinctive approach to progress and its limits in world politics. Members of the School reject the Hobbesian perspective without underestimating the potential for violence which invariably lurks beneath the surface of the most peaceful eras of international politics. They argue that to reduce all statecraft to strategic action which is concerned with controlling or at least with neutralizing principal adversaries is to neglect the extent to which states have learned to create and preserve order in anarchical societies. Watson's claim that all past systems of states have evolved into international societies captures this essential point.

The English School has often doubted that states can do more than agree on pluralist rules of coexistence although Bull, Vincent and Watson commented on growing support for transcultural values in recent times. They rejected the Kantian tradition with its progressivist faith in the human capacity to agree on universal norms which would secure the passage from a system of states dominated by power and force to a world community governed by dialogue and consent. The idea of moral learning is not embraced by the English School, and most of its members would have little sympathy for a notion which they would regard as prone to degenerating into self-righteousness which leads to needless interference in others' internal affairs. Members of the School have written about the advance of the universal human rights culture and the contraction of the sphere of domestic jurisdiction while being divided over the matter of whether the society of states can and should build new norms of humanitarian intervention into its normative structure. Bull's references to increasing cosmopolitan moral sensibilities, and Watson's remarks on the development of transcultural values and ethical standards, invite the discussion of whether visions of a universal community of humankind may yet come to have an unusual influence on world affairs. These dimensions of English School analysis suggest that states do not learn only in the sphere of strategic action (where they master new techniques for outmanoeuvring or overpowering each other) or in the sphere of communicative action (where they establish principles of coexistence through diplomatic dialogues); they also learn in the moral sphere (most obviously by evolving more demanding tests of the legitimacy of global political and economic arrangements which can then shape political action).

A final comment is that Bull and Wight regarded Kant as a member of the revolutionist tradition; however, several members of the English School have gravitated towards a more Kantian approach to international relations by arguing that modern states and peoples may be developing more searching and sophisticated moral tests of the legitimacy of global economic and political arrangements. Bull and Wight's characterization of Kant's perspective (which was often misleading) deflected attention away from the respects in which his approach extended the Grotian perspective – most obviously by reflecting, in Bull's terms, on how international order can be remade to contribute to the deeper value of world order. The aim of the next chapter is to remove the revolutionist label from Kant's writings and to explain their relevance for efforts to develop solidarist tendencies in the English School.

5 Cosmopolitanism and the harm principle in world politics

Wight (1991) maintained that rationalism was the *via media* between realism, which argues that states are condemned to take part in relations of competition and conflict, and revolutionism which believes in the possibility of replacing the states-system with a form of world political organization which realizes the ethical ideal of the unity of humankind. He claimed that rationalism went beyond realism which underestimated the importance of international society but it also superseded revolutionism which committed the opposite offence of overestimating the prospects for the progressive transformation of world politics. Wight argued that the ongoing conversation about international relations would be impoverished without the revolutionist's continuing protest against the moral deformities of world politics.[1] On this argument, rationalists should remain open to the revolutionists' claims about the moral imperfections of the international states-system while steering clear of their naively utopian solutions.

A group of scholars who aim to understand the foundations of international society and who share some of the realist's pessimism about the prospects for ending violent war must nevertheless deal with the revolutionists' criticism that sovereign communities can progress beyond international society by agreeing on the means of giving political expression to the ancient ideal of the universal community of humankind. It is no surprise then that leading members of the English

---

[1] Wight's interest in revolutionism had its roots in his early pacifism (on the latter, see Thomas, 2001). On his general position on the rationalist conception of the relationship between morality and politics, see Wight (1991: 243) where he argues that ideals 'are never realized, but should be striven for; the fundamentals wherein we believe will not be carried out, but it is necessary to affirm them: here is the moral tension with which Rationalist statecraft is conducted'.

School have been especially interested in their visions of global political progress (Wight, 1991; Bull, 2002: part 3). The fact that revolutionism had also influenced the early history of the European states-system (and has been one of the main theoretical and practical voices throughout its development) was an additional reason for taking revolutionism seriously. Revolutionism has often inspired diplomatic efforts to reduce human suffering whether caused by civil or inter-state war, intervention, natural disaster or economic collapse.[2] The abolition of slavery and the slave trade, the development of the laws of war and the rise of the human rights culture, demonstrated that international society gave at least partial expression to the ideal of universal human solidarity in a world where sovereign states commanded popular loyalty. A further reason for analysing the doctrine was that it held the key to understanding the tendency for the European society of states to fracture along transnational lines. Here it is important to remember Wight's observation that the modern states-system has known international revolution (in which transnational ideological or religious movements compete to impose universal political goals on the whole of humanity) and generalized warfare in almost equal degree (Wight, 1978: 92). To comprehend the repeated transnational fragmentation of European international society, it was essential to understand the appeal of revolutionism (which was itself a standing reminder that the European political order emerged in a region with significant cultural and political unity). The merits of its claims about the moral inadequacies of the states-system had to be acknowledged but its role in engulfing the society of states in violent transnational conflict was a central reason for Bull and Wight's consistent opposition to revolutionism.

Wight believed that the disciplinary preoccupation with the tension between utopianism and realism in the interwar years had oversimplified

---

[2] Bull (1991: xvii) claims that 'there are moments when Wight seems as much drawn towards the Kantian tradition as towards the Machiavellian or the Grotian'. He saw 'that the belief in progress is not the deepest element in the Kantian tradition. The deepest element – the element that must draw us to it – is the moral passion to abolish suffering and sin.' The importance of the harm principle is stressed in the current work because it provides a bridge between Wight's rationalism and Kant's so-called revolutionism. Wight's reference to the fact that 'political expedience itself has to consult the moral sense of those who it will affect' (Wight, 1966b: 128) leaves unclear the precise boundaries of the human constituency whose interests should be taken into account. What has been called 'critical international society theory' understands the moral constituency to include humanity as a whole. See Chapter 7.

the history of international thought. He introduced the category of rationalism to capture the greater complexity of thinking about international relations and to restore the Grotian tradition to its rightful place.[3] This was linked with the hope that its analysis of international affairs would continue to exercise its 'civilizing' role in world politics.[4] The idea of revolutionism was introduced to call attention to the rich diversity of utopian or dissenting approaches which a concentration on Western idealism or liberal internationalism had obscured, but gathering such diverse approaches as Marxism-Leninism, liberalism, fascism and pacifism under one broad heading created its own problems. For that reason, Wight divided revolutionism into several sub-types. 'Inverted revolutionism', which referred to the pacifist tradition, embraced thinkers such as Gandhi and Tolstoy. This was distinguished from the revolutionism of Marxism-Leninism or fascism which saw violence as a necessary instrument of political change. The 'evolutionary' revolutionism of those such as Woodrow Wilson who believed in the possibility of the peaceful transformation of world politics was distinguished from the 'revolutionary' revolutionism of Marxism-Leninism and fascism as well as from the pacifist tradition (Wight, 1991: 159–60).

Realism and rationalism were no less heterogeneous traditions, and this led Wight to subdivide them and also to identify respects in which they overlapped with different forms of revolutionism. It was important not to confuse the 'moderate realism' of Kennan and Morgenthau with the 'extreme realism' of Hitler, and essential to note how the more 'realist' forms of rationalism merged with 'moderate realism'.[5] The

---

[3] Wight (1991: 266–7) maintained 'the two-schools analysis of international theory' was to be lamented, but the 'recent fashionable division of international theory into two schools' (realism and utopianism) had occurred because 'rationalism, which used to be an orthodox, traditional, and respectable school of international theory, has grown steadily weaker, steadily dissolved, shedding its strength and support to the schools on the flanks'. See Wight (1991: 15) on rationalism as 'the *broad* middle road' (italics in original).

[4] On the civilizing role of rationalism, see Wight (1991: 268).

[5] Wight (1991: 161) distinguishes between the realist and idealist strands of Grotianism. Churchill, Acheson and Morgenthau are associated with the first position; Gladstone, late Nehru and Lincoln are associated with the second one. Morgenthau is described as a realist Grotian in Wight (1991: 160). See the further reference to Morgenthau in Wight (1991: 267) where Kennan is described as 'really a Rationalist'. Wight (1991: 126) maintains that 'Morgenthau, like Kennan, has one foot planted in Rationalist territory'. Significantly, Wight (1991: 162) distinguishes Kant from the Kantian who believes the end justifies the means. See Wight (1991: 15) on Kant's apparent rationalism.

157

'soft revolutionism' of Wilson with its preference for gradual political change had to be distinguished from 'hard revolutionism' with its preference for violent transformation. It was also important to recognize that, at certain points, the rationalist tradition converged with 'soft revolutionism' (Wight, 1991: 46–7). Far from being monolithic doctrines, realism, rationalism and revolutionism overlapped then in important ways. Wight was careful to add that the three main perspectives were useful organizing devices rather than exact replicas of unbroken and self-contained theoretical traditions. No thinker of substance, he argued, could be easily assigned to any one perspective; the deepest insights into the nature of international political life invariably resulted from combining elements from different persuasions, even though one voice might have the greatest influence in the final argument. But to know this, one had to separate different intellectual tendencies in the history of international thought and understand their distinctive anatomies.

Wight (1991: 268) confessed that all three traditions held some attraction for him but, due to its focus on international society, the rationalist persuasion was the most compelling of all.[6] The influence of realism is clearly present in his thought, which has been described as a version of 'soft' realism (see Wight, 1966; Bull, 1972b: 39).[7] The influence of revolutionism is harder to detect, but recent analyses of his intellectual development stress not only his early pacifism and religious conviction, but his almost revolutionist stance on the moral imperfections of international politics.[8] Wight's complex rationalism is a perfect illustration of his point that no thinker of any sophistication is so totally subsumed within one tradition as to be deaf to all external influences.

It has been argued that members of the English School depict realism and revolutionism in such unflattering terms that rationalism prevails effortlessly as the irresistible middle ground (Walker, 1993: 32). This

---

[6] Bull (1991: xv) maintains that 'Wight was too well aware of the vulnerability of the Grotian position ever to commit himself to it fully. He understood that "it is the perspective of the international establishment"'.

[7] Bull (1991: xiv) maintained it would be 'wrong to force Martin Wight into the Grotian pigeon-hole. It is a truer vision of him to regard him as standing outside the three traditions, feeling the attraction of each of them but unable to rest within any one of them, and embodying in his own life and thought the tension among them.' In the conclusion to his lectures, however, Wight (1991: 268) claims, 'my prejudices are Rationalist'.

[8] See Thomas (2002) on Wight's 'idealism without illusions'.

interpretation raises the question of whether revolutionism serves as a foil for the rationalist position and, in response, it must be emphasized that there have been times when the effort to defend rationalism was bound up with a crude and misleading interpretation of Kant and the larger Kantian tradition. This is especially true of Bull's writings which castigate the Kantians not only for ignoring the existence of international society but also for advocating intolerance and fanaticism in world affairs. Serious distortions of the Kantian perspective served to underline the greater reasonableness and superior practical wisdom of the Grotian tradition, but at the cost of neglecting affinities between the more solidarist tendencies within the English School and particular strands of reformist international thought. With the strengthening of these tendencies over roughly the last two decades, it is timely to consider these affinities in more detail and to reflect further on the significance of Kant's thought for the unfinished task of radicalizing rationalism.

The first part of this chapter interprets Kant as a thinker who stands at the radical end of the Grotian perspective rather than at the beginning of a separate tradition which dismisses international society on moral grounds and which offers the false hope of a cosmopolitan community of humankind. The second part identifies various respects in which Grotian thinking and Kant's theory of the state and international relations are united in regarding the harm principle as central to the theory and practice of world politics.[9] The argument is that whereas the English School has been largely concerned with how the harm principle can contribute to order between states, Kant's international theory was more centrally interested in how the society of states can evolve in conjunction with the cosmopolitan moral ideal that individuals everywhere are entitled to the protection of the harm principle in their own right. This is one crucial point where Kant's thought and solidarist thinking in the English School converge and are united in reflecting on the normative question of how international order can be made to work for, rather than against, world order. Extending the social realm in which the harm principle applies is one

---

[9] In this work the harm principle is used in Feinberg's sense to refer to the belief that the liberty of agents should only be restricted when actions harm others. See Feinberg (1984). The discussion of harm in the remainder of this work is a prelude to the more extensive discussion offered in Linklater's, *The Problem of Harm in World Politics* (in preparation).

way of bringing together these two spheres. This consideration will be addressed in the final section of this chapter.

Kant's radicalized rationalism

Another of Wight's taxonomies of different species of revolutionism must be added to those described earlier. The first form is cosmopolitanism which Wight described as the perspective that defends the idea of a 'civitas maxima . . . by proclaiming a world society of individuals, which overrides nations or states, diminishing or dismissing this middle link. It rejects the idea of a society of states and says that the only true international society is one of individuals . . . This is the most revolutionary of Revolutionist theories and it implies the total dissolution of international relations' (Wight, 1991: 45). Wight (ibid.) added that this perspective is 'theoretically the least important' version of revolutionism: 'no major work of international theory propounds such a doctrine' but 'in practice it is influential'. A second form of revolutionism, exemplified by Stalinism, favours 'doctrinal imperialism' through the efforts of a great power 'to spread a creed and impose uniformity' (Wight, 1991: 43). A third form which was attributed to Kant favours 'ideological homogeneity' (Wight, 1991: 41–2). This standpoint is said to be evident in Kant's belief that perpetual peace will only exist when international society consists exclusively of republican states.

Wight maintained that some forms of revolutionism have exercised a civilizing role in world politics by virtue of questioning the state's right to use force or defending constraints on violence in accordance with ethical commitments to universal values but, as mentioned earlier, the belief that revolutionism has often posed a threat to peace and to the survival of international society is an equally strong, if not more powerful, theme in his writings.[10] Each form of revolutionism outlined earlier is associated with some conception of the ideal society or good life which devotees regard as universally valid and which they may be determined to impose on others. Competition between transnational religious or political movements to realize their clashing visions of how the human race should be organized has often resulted

---

[10] Bull (1991: xvi) stressed Wight's personal revulsion towards progressivist approaches to world politics, the secular 'debasements' of eschatological approaches to history.

in fragmenting international society along horizontal divisions (Bull, 2002: 24). Bull's sketch of the Kantian tradition criticizes it for threatening the brittle structure of international society. He maintained that its foundational claim was that a 'horizontal conflict of ideology ... cuts across the boundaries of states and divides human society into two camps – the trustees of the immanent community of mankind and those who stand in its way, those who are of the true faith and the heretics, the liberators and the oppressed' (Bull, ibid.). Standard diplomatic conventions have no place in this world-view which dispenses with the customs and conventions of international society – including respect for the sovereignty of others – on the grounds that they are worthless impediments to the moral and political unification of humankind. 'Good faith with heretics' has only 'tactical convenience' for a world-view which is committed to the general principle that 'between the elect and the damned, the liberators and the oppressed, the question of mutual acceptance of rights to sovereignty or independence does not arise' (Bull, ibid.).

Bull's comments are a fair portrait of 'revolutionary revolutionism', but a misleading summary of Kant's (or the Kantian) theory of international relations. As Hoffmann (1990: 23) has argued, Kant 'was much less cosmopolitan and universalist in his writings on international affairs than Bull suggests' and, as Hurrell (1990) has observed, Bull was wrong to include Kant amongst the advocates of world government since his clear preference was for a loose confederation of states united by a covenant to advance together towards perpetual peace.[11] Interestingly, contemporary theorists of cosmopolitan democracy who belong to the Kantian tradition find his conception of world citizenship disappointing precisely because it is confined to defending the moral duty to extend hospitality to travellers and stops short of offering a bolder vision of the rights and duties which individuals should have as members of a universal community with effective global legal and political institutions (Habermas, 1997). Underpinning Kant's defence of world citizenship is a conception of an international society in which the sovereign equality of its constituent parts and, crucially, the duty of non-intervention are universally respected.

---

[11] Inaccurately, Bull (2002: 253) refers to 'the case for world government, as it is made out by Kant and others'. Yost (2004: xxv–xxvi) has observed that Wight includes in the Kantian or revolutionist tradition various ideas that are not found in Kant's writings.

At no point then did Kant celebrate the right of any enlightened transnational elite to use force to impose its will on the rest of human-kind; instead, he envisaged an international society which would respect individual human rights, and to that extent his position was solidarist in the sense of defending cosmopolitanism although he did not support 'cosmopolitan law enforcement'. His defence of the principle of non-intervention reveals that he did not break entirely with the pluralist conception of international society, fearing that global despotism was the most likely alternative to a world based on territorial sovereignty (Kant, 1970b: 223). Significantly, Jackson's claim that universal values including respect for human rights are best promoted within a pluralist framework rather than by breaching terri-torial sovereignty is not far removed from Kant's position (see above, pp. 141ff). Troubled by the consequences of transgressing sovereignty, Kant envisaged a transnational elite of enlightened *philosophes* who would seek to improve international society by bringing violations of human rights anywhere to the attention of the whole world. Moral suasion which relied on 'the power of the pen' (MacMillan, 1998) would effectively shrink domestic jurisdiction without directly attacking sovereign rights. To translate this into contemporary par-lance, Kant found a solution to the tension between pluralist and solidarist principles in the development of a rudimentary global public sphere in which non-state actors would take the lead in 'constructing world culture' (Bolis and Thomas, 1999).

These comments indicate that Kant did not belong to the cosmopol-itan branch of revolutionism with its vision of 'a world society of individuals, which overrides nations or states, diminishing or dismiss-ing this middle link' (see above, p. 160). There are also difficulties in associating him with those that long for 'doctrinal uniformity' notwith-standing his belief that republican states had a unique potential for achieving perpetual peace. Kant does not seem to have thought that republican regimes were an essential prerequisite for membership of the society of states; and he certainly did not formulate a liberal version of Burke's argument that a departure from his ideal system of government was a crime against international society which justi-fied military intervention (Macmillan, 1995).[12] His criticism of the treatment of Japan and China by the European powers, his sympathy

---

[12] Compare this with Wight (1991: 42) that Kant believed there 'could be no international peace until all governments were of the same ideological compulsion'.

for their desire to limit contact with the outside world, and his hostility to the cruelty that 'the Hottentots, the Tongas, or most of the American Indians' had suffered in the course of Europe's colonial expansion, does not suggest a vision of international society in which republican states are free to do as they please in their relations with non-liberal societies (Kant, 1965b: 126; Kant, 1970b: 215–16). They suggest instead a vision of international society which is heterogeneous in its membership, one that mirrors Wight's conception of a society of states in which diverse forms of government find common ground in upholding a principle of mutual tolerance.[13] Kant's vision of a world order which combines sovereignty with respect for human rights and cultural diversity is very different from the cosmopolitanism which Wight described, and it has nothing in common with the other forms of revolutionism described earlier (although the notion of 'evolutionary' revolutionism is not unhelpful in describing his position).[14] Bull and Wight would have been closer to the mark had they regarded Kant as a dissenting voice within the Grotian tradition and as one of the great exponents of a radicalized form of rationalism which envisaged the progressive application of the harm principle in international affairs – its extension, in short, from interaction between members of the same state to relations between all states, and in time, to relations involving all sections of humanity (see also Linklater 1982/1990: part two).

It is important to note that Wight described Kant's theory of the state and international relations as one of the least dangerous species of revolutionism, and that he compared him with the rationalist who is, above all, 'a reformist, the practitioner of piecemeal social engineering' (Wight, 1991: 29).[15] Wight (1991: 73) referred to the parallel with Grotius who thought in terms of harmonizing obligations to the state, international society and humankind rather than replacing national

[13] By distinguishing between an inner ring of enlightened republican states and an outer ring of non-republican peoples, Kant can be said to have developed a secularized version of the Grotian 'dual conception of international society' (see Wight, 1977: 125–8). Like Grotius he believed universal laws of reason should govern relations between all human societies. It is unclear whether he believed that republican states could ever have the right to intervene to prevent violations of human rights in the non-republican world but there can be little doubt that he would feared the possibility of despotism.

[14] Wight (1991: 160) distinguishes between evolutionary and revolutionary Kantianism. Interestingly, Kant does not appear under either heading.

[15] He could have added that Kant would not have disputed his contention that 'the fundamental task of politics at all times [is] to provide order, or security, from which law, justice and prosperity may afterwards develop' (Wight, 1977: 192).

loyalties with international and cosmopolitan responsibilities. Kant thought the ideal form of world political organization should recognize the importance of three legal spheres which correspond to those different tiers of moral and political obligation. The three spheres were: the civil law of the state, international law which creates order between sovereign associations, and cosmopolitan law which expresses the moral equality of all human beings.[16] Pluralists such as Jackson (see below, p. 228) are at one with Kant in thinking the central ethical challenge in world politics is how to balance national, international and humanitarian responsibilities which correspond with three basic forms of moral community and objects of human loyalty. Recent solidarists such as Wheeler (2000) have a similar conception of the key ethical challenge, siding with Kant on the importance of strengthening cosmopolitan law, but moving beyond his perspective by allowing for humanitarian intervention in supreme humanitarian emergencies. The fact that Kant's cosmopolitanism is modest by comparison makes the decision to locate him in the revolutionist tradition rather than at the radical end of the rationalist perspective all the more peculiar and perplexing.

None of this is to deny that important differences exist between Kant and Wight's approaches to international relations. Kant believed in the possibility of perpetual peace; Wight (1978: 137) thought 'war is inevitable', even though 'particular wars can be avoided'.[17] That was one reason why Wight thought the conviction that the modern society of states could evolve into a peaceful international anarchy was a flawed, if admirable, moral ideal which placed revolutionists at odds with the realist and rationalist's more worldly appreciation of the imperfectibility of world politics. Kant regarded the balance of power as a mere 'chimera' in which only the deluded would invest their faith although he thought it could be a useful temporary staging post in the movement towards perpetual peace (Kant, 1965b: 119; Kant, 1970b: 198).[18] His belief that republican states could coexist in perpetual peace denies that the balance of power is necessary for the maintenance of international order. Wight did not see the balance of power as a

---

[16] Kant (1970b: 206) refers to *ius civitatis* (civil law), *ius gentium* (international law) and *ius cosmopoliticum* (cosmopolitan law).

[17] Suganami (1996) criticizes this standpoint on the grounds that if particular wars can be avoided then war itself cannot be deemed to be inevitable.

[18] Wight (1991: 177–8) recognizes that Kant did not reject the balance of power outright but regarded it as 'a necessary step' towards 'progress'.

panacea for the deficiencies of international politics – it would almost certainly collapse as the major powers drifted into war with depressing predictability – but he clearly thought that revolutionists failed to recognize that there is no alternative to the balance of power as long as independent political communities remain in the condition of anarchy.[19]

It is important to note that Kant's analysis of world politics cannot be separated from a secularized eschatological view of history which was anathema to Wight (see above, note 10, p. 160). There is no doubt that Kant believed that nature or providence – a notion with parallels with Hegel's idea of the cunning of reason or Smith's idea of the invisible hand – would cajole the human race into collaborating to achieve perpetual peace under conditions of increasing global interdependence. Writers such as Carr believed such approaches were typical of the study of international relations in its infant years when moral purpose was a substitute for dispassionate analysis (Carr, 1946: ch. 1), and Wight may have had some sympathy with this standpoint. Despite their differences, Wight was as enthusiastic as Carr in contrasting the utopian temperament with the dispassionate analysis of the role of power in international politics and with the detached investigation of the tensions and rivalries between the great powers which have repeatedly erupted into war. But Wight's emphasis on the precarious nature of international order places him somewhat closer to Burke than to Kant or Carr.[20] In Wight's thinking, there are echoes of the conservative's fear that the radical spirit can rapidly erode fragile constraints on violent conduct which have developed slowly and laboriously over decades or centuries, and there are particular parallels with Burke's theme that the radicals' concentration on the imperfections of political life breeds disdain for arrangements which have the

---

[19] The differences between Kant and Wight have renewed significance given the hegemonic qualities of American power. Dunne (2003) returns to the question of whether international society is possible without the existence of a balance of power. Watson (1992) argues that it is more or less inevitable that great powers will seek hegemony but there is no explanation of why this is necessary. Admittedly, it is wise to recall Acton's dictum that 'power corrupts, and absolute power tends to corrupt absolutely', but the checks on such tendencies need not be external. Constitutional checks on the abuse of executive power – both nationally and at the international level – are an alternative. Of course, the idea of a liberal peace explicitly denies that states cannot maintain international order without the constraining role of the balance of power (see below, p. 166).

[20] On the more utopian dimensions of Carr's thought, see Linklater (2000a).

merit of having been tested in the unforgiving circumstances of conflict and distrust.[21] It would be wrong, however, to conclude that the essential difference between the two thinkers is that Wight believed responsibility in politics requires the careful labour of preserving (and where possible improving) brittle and imperfect global arrangements whereas Kant failed to appreciate the scale of the obstacles to global reform and argued naively for refashioning structures for what Burke called the senseless gratification of visionaries (see Mitrany, 1966: 150).[22]

The fact Kant did think that force could be reduced and possibly entirely eradicated from relations between states may seem a good reason for assigning him to the revolutionist tradition, but here too it is important to proceed with some caution. The powerful scepticism that runs through Bull and Wight's approaches is echoed in Kant's remark that 'from such crooked wood as man is made of, nothing perfectly straight can be built' (Kant, 1988: 419).[23] Kant's major reservations about the idea of human perfectibility were linked with the belief that the ethical ideal of perpetual peace might only be approximated rather than completely realized after several centuries of strenuous and often unrewarded effort (Kant 1965b: 124). Elements of scepticism attend Kant's cosmopolitanism, and they are displayed in his discussion of the claim that the central problem of international politics is (to return to themes raised in Chapter 4) how to make the arduous journey from a system to a society of states, and then to an international society strongly influenced by duties to humanity.

Kant's condemnation of the balance of power might seem to provide a more reliable basis for describing his position as revolutionist, but students of the liberal peace and security communities may protest that Kant's argument has the advantage over Wight's claim that international order ultimately depends on the balance of power. The upshot of Wight's position is that international order will not survive if it is made to rest simply on the self-restraint of the component parts. States will not be restrained effectively unless there are external military

---

[21] The parallels with Burke should not be pressed too far since Wight believed revolutionism was, as stated earlier, an important voice in an endless conversation about international affairs.

[22] See Kant (1965b: 119) for the defence of gradualism and opposition to 'revolutionary methods' of promoting change.

[23] On Kant's reference to the human propensity for evil, see R. J. Bernstein, 'Radical Evil: Kant at War with Himself', in Maria Pia Lara (ed.), *Rethinking Evil: Contemporary Perspectives*, University of California Press, Los Angeles, 2001, ch. 4.

constraints in the shape of the balance of power. Kant attached less importance to military equilibrium, believing that strong liberal convictions would provide the deeper motivation for self-restraint in foreign policy. Parallels exist with studies of the liberal peace and with analyses of security communities which stress the existence of forms of social learning – specifically, learning how to resolve differences peacefully and to eliminate all prospect of force – which orthodox approaches to international relations have tended to ignore. Far from displaying traits which reveal the discipline in its infancy when normative or metaphysical commitments prevailed, Kant's study of perpetual peace offered deep insights into the prospects for global political progress (and its limits) which have been taken forward in the analysis of security communities and the democratic peace.

What is radical about Kant's rationalism is his belief that the limits on progress are not as unyielding as the more sceptical, pluralist members of the English School suggest. From this follows a distinctive political project which has been recovered by the more solidarist or cosmopolitan members of the English School in recent times. Kant believed there is nothing etched into human nature, inscribed in sovereignty or inherent in international anarchy which abandons humanity to a condition of political stagnation and ineradicable war. As noted, Wight held a different perspective since he believed warfare is 'inevitable' even though particular wars can be avoided (see above, p. 164). But why war is inevitable rather than probable given past historical experience was not explained and, as mentioned earlier, for many scholars, the record indicates that liberal-democratic states have made major progress in eliminating war between themselves – progress that is, in principle, capable of spreading across international society as a whole.

At this point it is worth recalling Wight's emphasis on different tendencies within rationalism. The strand which gravitates towards realism proceeds from the assumption that the society of states is almost certain to fail in the attempt to eradicate inter-state violence; the survival of commitments to pluralism is the most that can be hoped for. The strand that inclines towards revolutionism maintains that independent political communities have the capacity to learn how to resolve their political differences without resorting to war; that they will make further progress in developing commitments to solidarism is therefore to be hoped for (see Chapter 7). The differences between these tendencies are largely about the empirical question of how far states can pacify international society (see Chapter 2), but they are also connected with important questions about whether the English School should be explicitly committed to moral and political advocacy. These questions have not been debated at length within the School but, arguably, Cox's distinction between problem-solving and critical theory still neatly captures what is at stake in the discussion (Cox, 1981).

It is arguable that the pluralist approach is mainly concerned with a problem-solving analysis of how international order can be made to function as smoothly as possible – although it is important to add that the English School would reject any suggestion that this standpoint involves indifference to human suffering – and the critical approach with identifying and defending the higher normative possibilities that are latent or immanent within current global structures and practices. This has implications for foreign policy analysis, as we will see in Chapter 7 – most obviously by considering what states can and should do as good international citizens. Opposition to moral and political advocacy which was a recurrent theme in Bull's thought (Bull, 1972b; 2002: xv) is present throughout the history of the English School but, drawing on Cox's argument, it is possible for its more cosmopolitan members to argue that pluralism fails to reflect deeply enough on what can be done to improve deeply flawed global arrangements.[24] What is missing in other words from pluralism is the equivalent of Kant's inquiry into progressive possibilities in international relations which included the spread of republican government and the growth of the modern human rights culture; what is missing is a counterpart to Kant's discussion of the maxims of foreign policy which could help bring a more ethical international society into existence. To be fair, the English School's analysis of human rights and humanitarian intervention can be read as offering a normatively grounded empirical analysis of the immanent possibility of a radically improved world order, although the philosophical justification for this solidarist venture has been largely unexplored. Even so, the effort to combine normative

---

[24] One might note here Vincent's claim that Bull became more preoccupied in his later writings with the extent to which order was not neutral between different societies but upheld the dominant Western economic and political interests (Vincent, 1990b: ch. 3). If order is 'always for someone and some purpose', to borrow an expression used by Cox (1981) in connection with international theory, then it is desirable to consider the moral principles which would underpin a more just world order (see also Vincent, 1990b: 48). This is what Vincent (1986) began to do in his radicalized version of rationalism.

vision with rigorous empirical analysis in discussions of human rights and humanitarian intervention marks the point where radicalized rationalism is closer to the Kantian approach than to pluralist alternatives. One theme that unites them is an interest in how existing commitments to the harm principle can be developed so that international society becomes the site for ambitious cosmopolitan political projects. Analysing immanent possibilities for normative development distinguishes the traditional from the critical approach to international society.

The harm principle in international relations

In *Politics as A Vocation*, Weber (1948) refers to 'the ethic of conviction' which holds that fundamental ethical principles must be observed irrespective of the consequences – justice must be upheld even though the whole world should perish. Kant's moral philosophy is often thought to have this unbending quality. The duty not to lie, for example, had to be observed without regard for the social consequences.[25] Realists subscribe to what Weber (ibid.) called 'the ethic of responsibility' which requires state officials to depart from moral conventions – such as the duty not to lie – when blind compliance would damage the interests of the state (see Wolfers, 1962a: ch. 4). The question of whether Kant's moral philosophy lacks 'realism' or regard for consequences lies outside the current inquiry, but his discussion of the maxims of foreign policy in *Perpetual Peace* carefully distinguishes between principles which are immediately binding (they include dispensing with the 'hellish art' and 'dishonourable stratagem' of the assassin and the poisoner) and more flexible principles which can be realized gradually over time (these include the goal of abolishing standing armies). This distinction hardly suggests that the Kantian project of moving from an international system to an international

---

[25] On Kant's 'rigorism' and on the fact that the categorical imperative does not require a morality without 'exceptions', see Acton (1970: 64). Paton (194: 76) argues that Kant has been misinterpreted – or allowed himself to be misinterpreted – on this particular point. Kant believed that moral agents should ask themselves whether they can universalize the maxims which inform their actions. They should not start with estimating consequences or make morality dependent solely on expected consequences. But that is not to say that moral agents should ignore consequences – only that such calculations are not the essence of moral action. For a more recent discussion, see Cummiskey (1996).

society imbued with cosmopolitan values is ignorant of profound constraints on political actors or blind to the significance of consequences for moral action. A more accurate interpretation would be that Kant's reformist project combined ethics with prudence regarding political context and consequences. For this reason, the general direction of Kant's approach to the normative development of international society has considerable relevance for the task of strengthening the links between 'idealist' Grotianism and 'evolutionary' revolutionism.

The liberal idea that individuals and societies do not share any one conception of the good life but can still agree on the need for some basic social constraints or rules of forbearance which give agents the freedom to pursue diverse ends is central to Kant's political philosophy and important in the writings of the English School. It is worth considering this area of convergence before proceeding further. In his summation of rationalism, in Wight's sense of that term, Donelan (1990: ch. 4) suggests the main principles of the approach can be reduced to the negative duty to minimize injury to others. Illustrating the point, Jackson (2000: 20) offers a strong defence of prudence which is the 'political virtue' which requires human beings 'to take care not to harm others'.[26] The harm principle is not the core tenet of Kant's moral philosophy but it features prominently in *Perpetual Peace* where he writes that a 'man (or a people) in a mere state of nature robs me of any security and injures me by virtue of this very state in which he coexists with me' (quoted in Hurrell, 1990: 186).[27] From this premise, Kant derives the obligation which binds independent political communities, just like individuals in the original state of nature, to exchange a condition of lawlessness for the condition of civil society which offers each party equal protection from the injurious actions of others. Several moral philosophers, some Kantian, regard the harm principle as the foundation of morality, and they regard it as a *prima facie* obligation

---

[26] See Jackson (2000: 154) on the fact that prudence requires us to 'take full responsibility for our actions by taking into consideration *all who might be harmed needlessly'*, and also the discussion of security in Jackson (2000: ch. 8). See also Wight (1966b: 128–9) for the case for prudence as 'a moral virtue' which involves 'the refusal to exploit an advantage' and the desire, which was noted earlier, to soften political expedience by *'consult(ing) the moral sense of those whom it will affect'* (emphases added).
[27] Kant (1970b: 206) proceeds to argue that it is 'the lawlessness of his condition (*statu iniusto*) which constantly threatens me, and I can compel him either to join me in a social (*legal*) state, or to move away'.

since there are times when harm to others is justified, for example in self-defence.[28] Others have stressed Kant's insistence not only on the negative obligation to avoid harm but on the positive virtue of beneficence towards others.[29] Kant makes it clear that altruism has its limits (individuals cannot be expected to make huge personal sacrifices for others) and he adds that humanity could survive without acts of beneficence,[30] but the important point for now is that his moral philosophy cannot be reduced to the harm principle. Nor for that matter do the English School's reflections on ethics and world politics disregard the importance of duties of beneficence, but whether they share Kant's enthusiasm for these more positive obligations is a moot point that need not detain us here.[31]

The consensus amongst Kant scholars would appear to be that his emphasis on the duty of non-maleficence – the principle that humanity could certainly not survive without – reveals the influence of Stoic cosmopolitanism. Acton (1970: 36) and Nussbaum (1997) suggest that Cicero may have been the greatest influence in this respect.[32] Cicero's cosmopolitanism is evident in his conviction that human beings have two sets of duties – as citizens of the city and as citizens of the world – and they include obligations to promote the good of others and to avoid causing unnecessary harm (Nussbaum, 1997: 31).[33] This was the common starting point for many theories of the state and international relations in the seventeenth and eighteenth centuries including those of Pufendorf and Vattel as well as Kant. All posed the question of how

---

[28] Ross (1930: 21ff) maintains that the *prima facie* duty of non-maleficence is the most fundamental of all moral duties. See also the discussion in Verkamp (1993: 90ff). The importance of the *prima facie* duty to avoid harm for contemporary discussions of ethics and foreign policy and good international citizenship is discussed in Chapter 7.
[29] See Cummiskey (1996: 49).
[30] Kant (1965a: 98) writes: 'Now humanity could no doubt subsist if everybody contributed nothing to the happiness of others but at the same time refrained from deliberately impairing their happiness.' Kant proceeds to argue that everyone should however endeavour, 'so far as in him lies, to further the ends of others'. See also Cummiskey (1996: esp. 8).
[31] Jackson (2000: 139) also distinguishes between 'the negative responsibility to forbear from inflicting needless and unjustified hardship or damages or suffering on others . . . and the positive responsibility to come to the assistance of others when the occasion demands and it is possible and wise to do so'.
[32] See Cicero (1967: 144): 'And not only nature, which may be defined as international law, but also the particular laws by which individual peoples are governed similarly ordain that no one is justified in injuring another for his own advantage.' See also Acton (1970).
[33] See Rowe and Schofield (2000: ch. 24).

such obligations should be honoured in a world which was divided into separate states, and they hoped for a condition in which individuals would identify closely with their own societies without failing in their duties to the rest of humankind. Stoics such as Cicero suggested an answer by arguing that while it is reasonable for the members of different communities to promote their own welfare, none has the right to secure an advantage by injuring others.

Kant's own judgement was that the 'miserable comforters' (Grotius, Pufendorf and Vattel) failed to take their professed moral commitments seriously,[34] and in this regard his basic argument was anticipated by Rousseau (1970a: 174) who mocked the 'legal experts' for advising citizens to lament the miseries of the original state of nature, to admire the peace and justice provided by the civil order, and to 'bless the wisdom of public institutions'. Only on the surface of things had the human race acquired additional security by departing from the original state of nature and by exchanging natural freedom for civil freedoms grounded in the rule of law. The realities of inter-state war, which were far more injurious than isolated conflicts between individuals in the first state of nature, shattered the myth that the transition to civil society provided human beings with greater security.[35] Similar sentiments led Kant to question the rationale for creating separate political communities when the problems that individuals confronted in the original state of nature were bound to surface – but more violently – yet again.[36] The problems would not be solved by establishing world government – on this much Pufendorf, Vattel and

---

[34] See Pufendorf (2002: 344) on the natural obligation to avoid injury to others. See Vattel (1970: 113) on the fact that injury must have occurred or be threatened before a state can use force with a just cause.

[35] The reality for Rousseau was that the transition to civil society increased the level of harm in human affairs to previously unimaginable levels. Looking up from the works of the legal experts who suggested individuals could console themselves for being men by recalling their rights as citizens, Rousseau claimed all one would see were 'unfortunate Nations groaning under yokes of iron, the human race crushed by a handful of oppressors', 'the face of death everywhere', all being the result of war. A new state of nature 'a thousand times more terrible' than the original one had come into existence with the partition of the human race into sovereign states. See Rousseau (1970a: 174; 1970b: 132). The apologists for these allegedly 'peaceful institutions' were advised to read their arguments on 'the field of battle'.

[36] 'What avails it to labour at the arrangement of a Commonwealth . . . [when] the same unsociableness which forced men to it, becomes again the cause of each Commonwealth assuming the attitude of uncontrolled freedom in its external relations' (Kant, 1970b: 183).

Kant agreed. But such problems were exacerbated in Kant's view by Pufendorf and Vattel's decision to grant states the right to decide the scope of their international obligations and also by their failure to rage against the institution of war. Kant's argument was that support for the harm principle required more radical moral qualifications of sovereign rights than Pufendorf or Vattel entertained. This led to a vision of world order which stressed obligations to cooperate to eradicate force as well as responsibilities to observe universalizable moral principles which would ensure that all human beings are treated as ends in themselves. Kant radicalized the rationalist tradition by envisaging an international society built on sovereignty, yet holding states responsible for observing global moral principles which conformed with Cicero's dictum that an individual 'who sees no harm in injuring others abolishes what is human in man' (Acton, 1970: 36). Kant's idea of a 'cosmopolitan condition of general political security' – a condition in which the rights of individuals everywhere as well as their communities would be respected – distils the essence of his radicalized rationalism (Kant, 1970a: 49).

Kant therefore criticized earlier natural lawyers for compromising the harm principle in the course of shifting their gaze from relations within, to relations between, states. He believed the duty to live together under a civil constitution arose whenever individuals were in a position to harm each other. His cosmopolitan project of enlarging the political domain in which the harm principle applies is precisely what the characterization of his position in several works of the English School has missed.[37] The Kantian project which focused on the possibilities for weaving cosmopolitan principles into a society of republican sovereign states (and on the prospects for achieving greater harmony between obligations to the state, international society and humanity) is the main precursor to the 'critical international society' perspective. Ethical claims (such as Bull's) about the duty to promote a world community and about the priority of world order over international order – claims that sit uneasily alongside Bull's opposition to moral and political advocacy – are Kant's decisive point of departure. His cosmopolitan approach starts with an investigation into the categorical imperative, and might therefore be said to judge states by

---

[37] The harm principle applies for Kant not only to relations between Europe's republics but, importantly, to their relations with the non-European world. See above, p. 162.

principles which lie outside current practices, but it is crucial not to forget that he appealed to principles – such as the duty of non-injury – which are already embedded in national societies, and in international society to a lesser extent.[38] The key point is that Kant's approach contains an immanent critique of the modern states-system. His cosmopolitan project argued for deepening political commitments to the harm principle so that international order would respect not only the equal rights of all states but also the moral standing of non-sovereign communities, including indigenous peoples, and all human beings as ends in themselves.

We can further explore points of convergence between Kant and Bull by noting that they agreed that progress from an international system to the most basic pluralist form of international society contributes to world order because it affords individuals some protection from the miseries and hardships of war. The principal difference between the original state of nature and 'that which exists between nations' led Kant to identify three areas in which international order could work for the benefit of world order. He argued 'that the Law of nations is concerned, not only with *the relationship of one state to another, but also with *relationships of individuals in one state to individuals in another* and of *an individual to another whole state*' (Kant, 1965b: 115; emphasis added). (Put more simply, the first two realms are concerned with issues arising in classical international politics and in the transnational or world society which was expanding in Kant's era; the third realm is concerned with relations between the members of one state and foreign governments, an example being the international efforts to protect human rights.) Regarding the first domain, states could contribute to world order, in Kant's view, by avoiding cruelty and unnecessary suffering in war, by striving to act in accordance with principles which can command the consent of the whole of international society, and by doing nothing to damage the 'mutual faith that is required if any enduring peace is to be established in future' (Kant, 1965b: 120–1). Regarding the second domain, the state's contribution to world order consisted in supporting 'world law' which preserved the right of free movement (Kant, 1965b: 125). Finally, regarding the relationships between another state and its nationals, sovereign governments could most obviously extend respect for the

---

[38] See Neiman (2002).

harm principle by protesting against human rights violations wherever they occurred. The ethical development of international society could be promoted by applying the harm principle which was first articulated by the Stoics and defended by more recent theorists of the state and international law to these three domains of social and political interaction.

It is possible to find counterparts for each domain in the writings of the English School although there has been less attention to the sphere of transnational relations or world society in large part because of an earlier neglect of international or global political economy (Buzan, 2004). In some respects this is surprising given Wight's interest in the part that commerce may have played in the formation of international states-systems, and because of Bull's claim that Grotians regard trade – and 'more generally, economic and social intercourse between one country and another' – as the 'international activity' that 'best typifies' the existence of a society of states (Wight, 1977: 33; Bull, 2002: 25). It must also be repeated that parallels between Kant and Bull's perspectives on international relations exist alongside very different philosophical standpoints. Kant believed the moral law created the duty to extend the sphere in which the harm principle applied; Bull believed that philosophical efforts to find principles which could apply globally have failed to uncover the basis for a previously elusive moral consensus. Consequently, his emphasis was not on the fundamental ethical obligations which might underpin international or world society, but on the utilitarian calculations states make about the need for a political order in which respect for the harm principle regulates their interactions. Bull (1984a) was aware that moral concerns about the plight of the suffering in other societies could strengthen the cosmopolitan culture which he regarded as having a major role to play in the survival of the first universal international society. His claim that its continuation increasingly depends on collective efforts to develop global arrangements which command the respect of the least privileged peoples and states may seem pragmatic and instrumental when compared with Kant's deontological defence of a fundamental moral obligation 'to woo the consent' of the rest of humankind at all times. The differences are less stark when it is remembered that Bull thought progress in creating a 'world community' was a value in its own right. This normative claim can be strengthened by incorporating Kantian ethical themes within future studies of international society. Some possibilities are considered in the next section.

Applications of the harm principle in world politics

The argument thus far has stressed the English School's sociological interest in the arrangements states have created to reduce the harm they do to each other. The discussion has analysed developments which have led the modern society of states to expand its interest in harm to include the mistreatment of citizens by national governments. The English School's empirical analyses of these phenomena have often been developed in the spirit of value-freedom. Revolutionist visions of alternative forms of world order have often been regarded as threats to the survival of international society, although it is recognized that no account of the rise and development of the modern society of states is complete without the careful analysis of revolutionist influences. Bull and Wight regarded Kant as a revolutionist who supported the division of international society between the 'elect' and the 'damned', but a more judicious view would have stressed his place at the radical end of the Grotian or rationalist tradition. There are clear parallels between his philosophical and sociological interest in the normative development of international society and contemporary solidarist analyses which build on Vincent's discussion of human rights, an inquiry which marked the start of a process of greater engagement with moral and political philosophy. It has been suggested here that the harm principle has special significance for future normative and sociological analyses of international society undertaken by members of the English School – and not only because developments in world politics have shown how the pursuit of national responsibilities in the aftermath of the terrorist attacks of 11 September can be in tension with international and humanitarian obligations to avoid unnecessary harm. The discussion now proceeds to develop this claim in more detail before commenting briefly on some developments in contemporary international society which are important for a critical analysis of global normative possibilities (as opposed to a more problem-solving inquiry into how the inter-state order might be made to function more smoothly). Since this is a large area of investigation in need of more extensive research, the discussion concentrates on a small number of developments in the three domains highlighted by Kant's remarks on the law of nations.

There are three reasons why the harm principle has an important role to play in a critical approach to international society; each finds some measure of support in the English School. First, the historical evidence indicates that the willingness to inflict harm on other peoples has been a central feature – perhaps *the* central feature – of relations between independent political communities over the last five millennia. Dissuading states from using their 'power to hurt' – rather than encouraging them to become more charitable or altruistic – has been the perennial problem in international relations.[39] This has been a key element in the study of international society, most obviously in analyses of constraints on the use of force. A second theme, and a related one because it also addresses the constant and universal fact of human vulnerability to mental and bodily harm, is that throughout much of this period human beings have identified with bounded political communities. The political challenge has been – and still is – how to contain the 'damaging effects' of 'limited sympathies' (see below, p. 235) or 'limited altruism' (Keal, 1983: 196) or 'confined generosity'.[40] A third reason for stressing the importance of the harm principle is provided by an important strand of political theory which contends that societies and individuals have competing and often irreconcilable visions of the good life, but such value-conflicts do not always block agreements on the need for eliminating or controlling injurious action. Individuals and groups have often been able to agree that the 'furtherance of virtually any conception of the good' requires some degree of consensus about the need to protect 'vital interests' such as security against 'the deliberate infliction of injury and death' (Barry, quoted in Matravers, 1998: 114). There are clear parallels between this last argument and Bull's discussion of the primary goals which virtually every political order seeks to protect – and equally strong parallels with his remarks about the reality of firm agreements about the basic ingredients of international order notwithstanding radical divergences of opinion about the meaning of justice. The upshot is that states have reached shared understandings about a range of matters which belong to a lower moral register than visions of some supposedly universalizable conception of the good; they have been able to agree on a limited but important set of issues by regarding the vulnerability of human

---

[39] This theme is captured by Mill's claim that 'a person may possibly not need the benefits of others; but he always needs that they should not do him hurt', quoted in Mackie (1977: 135).
[40] Hume refers to 'confined generosity' (see Mackie, 1977: 110).

beings to mental and bodily injury as the starting point for an account of international obligation.[41]

Of course, there are clear bounds to this agreement because states do not always agree on what constitutes injury, or unwarranted injury, as seemingly irreconcilable debates about the rights and wrongs of 'female genital mutilation' make clear. Even if states did agree about where precisely the boundary between harmful and harmless action lies, there would be good reason to doubt that observing the harm principle fulfils all human moral obligations or exhausts international morality. Straightforward compliance with the harm principle may do nothing, it has been argued, to help the victims of genocide or natural disaster – it might also be claimed that it is perfectly compatible with the ungenerous view that needy individuals and groups should fend for themselves rather than burden others.[42] We have seen that Kant believed that moral agents should recognize positive obligations of benevolence as well as negative obligations to avoid injury, a theme also endorsed by such members of the Grotian tradition as Vattel (1970: 97–8) and Jackson (2000). Kant is no different from them – or from many recent moral philosophers – in thinking that the positive duty of assistance has to be limited by obligations to co-nationals and close associates. The main differences between moral persuasions are often about where the line should be drawn between actions that do not deserve praise because they are no more than what any human being should do for another, and actions that go beyond the 'call of duty' and are rightly acclaimed as heroic or superorogatory.

Recent discussions about humanitarian intervention have raised important questions about how far one state should sacrifice the interests of its citizens for the purpose of 'saving strangers'.[43] Here one

---

[41] On the need for mutual forbearance in the context of 'human vulnerability', see Hart (1961: ch. 9, section 1).

[42] For the argument that the harm principle urges individuals to respect the negative obligation of avoiding harm to others but does not create the positive obligation to help them, see Geras (1998: part 3). On whether failing to help might itself be regarded as harm, see Feinberg (1984: ch. 4). We come back to this question in Chapter 7 where it will be argued that failures to rescue and forms of indifference to the suffering of others can be criticized for, *inter alia*, causing 'dignitary harm' or harm to self-esteem.

[43] A robust defence of cosmopolitan obligations can be found in Kaldor (1999). Within the English School, Wheeler (2000) has been especially concerned with the question of how much citizens should be prepared to do (and how much self-sacrifice should be expected from military personnel) for the sake of 'saving strangers'. The ethical issues await more detailed analysis in the study of international society. Leaving aside ethical matters, the very fact that modern populations are unwilling to make major sacrifices for

might recall Kant's claim that human society might well survive without acts of benevolence, but it cannot survive without prohibitions on harm. A similar conviction is found in Bull's argument that order between states is made possible by common recognition of the need to protect certain primary goals or, to put this differently, by their ability to agree on measures designed to protect societies from vulnerability to harm given the reality of limited altruism.[44] The pluralist society of states can be regarded as the global expression of an ethic which privileges negative over positive obligations in the attempt to reduce the Hobbesian features of international politics. What might be called *international harm conventions* – conventions which are designed to prevent harm in relations between states – can work to the advantage of the inhabitants of those states, but this is not always the case and it is therefore essential to develop *cosmopolitan harm conventions* which protect individuals in and of themselves (Linklater, 2001).[45] The question raised by Kant and by recent solidarists is whether the modern society of states can be changed fundamentally in light of the conviction that individuals rather than states are the fundamental members of international society – the main agents with moral standing. In line with Kant's approach to the law of nations, this question requires consideration of three areas: protection from unnecessary injury in warfare, security from human rights abuses caused by national governments, and protection from the wrongs that occur within world society.

To begin with warfare, many of the leading works by members of the English School have been concerned with international as opposed to cosmopolitan harm conventions. Wight's *Power Politics* is one work

strangers indicates that states are more concerned with harm to fellow-citizens than with the suffering of strangers (for an interesting discussion of this point, see Ignatieff, 2000). The corollary is that states are more likely to agree on principles which are designed to protect their respective populations from harm than to arrive at a global consensus about new duties of self-sacrifice. It is worth recalling that the principle affirming the moral duty to avoid harm to civilians in war has not only been central to public debates about the use of force in Afghanistan and Iraq but may actually be stronger as a result (see Wheeler, 2002).

[44] The emphasis here is on the three primary goals which Bull regarded as universal: protection from violence, respect for property and keeping promises (see above, pp. 56ff). In securing these goals, societies (domestic and international) recognize the vulnerability of human beings, or states, to three different forms of harm.

[45] To give one example, international harm conventions may not include the right of women to be free from rape in warfare. Indeed this omission seems to be the norm in international history. We come back to the general theme in the next chapter.

which mainly focuses on the rules and institutions which modern states have developed for the purpose of regulating the outbreak, conduct and termination of war. As with Bull's *Anarchical Society* which was also essentially state-centred, *Power Politics* was not especially concerned with the historical development of cosmopolitan harm conventions (see Chapter 6). But if we turn to other works written by members of the English School or by thinkers who sympathize with their approach, we find a much greater emphasis on moral and legal principles which deal with the rights of the civilian in war or with international responsibilities to prisoners of war (see, for example, Best, 1994; Roberts and Guelff, 2000). One can see in the recent development of the international law of war the same phenomenon that Bull and Vincent considered in their discussion of human rights, namely the reappearance of the Grotian theme that individuals, not states, are the ultimate members of international society; and one might also note how concerns with 'superfluous injury' to individuals and with 'unnecessary suffering' became central to international legal thinking with the rise of total war.[46] It is no less important to stress that the cosmopolitan project of universalizing the harm principle has led to striking developments in international criminal law which encroach on territorial sovereignty and erode the principle of sovereign immunity. The point here is not to catalogue the main trends but to identify some respects in which the modern society of states has made significant progress in incorporating the Stoic principle that states and their representatives which harm individuals unnecessarily stand outside the human community.[47] Attaching the revolutionist label to Kant ignored the respects in which his radicalized rationalism already contained a version of this critical approach to the potentials for building such cosmopolitan attachments into international society.

It will be clear from the previous chapter that the English School comes close to the spirit of the Kantian project in a second area of inquiry which is concerned with the development of the universal human rights culture. The growth of the state's capacity to use violence against citizens – most destructively in the case of totalitarianism – and an increase in the number of regimes which have waged devastating

---

[46] 'Unnecessary suffering' and 'superfluous injury' are terms found in the Hague Conventions. For further discussion, see Wells (1992: ch. 1).
[47] The landmark discussion remains H. Arendt, *Eichmann in Jerusalem*, Penguin, Harmondsworth, 1994.

war against sections of their population have created pressures to design harm conventions which do not deal with relations between states but with the rights of individuals and national minorities. International legal developments including the notion of universal jurisdiction have given contemporary expression to the Kantian theme that human rights violations in any part of the world should be felt everywhere (see Weller, 1999). International law regarding genocide and torture has extended the cosmopolitan principle that all human beings should be free from violent abuse irrespective of citizenship or nationality, gender, sexuality, class or race. In the terms of the 1948 *Convention on the Prevention and Punishment of the Crime of Genocide*, the members of all 'national, ethnical, racial or religious groups' should be spared 'serious bodily or mental harm' – and this expression is repeated in several other international legal conventions (see Chapter 6). The more solidarist tendencies within the English School are broadly Kantian in combining an empirical analysis of such trends with explicit normative support for their further development. An increased emphasis on the position of indigenous peoples in the contemporary society of states can also be regarded as recovering the Kantian theme that peoples as well as individuals and states have the right to be free from unnecessary suffering (Keal, 1995, 2003). Members of the English School who have focused on the respects in which the universal human rights culture can bridge the gulf between international order and world order have contributed to the restoration of a Kantian cosmopolitan project which was once generally regarded as incompatible with the sophisticated study of international society.

We turn finally to the third domain discussed in Kant's analysis of world law. Reference has been made to the duty of hospitality which applies the harm principle to cross-border transactions comprising transnational or world society. Kant did not develop this theme in detail although its significance for his thinking is evident in his claim that modern warfare has become intolerable because of the damage it does to the activity which is emblematic of world society, namely international commerce. His position on hospitality has been extended in the form of international law on the treatment of refugees and, more significantly, in ethical reflections on the rights of refugees which lament practical failures to live up to the demands of a cosmopolitan duty of hospitality (see especially Derrida, 2000). For its part, the English School has tended to ignore world society and its economic dimensions in particular, an oversight which Buzan (2001, 2004) has sought to remedy. One central question that arises in this context is whether a critical approach to world society – and specifically one that asks how it can be improved by ensuring greater respect for the harm principle – needs to forge closer intellectual links with a perspective which members of the English School have regarded as silent on the core issues of international politics or as congenitally incapable of understanding them, namely Marxism.

The English School's neglect or dismissal of Marxism is hardly surprising. From the mid-1840s, Marx and Engels believed that capitalist globalization would reduce the significance of nationalism, geopolitics and war. Although such projections were reconsidered in later years, it remains the case that Marxism was drawn towards a 'paradigm of production' which seemed to add little or nothing to the understanding of war, diplomacy, the balance of power and the other international institutions or practices which have most interested the English School. Wight (1966a: 25) made this perfectly clear in a passing comment on the irrelevance of Marxism-Leninism, as did Manning (1962: 75). But the strengths of Marxism are to be found in other areas, most notably in its decision to shift the focus from the harm that states do to each other as participants in an anarchic political system to harm that has its origins in global relations of production and which is transmitted across world society by ever-expanding networks of financial and market interdependence.[48] Although Marxism tended to overestimate the causal importance of production and exchange, and to underestimate the significance of nationalism, the state, geopolitical rivalry and war, its great achievement was to identify the rise of diffuse, and often unintended, forms of harm which have become more central to the study of world politics in recent years, for example in analyses of the global risk society (Beck, 1992).[49]

Several thinkers have addressed crucial ethical issues which arise because of the development of world society and the universalization of social and economic relations. De-Shalit (1998), O'Neill (1991), Pogge (2002) and Shue (1981) have considered the question of

---

[48] Buzan (2004) perpetuates the English School's neglect of Marxism by largely ignoring its discussion of the harms caused by capitalist world society.

[49] Marx argued that although capitalists often intend to harm their competitors, the operation of markets caused harm that no one intended. This is what is meant by claiming that certain forms of harm are diffuse. See also Linklater (2002d).

'transnational' as opposed to inter-state or domestic justice because of the multitudinous ways that the organization of world society harms the most vulnerable members of humanity. Each of them makes a strong case for a cosmopolitan ethic that challenges the orthodox account of political community which maintains that the state's primary moral duty is to promote the welfare of conationals. Their point is not that insiders and outsiders should have the same rights in all circumstances, but that all human beings are equally entitled to protection from the harms and hazards that flow from the transportation of hazardous waste or environmental degradation, or result from unjust or 'coercive' global regimes (see Pogge, 2002). Running parallel to philosophical arguments for superseding communitarian or realist ethics (see O'Neill, 2000: part 2) are serious political efforts to ensure that multinational business enterprises show due care in their dealings with vulnerable peoples (see Richter, 2001) and do not neglect their responsibilities to the environment. These have not been the most influential developments in international law; however, declarations that sovereign rights should not be exercised in ways that harm the global commons or the physical environment of neighbouring societies reveal how the international legal system might make further progress in making the harm principle a central ethical reference point for all social and economic relations within world society.[50]

The issue of transnational as opposed to inter-state justice has not been central to the English School although it arose in interesting ways at the edges of Vincent's major book on human rights whose main objective was defending the universal right to be free from starvation and malnutrition. A central part of the argument was that independent political communities should be more strongly committed to helping those who experience severe economic deprivation – however their plight may have been caused. But Vincent also stressed the need for the members of affluent societies to reflect on how these afflictions are in many circumstances caused by – or possibly exacerbated by – the operation of the world economy. In an important passage, he argued that 'in regard to the failure to provide subsistence rights' it may not be

---

[50] For a general discussion, see Mason (2001). Jackson (2000: 175–8) notes that Kant's idea of world society and cosmopolitan law is 'an early intimation of responsibility for the global commons' and the new 'solidarist' international norm which requires states in particular 'to regulate activities within their own jurisdictions that are harmful to the environment'. See also Hurrell (1994, 1995).

any particular government which is at fault or 'whose legitimacy is in question, but the whole international economic system in which we are all implicated' (Vincent, 1986a: 127). The argument was that affluent societies should recognize special moral obligations to the victims because their well-being and the misery of others are not unrelated but are indeed closely intertwined, since the affluent are unjust beneficiaries of the operation of the world economy (Vincent, 1986a: 147). Vincent did not develop this theme in detail but his use of the term 'implicated' indicates that affluent societies should recognize that while they may not wish the victims of starvation and malnutrition any harm, they are frequently complicit in their suffering.

Vincent's line of argument raises complex issues since serious doubts exist about the extent to which complicity infringes the harm principle. Complicity is different from the phenomena discussed earlier (deliberate attempts to cause unnecessary suffering in war and human rights violations) because there is no intention to injure others or to cause pain and suffering. But the claim that those who have the greatest ability to rescue the vulnerable benefit from global arrangements that harm others, inevitably raises the question of whether a failure to assist is always different from, and less reprehensible than, deliberate harm. Feinberg (1984: ch. 4) argues persuasively that there are circumstances in which a failure to assist others when there is no danger of significant risk to one's self is no different from harm.[51] This may not alter the fact that cruelty is the worst thing we do (see Shklar, 1984) since a failure to assist another can result from cruel motives.[52] But how far inaction in the face of human suffering or 'bad samaritanism' should be a punishable offence under the criminal law is a contentious question to which different legal systems give different answers (Feinberg, 1984: ch. 4). We need not pause to consider these questions here (see Linklater, 2004 for further discussion). The main point is that the stress on complicity in the suffering of others can help to increase the sense of collective responsibility, not only for dealing with actions that grow out of malicious intent but also for reducing harm and suffering which are often the unintended consequences of the operation of global economic forces. There is a parallel between

---

[51] Feinberg (1984) gives the example of an accomplished swimmer who can easily assist a drowning stranger but chooses not to.
[52] The example Feinberg (1984) gives is the doctor who fails to offer appropriate medical care to a detested patient.

Vincent's position on human rights and Honderich's argument for accepting moral responsibility for the wrongs we do 'in our ordinary lives' (Honderich, 1980b: 59). It is important not to read too much into Vincent's remarks about the need for assuming greater humanitarian responsibilities, but his work had a prescient quality in that it raised moral issues which have grown in importance in recent years as a result of abundant information about the ways in which affluent groups benefit from, and are implicated in, the suffering and vulnerability of others (see also Chapter 7).[53]

The main purpose of a critical approach to international society is to analyse the prospects for the development of cosmopolitan harm conventions in the three domains considered above – and in this way the English School can most usefully build on Kant's normative approach to world politics. Reference has been made to the fact that Kant did not reduce cosmopolitan morality to the duty of non-maleficence but argued strongly for an ethic of benevolence.[54] However far the duties required by the harm principle extend, it is often thought that compliance with it may leave the victims of certain forms of suffering unaided; negative obligations to refrain from harmful acts must therefore be complemented by positive obligations of assistance.[55] As stressed earlier in this chapter, the English School has mainly focused on the ways in which societies of states have created prohibitions on harm, the assumption being that their

---

[53] Vincent's stress on the ethics of being 'implicated' was prescient in that moral concerns with socially responsible investment, fair trading, sweatshops particularly in the garment industry, child labour and ethical tourism (especially where tourism augments the revenue available to regimes that violate human rights) appear to have grown in recent times. Contemporary discussions about these issues call for the development of cosmopolitan sensibilities in world society, or for extending the harm principle so that individuals accept some degree of responsibility for outcomes which are too easily detached from their personal lives. For important discussions of some of these issues, see especially Kutz (2000) on complicity, and Cohen (2001) on attitudes towards moral responsibility. Dunne and Wheeler (1999) raise the general theme in their observations about the morality of arms sales to human rights violators.

[54] The notion of a duty of non-maleficence is found in Ross (1930: 21ff) where it is said to be the most fundamental of all moral duties.

[55] It is customary to argue that positive duties to assist others are not unlimited (see Feinberg, 1984: 162). For this reason the negative duty to prevent unnecessary suffering is often regarded as the more binding obligation. The question is how far the duties which are required by the harm principle extend. Geras, as noted earlier, maintains that the harm principle supports a thin conception of obligation while Feinberg argues that it gives rise to a thicker conception of obligation which includes the *prima facie* duty to relieve unnecessary suffering (see n. 42 above).

central purpose has been negative (avoiding war) rather than positive (developing altruism). But even in this limited manner its constituent political units build the equivalent of domestic prohibitions on harm in the global sphere. Kant's achievement was to show how such commitments to harm prevention could be worked through the three domains discussed earlier in the attempt to make international society progressively more compatible with the axioms of a cosmopolitan morality.

Stripped of duties of benevolence, this may seem a dismally thin morality but, as Vincent argued, the concern with avoiding complicity in human suffering has radical implications for the organization of international society – even the most modest interpretation of the harm principle which maintains that human beings are more likely to act to assist those they have injured, or from whose misery they unfairly benefit, has more dramatic consequences than may at first appear. Various theorists of transnational justice and cosmopolitan democracy have argued that states have a diminished capacity to protect their citizens from harm that originates outside their territorial borders. In their view, increased opportunities for cross-border or transnational harm in world politics mean that it is essential to reconstruct international society so that it complies with the cosmopolitan principle that all human beings have a right to be consulted about decisions which adversely affect them.[56] Some see this as the logical implication of defending a broadly Kantian morality in the modern world (Habermas, 1997) but it can also be said to be the logical extension of Bull's argument that the contemporary society of states needs to be reformed so that it rests on the consent of a majority of the world's population whose fate is to live in the poorest regions. Cosmopolitan harm conventions are no different from international harm conventions in that their legitimacy and therefore survival depend in large part on the extent to which they have the consent of those who are most affected by them. Whatever its limitations, the harm principle leads to a vision of a more democratic international society in which individuals and non-sovereign communities can exercise the right to protest against violations of its requirements in appropriate global institutions; the affluent have the greatest responsibility for bringing these institutions into existence (O'Neill, 1989). Members of the

---

[56] This principle finds support in the writings of Wight and Jackson as n. 26 above indicates.

English School have been relatively silent about the merits or demerits of cosmopolitan democracy, and one can see why they might regard it as a utopian ideal. The response is that it is a vision of world political organization which does not appeal to moral principles that are remote from current practice, but defends the globalization of a harm principle which is already part of the fabric of most bounded political communities and the international society to which they belong. The recent revival of security politics and the resurgence of state power do not diminish the importance of this crucial ethical ideal.

Conclusion

One of the main objectives of this chapter has been to detach Kant from the revolutionist tradition, to focus on his role as a founder of radical-ized rationalism, and to stress the continuing importance of his thought for an analysis of how international order can work more effectively in support of world order. Kant criticized Grotius, Pufen-dorf and Vattel for compromising the harm principle, and he argued that a commitment to that principle required the human race to bring a cosmopolitan condition of general political security into being. Kant's idea of the categorical imperative underpinned this argument, but his belief in immutable moral principles did not result in an approach to international political change which ignored the specificity of social context and the complexity of political consequences. Bull (2002: 276) referred in passing to a mode of empirical inquiry which focuses on trends that run counter to existing practices, and Kant's analysis of the cosmopolitan harm conventions which are already immanent within the society of states exemplifies this critical approach (see Chapter 6). The revolutionist label has distracted attention from his perspective on incremental global political change which foreshadows recent solidarism.

The claim that rationalism is the *via media* between realism and revolutionism needs to be rethought in the light of these comments. Advocates of the pluralist perspective might reasonably lay claim to that status, but an approach which focuses on the foundations of international order clearly does not exhaust the possibilities available to the English School. An alternative, critical approach (which is dis-satisfied with pluralism and opposed to violent forms of revolution-ism) can focus on the immanent possibility of a world order in which the harm principle is central to the three domains discussed in Kant's writings on the law of nations. Here the emphasis shifts from international harm conventions, which give sovereign states some protection from unnecessary harm, to cosmopolitan harm conventions which give individuals and non-sovereign communities and associations protection for their own sake. Two different ways of thinking about the sociology of states-systems and about the modern states-system in a comparative context are suggested by these final remarks. Analysing them is a task for the next chapter.

6 The sociology of states-systems

In the 1960s Martin Wight and his colleagues in the British Committee on the Theory of International Politics wrote several papers on the 'historic states-systems' of Ancient Greece, China in the Spring and Autumn, and Warring States period, and the modern world. A volume on the sociology of states-systems was planned – a successor to Butterfield and Wight's *Diplomatic Investigations* – but the project did not come to fruition (Dunne, 1998: 124ff). Wight's papers on the sociology of states-systems were published posthumously in 1977. Fifteen years later Watson (1992) produced a world-historical analysis of different types of international system which remains the most comprehensive over-arching sociological statement by a member of the British Committee. Recent publications indicate that interest in this realm of its intellectual endeavour is much greater than at any other time in the recent past; they also reveal that the influence of Watson and Wight's publications is evident in works by writers who have not usually been associated with the English School (Buzan and Little, 2000; Linklater, 2002b). Of the many reasons for current efforts to resume the work of the British Committee one of the most important is the desire to build on the 'sociology of states-systems' which some of its members initiated nearly four decades ago.

The revival of interest in this area is part of a larger intellectual movement in which many students of international relations have become interested in developing large-scale historical-sociological accounts of world politics (Little, 1994). Dissatisfaction with the ahistoricism of neo-realist theory is a major reason for this development. Several authors have maintained that historically, sensitive approaches to world politics reveal important differences in the nature of states and their moral purpose, in the conduct of their external relations, and in the character of international systems which neo-realism has neglected (Rosenberg, 1994; Reus-Smit, 1999). Whether or not it is possible to establish general propositions which are true of international relations in all times and all places remains in dispute (Fischer, 1992), but a growing number of scholars have been drawn towards historical-sociological approaches to the subject, and several works have already appeared which demonstrate what International Relations can contribute to the broader pursuit of developing connections between History and Sociology (Rosenberg, 1994; Hobden, 1998; Reus-Smit, 1999; Buzan and Little, 2000; Hobden and Hobson, 2002).

The rise of the historical sociology of international relations is to be welcomed for many reasons. Efforts to draw on the work of thinkers such as Braudel, Elias, Giddens, Mann, Skocpol, Tilly and Wallerstein have shown how the peculiar barrier between sociology and International Relations can be eroded; new bridges are being built between theoretical and historical analyses of world politics; finally, and most important of all for the current argument, historical-sociological approaches can develop new insights into the origins, evolution and transformation of international systems as well as an improved understanding of how far the modern international system is similar to, and different from, states-systems in the past.

From the 'first period' of sociological investigation promoted by the English School, Wight's *Systems of States* did most to create a grand vision of 'a comparative study' or 'sociology of states-systems' (Wight, 1977: 22, 33). The first part of this chapter argues that Wight's pessimism, which is very evident in that volume, supports a particular sociological approach to states-systems. This is the Hobbesian or Machiavellian approach which concentrates on long-term historical processes that include the rise and fall of hegemonic powers and the final violent destruction of states-systems. However, the outlines of a rather different sociological approach can be identified in Wight's essays. This might be called the Kantian approach which focuses on long-term historical processes in which visions of the unity of the human race influence the development of states-systems.[1] The broad

---

[1] This dualism is unsurprising given that the rationalist tradition is divided between its more Hobbesian and more Kantian wings, and because the English School is divisible into pluralist and solidarist standpoints. It should be stressed here that English School sociology has been principally concerned with the bases of international order and, especially, with the foundations of order in the modern world. This chapter distinguishes between the Hobbesian or Machiavellian and Kantian approaches because

outline of a Kantian standpoint can be extracted from Wight's interest – most pronounced in his essays on the international relations of Ancient Greece and on relations between Hellas and Persia – in the extent to which visions of a universal community of humankind made a mark on statecraft in the ancient world.[2] The second part of this chapter builds on Kantian insights discussed in the preceding chapter. The core argument is that a sociology of states-systems undertaken in the spirit of Kant's inquiry can most profitably analyse the role of cosmopolitan harm conventions in different international systems.[3] One of the aims of the chapter is to identify different forms of harm in world politics which have led political actors to create or to argue for cosmopolitan harm conventions which address the problem of human mental and physical vulnerability. What is important from this point of view is how far the constituent parts of different international systems were able to reach an agreement that harm to individuals is a moral problem for the whole of humanity – a problem that all states, individually and collectively, should endeavour to solve. The final part of this chapter turns to the question of whether the modern states-system can be said to have progressed in creating cosmopolitan harm conventions which indicate that unnecessary suffering is increasingly – and perhaps unusually – a moral problem for humanity as a whole.

Two concepts of historical sociology

Two interconnected features of Wight's approach are worth noting prior to discussing the differences between the Hobbesian or Machiavellian and Kantian approaches in more detail: the first is his distinction between different types of states-system with their individual forms

---

they offer different positions on the long-term fate of systems of states. Wight tends towards the first position which concludes that their fate is to be destroyed by force. The second approach has not been defended explicitly by members of the English School. Drawing on the argument of the last two chapters, it is introduced here as a counterweight to Wight's pessimism.

[2] Themes discussed in this outline will be considered in future work on the sociology of states-systems. For further reflections on possible research directions, see Linklater (2002b, 2002d, and 2004).

[3] As noted earlier, these are conventions which are designed to protect individuals everywhere from unnecessary suffering irrespective of their citizenship or nationality, class, gender, race, sexuality and other characteristics.

of 'communication and intercourse'; the second is his focus on the power struggle within societies of states and its allegedly unavoidable result – the destruction of the states-system and its replacement by universal empire.

Wight (1977: 23) maintained that a states-system exists when each state ('by "states" we normally mean "sovereign states"', political authorities which recognize no superior') claims 'independence of any political superior' and recognizes 'the validity of the same claim by all the others'. Three examples of states-systems are identified in world history: the modern Western, the Hellenic-Hellenistic or Greco-Roman, and the Chinese systems between the collapse of the Chou Empire in 771 BC and the establishment of the Ts'in Empire in 221 BC (Wight, 1977: 22).[4] A system of states is distinguished from a suzerain state-system in which one state is 'the sole source of legitimate authority, conferring status on the rest and exacting tribute or other marks of deference'. Wight (1977: 23) gives the examples of China, Byzantium, the Abassid Caliphate and the British Raj.[5] International states-systems are subdivided into two principal forms: primary states-systems whose members are states, and secondary states-systems whose members are 'not unitary sovereign states but complex empires or suzerain state-systems' (Wight, 1977: 25).[6] In each primary states-system various institutions were developed for the purpose of regulating relations between societies with different political interests and divergent cultural standpoints. 'Messengers, conferences and congresses, a diplomatic language and trade' have been some of the main institutions to appear in different states-systems (Bull, 1991: 16). Through the process of diplomatic dialogue, the members of these international systems were able to reach some consensus about the principles which should govern their relations not only with each other, but also with

---

[4] In *Systems of States*, the Chinese system is said to end in 221 AD (Wight, 1977: 22).
[5] Wight (1977: 24) adds that the word 'state' in international states-systems 'should be in the plural' but in the case of suzerain state-systems it must be in the singular. Moreover, while 'the fundamental political principle of the first will be to maintain a balance of power, for the second it will be *divide et impera*'.
[6] Wight (1977: 24) adds that there have been very few examples of secondary states-systems 'in the world at one time' although the 'relations between the Roman Empire and the Persian empire in its successive manifestations (Parthian, Sassanian, Abassid Caliphate) might provide a test-case'. The international system of the Near East in the latter half of the second millennium BC is cited as a possible example, and the nearest 'analogue' in modern times is said to be the international society which existed in the Mediterranean in the twelfth and thirteenth centuries AD (Wight, 1977: 25).

peoples deemed to lack the level of cultural and political sophistication required for full membership of international society.

On the subject of different configurations of military power, Wight (1977: 179) wrote that triangles, 'like duels, are relationships of conflict, and are resolved by war. The triangle of Russia, China and the United States has not yet been so resolved, but the historical precedents permit no other generalization.' And again, it 'might be argued that every states-system can only maintain its existence on the principle of the balance of power, that the balance of power is inherently unstable, and that sooner or later its tensions and conflicts will be resolved into a monopoly of power' (Wight, 1977: 44). Questions about whether there has ever been a states-system which did not end in empire, and about whether there is anything that suggests that the modern international order can avoid the fate of its predecessors, are prominent in his approach (Wight 1977: 44). As far as the second question is concerned, one does not encounter much optimism in Wight's essays that the modern states-system is poised to break the historical mould.[7] Indeed, the current phase of American military hegemony invites renewed discussion of Wight's claim that international relations is essentially a succession of hegemonies; and it invites renewed consideration of the claim that international society ultimately depends on the balance of power and invariably enters a precarious phase when one state acquires the military capacity to seek 'to lay down the law' (Dunne, 2003). Tentatively, Wight suggested all societies of states seem to follow similar patterns of evolution, beginning with the gradual destruction of large numbers of independent political communities which is followed by increasingly violent relations between the few surviving great powers and the final struggle to dominate the system as a whole.[8] In line with this approach, Wight was strongly inclined to develop a sociology of the contemporary states-system which looks for

[7] Wight (1966a: 22) took issue with Toynbee's belief that the modern society of states might end in a stable international anarchy rather than in universal empire.

[8] Wight reaches this judgement in connection with the three states-systems mentioned at the start of this chapter. More recently, Wilkinson (2000: 60) refers to a total of twenty-eight states-systems, and adds that the modern states-system has outlived its predecessors as well as all twenty-three universal empires. Wilkinson's comment raises the question of how many states-systems there have been in human history (according to Wight's definition of this term) and whether Wight's focus on three states-systems is, in the end, arbitrary.

signs of its possible or probable replacement by a single 'monopoly of power'.[9]

Watson's *The Evolution of International Society* with its apparent predilection for a cyclical view of history is a second example of the realist tendency in English School sociology of international relations. Watson (1992: 4) argues that a 'system of absolutely independent states, and a heterogeneous empire wholly and directly administered from one centre, are theoretically extreme cases. In practice all known examples of organizing diverse but interconnected communities have operated somewhere between these two extremes.' Two recurrent logics are identified in international history: the first is the centripetal tendency towards dominion and suzerainty in international societies;[10] the second is the centrifugal struggle for independence or autonomy in centralized forms of world political organizsation. The stress clearly falls on the struggle for military power, but in the analysis of the 'pendulum effect' in world history Watson (1992) attaches considerable importance, in true Grotian fashion, to the rule-governed nature of international interaction and to global principles of legitimacy which lend international systems their individual identities.[11] As noted earlier, Watson's remark that modern states may be progressing towards a global agreement about transcultural principles would seem to clash with Wight's deeply pessimistic interpretation of international relations but these are not necessarily incompatible propositions. The view that the pendulum effect will finally prevail as one of the great

[9] One might also note in this context Adam Roberts' comment that in Wight's approach to the three traditions, 'too little room is left for evolutionary, or even teleological, views of international relations' (see Wight, 1991: xxv).

[10] Watson (1992: 15–16) distinguishes between 'hegemony' where one state dominates other states which remain 'domestically independent'; 'suzerainty' where all or most states accept hegemony as legitimate; and 'dominion' where an imperial authority 'to some extent determines the internal government of other communities, but they nevertheless retain their identity as separate states and some control over their own affairs'.

[11] This is a reminder of how the English School differs from Waltzian neo-realism which argues for omitting culture and belief from a theory of international politics. See Waltz (1979: ch. 5). It is also important to stress that Wight (1966a: 26) does not argue that the recurrent and repetitive nature of world politics is found only in the formation of alliances and the struggle for power. Patterns might also be found in the existence of 'universal doctrines contending against local patriotism' and in the tension between 'the duty of intervention' and 'the right of independence' in different states-systems. His brief remarks about whether tensions between the three traditions of international theory have arisen in different states-systems raised the question of how far there are intellectual patterns in international history.

powers resumes the struggle to impose its will on the states-system and eventually realizes its purpose suggests that a global agreement about transcultural values may prove to be temporary. Even so, Watson's point about transcultural values invites analysts to ask whether the modern states-system is developing an unusual, if not unique, commitment to cosmopolitan principles of international legitimacy and whether this process may yet validate the Kantian belief that it is not bound to repeat the historical pattern of violent implosion followed by empire.[12] In this context, it is important to note that the hegemonic qualities of the contemporary international order do not necessarily mark the end of commitments to cosmopolitan principles, but may have the opposing long-term effect of consolidating them (Hurrell, 2002).[13]

The notion of the *via media* suggests that the realist emphasis in Wight and Watson's writings is not the only approach to the historical sociology of international states-systems that can be developed from the resources of the English School. Bull's observation that 'international society is no more than one of the basic elements at work in modern international politics, and is always in competition with the elements of a state of war and of transnational solidarity or conflict' is worth stressing at this point, as is his claim that it 'is always erroneous to interpret international events as if international society were the sole or the dominant element' (Bull, 2002: 49). In 'different historical phases of the states system, in very different geographical theatres of its operation, and in the policies of different states and statesmen', one of three perspectives (the Hobbesian approach with its emphasis on 'war and struggle for power among states', the Grotian approach with its specific focus on 'cooperation and regulated intercourse', and

---

[12] Progressivist tendencies resting on a strangely optimistic interpretation of the United States' capacity for good international citizenship are evident in Watson's claim in 1997 that if 'the pendulum keeps swinging in its present direction, the great powers, and especially the US, are likely to become increasingly *the joint trustees and executors of a general will of mankind*' (Watson, 1997: 141; emphasis in original). Ethical criteria for assessing good international citizenship and trusteeship are considered in the next chapter.

[13] Hurrell (2002: 202–3) maintains that 'effective hegemony requires acceptance by the others of the hegemon's leadership and authority', and that US claims for exceptionalism have thus far intensified counter-hegemonic moral and political commitments rather than an acceptance of the great power's ability to lay down the law on which effective hegemony ultimately rests. Of course, the counter-hegemonic response is concerned in large part with trying to persuade the United States to comply with its own liberal values.

the Kantian approach with its distinctive preoccupation with 'the element of transnational solidarity and conflict') 'may predominate over the others' (see also Bull, 2002: 39).[14] In addition to summarizing tendencies in the history of modern international society, this observation has the added value of capturing important tensions and dynamics within the current global order.

As the *via media*, rationalism must be concerned with geopolitical competition and war in the global society of states and in its different theatres of operation. The side that inclines towards realism must be watchful for the early appearance of the logic of destruction which may transform the society of states into universal empire; but it must also analyse developments which especially interest those at the Kantian end of the theoretical spectrum. Crucial here is the impact that visions of a universal community of humankind have had on past states-systems and on the development of modern international society. Wight did not deal with these matters in any detail. As previously noted, he stressed the respects in which moral and political universalism have had a civilizing effect in international relations, but he was as – and perhaps more – inclined to stress its 'decivilizing' role in promoting transnational schism and revolution. Nevertheless, his observations about the extent to which visions of the human community influenced international relations in the ancient world can be read as containing in broad outline the basic elements of a Kantian approach to the sociology of states-systems. These comments warrant brief consideration prior to assessing their significance for a mode of investigation which is informed by Bull's undeveloped observations about the ideal relationship between international order and world order.

Regarding the Hellenic states-system, Wight observed that loyalties to the polis were far stronger than loyalties to Hellas or to humanity at large. Ideas about the solidarity of the Hellenes and the unity of the human race existed but they were too hesitant to check egotism in

---

[14] Developing the point, Bull added that the Hobbesian approach to the sociology of international relations deserves special place in an attempt to explain the trade and colonial wars of the seventeenth and eighteenth centuries; the Grotian perspective is especially relevant to understanding the long peace after the Napoleonic Wars; and the Kantian approach has special importance when the task is to understand periods of revolutionary upheaval such as the religious wars leading up to the Peace of Westphalia. None of this should alter the view that Bull, like Wight before him, was most interested in the nature of international society.

foreign policy.[15] Wight noted that, according to Aeschines, members of the Delphic Amphictyony were bound by an oath 'not to destroy any *polis* of the Amphictyons, nor starve it out, nor cut off its running water in war or in peace' although it seems this oath was rarely effective (Wight, 1977: 50). Thucydides' great work on the Peloponnesian war seemed designed, according to Wight (1977: 51), to show that 'the customs of war were minimal' and that 'the only restraints on savagery were not accepted custom or agreed law, but a dim fear of committing impiety on the part of the conservatives, and prudential calculations on the part of the progressives'. But that was not to say that Greek city-states belonged to a system as opposed to a society of states in Bull's sense of these terms (see above, pp. 53ff). Conceptions of Hellas were not so exclusionary as to prevent the enlargement of the society of states to embrace, at least partially but not unproblematically, Persia (Wight, 1977: 88). Although the Greeks distinguished themselves from the barbarian or *barbaros* (literally the non-Greek-speaking peoples), and although the concept of the barbarian acquired a more xenophobic meaning as a consequence of the Persian Wars, that term was never strong enough to extinguish their sense of the wider unity of humankind (Wight, 1977: 85–6).[16]

Wight thought that the sense of human unity was reflected in the belief, which has been attributed to Eratosthenes, that the Carthaginians displayed their barbarism by repelling strangers and drowning foreign sailors stranded in waters nearby. Wight proceeded to cite the peace with Carthage in 480 BC in which Gelon 'included a prohibition of the practice of sacrificing children to Moloch' as an early example of an unequal treaty resting on a belief in a transculturally valid moral standard (Wight, 1977: 103–4). However, if Wight is correct, the modern ethical conviction that certain violent acts of state so shock the conscience of humankind as to demand intervention had no counterpart in the ancient world – nor was there a Greek equivalent to the modern international law of war or to the universal culture of human rights. Significantly, 'no Greek Vitoria or Grotius' emerged to reflect in a systematic manner on the normative foundations of ancient international society or to consider the ethical principles which

---

[15] This description can be found in Mann (1986: ch. 7).

[16] See also Mann (1986: 223ff) on the importance of the polis, Hellas and humankind ('the triple power network') in Ancient Greece.

members should observe in their dealings with non-Hellenic peoples (Wight, 1977: 52). Appeals to world public opinion had little moral force in the Hellenic system (Wight, 1977: 71–2). The Greeks' horror at what they regarded as the barbarous actions of the Carthaginians revealed they had some respect for human life outside the state of war, but the sense of loyalty to the community of humankind was not powerful enough to encourage them to create an international society furnished with cosmopolitan conventions designed to protect all individuals – or all Greeks – from unnecessary suffering.[17]

Wight was not persuaded by any version of cosmopolitan ethics, but he was certainly interested in the sociological question of how far, or how little, visions of universal solidarity had influenced the long-term development of earlier states-systems. Key foundations for an approach to the sociology of states-systems which analyses cosmopolitan tendencies are evident in his brief, but insightful, observations about cruelty and compassion in the international relations of Ancient Greece. His illuminating comments can be extended further by analysing the extent to which cosmopolitan, as opposed to international, harm conventions have influenced long-term patterns of change in different international systems. This is to ask how far the historic states-systems developed moral conventions which reveal that human sympathies need not be confined to members of one's own society but can expand to include the whole human race. In Bull's terms, it is to inquire into the extent to which different international political orders contributed to world order by drawing on the idea of a universal community to create mechanisms for protecting individuals and non-sovereign communities from unwarranted suffering.

[17] The notion that the strong do what they can and the weak must suffer as a result was deeply ingrained in Greek culture according to Thucydides. In this context it is worth noting the comment that few writers in the ancient world 'ever denied (and no Greek would have done so) that in warfare one has an obligation to inflict maximum damage on the enemy while producing maximum advantage for one's own side' (see Blundell 1991: 52). Konstan (2001) provides a fascinating account of the limited role of pity in the ancient world. However, the sense of a community wider than the polis – though admittedly still largely limited to Greek civilization rather than to humanity at large – is evident in Plato's claim that 'the enslavement of Greeks by Greeks, the stripping of corpses on the battlefield, the ravaging of land and the burning of houses, ought to be abolished' (Wight, 1977: 51).

Towards a sociology of cosmopolitan harm conventions

Wight's pessimistic interpretation of world politics has to be placed in its historical context. Two major wars followed by the tensions and conflicts of the Cold War era hardly encouraged optimism about the future of international relations. In the immediate aftermath of the bipolar era, a growing literature on the liberal-democratic peace and on the obsolescence of force between core states in the world economy raised serious problems for Wight's fatalist position. Of course, developments since the terrorist attacks on the United States in September 2001 and the war against Iraq in 2003 may yet confirm his suspicion that the modern states-system will follow the path of its predecessors by ending in a 'monopoly of power'. Analysts can only speculate about possible long-term trends. It is important not to lose sight of the literature on the obsolescence of force between the industrial powers because this raises the intriguing idea that modern international society may yet succeed in creating permanent constraints on the use of force which are unrivalled historically. The pacification of core areas of the international system invites a discussion of whether the cosmopolitan's faith in the ability of human beings to extend compassion across national boundaries may yet come to have unparalleled success; it raises the question of whether the development of cosmopolitan harm conventions may yet prevent the logic of domination which destroyed past states-systems. Here one might note the particular importance of the principle of non-combatant immunity in recent international conflicts such as the war against the Taliban and Iraq (Wheeler, 2002: 210–11).[18] In this context, it is important to ask if Wight focused rather too much on the political dangers inherent in cosmopolitan doctrines which supported the withering away of the state and the dissolution of national sentiments, and too little on varieties of cosmopolitanism which are consistent with, and indeed complement, his rationalist position. Forms of cosmopolitanism exist which do not endorse his

---

[18] Its significance is all the more important if Toynbee was right that international societies entered their final phase when the great powers felt they were at liberty to set aside the rules of war (see McNeill, 1989: 160ff). Wheeler (2002) argues that 'the norm of non-combatant immunity has become the legitimating standard against which military operations have to be justified'. Following the war against the Taliban, the norm was strengthened, 'raising expectations that war can be fought in a relatively bloodless manner for civilians in the target state'.

belief in the basic 'incompatibility of the cosmopolitan ideal with the existence of any states-system' (Wight, 1977: 87–8).

The *Oxford English Dictionary* usefully distinguishes between two forms of cosmopolitanism which are relevant to the current discussion. The first mirrors Wight's definition of cosmopolitanism as that doctrine which believes that provincial political loyalties should give way to an allegedly higher ethical identification with humanity, and that international society should be sacrificed in the process. The second definition does not support the elimination of national ties but criticizes the way in which parochial loyalties often lead to deliberate harm to outsiders, to neglect of their legitimate interests, and to general indifference to their suffering. Illustrating this second approach, the *Oxford English Dictionary* defines the *cosmophil* as someone who is 'friendly to the world in general' rather than hostile to special ties to bounded political communities. According to this reasoning, the members of separate states should not defend national affiliations or celebrate cultural differences when these impose terrible burdens and hardship on the members of other societies. The Stoic-Kantian belief that human beings have special duties as citizens of particular cities *and* general obligations to avoid injuring other members of a universal commonwealth is a perfect illustration of a cosmopolitan approach which endeavours to balance different human loyalties (see above, pp. 163–4).

A focus on the sociology of cosmopolitan harm conventions is one way of building on Wight's interest in how far the members of different states-systems felt the pull of obligations to humanity in addition to duties to their own inhabitants and to international society. It is to recognize one of the main strengths of Wight's approach which Bull summarized as a commitment to moving beyond 'those studies of states-systems which view them as determined purely by mechanical factors such as the number of states in the system, their relative size, the political configuration in which they stand, the state of military technology' to a position which concentrates instead on 'the norms and values that animate the system, and the institutions in which they are expressed' (Bull, 1991: 17). It is to seek to extend that broadly constructivist approach in the following way (see Chapter 3). For the most part, Wight's focus was on the norms, values and institutions which revealed how bounded political communities have understood their rights against and duties to each other – his primary concern was to understand moral and cultural understandings of the relationship between the state and international society or international order. But, mindful of Wight's remarks about whether the idea of the equality of all human beings exerted much influence on international relations in the ancient world, it is necessary to do more to analyse the norms, values and institutions which have been less concerned with encouraging the sense of obligations to the society of states than with strengthening individual loyalties to the human race as a whole. Shifting the emphasis from the foundations of inter-state order to how far ethical commitments to protecting all individuals from unnecessary suffering developed in different states-systems is the central task for a historical-sociological approach which falls squarely within the Kantian tradition.[19]

Some further comments about harm or injury are required before considering the different forms of harm which are important for the sociology of cosmopolitan harm conventions. It is useful first of all to recall Bull's argument that a key purpose of social order is to protect individuals from 'violence resulting in death or bodily harm' (Bull, 2002: 4) as well as from hardship caused by property theft or the breach of agreements. This formulation suggests that harmful actions can be placed along a spectrum. Actions that can lead to the loss of life or cause severe physical pain and mental anguish, and actions that result in 'setbacks' to interests because they bring economic disadvantage or breed insecurity about the future (but do not threaten survival or inflict great pain), lie at different points on a spectrum.[20] As Bull implies in his discussion of primary goals, all societies possess harm conventions which recognize the vulnerability of human beings to different forms of harm. This point can be extended by noting that in order to function effectively, societies need to develop some basic understandings about what counts as injury, and about where the boundaries are best drawn between deserved and permissible harm (e.g., systems of punishment) and proscribed harm (e.g., unauthorized acts of violence). Of course, these are only formal similarities between societies. Different social systems answer the question of where the line should be drawn between harmful and harmless acts, and between

---

[19] It is only one element because of the importance of beneficence for Kant's thinking (see above, p. 171). A more comprehensive sociology would need to investigate the role of positive obligations of assistance in different states-systems to the extent that these can be separated from the negative obligation of avoiding injury to others.

[20] See Feinberg (1984: 33–4) on harm as involving setbacks to interests.

legitimate and illegitimate harm, in radically different ways. This is also inevitably true of international states-systems.

Before developing this last point, one general tendency across all human societies should be noted. The recurrent practice in the history of political communities is that prohibitions on harm between members of the same social group rarely apply – or hardly ever apply with the same force – in relations with other groups. Most societies have punished violations of the duty of non-maleficence within the group while not only condoning but, especially in times of war, actively encouraging violations of this principle in relations with other communities. Referring to the modern world, Elias (1996: 154ff) described this phenomenon as 'the duality of nation-states' normative codes' although, like Bergson who influenced his argument, he recognized that tensions between the moral principles which apply within and between societies predated the rise of the modern states-system.

The existence of a society of states testifies to the fact that separate political communities have often recognized that mutual vulnerability makes it valuable to agree on basic harm conventions which afford them some protection from excessive violence or unnecessary injury. As with relations within bounded communities, a society of states rests on shared understandings about where the line should be drawn between harmful and harmless actions, and also about what counts as permissible harm (e.g., the use of force in self-defence) and proscribed harm (e.g., the unauthorized breach of territorial sovereignty). An international society modifies the duality of normative codes, or mitigates its effects, by developing harm conventions which express the recognition that obligations between citizens do not exhaust human morality. As noted earlier, the English School analysis of international society has been primarily concerned with understanding international harm conventions, conventions which are concerned most of all with the interests of states. If the School has paid less attention to cosmopolitan harm conventions, it is because they have had much less impact on the long-term development of international societies. A society of states necessarily contains international harm conventions (this is a large part of what it is) but it is, in principle, possible for a society of states to have no cosmopolitan harm conventions. Analyses of human rights and humanitarian intervention indicate how the dual structure of political morality has been modified in the modern society of states because of the sense of belonging to a world community in addition to pragmatic interests in preserving international order. The study of human rights marks the point where the English School most obviously shifts its attention from a traditional preoccupation with international harm conventions to the relatively neglected realm of cosmopolitan harm conventions.[21]

It was suggested in the last chapter that international harm conventions are concerned with national or state security whereas cosmopolitan harm conventions address threats to human security. Of course, this is not an absolute distinction because national security is now usually regarded as a means of promoting individual security, but it is not necessarily the case that agreements about preventing or minimizing harm to states will automatically promote the security of all individual members – or are designed to have that end. When Eglantyne Jebb, the founder of *Save the Children*, argued that there was 'no such thing as an enemy child', she appealed to a notion of security much broader than the one that was dominant in the thinking of European governments during World War I (Finnemore, 1999). To repeat, international harm conventions have been designed to protect states rather than all vulnerable groups or individuals from unnecessary injury: they have not been concerned with reducing human vulnerability to harm in its manifold forms.[22]

Jebb's efforts to extend human sympathies and solidarity are a clear reminder that war and conquest have been principal causes of unnecessary suffering for millennia. Other forms of harm which have often concerned international society as a whole have resulted from state-building, the most obvious being the forced movement of peoples (see Rae, 2002). Warfare, conquest and state-building have frequently created or intensified pernicious distinctions between human groups which are used to justify violations of taboos against killing. Throughout human history supposedly 'ontological differences' between human beings have led some groups to claim an unlimited right to hurt and humiliate others; at times, allegedly natural inequalities between human groups have been linked with the pseudo-scientific

---

[21] Of course, the literature on human rights has been concerned with contemporary world politics. The influence of notions of human dignity in earlier historical periods has not been a principal area of research for members of the English School.

[22] The distinction between international and cosmopolitan harm conventions is most relevant when states are the private property of their rulers, and when harm conventions are best regarded as agreements between ruling elites rather than peoples and do not address the problem of human suffering across international society as a whole.

view that 'inferior' peoples do not feel pain to the same extent as the more delicate members of 'civilized' humanity (Bending, 2000). From the beginning of the Industrial Revolution, the globalization of economic and social life has been an increasingly important source of long-distance, and often unintended, harm to the inhabitants of remote communities. Discussions about cosmopolitan morality have been enlarged during the last two centuries of economic globalization to add the problem of indifference to the suffering of other peoples (including the suffering in which the affluent are clearly implicated in the manner suggested by Vincent)[23] to earlier concerns about human cruelty and excessive force.

All such forms of harm provide the rationale for building cosmopolitan harm conventions into the structure of international society and for ensuring that the global political order advances the interests of as large a proportion of the human race as possible.[24] From the elementary classification of different types of harm in world politics set out in the preceding paragraph follow some basic questions that the sociologist of cosmopolitan harm conventions must try to answer. The first cause of harm mentioned earlier raises the issue of how far different states-systems (primary and secondary) have developed moral conventions such as the category of non-combatant immunity which were designed to spare the 'innocent' unnecessary suffering. Sociological analysis can explore how far different international systems recognized the particular vulnerability of women and children in wars of conquest and inter-state conflict in addition to attempting to protect combatants and enemy prisoners from excessive cruelty in war. The second source of harm requires a discussion of how far different societies of states concluded that the harm that governments do to their citizens is not a purely domestic matter, but the legitimate business of international society as a whole. It is then important to ask how far member states believed that they were entitled or even obligated to intervene to protect peoples from suffering at the

---

[23] See below, p. 250.

[24] The argument is influenced by Carr's claim that the 'driving force behind any future international order must be a belief, however expressed, in the value of individual human beings irrespective of national affinities or allegiance and in a common and mutual obligation to promote their well-being' (see Carr 1945: 44). The argument as it stands is anthropocentric, and a more complete analysis would need to consider the ways in which concerns about animal suffering have made additional demands on international order.

hands of their own rulers. The third cause of harm requires an analysis of the extent to which all states-systems have regarded pernicious distinctions between peoples, and especially between the allegedly civilized and the supposedly barbaric, as the reason for unnecessary violence and humiliation which all societies should strive to eradicate. The fourth source of harm leads to a discussion of whether all states-systems developed conventions which were designed to protect individuals from long-distance harm, whether deliberately inflicted or accidental and unintended.[25] In this last example, the discussion shifts from how societies of states have dealt with acts of deliberate cruelty to how they have dealt with indifference to setbacks to the interests of all peoples in which they are implicated.

To return to themes raised in the previous two chapters, a sociology of cosmopolitan harm conventions explores the middle ground between the Hobbesian portrayal of international politics and diametrically opposed positions which believe that it is possible to bring the whole of humanity under a universal state or to progress towards a condition in which violent conflict is abolished. In the sociological project just described, cosmopolitanism does not come with a naive view of the prospects for global political progress or suffer from the negative connotations which Wight attributed to it. Its moral purpose is not to devalue the national bonds which stand between the individual and humanity, but to question the moral relevance of distinctions between citizens and outsiders in world politics and to defend the right of all human beings to be free from the varieties of unnecessary harm described earlier – from types of harm which will persist as long as the Hobbesian 'struggle for power among states' survives. Its

---

[25] Three of the four sources of harm correspond with Kant's discussion of the reasons for creating world law mentioned in the preceding chapter. Three other points need to be made at this stage. Firstly, admittedly it is difficult to compare how different states-systems have responded to long-distance harm because earlier systems did not experience the level of global interconnectedness which exists at the present time. Different levels of border interaction in premodern and modern international systems are discussed in Buzan and Little (2000). Secondly, the widespread institution of slavery in world history does raise questions about how far concerns about moral indifference, or guilt about benefiting unfairly from the vulnerable, or anxieties about being complicit in the suffering of others have appeared in different states-systems. Thirdly, the extent of efforts to control forms of private international violence such as piracy or involving mercenary armies also provides interesting points of comparison. These last two points raise issues that go well beyond the present discussion but they are important for a more comprehensive discussion of the variety of sources of cross-border harm and the harm conventions with universal scope to which they may (or may not) give rise. On this matter, see Linklater (2002b).

aim then is to address what the philosopher, Geoffrey Warnock (1971: ch. 2) has called the 'damaging effects' of 'limited sympathies' – that is, the historical tendency for loyalties to particular groups to result in cruelty to the members of other societies or to indifference to the ways in which efforts to promote group interests harm other peoples. To ask how far different international societies developed commitments to cosmopolitanism is to aim to understand how far the effects of the dual structure of normative codes were moderated by a widespread belief in moral obligations to avoid, prevent and reduce unnecessary harm. It is to examine the extent to which societies of states have been influenced by 'cosmopolitan forms of legitimation' (Shapcott, 2000: 156) which are in keeping with the meliorist approach to world politics which Wight (1991: 207) supported. On such foundations it is possible to build a comparative study of societies of states which analyses the extent to which cosmopolitan ethical commitments shaped their long-term development; and on such foundations it is possible to build a more specific inquiry into whether or not the modern society of states is making commitments to globalizing the harm principle which clearly set it apart from its predecessors.[26]

Modernity and progress

Wight's comparative approach aimed to uncover universal laws or tendencies such as the gradual elimination of significant numbers of separate states and the drift towards the major wars which destroyed past states-systems. The two earlier examples of states-systems which Wight discussed (the Chinese and Hellenic) did not survive long enough for cosmopolitan moral principles to have much impact on foreign affairs, and conceivably they would not have acquired significant influence even if these states-systems had survived for a longer period. Be that as it may, the rise and fall of hegemonic powers and incessant conflict meant that cosmopolitan moral beliefs did not enjoy much practical success. Wight may have thought the modern states-system was nearing its end given the reduction in the number of

---

[26] The study of cosmopolitan harm conventions is an essential part of the study of how far visions of the community of humankind have shaped the development of international order and also how far they have influenced conduct within world society – the domain comprising all manner of non-state interaction – as discussed in Buzan (2004).

great powers and ensuing tensions between the remaining adversaries. It is intriguing, however, that Wight maintained that the idea of progress had been one factor in the British Committee's decision to select states-systems as its principal object of inquiry.[27] We have seen how Jackson takes this point further by arguing that the society of states is the most successful form of world political organization yet devised for the purpose of creating orderly relations between independent political communities.[28] From this standpoint, states-systems are to be preferred to other forms of global political organization despite their propensity for violent destruction.[29] Reference has been made to contemporary approaches which cast doubt on this last claim on the grounds that the most recent phase of globalization may have sown the seeds of long-term patterns of change. This includes the obsolescence of force as a means of resolving disputes at least in relations between the technologically advanced liberal democracies. The question which immediately follows is whether global economic and social change has the capacity to extend the life-span of modern international society and to provide unusual opportunities for cosmopolitan ideas to shape future developments.

Complex questions are raised by the suggestion that it is worth comparing modern international society with past states-systems in order to understand whether or not the former is making significant progress in developing global commitments to the harm principle in the dimensions of social and political life mentioned earlier. Sceptics will ask whether there is a transculturally acceptable definition of

[27] Wight (1977: 44) refers to the judgement which 'underlies our choice of states-systems as a subject of study'. He adds: 'For what reasons are we inclined (as I think we probably are) to judge a state-system as *per se* a more desirable way of arranging the affairs of a great number of men than the alternatives, whatever these may be'. Wight proceeds to refer to Orwell's vision of 'three totalitarian great powers, locked together in interdependent hatred', and to note that 'some of the historic generations which have experienced the *end* of a states-system have done so with relief and rejoicing'. Wight proceeds to refer to St Augustine's belief that 'the world would be a better place without empires' since, in Augustine's words, 'it is greater felicity to have a good neighbour at peace, than to subjugate a bad one by war'.

[28] See above, pp. 41–2. Arguably, a somewhat similar sentiment exists, albeit implicitly, in Bull and Watson (1984). Their joint contributions to that volume suggest progress has occurred in that non-Western civilizations have exchanged their 'hegemonial concept' of international relations for a belief in the Western conception of an international order based on sovereign equality (see Bull and Watson, 1984: 3ff).

[29] Jackson's observation about the unprecedented achievements of the modern pluralist society of states would appear to imply that modern states have acquired the capacity to avoid the fate of all previous states-systems.

harm or injury which can be used to make meaningful historical comparisons. The danger, it will be argued, is that particular under-standings of injury which prevail, say, in the liberal-democratic West will be used to compare different international systems and to con-clude that earlier states-systems are clearly inferior. An additional concern, it might be added, is that contemporary societies that do not share liberal conceptions of unnecessary suffering will be deemed to lag behind supposedly more civilized areas. On this argument, histor-ical comparisons should be resisted, because they will rest on arbitrary ethical yardsticks which favour modern social and political arrange-ments and which may have pernicious implications for practice – of the kind that poststructuralists have highlighted in analyses of constructions of otherness.

To try to answer the question of whether it is legitimate to make such comparisons, or wise to concentrate instead on comparing differ-ent stages in the history of the modern states-system, is to go beyond the parameters of the current discussion. These are matters for future investigation. Suffice it to add that three approaches to the question of progress in world politics would seem to warrant close attention in the course of that inquiry. The first two approaches are broadly compatible with certain tendencies in the English School but, arguably, it is the third approach which comes closest to its meliorist standpoint.

The first approach is the 'progressivist interpretation of international relations' which Wight (1978: 30) famously rejected, not least in his claim that the 'most conspicuous theme in international history is not the growth of internationalism . . . It is the series of efforts, by one power after another, to gain mastery of the states-system – efforts that have been defeated only by a coalition of the majority of other powers at the cost of an exhausting general war.' Exponents of progressivism have maintained there have been gradual advances in world politics not just in recent decades but over the longer course of human history. Studies of the unique liberal-democratic peace and analyses of the growth of the universal culture of human rights are the best known contemporary examples of this approach.[30]

The English School is usually thought to be at odds with progressiv-ism, and this is clearly true where the approach suggests unilinear,

---

[30] Kant (2002: 429) maintained that 'various evidence suggests that in our age, as compared with all previous ages, the human race has made considerable moral progress, and short-term hindrances prove nothing to the contrary'.

irreversible progress towards a global moral consensus. However Bull (1984a: 125) defended a milder version of this doctrine when he claimed that 'the first stirrings of internationally organized action about human rights in relation to the abolition of the slave trade, and new ideas about disarmament and the peaceful settlement of international disputes' demonstrated that European international society was in 'a state of progressive development' in the late nineteenth century. Bull, Vincent and Wheeler all referred to progress in the area of human rights in recent times – and, of course, the very existence of a society of states can be regarded as evidence of progress in controlling the use of force and in developing shared understandings about the ingredients of order (see Chapter 3).[31] Progressivist tendencies in the English School are not unqualified given its members' stress on the precarious nature of international societies. Throughout its history, moreover, the English School has stressed that what we have called cosmopolitan harm conventions such as human rights declarations are controversial in their design and application. The case for treating the idea of the liberal peace with some care is perhaps implicit in Wight's critical comments on the idea of doctrinal uniformity which holds that societies should be united in upholding the same principles of government.[32] The argument, which is found in the literature which explores the idea of the liberal peace, is that there is a danger that the zone of peace will be grounded in the liberals' sense of superiority to the non-liberal world, in apathy towards the suffering of non-liberal peoples, and in the conviction that principles that apply in relations between liberal states can be set aside when liberals wage war against illiberal regimes (see MacMillan, 1995).[33] Of equal importance is the

---

[31] Roberts maintains that Wight notes 'albeit briefly that there has been progress, not least in the emergence of a universal society of states' (Wight, 1991: xxv). This position is taken further in the contention that international society ought to play a civilizing role (see Buzan 2001: 482). International society, it is argued, 'has to take over from imperialism as the next phase of the transition to modernism . . . that all parts of the world except the West still have to go through'. The seeming Eurocentrism of this statement is moderated by the comment that movement towards a 'similar end result' must be 'compatible' with non-Western cultures. Large ethical issues arise here as discussed by Brown (1988) and others.

[32] But explicit in Butterfield (1953).

[33] The key here is Wight's claim that order and society between states have always relied on the fact of external 'cultural differentiation', that is on distinctions between the civilized and the uncivilized world (Wight, 1977: 34–5). It is a short step from here to the observation that the order and society between liberal states may rest on similar dichotomies of the kind discussed by Goldgeier and McFaul (1992) and Sadowski (1998). Doyle (1983) highlights the general problem.

danger that the affluent liberal world will strive to isolate itself as far as possible from 'the criminalized and brutal hinterland' of actual or potential failed states.[34] This is not to deny there is progress in the relations between states, or to suggest that movements in the sphere of human rights are reducible to power politics rather than evidence of the normative development of international society. But it is to suggest that notions of progress should always be used with caution because they can be used to reconfigure rather than to eliminate the dual structure of morality mentioned earlier. There are some echoes in these considerations of Foucault's influential claim that everything may not be bad, but everything is potentially dangerous (Rabinow, 1986: 343).

A second approach to the assessment of modernity is the anti-progressivist standpoint which maintains there have been no lasting advances in the history of relations between states, only short-lived departures from persistent trends. On this view, which appears to unite Wight with Toynbee, there is no reason to think the modern society of states has superseded earlier states-systems in its zeal for abolishing cruelty and reducing suffering.[35] Human rights advocates may protest that the modern states-system does not specialize in physical cruelty in the ways that many past empires and civilizations, or the Greek city-states system, clearly did.[36] They are in broad agreement with Elias (1978: 190ff) that aggressive impulses have been tamed, and the pleasure derived from public acts of cruelty largely suppressed, because of the 'civilizing process' in the modern West. These are contentious issues as Foucault (1977) and Bauman (1989) have contended. For Foucault, modern societies have replaced public cruelty with new forms of panoptical power, and this very fact is hard to reconcile with the idea of moral progress. For Bauman, modernity introduced new opportunities for the industrialized killing and bureaucratized violence which were exemplified by the Holocaust. Critical interpretations of narratives that portray modernity as more

---

[34] Mayall (2000a: 73) who makes this point refers to the importance of maintaining diplomatic fora 'where the special difficulties of the weaker states can be examined'. The 'alternative will be the creation of a democratic affluent citadel, surrounded by a criminalized and brutal hinterland, whose unfortunate population will have to be kept out – indeed, are already being kept out – by force'. See also Hurrell (1999: 291).
[35] See Toynbee (1978: 590).
[36] See Kyle (1998: 134ff).

advanced than earlier epochs all suggest that 'civilizing processes' expand potentialities for evil as well as good.[37]

The third approach combines elements of the first two perspectives by keeping faith with the idea of progress while stressing the dark side of modernity and the dangerous tendencies mentioned earlier.[38] In this case, the emphasis shifts to global standards of legitimacy which have developed in response to violence in the modern world. The crucial question is whether modern states are judged by higher moral standards than states in the past.[39] Starting with Luard's distinction between 'the *principles* on which international society [is] based' and 'the *procedures* by which such principles [are] formulated and conflicts resolved' (Luard, 1976: 381, italics in original), this question can be divided into two parts: the first is whether higher standards of legitimacy are evident in contemporary rules and understandings about how authoritative decisions in world politics should be taken; the second is whether higher ethical standards are evident in concrete decisions about what is permissible and what is forbidden in contemporary international affairs.[40]

The English School has been especially interested in standards of legitimacy which define the conditions which must be satisfied before political actors can enjoy membership of international society. Wight (1977: ch. 6) explained in an important essay on international legitimacy how the prevalent understandings about rights of representation in world politics had changed in the history of the modern

---

[37] Progress in the last few decades in the area of human rights and in promoting the humanitarian law of war also has to be viewed against a background of human rights violations and civilian casualties in war which have few parallels in human history. Toynbee's argument that nothing has progressed outside the technological field stresses the appalling cruelty in the wars of the twentieth century. See Toynbee (1978: 576ff).

[38] Bull (1991: xvii) refers to Wight's claim that a revolutionist argument which is 'grounded in utter despair deserves respect' but should not be regarded as 'a good argument'.

[39] Wight (1977: ch. 6) analysed the changing nature of international legitimacy, but his study focused on the principles that govern membership of the society of states. Bull (1983b) extends the analysis when he argues that the modern society of states will not solve its legitimation problem until it commands the support of the majority of the world's peoples. For the case for taking the study of international legitimacy more seriously, see Vincent and Wilson (1993). For recent overviews of the important issues at stake, see Clark (2003, 2005). For the purposes of the present argument, the principles of legitimacy which are most important are those that proscribe specific forms of harm.

[40] Hurrell (1999: 300) distinguishes along similar lines between a 'procedural' and a 'substantive value consensus'.

states-system.[41] Luard (1976: ch. 6) argued that dynastic rulers made foreign policy by and for themselves in the Ancient Chinese states-system, as did the absolutist states of early modern Europe. Clark (1989: 126ff; 2005: ch. 5) has explained how new standards of legitimacy emerged at the end of the Napoleonic Wars when the great power concert decided to institutionalize consultation about matters of common concern. More recent developments concerning membership and decision-making procedures include support for the idea of national self-determination at the end of World War I, the anti-colonial revolution in the second half of the twentieth century, and continuing pressures from indigenous peoples, stateless nations and international non-governmental associations for representation in world affairs. These developments – along with the idea that individuals should enjoy international legal personality in their own right, and parallel movements in the sphere of international criminal law – confirm the judgement that the idea of human equality is more important in the modern society of states than it was in past states-systems (Buzan and Little, 2000: 340; see also Crawford, 2002). As a result of these developments, it is no longer eccentric or extraordinary to argue that global decisions should have the consent of everyone who may be harmed by them, however much the gulf between principle and practice persists. The gulf between high ideals and political reality does not alter the fact that the modern states-system has built egalitarian principles into its standards of international legitimacy and is, in consequence, more open than earlier states-system to the ethical ideal that decisions about world affairs should be judged by their effect on individuals and communities everywhere.[42]

---

[41] The modern states-system may have progressed beyond its predecessors by introducing several institutional innovations for controlling conflict (see Little, 2000: 410). Wight (1977: 30) stressed the modernity of the institution of 'the resident ambassador' and asked whether any other states-system had developed the institution of the balance of power, the 'natural aristocracy' of the great powers, and the effort to transform them into 'great responsibles' (Wight, 1977: 42). Bull (2002: 137) added that the place of international law in the modern society of states 'gives it a distinctive stamp'.

[42] Democratic principles of government are more firmly entrenched in the modern society of states than in any of its predecessors. They are proclaimed within the respective territories of a large number of member states and they are regarded (by states, social movements and political theorists) as principles which should govern not only relations between sovereign states but all global social and political relations. There is no evidence that similar commitments to democratic legitimacy played any part in the evolution of earlier international systems. Whether the modern society of states will realize seemingly unique possibilities for developing more democratic forms of world

The second part of the question posed earlier shifts from procedural matters to substantive principles and asks if the modern states-system differs from its predecessors by displaying stronger ethical commitments to the harm principle. Elias's study of the civilizing process suggests ways in which the English School can develop this part of the analysis of changing principles of international legitimacy. Elias made several contrasts between warfare in Ancient Greece, the Middle Ages and the modern world. 'The Ancient Greeks', he wrote, 'who are so often held up . . . as models of civilized behaviour considered it quite a matter of course to commit acts of mass destruction not quite identical to those of the National Socialists but, nevertheless, similar to them in many respects' (Elias, 1996: 445).[43] Human emotions in the Middle Ages were 'wild, cruel, prone to violent outbreaks, and abandoned to the joy of the moment' (Elias, quoted in Fletcher, 1997: 17). Wars in modern Europe in the seventeenth century 'were cruel in a somewhat different sense to those of today . . . Plunder and rapine were not merely permitted, but demanded by military technique. To torment the subjugated inhabitants of occupied territories . . . was, as well as a means of satisfying lust, a deliberate means of collecting war contributions and bringing to light concealed treasure. Soldiers were supposed to behave like robbers' (Elias, 1998a: 22–3). Writing especially about the Ancient Greek city-state system, although he makes a similar observation about the Middle Ages, Elias noted that 'this warlike behaviour was considered normal . . . The way the conscience is formed in European societies – and, indeed, in large parts of humanity – in the twentieth century is different. It sets a standard for human behaviour against which the deeds of Nazi Germany appear abhorrent, and are regarded with spontaneous feelings of horror' (1996: 445). Because of the European civilizing process which began in the fifteenth

---

politics remains unclear, but this is one of the central issues at stake in recent discussions about unilateral tendencies in contemporary American foreign policy – and one reason why the analysis of the preconditions of good international citizenship is important. We turn to this last matter in the next chapter.

[43] Wight (1966b: 126) suggests there is some truth in this remark as the following quotation indicates: 'Perhaps modern Europe has acquired a moral sensitiveness, and an awareness of the complexities, denied to simpler civilizations. The Greeks and Romans gave small thought to political ethics, still less to international ethics.' Wight makes this comparison immediately after discussing Churchill's disgust at Stalin's flippant remark or serious suggestion that the German General Staff should be liquidated at the end of World War II. Even so, Elias's portrayal of Ancient Greece is not problem-free. For further discussion, see Shipley (1993) who argues that 'annihilation was rare and usually exemplary' given the interest in exacting tribute from defeated warriors.

century,[44] 'certain minimum rules of civilized conduct [are] generally still observed even in the treatment of prisoners of war. With a few exceptions, a kernel of self-esteem which prevents the senseless torturing of enemies and allows identification with one's enemy in the last instance as another human being, together with compassion for his suffering, did not entirely lapse' even during World War II (Elias 1998a: 114).[45]

As Fletcher (1997: 19) has argued, Elias believed that a significant 'change in attitudes with regard to the perpetration of violent acts causing harm to other people' occurred in Europe from the fifteenth century onwards because of the rise of stable monopolies of power and growing interdependence between the members of society. These phenomena created the need for greater self-restraint in social life and the ability 'to think from the standpoint of the multiplicity of people' (Elias, 1994: 140). This process was much more advanced within states than in relations between them with the result that 'a curious split runs through our civilization': violence within domestic societies is 'tabooed and, when possible, punished' whereas in international relations the perpetrators of violence are 'extremely highly valued, and in many cases praised and rewarded' (Elias, 1996: 177). If there is little in the way of a civilizing process in international relations in Elias's judgement,[46] this is because the 'comparatively strong aversion to the use of force in intra-state relations' is not yet duplicated at the global level (Elias, 1996: 461). Moreover, as two world wars revealed, 'the sensitivity towards killing, towards dying people and death clearly [can evaporate] quite quickly in the majority of

---

[44] The phrase, 'the European civilizing process', is used here to avoid the impression that civilization is somehow uniquely Western. As Goudsblom (1994) notes, Elias observed that all societies contain civilizing processes in that they develop means of dealing with violent outbursts on the part of their members. See Mennell (1996) on ways of applying the idea of civilizing process to Asian societies. It is also important to note that Elias (1996) was well aware that civilizing processes have decivilizing effects. One might argue that the sociology of states-systems is in large part a study of different civilizing and decivilizing processes. This is a theme for future research. Some of these issues are discussed in more detail in Linklater (2004).
[45] Elias's comments pertain to wars within Europe. As Kiernan (1998) and Wesson (1978) have argued, different rules applied in relations with the non-European world.
[46] Elias was perhaps too inclined towards a Hobbesian approach to international relations, and to think that the problem of order would not be solved until there was a world state, although his remarks on the development of cosmopolitan sympathies point in a different direction. For the most part, Elias (1996: 3–4), rather like Wight, thought that states-systems tended towards 'elimination contests' which culminate in the establishment of larger monopolies of power.

people' when security fears run high (Elias, 2001: 51). The question then is whether the normative claims embedded in the dominant principles of international legitimacy promise to heal the 'curious split' that runs through modern civilization. To consider whether these principles do demonstrate a greater aversion to violence, whether they provide the vulnerable with moral resources which they can use to promote global change, and whether they promise further progress in overcoming one of the major tensions within modern civilization, it is useful to return to the four sources of harm described earlier.

Evidence of a global civilizing process is provided by assorted international legal obligations to avoid 'unnecessary suffering' or 'superfluous injury' to individuals in the course of waging war, in the aversion to physical cruelty captured in the idea of crimes against humanity introduced by the Nuremberg Charter, in the erosion of the principle of sovereign immunity, in the establishment of international criminal tribunals, in the movement towards the creation of an International Criminal Court, and in United Nations Security Council resolutions which add rape in war to the list of crimes against humanity. These legal developments enlarge the domain of cosmopolitan or world law which begins with the rights and duties of individuals (as opposed to classical international law which is centred on the rights and duties of territorial states). They are further evidence for the claim that the idea of human equality has a more central place in the normative constitution of the modern states-system and in discourses of legitimation than it had in earlier times (see also Crawford, 2002).[47]

Principles of legitimacy that codify an aversion to physical cruelty have been extended to include acts of violence which governments perpetrate against their own citizens as well as unnecessary harm in the conduct of war or in the establishment of empire (on this last point, see Crawford, 2002). Important changes in the normative constitution of international society are evident in international legal conventions concerning the suppression and punishment of the crime of apartheid, genocide and torture, and in the United Nations *Declaration on the Elimination of Violence against Women*.[48] As noted earlier, each of these

[47] Strong endorsements of the principle of non-combatant immunity in recent international conflicts demonstrate that hegemonic power or claims for exceptionalism are not incompatible with further developments in this area.
[48] See also Armstrong (1993: 78): 'International society has developed a greater sensitivity concerning human rights, racism, colonialism, self-determination, and

legal documents outlaws 'serious bodily or mental harm'. Several also confront the problem of pernicious distinctions between human groups – necessarily because acts of violence and humiliation are often predicated on assumptions about one group's superiority over others.[49] These legal stipulations suggest that the modern states-system is different from its predecessors because of broad commitments to the Kantian principle that a violation of human rights in any part of the world should be felt everywhere, and because of complementary decisions to contract the sphere of domestic jurisdiction accordingly.[50]

On the subject of pernicious distinctions between human beings, it is important to recall Bull and Watson's claim that morally relevant differences between the civilized and the barbarian featured in each of the regional international systems which have come together in recent centuries to form the first truly global international society. A central question about the development of modern international society has been whether the different regional systems have broken with the hierarchical conceptions of human differences which shaped their relations with the outside world over preceding centuries. As we have seen, Bull and Watson maintained that the globalization of

undemocratic practices to a point where they may be said to have amended the general principle of international legitimacy: international society's collective judgement about what it expects from its members for them to qualify for full and undisputed membership.'

[49] Reference to the issue of 'serious bodily or mental harm' to 'national, ethnical, racial or religious groups' in the 1948 *Convention on the Prevention and Punishment of the Crime of Genocide* was made earlier (Evans, 1994: 37). These themes are repeated in the 1993 Statute establishing the tribunal authorized to prosecute persons responsible for violations of international humanitarian law in the former Yugoslavia (Evans, 1994: 393). Also important is Article II of the 1973 *International Convention on the Suppression and Punishment of the Crime of Apartheid*, which condemns efforts to maintain racial supremacy by inflicting 'upon the members of a racial group or groups serious bodily or mental harm by the infringement of their freedom or dignity, or by subjecting them to torture or to cruel, inhuman or degrading treatment or punishment' (Evans, 1994: 218). See also the *Declaration on the Protection of All Persons from Being Subjected to Torture and Other Cruel, Inhuman or Degrading Treatment or Punishment*, in Rodley (1987: Annex 1) and Article 1 of the 1993 United Nations General Resolution adopting the *Declaration on the Elimination of Violence against Women* which defines 'violence against women' as 'any act of gender-based violence that results in, or is likely to result in, physical, sexual or psychological harm or suffering to women, including threats of such acts, coercion or arbitrary deprivation of liberty, whether occurring in public or private life'. On this last point, see Stamatopoulou (1995: 39–40).

[50] Against this, one has to note inaction in the face of genocide in Rwanda and the widespread feeling that this remains one of the great scars on international society because of the failure to take its own moral and legal principles seriously.

the principle of equal sovereignty represented progress in breaking down pernicious distinctions between Europe and the rest of the world; agreements to abolish the slave trade and slavery and to promote the idea of racial equality constituted an advance in seeking to end forms of discrimination based on skin colour (see Vincent, 1984b). One possible implication of Bull and Watson's analysis is that no other states-system has gone as far as modern international society in developing principles of legitimacy which reject efforts to place hierarchical conceptions of human differences at the centre of international order and at the heart of social and political organization in the constituent parts (Bull and Watson, 1984, especially the introduction).[51]

A comparative sociology of states-systems may well reveal that modern international society has progressed beyond its predecessors by developing principles of legitimacy which prohibit excessive violence but the realist or sceptic will be quick to point out that societies of states should not be judged simply in terms of their professed normative commitments. Rousseau's comment about the tension between 'the boundless humanity of our maxims and the boundless cruelty of our deeds' is worth recalling at this point (Rousseau, 1970b: 135–6), as is the gap between ideals and practice exemplified traditionally by the great powers' selective regard for international law. One of the hallmarks of the English School is its belief that principles of legitimacy are not merely decorative but usually constrain state behaviour – breaches of international legal conventions rarely pass unnoticed (see Wheeler: 2000). Principles of international legitimacy are important because they provide moral resources which states, non-governmental organizations and other political actors can use in protests against cruelty or indifference to human suffering (see Hurrell, 1999: 299). From the tension between principle and practice more ambitious efforts to transform international society may grow.[52]

---

[51] More research is needed in this area. It is important to stress that ethnic and cultural hostility seem to have been universal features of international relations, but racial differences in particular have not always had the moral and political significance which they acquired with the rise of the modern world. On this subject, see Lewis (1990). It is important not to congratulate modernity on breaking with forms of racial discrimination which reached their most destructive levels in the twentieth century in modern Europe.

[52] Kant (2002: 429) argued that 'the outcry about man's continually increasing decadence arises for the very reason that we can see further ahead, because we have reached a higher level of morality. We thus pass more severe judgements on what we are, comparing it with what we ought to be, so that our self-reproach increases in

Dominant standards of legitimacy in the modern states-system demonstrate the aversion to violence, and disgust with the notion that pleasure can be derived from cruelty, which Elias believed was the key to the civilizing process in modern Europe. But this is not the only yardstick that can be used to judge different states-systems. It is also important to ask whether the modern states-system is any more advanced than its predecessors in the extent of its moral obligations to those that are most exposed to the harmful consequences of global economic forces and whether it is more refined in its sense of duty to the victims of malnutrition and starvation, however their circumstances may have been caused. Addressing this subject, Elias (1991: 262–3) maintained that 'if humanity can survive the violence of our age' then 'our descendants' might come to think of us as the 'late barbarians'. He added that the affluent regions are more conscious than ever before of large numbers of humanity living on the edge of starvation – 'the feeling of responsibility which people have for each other is certainly minimal, looked at in absolute terms', but it has 'increased' in recent times (Elias, 1996: 26). Somewhat similar sentiments, as noted earlier, are encapsulated in Vincent's statements about the advance of welfare internationalism (see above, pp. 149ff).[53]

The question of whether the modern states-system represents a major historical advance in demonstrating what Hegel called greater 'anxiety for the well-being of humankind as a whole' (quoted in Elias, 1996: 262) cannot be answered then by focusing only on how far prevailing standards of legitimacy deal with the problems of inter- and intra-state violence or with the question of supposedly ontological differences between human groups: it is also important to ask whether these global principles confront the problem of global inequality and deprivation associated with environmental degradation. Of course, the very high levels of interdependence in the modern world compound the problem of making meaningful comparisons between different international systems.[54] What might be suggested, however, is that

---

proportion to the number of stages of morality we have advanced through during the whole of known history.'

[53] Barkan (2000) regards the modern phenomenon of restitutive justice as evidence of the development of a new international morality. Barkan's discussion includes German reparations to the Jewish victims of the Holocaust, the campaign against the Swiss banks regarding 'Nazi gold' and pressure on Japan to apologize and make amends to the 'comfort women'.

[54] But as noted earlier, a comparative analysis of attitudes to slavery might be insightful.

modern principles of legitimacy reveal progress in expanding what O'Neill (2000: 188ff) has called the 'scope of moral concern'. This is to argue that there have been advances in enlarging the circle of those with equal rights to be free from unnecessary violence, and progress in the level of global support for an ethic which puts cruelty first (Shklar, 1984). There has been significantly less progress, however, along a second axis which allows comparisons about the depth as opposed to the scope of moral concern – less progress, that is, in recognizing the right of all human beings to be protected from the disadvantages caused by global economic forces or environmental degradation as well as from the threat or use of violence and deliberate acts of humiliation and degradation.[55]

Matters pertinent to this second axis have not been the most central preoccupations of the English School although Donelan (1990) and Hurrell (1994, 1995) in addition to Vincent have drawn attention to these additional moral challenges confronting contemporary inter-national society – challenges which first became central to social and political thought in the eighteenth century when 'concerns for distant others' developed in tandem with the expansion of global 'commercial society'.[56] No doubt, the relative neglect of these issues by the English School illustrates Jones' point about its intellectual insularity and lack of engagement with political philosophy and international political economy (Jones, 1981). One might note here its broad hostility to Marxist and neo-Marxist perspectives which have been concerned with the unintended harmful consequences of the global capitalist economy rather than with intentional violence committed in warfare or during state formation; and one might also note in passing the importance of the Marxian claim that advances in prohibiting cruelty and in challenging pernicious representations of human differences

---

[55] The crucial point here which has been made in feminist interpretations of human rights is that these have been concerned with 'state-sanctioned or -condoned oppression' which takes place in the public as opposed to the private sphere (see Peters and Wolper, 1995: 2). On the more specific issue of international legal conventions which deal with harms caused by environmental degradation, see Mason (2001).

[56] Donelan (1990: 69–70) addresses the problem of harm in the form of the 'blight of mass tourism' and the 'depletion or pollution of earth, sea and sky'. States, he adds, abet these injuries by indulging corporations. Liberal states are especially culpable through their 'indiscriminate encouragement of most forms of international traffic, regardless of the nuisance caused'. See Tronto (1994: 20 and ch. 2) on changing ethical sensibilities in the eighteenth century as reflected in the ideas of the leading philosophers of the Scottish Enlightenment.

219

have taken place, and not coincidentally, in an era in which affluent Western societies are increasingly free to promote their interests in a manner that exposes an increasing proportion of the human race to the vagaries of a liberalized world economy. The Marxist tradition draws attention then to serious limitations in a global ethic that puts cruelty first.[57] The upshot is that standards of international legitimacy will remain inadequate and incomplete unless progress is made in ending widespread indifference to economic and social vulnerability to global forces in the poorer regions of the world as well as in eradicating excessive force and physical cruelty.[58]

The modern states-system is unique in having to deal with the great diversity of forms of harm caused by war, state-building, invidious distinctions between peoples and relentless economic and cultural globalization. The shifts in human consciousness which Elias regarded as integral to the civilizing process are clearly visible in world politics

---

[57] Marx suggested that the two axes were connected in the following way. His argument was that capitalist globalization had begun to destroy allegedly natural hierarchies of status and rights, and to spread the idea of the free and equal individual across the world. This long-term process of change would mean that human beings would be less likely to suffer cruelty and experience violence on account of their national, racial and other related differences. But the decline in suffering caused by war and national hostilities was connected with the rise of suffering at the hands of the world market. For a contemporary formulation of this thesis, see Geras (1998). The implication of Marx's argument is that 'putting cruelty first' is the logical outcome of the process of constituting human beings as free and equal subjects whose social relations are essentially contractual in nature. It is the rise of contractual relations which makes violence increasingly problematic in modern society, but the ethic of putting cruelty first needs to be complemented by an ethic which addresses harms caused by global economic processes over which nominally free and equal individuals have little or no control. For a summary of Marx's discussion of how individuals acquire greater personal freedom only to become dominated by impersonal forces and 'abstractions', see Linklater (1990a: ch. 2).

[58] It is also important to note how developments within the global political economy affect domestic stability in the less affluent regions of the world. Sadowski (1998) has criticized the belief that the United States should resist the temptation to be drawn into the quagmire of foreign ethnic conflicts on the grounds there is little it can do to end the atavism of tribal hatred. What the stress on irrational or premodern conflicts conveniently overlooks is the extent to which many civil conflicts have been fuelled by global financial institutions and structural adjustment policies which increased economic inequalities in the societies involved. Sadowski's point is the United States and global financial institutions have a moral responsibility to ensure that their policies and decisions do not compound what are often regarded as purely domestic 'ethnic' conflicts. In the terms of the present argument, Sadowski highlights a tendency to believe that societies torn apart by civil conflict have yet to develop liberal prohibitions on cruelty. Affluent societies and powerful international organizations thereby overlook their own failure to develop obligations to the poorer societies which progress in the depth of moral concern requires.

in the construction of standards of legitimacy which are concerned with the use of force and the abuse of human rights. New conceptions of international obligations with respect to environmental, economic and social issues are discernible, but they are still much weaker than the international duties which have developed in these other domains. Sociological analysis of the extent to which societies of states have drawn on the idea of the unity of humankind to reduce unnecessary suffering requires specific inquiries into the principles governing global economic relations in the contemporary world (and not least because of the many ways in which the affluent benefit unfairly from the vulnerability of others).[59] The continuing tension between principle and practice in world affairs leads inevitably to the question of how far dominant economic and political interests need to comply with, and advance, cosmopolitan moral principles in order to shore up their legitimacy. It also raises the question of whether political actors with a cosmopolitan bent can persuade powerful groups to create more demanding cosmopolitan harm conventions and more robust forms of collective implementation and enforcement. The larger point, however, is that analysing the extent to which the modern states-system is unique in developing cosmopolitan principles of legitimacy which prohibit 'serious mental and bodily harm' – and reflecting on the extent to which this commitment stretches across all sectors of international economic and political life – is a novel way of building on the sociology of states-systems which the British Committee inaugurated four decades ago.

Conclusion

The argument of this chapter has been that two different sociological approaches to long-term processes of change in states-systems can be developed from the intellectual resources of the English School. The dominant approach focuses on how different international systems have sought to preserve order between independent political communities. Its advocates stress that no society of states has ever succeeded in eradicating inter-state violence. War destroyed all previous societies of states, and it would seem to have been Wight's view that war will

---

[59] Gonzalez-Pelaez and Buzan (2003: 327ff) are exemplary in describing 'the normative evolution of the right to food within international society'.

most probably destroy the modern international order. An alternative, Kantian approach can also be derived from the English School's sociology of states-systems. The task here is to develop Wight's interest in the extent to which cosmopolitan principles influenced the development of states-systems; more specifically it is to analyse different commitments to establishing cosmopolitan harm conventions which express the sense of membership of a universal moral community. Whether the modern states-system has made significant progress in creating cosmopolitan conventions which are designed to protect individuals and non-sovereign communities from unnecessary harm is a central question for the Kantian approach. Virtually uncharted territory, this is one way of building on the intellectual legacy of the British Committee.

This approach to the sociology of states-systems leads inevitably to an analysis of foreign policy behaviour, and especially to an inquiry into principles which promise to reduce the gulf between ethical ideals and political practice and also to realize the normative possibilities that are latent within the modern states-system. The question of what states can do to create a more just international order was central to Kant's radicalized rationalism. It has been central to recent English School discussions of ethics and foreign policy which focus on the nature of and prospects for 'good international citizenship'. These are matters to consider in Chapter 7.

7 The good international citizen and the transformation of international society

In an important essay on the balance of power Butterfield (1966a: 147) maintained 'that an international order is not a thing bestowed upon by nature, but is a matter of refined thought, careful contrivance and elaborate artifice. At best it is a precarious thing, and though it seems so abstract it requires the same kind of loyalty, the same constant attention, that people give to their country or to the other private causes which only the international order enables them to follow.' Elsewhere he observed that what a historical survey of societies of states provides is 'an impression of the tremendous difficulty of actually creating an international order where no firm basis for it previously existed. It looks as though (in the conditions of the past at least) a states-system can only be achieved by a tremendous *conscious* effort of reassembly after a political hegemony has broken down' (quoted in Dunne, 1998: 125–6). Once established, international orders have faced the difficult challenge of how to admit 'new units', the best-known example being the way the Western powers dealt with pressures from Turkey, China, Japan and the former colonial territories to join international society during the twentieth century.

These comments illustrate the differences between the English School analysis of international society and the neo-realist approach to the international system – in particular, their very different conceptions of the importance of agency in world affairs. Neo-realists stress the extent to which political units are compelled by the anarchic structure of international relations to behave in such a way as to reproduce the states-system. As Butterfield's comments indicate, the English School does not take the view that international society is more or less bound to be reproduced indefinitely. Its members are more inclined to stress the great powers' ability to weaken or destroy

223

that society than to dwell on the respects in which anarchy forces states to behave in much the same manner. The claim that the society of states owes its existence to the 'tremendous conscious effort' of states calls attention to the comparative rarity of states-systems, their susceptibility to violence, and the recurrent problem of ensuring compliance with global agreements in the context of anarchy.[1] For these reasons, the English School has been understandably keen to emphasize the crucial role of human agency not only for preserving delicate global arrangements but also in adapting them to ever-changing circumstances.[2]

As noted in Chapter 2, the English School has been centrally concerned with structural, functional and historical analyses of international society. None of these is interested in developing a global ethic from which it is possible to derive practical recommendations about how states should behave. However, the rudiments of such an ethic from which it is possible to derive moral judgements about right conduct in foreign policy and appropriate responsibilities to international society are implicit in its overall approach. Identifying its key elements is the principal aim of this chapter.

There may be objections to the claim that the English School has an implicit ethical position on what it means for states to be responsible members of international society underestimates the seriousness of, for example, Bull's aspiration for value-free analysis. It might be argued that when he maintains that states should respect certain principles and practices with a view to preserving international order, he advocates hypothetical rather than categorical imperatives in Kant's use of these terms. Hypothetical imperatives according to Kant have a conditional status. They have instrumental value; agents only need to comply with them if they wish to achieve particular ends. In contrast, categorical imperatives are unconditionally binding; their claim on agents does not depend on the contingent fact that they

---

[1] The compliance problem is a central feature of neo-liberal institutionalism which, reflecting the influence of neo-realism, seeks to explain how cooperation is possible between rational egotists (see Chapter 4). Members of the English School do not start with the postulate of rational egoism but with the assumption that state behaviour is always moderated, at least to some extent, by the existence of international society. The English School locates the compliance problem, then, within a different theoretical system.

[2] For a recent discussion of foreign policy agency which stresses the importance of responsibility to the members of the national community and to 'a perceived community of a much wider ambit', see Hill (2003: ch. 1).

happen to want particular goals.[3] If we apply this distinction to reflect on the principle of respect for sovereignty, it would appear that this is a hypothetical imperative for Bull; it is contingent on the fact that independent political communities want to preserve their separateness and also attach great value to international order; respect for sovereignty would lose its importance if states were to decide at some future point to replace the international states-system with a world political authority to which they willingly transferred many of their powers. For Bull, then, sovereignty is not an unconditional value or an eternal political ideal.

Vincent (1986a) maintained that the development of an international obligation to end starvation and malnutrition could strengthen international society: it could help overcome some of the differences between North and South, and it could bring Western capitalist democracies and state socialist societies together in a global political project which recovered for modern times the humanitarian spirit which animated the attempt to eradicate slavery in the nineteenth century. But Vincent did not regard cooperation to end starvation as only a hypothetical imperative which states should follow because they wanted to preserve international order. The right to be free from starvation is a fundamental human right in his view. Although he did not draw on Kantian terminology to describe his perspective, collective action to secure that human right is a categorical rather than (or in addition to) a hypothetical imperative.

At the time of its publication, Vincent's book on human rights was unusual within the English School in foregrounding such ethical claims, but it would be erroneous to think that all of the principles and practices which feature in Bull's own analysis of the preconditions of international order are reducible to hypothetical imperatives. As we have seen, his contention that order between states is an important value in current circumstances but far from a permanent ethical ideal does seem to come with the implication that respect for national sovereignty is a hypothetical imperative. But the fact there is no alternative to the multi-state order at the present time appears to have stronger implications for Bull, namely that national representatives have important legal and moral obligations to preserve and

---

[3] To explain, attending lectures is a hypothetical imperative, contingent on the desire to obtain a good degree. Respecting others as ends in themselves is a categorical imperative which is not contingent on the existence of such ends.

strengthen an international society which, in Butterfield's words, 're-quires the same kind of loyalty, the same constant attention, that people give to their country or to the other private causes which only the international order enables them to follow' (see above, p. 223). The moral significance of international order for Bull is strengthened by his claim that it should be valued not only for its own sake but also because it contributes to world order which has higher ethical stand-ing in his view. Bull's comments about the poverty of the super-powers' moral imagination, and his writings on the need to combine order with global social justice, are further evidence of the strong ethi-cal commitments running through his analysis of modern international society.

Bull maintained that order was only one value worth promoting in international relations – on occasion the commitment to order might be overridden by other considerations such as the desire to advance justice. In making this claim, Bull offered an empirical observation about the moral principles which influence state behaviour: he did not advance a normative judgement about how states should act (see Chapter 3). Bearing in mind his belief that moral philosophers are unlikely to succeed where diplomats have repeatedly failed – that is, in developing a moral code which is acceptable to all or most socie-ties – it is unsurprising that he did not share Walzer's enthusiasm for reflecting on the moral principles which should weigh most heav-ily on the minds of actors confronting questions of 'just and unjust wars'.[4] In an interesting passage Bull (2002: 266) briefly referred to a sociological project which aims to identify trends running counter to the existing order of things – a project with obvious affinities to a critical investigation of immanent possibilities in international society – but he did not develop an approach that so clearly complements ethical claims about the duty to work for the establishment of a world community which exist elsewhere in the same work.[5] One must look to a new generation of writers in the English School – strongly influenced

---

[4] The reference here is to Walzer (1980). In his review of that work, Bull commented on the lack of a coherent moral and political philosophy, a point that can be made about Bull's own work, as Vincent (1990b: 48) argued.

[5] Bull (2002: 266) associated this approach with the writings of Richard Falk. Bull was quick to add that the problem with it is that it runs descriptive and prescriptive analysis together. Moreover, 'trends making against the states system may be strengthened by being recognised and dramatised but only so far; there are certain realities which will persist whatever attitude we take up towards them'. The nature of these 'realities' which will persist whatever we think of them is not specified.

by the solidarist tendencies in Bull and Vincent's last writings – for a discussion of what the good international citizen can do to promote the transformation of world politics (see Wheeler and Dunne, 1998, 2001). The question of how the good international citizen can release existing potentialities in world politics and, in so doing, reduce and eradicate human suffering (particularly suffering caused by the gross violation of human rights) is a central dimension of their 'critical international society' approach.[6]

It is worth pausing at this moment to make some comments about the idea of good international citizenship, an expression which was first used in Australia in the late 1980s by the then foreign minister, Senator Gareth Evans, to describe a vision of a more internationalist Australian foreign policy in which the promotion of legitimate national interests and goals would be moderated by what Bull (1973) called 'purposes beyond ourselves'. Wheeler and Dunne (1998: 856) have argued that the idea of good international citizenship 'can clearly be placed within the international society tradition or English School'; they connect it with Bull's liberal conviction that one of the state's principal global responsibilities is to strive to reconcile the need for order with the desire for justice. For several years, the idea of good international citizenship has been central to their writings on morality and world affairs which include a critical appraisal of the first Blair Government's commitment to strengthening the ethical dimension of foreign policy. There is perhaps a danger in these writings that good international citizenship may seem to be the private property of advocates of the solidarist conception of international society. But if the idea of good international citizenship belongs to 'the international society tradition' as a whole, then the proponents of the pluralist conception of international society have every right to harness the concept to their cause (see Jackson, 2000: 114). Solidarists are not alone then, in having, or being able, to develop an account of what it means for a state to be a good international citizen. With this point in mind, the present chapter will suggest that a systematic position on ethics and foreign policy can be extracted from the pluralist's belief in the cardinal importance of sovereignty and the principle of non-intervention in global politics (and from deep scepticism about

---

[6] See in this context Adorno's reference to 'the need to lend a voice to suffering' and Horkheimer's plea for solidarity which takes the form of 'universal compassion among all suffering creatures', quoted in D. Rasmussen (ed.), *The Handbook of Critical Theory*, Blackwell, Oxford, 1999, pp. 150 and 196.

the possibility of progress in world affairs).[7] Bull (1966b: 73; 2002: 232) took the view in the 1960s and 1970s that the solidarist conception of international society was 'premature', although his position is often said to have become more solidarist in his last writings. Along with Vincent's work on human rights, Bull's more explicit normative standpoint has been the starting point for recent efforts to use the idea of good international citizenship to develop the case for a solidarist international society. This chapter aims to build on these developments.[8]

Prior to the explosion of interest in human rights in the 1970s and 1980s, the English School was mainly concerned with defending prudence in foreign policy, and this remains a central theme in contemporary pluralist international theory (see Jackson 2000: ch. 7). This emphasis on the virtues of prudence is best seen in conjunction with Wight's claim that most states recognize that they are answerable to three separate moral constituencies (conationals, international society and humanity), a claim which Jackson develops in his analysis of the state's need to balance national, international and humanitarian responsibilities.[9] Many of the more important developments within the English School over the past twenty years – and some of the most instructive debates between its members – have revolved around the question of whether there was less need for scepticism and caution in foreign policy in the immediate aftermath of the collapse of bipolarity and whether it is realistic to expect foreign policy makers to add more onerous humanitarian responsibilities to existing national and international obligations. It is hardly surprising that the English School emphasized the importance of national responsibilities to international society in periods when superpower rivalries demonstrated the centrality of more parochial concerns. Geopolitical competition did not augur well for major diplomatic breakthroughs at the level of humanitarian responsibilities. No doubt this reinforced Bull's

---

[7] See Jackson (ibid.) for a related argument.

[8] It should be noted that pluralism and solidarism are used in this chapter to describe normative positions on how international society should be organized. This usage is now firmly embedded in the literature, as earlier comments about Jackson's defence of pluralism and Wheeler's defence of solidarism reveal (see Chapter 4). Whether this is strictly in keeping with Bull's use of these terms is a matter which was discussed in Chapter 1.

[9] Wight (1991: 69ff). See Jackson (1995) on the three types of responsibility, increased (in Jackson 2000: 169–78) to include the important, new 'responsibility for the global commons'.

conviction that normative international theory was a diversion from the empirical task of understanding challenges to, and changes in, the contemporary society of states (although it should be noted that members of the World Order Models Project were not so timid about reflecting on the ethical principles which should inform foreign policy even in such unpropitious circumstances).[10] Vincent's defence of human rights in the 1980s, and Wheeler's discussion of the importance of the principle of non-combatant immunity in recent years, maintained an emphasis on the prospects for strengthening humanitarian responsibilities at a time when many may have thought that the central challenge is to defend pluralist arrangements from challenges emanating from the short-sighted pursuit of national security objectives (Vincent 1986a; Wheeler 2002, 2003).

In the period since Bull and Vincent commented on the improved prospects for solidarism, interest in international ethics and support for increased humanitarian responsibilities has grown dramatically. Various features of the post-bipolar era encouraged the development of normative approaches to foreign policy and world politics. Among the more important are the seeming obsolescence of force in the core areas of the world-system; widening global inequalities and corresponding popular demands for global justice and humane global governance; the growing importance of international civil society actors committed to human rights as well as to obligations to future generations, the natural environment and non-human species; movements in the politics of recognition exemplified by various changes in international law which signify progress in thinking that international society should respect the rights of indigenous peoples and minority nations; and, finally, as the establishment of war crimes tribunals following conflicts in the former Yugoslavia and Rwanda and the creation of an International Criminal Court reveal, the creation of new legal institutions for punishing violations of international humanitarian law. Such global developments have applied great pressure to the idea that states cannot advance significantly beyond a pluralist conception of good international citizenship although, as noted in Chapter 4, the English School is still sharply divided over the extent to which solidarism remains premature.[11]

---

[10] See, in particular, the pioneering discussion in Johansen (1980).

[11] Here it is important to recall Jackson's critique of the solidarist defence of human rights where humanitarian intervention to end human rights abuses is thought to be

Many of the global changes which have occurred since the end of the bipolar era have encouraged some members of the English School to analyse the nature of good international citizenship and to defend humanitarian responsibilities which go significantly beyond Bull and Vincent's cautiously solidarist statements in the 1980s. A striking illustration of Wheeler and Dunne's argument is that good international citizens have a responsibility to use force to 'prevent or stop genocide and mass murder' – an obligation which is best discharged by multilateral action authorized by the United Nations. In a major departure from Bull and Vincent's position, they add that the good international citizen can exercise the right to act alone 'in exceptional cases' even though unilateralism 'weakens the rule of law in the society of states' (Wheeler and Dunne, 1998: 869). Recognizing the danger that intervening states usually prefer to risk increased civilian casualties in the target state rather than endanger the lives of their military personnel, they advance the highly controversial point that in 'killing to defend human rights, the good international citizen must be prepared to ask its soldiers to risk and, if necessary, lose their lives to stop crimes against humanity' (Wheeler and Dunne, 2000: 184). This is by far the strongest argument for upgrading humanitarian responsibilities relative to national and international obligations which has been put forward by representatives of solidarism in recent times. The notion that good international citizenship requires this form of self-sacrifice goes well beyond the English School's traditional thinking about such matters – and many would argue, with recent wars and interventions in mind, far beyond what is currently achievable in practice.

Writing about British foreign policy, Wheeler and Dunne (1998: 856) refer to Bull's argument that solidarists believe that states should be

more important than preserving order between the great powers (see above, p. 175). From the pluralist vantage point, it is easy to exaggerate the importance of the end of bipolarity, and many would argue that the pluralist ethic needs to be restated in the light of the relaxation of earlier constraints on intervention, NATO's decision to wage 'humanitarian war' without the consent of the United Nations Security Council, and the current realities of American military superiority and ensuing unilateralist tendencies. But as noted in Chapter 4, recent events in world politics have also strengthened solidarist commitments in various parts of the world. There is no obvious rationale for concluding that recent developments demonstrate the priority of defending pluralist arrangements rather than intensifying solidarist commitments in response to hegemonic strategies and inclinations.

'burdened with the guardianship of human rights everywhere'; they argue that this is 'the litmus test for judging Britain as a good international citizen'. The pluralist will reply that the problem with this formulation is that there are circumstances when the promotion of human rights clashes with vital national goals and with international order. Wheeler and Dunne recognize the force behind Bull's argument that foreign policy makers regularly confront 'agonising choices' and can only realize some values by sacrificing others of comparable importance. The upshot of Bull's point is that the good international citizen must guard against the temptation to make any single ethical value, such as the protection of human rights, the litmus test of an ethical foreign policy. An alternative starting point is that aspiring good international citizens have to conduct relations with very different types of states occupying a number of different points along a spectrum that stretches from 'amity to enmity' (Wolfers, 1962b). It is important that the analysis of good international citizenship reflects the fact that foreign policy has to deal with such diversity which now includes the threats that a new distinct breed of terrorist organization poses to national and personal security.

It has been argued elsewhere that the modern society of states remains essentially pluralist in character although solidarism has become a prominent theme in relations between core liberal-democratic powers and also in the standpoints they adopt in their dealings with the rest of the world. It was also argued that 'neo-medieval' or 'post-Westphalian' themes are particularly important in the European Union where the link between nation and state, and attachments to territorial sovereignty, are less strong than they were only half a century ago (Linklater, 1998: ch. 6). It follows that liberal-democratic societies which aspire to be good international citizens must develop principles of foreign policy which are relevant to relations with very different types of state. Some will be actual or potential adversaries; some will be strongly committed to pluralist principles of international relations and therefore hostile to external interference in domestic affairs; some, attached to solidarism, may have relinquished some traditional monopoly powers to substate and transnational authorities.[12]

---

[12] This is not to suggest that only liberal-democratic states can be good international citizens. In the following discussion, however, the emphasis will be on their international obligations.

Mindful of such diversity, this chapter builds on recent reflections on the good international citizen. Part one considers the principles of good international citizenship which are relevant to a condition in which great power rivalries suggest that agreement on pluralist rules of coexistence, or on some basic international harm conventions, is all that can reasonably be hoped for. Part two turns to the principles of good international citizenship where like-minded states are capable of progressing beyond a pluralist contract to a solidarist agreement to establish cosmopolitan harm conventions which protect individuals and non-sovereign communities from unnecessary suffering. Part three reflects on the principles of good international citizenship which apply in circumstances where societies which are evolving in a broadly solidarist direction have relations with weaker societies which are committed to pluralism and which resent or fear efforts to make them comply with what they see as alien notions of human rights. Although rather different principles of good international citizenship are required in these varied circumstances, one theme unites them. This is the ethical aspiration to build a global community that institutionalizes respect for the harm principle and grants all human beings the right to express their concerns and fears about injury, vulnerability and suffering.

Two additional points need to be made before proceeding further. First, the central objective of this chapter is to consider principles of foreign policy which can promote the moral ideal of the unity of humankind without jeopardizing international order. To proceed in this manner is to stress the continuing relevance of Kant's philosophy of international relations for the project of radicalizing rationalism. It is to note how his analysis of the maxims of an ethical foreign policy had no illusions about the scale of the achievement involved in creating order between states or about the obstacles to adding cosmopolitan harm conventions – notably in the sphere of human rights – to pluralist rules of coexistence.[13] Of course, sceptics will doubt the value of endeavouring to systematize principles of good international citizenship in the manner of Kant's essay on *Perpetual Peace*. Such a project may seem utopian to those who wish to emphasize the need for flexibility in foreign policy and the naivety of supposing that national governments can be bound by one set of ethical rules and principles. But it is

---

[13] Kant (1970b: 200ff) identified six 'preliminary articles of perpetual peace' or six principles of good international citizenship.

important not to press this objection too far. An absolutely crucial distinction exists between an approach to foreign policy which holds that 'everything is permitted' under conditions of national insecurity and an approach which endeavours to set out basic *prima facie* international and humanitarian responsibilities. The notion of *prima facie* obligations recognizes that diplomacy is a complex practical activity in which difficult and often controversial judgements have to be made (frequently under conditions of great uncertainty) about the relative importance of national, international and humanitarian responsibilities and values.[14] We return to this theme later.

The second point is some neo-Kantian philosophers have used the notion of *prima facie* obligations, including the duty not to harm others, to avoid the ethical rigorism which many detect in Kant's moral philosophy (see above, p. 169). Neo-Kantians such as Ross (1930) argued that obligations such as the duty of non-maleficence are *prima facie* duties because they may clash with, and have to yield to, other moral principles. In the case of a conflict between the right of self-defence and the duty not to harm others, the first principle may prevail (subject to the condition that action taken in self-defence is not disproportionate to the threat posed). The crucial point here, as this example and the proviso indicate, is that the burden of proof falls on the agent who violates a *prima facie* moral obligation to show that the breach of a normally binding principle can be justified. The argument of this chapter is that this neo-Kantian approach can contribute to the English School's use of the idea of good international citizenship to reflect on the prospects for an ethical foreign policy. Returning to an earlier theme, the notion of good international citizenship recognizes the importance of agency in world politics, specifically, the decisive role that states have in determining the relationship between national, international and humanitarian responsibilities in the society of states. The task of foreign policy, it might be argued along Kantian lines, is to develop support for international and humanitarian responsibilities, wherever possible, including respect for the *prima facie* duty to

---

[14] One might add that the rationalist in the Grotian sense is deeply hostile to 'rationalism in politics' in the Oakeshottian sense which involves the mechanical application of principles to worldly affairs. See Oakeshott (1974: ch. 1). As noted earlier, Kant's distinction between principles which 'are valid without distinction of circumstances' and principles 'which have a certain subjective breadth in respect of their application' also implies hostility to rationalism in the sense of applying moral principles without regard for context and consequence.

avoid harm; the parallel task of a critical inquiry into foreign policy behaviour is to ascertain, given the options available to them, whether states make decisions which balance the pursuit of their own legitimate interests with their moral responsibilities not to harm other peoples.

Pluralism and beyond

Rousseau (1968b: 247) asked, What would be the point of being a citizen of a particular state, if foreigners could claim the same legal and political rights? The upshot of Rousseau's remark is that the state's principal obligations are to its own citizens and not to the members of other societies. Starting with this premise, many varieties of realism have denied that states have any duties towards other peoples unless national goals benefit from honouring international obligations. Characteristically, Machiavelli argued that when the safety of the country is at stake 'no attention should be paid either to justice or injustice' or 'to kindness or cruelty, or to its being praiseworthy or ignominious' (quoted in Wight, 1991: 248). Wight (1991: 253) suggested that revolutionists 'can be expected to be as opportunistic' as such realists, and one frequently discovers that exponents of these different perspectives are united in the belief that 'the end justifies the means'. In an intriguing passage, Wight (1991: 242) distinguished the rationalist position on international ethics from these other perspectives by linking it with an ethic of justice as opposed to an ethic of charity in world affairs. The ethic of justice followed logically, in his view, from the belief that the state is a trustee for its citizens, and is obliged to think first about their welfare. From this standpoint, 'it is admirable for an individual to give away his money for philanthropic purposes, but not for the trustee to give away the money of his ward . . . The trustee should not be indifferent to the rights of others besides his ward, and it would be wrong for him to seek to gain more than the ward is entitled to in strict justice.' Applied to statecraft, this principle led to the view that states 'are there to secure the interests of the peoples they serve; they should respect the rights of other states and not seek to gain more for their people than is just, but they are bound also not to give away anything that their people may in justice claim. Governments cannot be expected to act continuously on any other grounds than national interest tempered by justice, and they have no right to do so, being agents and not principals. Hence it follows that the Rationalist tradition affirms a double standard of morality: the ethic of charity in private morality; the ethic of justice in state morality. This is not to say that private morality is moral and state morality is immoral; the validity of the ethical is maintained in both fields' (Wight, 1991: 242).

Wight's claim that special ties between citizens should not lead to indifference 'to the rights of others' is the rationalist counterpart of Warnock's argument that human associations should be acutely aware that 'limited sympathies' can have damaging effects on the members of other societies (see above, p. 177). One implication of this moral stand-point for the current discussion is that the negative duty of non-maleficence is a fundamental obligation of the good international citizen.[15] The special ties that bind the state to its ward place essential limits on acts of charity towards the outside world although, according to Wight's formulation of the rationalist position on morality and foreign policy, they do not permit violations of the ethic of justice. It is worth noting here important differences between Wight's position and Jackson's claim that the 'first duty of a government is to protect its own people. After that it can try to help whomever else it can' (Jackson, 1995: 122). Taken literally – and admittedly this may not be Jackson's intention – this formulation implies that states need only give consideration to the interests of the members of other societies when they have done all they can to assist their citizens. It follows that in war a state need only think about the suffering it inflicts on another people (non-combatants as well as combatants) when it has done everything in its power to secure the interests of its own population. What is missing from this theme is the recognition that the trustee has, in Wight's terms, duties not to 'gain more for their people than is just'. On this view, duties to safeguard the interests of one's population do not allow national governments to impose terrible costs on outsiders.[16]

---

[15] See Warnock (1971: esp ch . 2 and 80ff) on the claim that a duty of non-maleficence is 'a' but not 'the' foundation of morality. Warnock adds benevolence, fairness and the duty not to deceive to his list of universal moral principles. Warnock's claims about ethical universality can be found at pp. 147–50. For a related discussion influenced by Warnock, see Mackie (1977: part two).

[16] Wight (2004: 33) refers to the moral maze that exists where decisions must be made about whether to kill civilians and indeed what proportion can be killed 'without exceeding the bounds of necessity'. It is interesting to note how Wight characterizes the three traditions of international thought with respect to the 'maze in which we are lost' in such circumstances. Grotius, he adds, 'reflects more accurately this morally multidimensional character of our experience than, arguably, any other writer on the subject . . . To simplify crudely: if you are apt to think the moral problems of international politics are simple, you are a natural, instinctive Kantian; if you think they

These duties find expression in international legal conventions which prohibit unnecessary cruelty in war.[17]

The belief that each government's 'first duty . . . to protect its own people' and then to 'try to help whomever else it can' does not give the harm principle the importance it deserves from the standpoint of an ethic of justice. It does not consider whether in the course of doing the best for its citizens, the state poses unreasonable costs on other peoples – in times of war, for example – and whether dubious claims about necessity are advanced in the process.[18] However, the question for many is whether the demands of an ethical commitment to avoid unnecessary suffering go far enough. Kant, it was noted earlier, believed that moral agents have positive duties of benevolence as well as negative duties to avoid harming others (see above, p. 171). Geras (1998: 49ff) criticizes the harm principle because its emphasis is solely on avoiding harm; it does not defend forms of universal solidarity which create obligations to rescue the victims of genocide. Within the English School, Dunne and Wheeler endorse a similar notion of universal solidarity when they argue that the good international citizen should be prepared to risk the lives of co-nationals in order 'to stop crimes against humanity'. As Kant (see Cummiskey, 1996) and Geras (1998) recognize, complex questions arise here about the extent to which moral agents can be expected to put themselves at risk for the sake of others. The widespread belief that obligations to rescue others are not open-ended informs the distinction between heroism and justice. But wherever one wishes to draw the line between charity and justice, the reality is that states usually act on the assumption that national responsibilities have priority over international and humanitarian obligations. When national security is at risk, states have often argued that there is no choice but to arrange obligations in a hierarchy

are non-existent, bogus, or delusory, you are a natural Machiavellian; if you are apt to think them infinitely complex, bewildering, and perplexing, you are probably a natural Grotian.'

[17] The harm principle has the advantage over the notion of 'citizens first, foreigners second' because it foregrounds the duty to respect the principle of non-combatant immunity in war and to hold conationals accountable for violations of the law of war. Taken literally, the doctrine of 'citizens first' clashes with the idea that conationals should be punished for war crimes. But in such cases, the overriding moral obligation is to ensure justice for the victims of war crimes rather than to protect conationals.

[18] Walzer (1980) contains an exemplary critical analysis of necessity claims with respect to the strategic bombing of German cities and the use of the A-bomb against Hiroshima and Nagasaki. Butler (2004) provides a critique of the indefinite detention of terrorist suspects on the grounds of necessity.

of this kind. But this does not mean that the question of what it means to be a good international citizen is redundant in such circumstances (see Linklater, 1990b). As noted earlier, necessity claims must always be analysed, debated and possibly rejected when the argument is made that national security must override other responsibilities.[19]

It is possible to identify a number of principles of good international citizenship which are relevant to a condition in which adversaries seek to make progress beyond relations which are purely strategic in nature or where there is hope of preserving the moral life from excessive claims about necessity (see above, pp. 123ff). The question is what a commitment to the harm principle entails in a world in which the establishment of a pluralist international order would constitute a major achievement. We can then ask how the harm principle can be embodied in forms of good international citizenship which explore the possibilities for building more demanding international and humanitarian responsibilities into the society of states. A central task is to consider how foreign policy commitments not to be 'indifferent to the rights of others besides [one's] ward' or 'to seek to gain more than the ward is entitled to in strict justice' can be embodied in forms of international society which are increasingly cosmopolitan in the terms described in Chapter 5.

This is not the occasion on which to try to list all the principles of good international citizenship which might guide foreign policy in circumstances where it is possible to make progress beyond purely strategic orientations. However, such a list should include: (1) the need for restraint in the pursuit of national objectives; (2) respect for the principle of reciprocity; (3) recognition of the existence of the security

---

[19] The analysis of necessity claims is a major element in Thucydides' history of the Peloponnesian war, particularly in his commentaries on the Melian Debate and the Mytilenean Dialogue. Indeed, one can regard his history as an analysis of the steady inflation of necessity claims to justify violations of the earlier conventions of war. Thucydides stressed that there is scope for moral deliberation where necessity is thought to dictate policy; he also analysed how the expansion of necessity claims led to the brutalization of Hellenic international relations. The scrutiny of necessity claims – especially when they are advanced by the great powers – is crucial then to the survival of international society. The significance of these themes for the current juncture of world politics will be apparent. Pouncey (1980) is a useful study of Thucydides' account of the 'decivilizing' effects of the arguments that were made from necessity during the war between Athens and Sparta. It also highlights Thucydides' belief that these destructive tendencies cannot be eradicated from relations between states, hence his claim that his history of the war was not a study of unique political circumstances, but a possession forever.

dilemma – specifically of how actions which are not intended to intimidate can generate fear and distrust;[20] (4) the commitment to a fair balance between national security and insecurity in the knowledge that a high level of security for one state will mean insecurity for others in conditions of fear and distrust.[21] A system of states which succeeds in building such principles into the conduct of foreign policy has made important progress towards a pluralist international society, albeit one that is heavily biased in favour of the dominant powers and indifferent to the interests of smaller states and minority peoples and to the victims of human rights abuses within national borders (see above, pp. 127ff). A central theme in the English School is that states can exercise 'foreign policy agency' to transcend this condition (Hill, 2003). Additional principles of good international citizenship can be used to create foreign policy orientations which aim to advance order and civility.

It is possible to derive several principles of good international citizenship from the English School's analysis of the pluralist conception of international society. Again, the following list is not exhaustive but it may be sufficiently comprehensive to capture key governing principles of a pluralist international order considered as an ideal-type. Principles of good international citizenship which enable states to make progress together in creating and maintaining pluralist arrangements include: (1) states are the basic members of international society; (2) all societies have a right to a separate existence subject to the need to maintain the balance of power; (3) intervention in the internal affairs of member states to promote some vision of human decency or human justice is prohibited; (4) states should relinquish the goal of acquiring preponderant power in the international system; (5) the duty to cooperate to maintain an equilibrium of power is incumbent on all states;[22] (6) diplomatic efforts to reconcile competing interests should proceed from the assumption that each state is the best

---

[20] Butterfield maintained the security dilemma arises where states, which mean 'no harm' to others and 'want nothing . . . save guarantees for [their] own safety', fail to appreciate the other's 'counter-fear' and lack of 'assurance of . . . intentions' (quoted in Dunne, 1998: 77).
[21] See Kissinger (1979) for a discussion of this theme in relations between the United States and the Soviet Union.
[22] Bull (2002: ch. 4) notes that this principle has often overridden the equal right of states to a separate existence in modern international society.

judge of its own interests;[23] (7) an 'inclusive' as opposed to 'exclusive' conception of the national interest should be pursued so that other states, and the society to which they belong, are not harmed for the sake of trivial national advantages;[24] (8) because of their unique military capabilities the great powers should assume special responsibilities which are determined by mutual consent for preserving international order;[25] (9) an essential purpose of an 'inclusive' foreign policy is to make changes to international society which will satisfy the legitimate interests of rising powers and new member states;[26] (10) force is justified in self-defence and in response to states that seek preponderant power;[27] and (11) proportionality in war should be

---

[23] Wight (1991: 120) argued that Kennan's claim that 'we should have the modesty to admit that our own national interest is all that we are really capable of knowing and understanding' is at the 'heart of Rationalist country'. Kennan was singled out as a figure who 'stands out in the public life of the West as a foreign policy publicist who was most scrupulous and respectful in considering the interests of Russia'. See also Wight (1991: 191). The English School's hermeneutic orientation is especially evident in the contention that one of the purposes of diplomacy is to endeavour to understand how the world appears from the vantage point of others (see Linklater, 1990a: ch. 1; Shapcott, 1994: Epp, 1998). Wight's remark about the importance of assuming that states are the best judge of their own interests might be said to encapsulate Vattel's claim that states should conduct war on the understanding that there is justice on both sides.

[24] Illustrating the point, Wight (1991: 123) argued that 'the difference between Chamberlain and Churchill . . . is that between an exclusive and inclusive conception of national interest'. For Chamberlain, Czechoslovakia was 'a far-away people of whom we know nothing'; for Churchill, she is one of the 'famous and ancient states of Europe' whose interests coincided with our own. Wight saw the 'refusal to exploit an advantage' and 'restraint in the exercise of power' as central to an inclusive foreign policy. See Wight (1966b: 129).

[25] For further discussion, see Bull (2002: ch. 9) on the great powers.

[26] This is a central theme in Bull and Watson (1984). The need for diplomatic inventiveness when dealing with new states or a new distribution of power was a central theme in Butterfield's writings, as noted in the introduction to the present chapter. Debates within the United States in the 1970s over whether the Soviet Union was a conservative or revolutionary power, and earlier debates about the motives and pliability of Nazi Germany, demonstrate the immense difficulties which arise here, and the painful choices which often await policy-makers. Of course, assembling general maxims of foreign policy is no substitute for practical wisdom in such circumstances. However, the importance of the sixth principle of good international citizenship is underlined by Wight's comment on Sir John Slessor's view that 'if the Russians wanted war [then] we should not allow our strategy to be deflected by weak-kneed fear of provoking them, or refrain from the use of force for fear of it leading to general war'. Wight (1991: 194) protested, 'This is the obverse of the Grotian's attempt to get inside and appreciate the other man's interests. It assumes a hostility and irreconcilability of views, discounting the other side's views in advance.'

[27] As recent events remind us, complex questions arise about when the intention to harm can be assumed, and a pre-emptive strike or preventive war is justified. It is useful to recall Grotius on the 'doctrine contrary to every principle of equity that justice allows us to resort to force in order to injure another merely because there is a possibility that

respected along with the principle that defeated powers should be readmitted as equals into international society.[28]

Vincent's claim that international politics is not a realm character-ized by 'the absence of morality' but is certainly one in which morality has very definite 'limits' is supported by this list of principles of good international citizenship (Vincent, 1986a: 114). The key point is that states can take the initiative in creating 'morality in the narrow sense' which provides 'a counterpoise to selfishness or excessively narrow sympathies' (Mackie, 1977: 134ff). Three moral deficits which are in-herent in what Vincent (1986a: 113ff) called 'the morality of states' were discussed in Chapter 4; they highlight the limitations of good international citizenship in pluralist conditions (the deficits are that its principles are centrally concerned with the prevention of harm to the great powers so small states have no guarantee of freedom from partition for the sake of the balance of power; non-sovereign commu-nities do not have moral standing in international society; harm that befalls individuals – human rights abuses for example – do not trouble the society of states as a whole). In short, the primary objective of maintaining order between the great powers is perfectly compatible with indifference to many forms of human suffering. Principles of good international citizenship in a pluralist international society are concerned with creating and preserving international harm conven-tions which work to the advantage of the great powers. These can work to the benefit of countless millions of people in these societies and elsewhere but they are not the same as efforts to develop cosmo-politan harm conventions which have the specific objective of extending protection to individuals and non-sovereign communities in their own right.

There can be no doubt that the survival of pluralist principles of good international citizenship was a considerable diplomatic achieve-ment in the face of superpower rivalries and tensions between North and South and, unsurprisingly perhaps, there was little consideration of alternative principles of foreign policy. The accent was placed

---

he may injure us' (quoted in Wight, 1991: 220ff) and also Vattel's standpoint as discussed on p. 132.

[28] Watson (1992: 161) claims this approach to defeated powers was an invention of the Italian city-state system, and especially of Lorenzo Dei Medici's foreign policy. It is worth noting that the notion of proportionality in warfare was central to Vattel's pluralist claim that war can be just on both sides.

appropriately on what Butterfield (1951b) called the tragic dimension of world politics and not on the essential malevolence of states. One of the chief merits of this approach is its sensitivity to the need for 'sacrifices of value' in order to achieve vital national security goals (for a related discussion, see Wolfers, 1962c: 58). An example is the decision to enter into unwelcome and hopefully temporary alliances with regimes that abuse human rights for national security reasons or to preserve the balance of power.

It is probably fair to add that foreign policy analysis has often been too heavily biased in favour of arguments about the persistent 'realities' which block progress in realizing cosmopolitan values. As far as the English School is concerned, this bias may betray a suspicion that the great powers are unlikely to shed their role as 'gangsters' which do not play a 'civilizing' role in world politics and to evolve into 'guardians' of cosmopolitan values (Wheeler, 1996; Dunne, 1998: xiv). It is intriguing that Wight (1991: 130) argued that since the rationalist 'fears and suspects power . . . he fears and suspects great powers more than small powers. He doubts whether great powers can be transformed into great responsibles, and believes that small powers have been truer spokesmen of civilised values than great ones.'[29] But as the *'via media'* between realism and revolutionism, the English School has an obligation not only to stress persistent realities but also to expose states which make exaggerated claims about 'necessity' to justify decisions which subordinate international and humanitarian responsibilities to national imperatives. Assessing the claims that states make to defend the sacrifice of international and cosmopolitan values is a neglected area within the English School.[30] It is here that the solidarist can develop a distinctive approach to foreign policy analysis, one that tries to ascertain whether states could have done – or could do – more on the evidence available to promote cosmopolitan objectives even in the

[29] Wight (1991: 130) maintains that the 'realist makes a presumption in favour of great powers'. Small powers are thought to 'lack the broad world-picture of great powers and are mainly devoted to intrigue, squabbling and horse trading'. Rationalist theory is an 'attitude' which leads to 'a presumption in favour of small powers'. They 'were the authors of whatever success the League of Nations enjoyed; the great powers sabotaged it'.

[30] See, however, Hurrell (2002) and Wheeler (2002) on the argument the Bush Administration advanced in support of a pre-emptive war against Iraq. Of course, the moral status of pre-emptive strikes has long been a central theme in the Grotian tradition.

most difficult circumstances. Vincent (1986a: ch. 4) was implicitly committed to this approach to foreign policy when he argued that the United States and other powers could have done more – than repeated observations about Cold War rivalries suggested was possible – to promote welfare rights (see also Dunne, 1998: xiv). We find the same emphasis in Dunne and Wheeler's analysis of the possibilities that the first Blair Administration could have accomplished more by way of protecting human rights in other societies, not least by suspending arms sales to repressive regimes such as Suharto's Indonesia (Wheeler and Dunne, 1998).

It remains the case that many, and perhaps most, members of the English School have doubted that the state's civilizing role is likely to extend beyond preserving the pluralist condition, however much a more cosmopolitan form of foreign policy is to be desired. Although he appears to have subscribed to this view, Wight stressed the need to defend the highest ethical ideals even though they may never be realized in practice (see above, p. 155). This position can all too easily succumb to defeatism unless accompanied by efforts to expose false claims to necessity and to highlight the possibilities for more cosmopolitan demonstrations of foreign policy agency. Solidarism is bound to remain premature without reflections – of the kind that Dunne and Wheeler have offered with respect to human rights – on the contribution that good international citizens can reasonably be expected to make to the development of a more ethical international society.

The solidarist ethic

Pluralist principles of good international citizenship might be regarded as a 'second best' morality – as the most that societies with competing political interests and divergent moral and cultural preferences can agree on. Bull and Vincent did believe that higher goals could be realized in the western regions of Europe. States in that region had accepted that domestic jurisdiction had to be contracted for the sake of human rights, and clearly this was where the 'best-established human rights institutions' were to be found (Vincent, 1986a: 95). Of course, defenders of the human rights culture have never claimed that such institutions only apply to already existing Western liberal democracies; they have argued that most societies agree on the need for answerability to global institutions which have humanitarian responsibilities for protecting individuals and minorities from violent regimes.

242

Pluralist arrangements build respect for the harm principle into the society of states; solidarist principles of good international citizenship demonstrate how existing normative commitments to minimizing harm can be pushed in a cosmopolitan direction.

Although Bull had clear doubts about the extent to which the liberal human rights culture could command universal support, he emphasized that some forms of assault on the person are so abhorrent – and are so regarded by most of the world's cultures – that 'it is possible for practical purposes to proceed as if [there] were natural rights' (Bull, 1979a: 89–90). In the aftermath of the Holocaust and World War II, liberal-democratic states created new legal conventions that made the individual's right to be free from 'cruel, inhuman or degrading treatment or punishment' a core principle of international society.[31] We can regard this as the *grund-norm* of the solidarist position on good international citizenship.[32]

From those English School writings which have considered current possibilities for transforming world politics in a solidarist direction it is possible to derive specific principles of good international citizenship. These are principles which can inform the foreign policies of states which wish to make progress together in creating a more ethical international society. But these principles can also be used to expose false claims about necessity and to highlight actual possibilities for more cosmopolitan foreign policy orientations. Among the more important principles are: (1) individuals and the various communities and associations to which they belong are the fundamental members of international society; (2) unnecessary suffering and cruelty to individuals and their immediate associations should be avoided in the conduct of war;[33] (3) pluralist commitments to sovereignty and sovereign immunity should be replaced by the notion of personal responsibility for infringements of the laws of war;[34] (4) superior orders do

[31] As set out in Article 4 of the 1948 *Universal Declaration of Human Rights* – see Evans (1994: 40).

[32] See Buzan (2004) for a view of solidarism which does not privilege human rights in this way, and p. 133 note 27 above for a counter-argument.

[33] This was a central principle of Grotius' solidarism as explained by Bull (1966b: 58) who states that 'according to Grotius' account the law of nations permitted belligerents to kill and injure all who are in enemy territory, including women and children; to destroy and pillage enemy property, even that which is held sacred; to kill captives and hostages; and to make slaves of prisoners of war (although it strictly forbade the use of poison). Grotius however makes clear his dissent from the existing state of law.'

[34] See Article 7 of the Statute of the International Tribunal for the Prosecution of Persons Responsible for Serious Violations of International Humanitarian Law Committed in the Territory of the Former Yugoslavia since 1991 (Evans, 1994: 393).

not justify violations of humanitarian international law;[35] (5) breaches of the laws of war should be punishable in domestic and international courts;[36] (6) the sovereignty of the state is conditional on compliance with the international law of human rights;[37] (7) sovereignty does not entitle states to be free from 'the legitimate appraisal of their peers' with respect to human rights;[38] (8) states have responsibilities as custodians of human rights everywhere;[39] (9) individuals have the legal right of appeal to international courts of law when violations of human rights occur; and (10) regard for human rights requires respect for non-sovereign communities and requires the society of states to protect minority nations and indigenous peoples from unnecessary suffering.

Pluralist principles moderate the effects of what Elias called the dual structure of nation-states' normative codes by defending the international responsibility to avoid unnecessary harm to other sovereign political communities (see Chapter 6, p. 202). Solidarist principles make further inroads into the dual structure of morality by defending the humanitarian responsibility to bring all members of the human

[35] The role of extenuating circumstances is recognized in the law of war (Evans, ibid.). For further discussion of current debates about the extent to which duress is permissible in defence of superior orders, see Meron (1998).

[36] A useful discussion of recent legal developments can be found in Weller (1999).

[37] 'It is not now enough for a state to be, and to be recognized as, sovereign . . . It must also act domestically in such a way as not to offend against the basic rights of individuals and groups within its territory' (Vincent, 1986a: 130).

[38] Vincent (1986a: 152) is the source of the section in quotes. He immediately adds that this 'does not issue a general license for intervention. International society is not yet as solidarist as that.' We return to the question of humanitarian intervention in the next section.

[39] Bull (1966b: 63) stresses the importance of this theme in Grotius' thought: 'kings, as well as being responsible for the safety and welfare of their subjects, are burdened with the guardianship of human rights everywhere'. Vincent (1986a: 103–4) argued that modern international society has already gone some way towards recovering Suarez's notion of the *ius gentium intra se* – that part of international law which is embodied in the domestic law of states. The case of *Filartiga* v. *Pena-Irala* – in which Pena was sued by Filartiga in an American court for torturing his son to death in Paraguay – was especially significant because a domestic court had prosecuted an alien for human rights abuses committed in another state (Vincent, 1986a: 103-4). The case was heard under the 1789 Alien Tort Statute. Vincent (1986a: 104) quoted Judge Kaufman's comment that 'the torturer has become – like the pirate and slave trader before him – *hostis humani generis* – an enemy of all mankind'. Vincent (1986a: 103) added that 'a revolutionary breach of the principle of state sovereignty as received from the nineteenth century' would occur if the legal philosophy invoked in that case were to find support in other domestic courts of law since then states would accept new international legal obligations to protect individuals everywhere, irrespective of their citizenship or nationality.

race under the protection of cosmopolitan harm conventions. Bull (1969: 42–3) was cautiously optimistic that Western European states could make further progress of this kind within their own region.[40] Western Europe might be the setting, he argued, for an unusual experiment in creating neo-medieval arrangements which would allow subnational and transnational authorities and loyalties to be liberated from 'the tyranny of the concepts' of nationalism and the state (Bull, 2002: 265).[41] Although he believed the time might be ripe to explicate principles of political organization that broke with the modern idea of the sovereign nation state, Bull (2002: 246) was quick to recall the violence of the medieval world and to stress that the decline of the territorial state might result in increased private violence. It would also be unwise to conclude that the 'Western European nations constitute a security community in the sense that war between them could not happen again' (Bull, 1983a: 163).[42]

The prospects for new forms of political community have improved in the period since Bull reflected on a possible neo-medieval future for Western Europe, and in this context it is possible to build on the solidarist principles listed earlier, at least for relations within the continent. Here it is useful to draw on Adler and Barnet's distinction between 'loosely coupled' security communities, where the sense of 'we-feeling' is stronger than in the pluralist condition but states retain their sovereign powers, and 'tightly coupled' security communities where societies come together in 'a system of rule that lies somewhere between a sovereign state and a regional, centralized government' (Adler and Barnet, 1998: 30). The solidarist principles of

---

[40] Bull (1969: 365) wrote positively about Deutsch's study of security communities (communities in which member states have a strong sense of 'we feeling' and an ability to resolve their differences without resorting to force), stating that it was 'pregnant' with implications for a more general theory of international relations.
[41] Bull's neo-medieval vision is evident in the following statement: 'We may envisage a situation in which, say, a Scottish authority in Edinburgh, a British authority in London, and a European authority in Brussels were all actors in world politics and all enjoyed representation in world political organizations, together with rights and duties of various kinds in world law, but in which no one of them claimed sovereignty or supremacy over the others, and a person living in Glasgow had no exclusive or overriding loyalty to any one of them. Such an outcome would take us truly "beyond the sovereign state" and is by no means implausible, but it is striking how little interest has been displayed in it by either the regional integrationists or the subnational "disintegrations"' (Bull, 2000b: 114). For further discussion, see Linklater (1998: ch. 6).
[42] See Bull (2002: 273–4) on the improbability of a global pluralist security community although such a thing was not a 'logical impossibility' and might 'provide a vision which offers hope' for the future.

good international citizenship which were listed earlier can underpin a loosely coupled security community where the desire to protect human rights weakens the significance of national sovereignty and where shared commitments to dialogue and consent replace the balance of power as the keystone of international order. But more radical principles of good international citizenship which promote the Kantian project of making the harm principle fundamental to the totality of social and political relations can inform the conduct of relations within Europe. Among the more important are the duty: (1) to create transnational democratic legal and political institutions which give individuals and their associations the capacity to influence all decisions which may adversely affect them; (2) to devolve political power to ensure advances in the public recognition of cultural and linguistic differences; and (3) to reduce material inequalities and unequal life chances in order to create meaningful forms of citizenship in a regional polity 'that lies somewhere between a sovereign state and a regional, centralized government' (for further discussion, see Linklater 1998). Incorporating these principles in political life is the most advanced means currently available of ensuring harmony between international order and world order in a region whose parts share commitments to liberal and social-democratic values.

Ethical challenges in relations between solidarists and pluralists

How societies which are making progress – or can make progress – in a solidarist direction should conduct their relations with vulnerable Third World communities which are strongly committed to pluralism is one of the most important normative questions in contemporary international society. The English School has answered this question in several discussions of humanitarian intervention and human rights. A central issue in these discussions has been how independent political communities should 'act as a moral trustee' not only for international society but for 'suffering humanity' (Wheeler, 1996: 124).[43] This section begins by considering English School reflections on trusteeship which focus on the rights and wrongs of humanitarian intervention. It then proceeds to consider how Wight's defence of an

---

[43] Wheeler (1996) regards this moral concern with suffering as central to the 'critical international society' theoretical project.

ethic of justice leads to principles of good international citizenship which seek to promote welfare internationalism.

In his earliest papers on human rights, Bull argued that Western societies do not have a monopoly of wisdom in this area. It was important that they remember that Western and non-Western societies are often divided 'over basic matters of principle' and that liberal-democratic constructions of human rights repeatedly fail to evoke a positive response elsewhere (Bull, 1979a: 88–90). Western governments had to recognize that their pronounced enthusiasm for civil and political rights led many newly independent countries to fear the imposition of new forms of colonial rule. Mindful of the partiality of their values, the powerful liberal democracies had a special obligation to ensure that the first universal society of states was respectful of non-Western cultural preferences which were often not only different from, but hostile to, values paramount in the West. The hermeneutic burden fell most heavily on the Western powers to understand different non-Western standpoints, to refrain from imposing their moral and political preferences on others, and to explore the possibility of 'transcultural standards and values' through open dialogue (see above, p. 120).

The language of such remarks is unmistakably pluralist – it inclines towards recommending that the good international citizen should recognize other states' right to a separate existence and abstain from interfering in their internal affairs. Bull's observation that certain actions are generally regarded as so abhorrent as to suggest the existence of some natural rights tends towards two principles of solidarist good international citizenship – that sovereignty does not mean freedom from 'the legitimate appraisal of their peers' and that liberal states should regard themselves as custodians of the universal culture of human rights. Bull did not go so far as to argue that state sovereignty should be conditional on compliance with the international law of human rights but, like Vincent, he argued that some human rights violations may be sufficiently serious to lead international society to take the view that the principle of non-intervention, while 'essential to world order', should be relaxed in exceptional circumstances (Bull, 1984b: 6, 187). Vincent was no more inclined than Bull to argue that good international citizens could claim a right, or duty, of humanitarian intervention,[44] but he believed the emergence of a

---

[44] In his major work on the principle of non-intervention, Vincent noted that the tolerance of intervention to prevent genocide had increased since the 1960s, and he

'world civil society' with responsibility for monitoring compliance with human rights law would be an effective compromise between pluralism and solidarism (Vincent, 1992: 291).[45]

The last point is a reminder that there are many ways short of military intervention in which the good international citizen can hope to influence a regime which is deemed guilty of violating human rights. The European Union, to take one example, has developed rules governing admission which express strong solidarist commitments with respect to human rights.[46] However, efforts to promote these commitments outside the region have been controversial. Dunne and Wheeler (1999: 24) cite efforts by the United States and the European Union to dissuade members of the Association of South East Asian Nations from admitting Burma because of its history of human rights abuse. The ASEAN response affirmed the principle of territorial

added that it might therefore seem curious 'to object to intervention on the ground of its want of impartiality, or of the impurity of the motives of the intervening state or states' (Vincent, 1974: 347). What should not be forgotten, he proceeded to argue, was that there is still no consensus in international society about the criteria which should be used in deciding when sovereignty could be overridden for the sake of human rights. In this condition, it was far from clear that states could trace 'a middle course . . . between a virginal doctrine of non-intervention that would allow nothing to be done and a promiscuous doctrine of intervention that would make a trollop of the law'. Until that course had been defined, it was perhaps necessary to conclude that non-intervention is the 'more dignified principle for international law to sanction' (Vincent, 1974: 348–9).

[45] In an insightful appraisal of the development of Vincent's reflections on human rights and non-intervention, Neumann (1997a: 46) argues that Vincent was especially drawn towards the 'revolutionist' rather than to the 'realist' challenge to universal human rights because it advanced 'the idea that there actually *may* be a number of signs that the transformations of world politics today *are* on the scale of those which had to be confronted by Grotius and others who lived through an early phase of the modern states system' (italics in original). Realists stood accused of 'missing a transformation from international relations to world politics as significant as that which established the society of states, and for which the idea of human rights is a kind of midwife' (quoted by Neumann, 1997a: 55–6). Vincent (1986a: 148) did not rule out economic sanctions as had occurred in response to human rights abuses in Amin's Uganda, but he suggested that Amin's vulnerability to a coffee boycott was 'unique' in contemporary international society.

[46] The European Union proclamation of 16 December 1991 regarding relations with the former Yugoslavia is an example of how human rights principles have been incorporated into its rules pertaining to the recognition of new states. Recognition was made conditional on respect for the democratic process and on constitutional 'guarantees for the rights of ethnic and national groups and minorities in accordance with the commitments subscribed to in the framework of the CSCE' (Akehurst, 1992: 210). This represented a shift from a 'declaratory' approach, in which recognition depends simply on the existence of an effective central government, to a 'constitutive' approach in which recognition is conditional on the observance of international standards of legitimacy (Akehurst, ibid.).

sovereignty which ruled out interfering in what governments do in their 'backyard'. Faced with a pluralist response of this kind, custodians of the human rights culture can argue that it is legitimate to apply moral pressure to delinquent regimes, especially when they are signatories to the relevant international legal conventions. Far more contentious, of course, is the question of whether the good international citizen is entitled to defend human rights by using force.

As Mayall (1996: 4–5) has argued, the constitution of the modern society of states as set out in the United Nations Charter incorporates conflicting positions on how international society should respond to gross violations of human rights. During the bipolar era, states such as Vietnam, Tanzania and India were careful not to defend their excursions into Kampuchea, Uganda and Bangladesh in solidarist terms. They asserted the right of national self-defence rather than the moral right or duty of humanitarian action (Akehurst, 1984). A marked increase in the use of solidarist language or rhetoric has occurred in the post-bipolar era,[47] but the tension between pluralist and solidarist principles of world politics is no closer to being resolved as debates over the morality and legality of NATO's intervention in Serbia revealed.

Sharp differences within the English School on the subject of NATO's military action over Kosovo (and on humanitarian intervention in general) indicate that there is no simple solution to the question of how the good international citizen should respond to gross violations of human rights (see Chapter 4). Solidarists can argue that good international citizenship justifies unilateral intervention to prevent genocide or a similar human tragedy (Dunne and Wheeler, see above, p. 230). The fact the United Nations Security Council did not authorize NATO's military action may be troubling (ideally the intervening power would be sure of its support) but the absence of authorization could not be the determining factor in deliberations about whether or not to intervene. Good international citizenship was displayed in the argument that 'the veto power of Russia and China must not be allowed to block the defence of human rights' in crises such as Kosovo;

---

[47] The debate surrounding the legitimacy of the war against Iraq may strengthen this trend. A British Government document states that 'where a population is suffering serious harm, as a result of internal war, insurgency, repression or state failure, and the state in question is unwilling or unable to halt or avert it, the principle of non-intervention yields to the international responsibility to protect' – see 'Blair seeks new powers to attack rogue states', *The Independent on Sunday*, 13 July 2003.

the 'unreasonable veto' leads to the argument that respect for the veto power in the Security Council, like respect for sovereignty, should be conditional on support for human rights law (Dunne and Wheeler, 2000: 74; Linklater, 2000: 490). The pluralist has several responses to this argument: that breaching the United Nations Charter is hardly an act of good international citizenship, that the unauthorized use of force may set precedents which damage international society, that intervening powers are vulnerable to the accusation that intervention is invariably selective and dependent on self-interested calculations, that their actions may encourage secessionist movements in other fragile nation-states, and that the bitter experience of involvement in intractable intra-state conflicts usually dissuades intervening powers from making necessary long-term commitments to the reconstruction of societies ravaged by civil war (Roberts, 1993; Mayall, 1996: 23–4; 2000b: 328ff).

One approach to resolving these differences envisages a global dialogue to consider the possibility of introducing new principles of intervention including a commitment from the permanent members of the Security Council not to exercise the veto to prevent action to end gross violations of human rights (see above, pp. 143ff). The stress on the obligation to initiate the quest for an agreement about the precise rules that would govern future humanitarian interventions – thereby reducing the dangers of unilateralism – is the great merit of this approach. To enter such a dialogue in good faith, however, the good international citizen would have to be willing to comply with the outcome which might well be to reaffirm pluralist principles of international order. Any other standpoint involving, for example, the claim to a reserve power to resort to unilateral intervention in supreme emergencies would place solidarist states above international society. This compromise of solidarist ethical aspirations can be condoned on two grounds. The first is that good international citizens can rely, as noted earlier, on many ways of defending human rights without resorting to force; the second is that the determination to convince others of the merits of humanitarian intervention is not the only litmus test of good international citizenship. Assisting weak and vulnerable communities is no less important a test of good international citizenship – and if Vincent is correct, it might even be a more important one (see also Gonzalez-Pelaez and Buzan, 2003).

A core feature of Vincent's argument is that starvation and malnutrition are the permanent but largely hidden emergency in world politics (Vincent, 1986a). The question of whether or not to use military force to prevent human rights abuses arises infrequently but dramatically in world politics; whether to assist the starving and the malnourished is a question that should arise for the good international citizen every single day. Vincent pre-empted criticisms of the argument that welfare rights should be at the heart of human rights diplomacy. Some opponents would protest that 'crucial human rights' – specifically liberal-democratic rights – might therefore be placed to one side 'on the ground that they are controversial'; others might go further and condemn the decision to privilege welfare rights as a 'sell-out to those who use the purported pursuit of economic and social rights as an excuse for suppressing, or ignoring, or at any rate putting off, civil and political rights' (Vincent, 1986a: 148). Vincent's reply was that Western liberal democracies and socialist states could hardly expect others to take their version of human rights seriously when the plight of 'the submerged 40%' of the world's population was largely neglected (Vincent, 1986a: 145, 150). Several responses to the terrorist attacks on the United States in September 2001 reveal that Vincent's argument has lost none of its importance in recent years.[48]

Vincent (1986a: 147–8) claimed the promotion of welfare rights promised to be 'a more neutral undertaking for international society' than the struggle for traditional liberal rights; it called for 'technical' solutions which did not engage 'the major ideologies in an argument about their superiority to the others', and it could proceed without 'mutual recrimination' about who should take responsibility for the plight of the most desperate members of humanity. But another, and admittedly less, central part of his argument points in a different direction. This is his observation that the affluent world cannot escape the fact that it has caused or contributed to the suffering of the starving, and has frequently benefited from poverty and vulnerability in many parts of the world.[49] Vincent (1986a: 128) argued that one of the strengths of his ethical 'minimalism' which privileged welfare rights was its 'realist' appreciation of the willingness of the society of states to take on new, but ultimately, uncontroversial humanitarian

---

[48] For details, see Linklater (2002b).

[49] Vincent (1986a: 147) stresses that 'disturbingly for us, [this] might require that we consider our direct responsibility for depriving people of their basic rights in foreign countries that we have economic relations with, which would raise questions about disinvestment and the like'.

responsibilities. But he was quick to admit that this 'turns out to look like maximalism' when the 'legitimacy' of 'the whole international economic system in which we are all implicated' is taken into account (Vincent, 1986a: 127–8). Efforts to end starvation which addressed the contributory role of the world economy would represent 'a colossal task for international society' as a whole (Vincent, 1986a: 172).[50] However, Vincent's central argument was that international society should place such complexities to one side and make the goal of eradicating one of the worst forms of human suffering its central moral priority.

The enduring strength of Vincent's argument lies in its implicit argument that disputes about the rights and wrongs of humanitarian intervention should not divert attention from the relative ease with which affluent states could demonstrate their good international citizenship by striving to end starvation and malnutrition (see also Pogge, 2002). One might go further by arguing that global strategies to end these forms of human suffering fall within the domain of Wight's rationalist ethic of justice – they fall within the realm of moral obligation rather than charity. This judgement follows from Wight's argument that the state which is a trustee for its citizens 'should not be indifferent to the rights of others' or 'seek to gain more for [its] people than is just' (see above, p. 234). Vincent's argument that with 'regard to the failure to provide subsistence rights, it is not this or that government whose legitimacy is in question, but the whole international economic system in which we are all implicated' strongly suggests that indifference to extreme suffering is especially intolerable under conditions of unjust enrichment.

One might add, although this is more controversial territory, that the global initiatives which Vincent defended are required by respect for the harm principle. This is not just because the affluent may have caused or contributed to the most serious forms of deprivation but because, as Feinberg (see p. 184) has argued, the failure to rescue those who are vulnerable when there is little cost to oneself can constitute

---

[50] Commenting on this passage, Neumann (1997a: 57) argues that 'one thing leads to another, however, and Vincent is thus tempted to include the right of humans to speak up in order to avoid being obliterated. Neither is he blind to the enormous consequences the seemingly modest expansion of the idea of human rights to include subsistence would have, if the whole range of steps necessary to rearrange the international economic system were to be taken into account.'

harm in itself. A related point, emphasized in the Holocaust literature, is that indifference harms the self-respect of the vulnerable by forcing them to conclude that they have no claims against communities which can alleviate their misery without much cost to themselves (see Wiesel, 1977). In this case, the lack of recognition constitutes 'dignitary harm' (Dan-Cohen 2002: 170, note 31) or damage to self-esteem. The harm principle has been criticized for its narrow emphasis on duties to avoid injury and for its failure to support an ethic of rescue, but it can be invoked to defend humanitarian responsibilities which are required by justice rather than deserving special praise because of their kindness.

With these points in mind, we can now turn to the principles of good international citizenship which can be pieced together from English School writings which have solidarist leanings, but appreciate the seriousness of non-Western concerns about interference in their internal affairs. The question which arises immediately is how far solidarists should apply the principles which pertain to relations between themselves to relations with pluralist societies (and, conversely, how far relations between solidarists and pluralists should be governed by distinctive principles of good international citizenship). Bull's remark that there is a broad consensus that certain acts are so abhorrent as to lend support to the idea of natural rights suggests two preliminary comments. The first is that there is no obvious reason why pluralist regimes should be exempt from solidarist principles regarding the conduct of war. The second, which addresses gross violations of human rights, is that there is no reason why pluralist regimes should be immune from close scrutiny by peers. The logic of these arguments is that the principles of solidarist good international citizenship listed earlier apply with equal effect to the solidarist's relations with pluralist states. (These were the principles granting individuals and non-sovereign communities ultimate membership of international society, stressing the duty to avoid cruelty and unnecessary suffering in war, requiring national leaders and military personnel to abide by the humanitarian law of war and justifying prosecution for breaches of the law, and, finally, asserting that the recognition of sovereignty is conditional on compliance with the international law of human rights and no longer means immunity from 'the legitimate appraisal' of peers.)

English School discussions of human rights require an additional seven principles of good international citizenship which are concerned with humanitarian responsibilities for minimizing harm to the members of vulnerable societies. They are: (1) subject to United Nations approval, solidarist states can exercise a collective right of humanitarian intervention when gross violations of human rights occur; (2) the good international citizen may believe there is a strong moral case for unilateral intervention, but doubts about legality require a global dialogue to ascertain whether states can agree that supreme humanitarian emergencies justify new principles of humanitarian intervention;[51] (3) solidarists have a *prima facie* duty to avoid being complicit in human rights violations in other societies;[52] (4) there is a related obligation to avoid exploitation (in the sense of 'taking advantage of the vulnerable') as well as profiting from unjust enrichment;[53] (5) there is a duty to protect vulnerable peoples from terrible hardship such as extreme poverty and curable disease; (6) affluent societies have global environmental responsibilities to ensure that vulnerable populations enjoy a safe natural environment;[54] (7) obligations to protect the vulnerable require the establishment of global political structures – involving close cooperation with international governmental and non-governmental organizations – that institutionalize the universal right to be able to protest against actual or potential harm.[55]

---

[51] It was suggested earlier that such a dialogue might have uncomfortable conclusions for solidarists not only because it might lead to the decision, which they would be bound to accept, to respect the principle of non-intervention (with the qualifications already noted) but also because they would no doubt be reminded of the many ways, apart from humanitarian intervention, in which they could demonstrate their good international citizenship. The principles which follow explore this larger sphere.

[52] Having quoted Chomsky's question, 'Do we really care about the human consequences of our actions?', Vincent (1986a: 147) adds that 'this might require that we cease aiding a society that deprived its citizens of their basic rights'. Developing this theme, Wheeler and Dunne (1998: 862) argue that Britain should not have sold arms and military equipment to the Indonesian government given evidence that the weapons were used for internal repression. They stress that aspiring good international citizens are not obliged to sacrifice 'vital security interests' but add that the onus is on them to show why certain sacrifices of moral value are justified for the sake of vital interests (Wheeler and Dunne, 1998: 861–2, 866). Wheeler and Dunne (1998: 865) claim that pressure on China on the human rights front could jeopardize its support for 'global non-proliferation norms'. As they argue in another context, there are times when 'prudence dictates a cautious response' (see Wheeler and Dunne, 2001: 179). For this reason, the obligation to avoid being complicit in human rights abuses is best regarded as a *prima facie* obligation.

[53] On this sense of exploitation, see Wertheimer (1996). Some examples of contemporary concerns about complicity and exploitation were noted in Chapter 6.

[54] Jackson is one of the main members of the English School to stress the importance of such global responsibilities (see above, note 9). See also Hurrell (1994, 1995, 1999).

[55] On the notion of 'protecting the vulnerable', see Goodin (1985).

The list of principles reflects an earlier part of the discussion (see p. 147) in which it was claimed that good international citizenship in relations between solidarist and pluralist societies must address not only the scope but also the depth of cosmopolitan morality. The introduction of a human right to be protected from cruel or degrading treatment is a major advance in the ethical development of international society, but a more extensive set of cosmopolitan harm conventions is required to protect the vulnerable from global market forces and environmental degradation. The principles outlined in this section assume the continuation of 'limited sympathies' but recognize duties to avoid indifference to the fate of others or to claim more for one's society than is permissible in terms of 'strict justice'. They invoke the ethos which informs Thucydides' (1972: Book 3.84) defence of those 'general laws of humanity which are there to give a hope of salvation to all who are in distress'.[56] They capture at least part of what it means for the good international citizen to develop humanitarian responsibilities that befit its role as a custodian for 'suffering humanity'.

Conclusion

The 'tremendous conscious effort' involved in creating and maintaining a society of sovereign states was the starting point for the current discussion of good international citizenship. The analysis began with some comments about how good international citizens can embed respect for the harm principle in a pluralist society of states. Starting with international harm conventions which are mainly concerned with averting war, the argument then turned to cosmopolitan harm conventions which protect individuals and communities from unnecessary suffering in war, from human rights violations committed by their own governments, and from injuries that have their origins in world society. The final section has argued that good international citizenship should be informed by a broad interpretation of the harm principle

---

[56] Wight (2004: 112) uncovered a related theme in the writings of Mazzini: 'Ask yourselves, as to every act you commit within the circle of family or country: If what I now do were done by and for all men, would it be beneficial or injurious to Humanity? And if your conscience tells you it would be injurious, desist: desist even though it seems that an immediate advantage to your country or family would be the result.' This might be regarded as an apt summary of a solidarist ethic.

which conforms with Wight's account of the rationalist ethic of justice. Complying with that principle involves the duty to avoid causing unnecessary mental and bodily harm, but observing that principle also creates the obligation to avoid indifference to the suffering of others or benefiting unfairly from their vulnerability, since inaction can cause dignitary harm. More detailed precepts have been derived from these broad principles to show how good international citizens can incorporate increasingly demanding conceptions of the harm principle in more ethical forms of international society.

The second part of this book opened with some reflections on the qualified progressivist interpretation of international politics which runs through English School writings and distinguishes the Grotian approach from other theoretical persuasions. This defining interest requires, it has been argued, further analyses of foreign policy agency, and specifically more systematic inquiry into spurious claims about necessity or limited opportunities for promoting global economic and political change. The moral reference point for such inquiries is not some notion of the good life or some vision of world politics which is far removed from the conduct of foreign affairs. The emphasis instead is on duties to avoid harm which are already recognizable features of international society and of the overwhelming majority of its constituent parts. The core question is how far states can construct foreign policies which take that principle more seriously, which deepen its meaning and implications, and which extend its application across the totality of global political and economic relations.

The method outlined here has been used in discussions of British foreign policy in the human rights area (see pp. 230ff) and in a recent analysis of the war against the Taliban which asks whether the American administration adopted a 'permissive interpretation of what counted as a legitimate military target' which justified 'excessive' force (Wheeler, 2002: 219). Many analyses of the war against the Taliban have asked whether 'the realist plea of necessity' (Wheeler, 2002: 214) has been exploited to defend security policies which violate international legal requirements to observe the principle of non-combatant immunity and to protect the rights of persons detained as Al Qaeda suspects. The war against Iraq has led to ongoing public debates about the extent to which the United States' duty to protect citizens from terrorist acts of violence led to the unwarranted departure from international responsibilities to work through the United Nations system and the neglect of humanitarian responsibilities to the civilian population of Iraq. In each case, the question is how far states fail the test of good international citizenship by using arguments about necessity to allow obligations to conationals to override international and humanitarian responsibilities; in each case, the question for a critical approach to foreign policy is how far states misrepresent the choices available to them and, in so doing, subordinate broader ethical responsibilities to considerations of national security.[57]

Analysing how the good international citizens can contribute to the improvement of international society may seem to duplicate the English School's narrow preoccupation with states and its neglect of other influential political actors. Its preoccupation with the state stems from its uncontroversial belief that the great powers have the greatest impact on international society. Discussions of good international citizenship have reflected this understanding of the ambiguous role of the great powers: of their capacity to acquire some of the qualities of the 'great responsible' and of their ability to become 'great irresponsibles' who play a decivilizing rather than a civilizing role in world affairs. The revival of national security politics since the terrorist attacks of 11 September 2002 has demonstrated the importance of reflecting on what it means for the state to be a good international citizen, but it is nevertheless the case that the modern states-system has recovered something of its earlier heterogeneity because of the diversification of non-state actors which can also influence the future of world politics. Transnational business corporations are no different from states in that they can be judged by notions of responsibility which highlight obligations not to benefit from unjust enrichment and more general duties of care in their dealings with the vulnerable. Conceptions of corporate responsibility stress possibilities for the moral exercise of agency, as do references to international and humanitarian responsibilities in approaches to good international citizenship which are concerned with the foreign policy of states. We do not know if the modern society of states can make progress in making human suffering a moral problem for the world as a whole; if it will distinguish itself from its predecessors by realizing existing potentials for making the harm principle central to the organization of

---

[57] The point is also how far the failure to comply with international and humanitarian responsibilities will have negative consequences for national security. We see this in recent discussions about how American policy may deepen anti-American sentiment which will find expression in future acts of terrorism.

global social and political affairs; and if it will move forward by strengthening the ethical commitment to universal answerability and to the collective legitimation of policies that affect the fate of humanity. These matters are at the heart of current debates about the recent course of American foreign policy and about its future direction. Analysing foreign policy agency remains important not only for understanding the 'conscious effort' involved in preserving international society in the face of the Hobbesian struggle for power and security but also for comprehending the great labour required to transform international society in accordance with Kantian ideals of human equality. The distinctiveness of the English School lies in its unrivalled discussion of the constant interplay between these tendencies in the troubled history of relations between independent political communities.

Conclusion

This book has aimed to give a comprehensive account of the English School's study of international relations and to explore how a historically based and normatively progressivist perspective may be extrapolated and developed further from its existing achievements. The discussion began with a detailed account of the changing identity of the English School. The range of questions the School's leading figures have addressed, and the answers they have suggested, were then outlined. And the book moved to a close scrutiny of the epistemological and methodological parameters within which the School's key authors have made contributions to the study of their subject-matter.

It is often enough stated that, in discussing the achievements of the English School, the question of 'who is in and who is out' is *not* an issue worth spending time on (Little, 2003: 444). The point of such a remark may be that any answer given to the question of which figures are more, or less, central to the story of the English School cannot but be arbitrary. Against this scepticism, Chapter 1 argued that, despite a remarkably diverse range of interpretations concerning the English School's identity which have been aired in the last twenty years or so, a defensible picture of the School's identity emerges when these contending interpretations are carefully scrutinized.

The English School, it was suggested, was a historically evolving cluster of so far mainly UK-based contributors to International Relations, initially active in the latter part of the twentieth century, who broadly agree in treating the international society perspective – or 'rationalism' in Wight's sense – as a particularly important way to interpret world politics. Their views and intellectual dispositions show significant family resemblance due partly to the exceptionally close personal or professional connections amongst them. These connections were initially formed at the LSE, but later extended to other academic institutions, and were also, to a large extent independently, cultivated within the British Committee on the Theory of International Politics.

Those who are central to this cluster of scholars have included Manning, Wight, Bull, James, Vincent, Watson, and perhaps also Butterfield, and, among the more recent contributors, Hurrell, Wheeler, Dunne, Jackson, and perhaps also Buzan and Little. While acknowledging that there may be slightly different, but more or less equally plausible, conceptions of the English School, the discussion proceeded on the premise that these are indeed the School's central figures. While acknowledging also that, in their view, the picture of the world as a society of states is not the only valid or useful representation of it, it was nevertheless argued that this representation was central to their conception of world politics and that therefore to characterize their approach as 'pluralistic' is to exaggerate the significance they attach to other representations. This, of course, is not at all the same as saying that those who wish to build on the achievements of the English School should not move in the direction of other representations. Such a move will constitute an important step in the historically evolving intellectual movement which the English School undoubtedly is (see, for example, Buzan, 2004).

In Chapter 2, the key texts emanating from the English School were divided into three kinds: those which identify the institutional structure of world politics organized as a society of sovereign states; those which assess how and how well the institutions of that society function in achieving some basic social goals (and, conversely, what values may or may not be pursued effectively in world politics organized as a society of sovereign states); and those which engage in a comparative study of historical states-systems and/or a study of the historical evolution of the modern states-system.

At an early stage, Manning, Wight, Bull and James made groundbreaking contributions to the first kind of study which effectively defined the central subject-matter of the English School's inquiry – the society of states. Bull, Vincent, Wheeler and Jackson have made significant contributions to the second area of investigation, and recently the discussion has entered a new, more explicitly normative, phase. Wight, Bull, Watson, Buzan and Little are the chief contributors to the third area of inquiry, and their works now form part of the growing body of literature on the historical sociology of world politics.

Chapter 2 also examined in detail the contrast between pluralism and solidarism – a subject of considerable importance in understanding current debates within the English School and for the development of the argument in the latter part of this volume.

Any distinction is drawn for a purpose, and a dichotomy is usually offered as part of a claim that one kind of thing is better than the other. The pluralist/solidarist division illustrates this well. Bull used it basically to show that in the area of the legal control of the use of force, the nineteenth-century 'pluralist' system of international law was better suited to the twentieth-century reality of international society than was the twentieth-century 'solidarist' system incorporating the distinction between unlawful and lawful resort to war, or 'delicts' and 'sanctions' in the language of Hans Kelsen (1967). This was so, according to Bull's empirical judgement, because the twentieth-century reality of international society lacked the requisite degree of solidarity that made the solidarist system of international law work effectively. Bull's argument was substantially the same as Vattel's defence of what the latter called 'the voluntary law of nations' (Vattel, [1758]1916: Bk III, ch. 12).

Although Bull himself continued to argue in the same way into the late 1970s, the article in which he first introduced the two labels contained some ambiguity. For example, pluralists were characterized as positivists while solidarists were said to believe in natural law as a source of law – a claim that does not withstand even a cursory study of the history of ideas about international law and institutions. Far more importantly for the later development of debates within the English School, Bull asserted that unlike pluralists, for whom only sovereign states had rights and duties in international law, solidarists subscribed to the view that individual human persons held such rights and duties. Subsequently, this came to be taken to mean that whereas pluralists are only concerned with the minimum goal of the orderly coexistence of states, solidarists, by contrast, hold the view that it is both realistic and morally right that the society of states should pursue the more ambitious goal of protecting human rights worldwide.

Bull himself never, of course, held the view that the welfare of individual human persons was morally unimportant. On the contrary, he defended the political organization of the world as a society of sovereign states precisely because he believed that this was an effective means of achieving 'world (as opposed to merely international) order' defined in terms of the attainment of basic social goals by individual persons making up the human race. In this sense, he was at heart a solidarist, but his relatively pessimistic empirical assessment of the degree of solidarity present in international society had made him a pluralist.

However, just as much as leading solidarists came to advocate (and, it appears, the label 'solidarists' came to denote those who advocate) that it is both morally right and practical/beneficial that the society of states should pursue the goal of protecting human rights worldwide even by recourse to humanitarian intervention, some pluralists came to advance the view (and the label 'pluralists' may have come to mean those who hold the view) that it is neither practical/beneficial nor even morally right that the society of states should pursue such a line. This polarization is clearly present in the debate between Wheeler and Jackson – the former arguing that it is morally right and practical/beneficial, in the present set of circumstances, for states to cooperate in pursuit of human rights and, under certain circumstances and within certain constraints, to legitimate the practice of humanitarian intervention, and the latter insisting that such an option is neither practical/beneficial nor even morally desirable.

In the contest polarized in this way, one plausible line to take might be to suggest that the solidarists are too optimistic in their empirical assessment and the pluralists are excessively anti-universalist in their normative pronouncements. But whatever may be one's judgement on these issues, it seems clear that the two parties need to go beyond the adversarial – and ultimately dogmatic – form of engagement.

Chapter 3 was written partly in response to the frequently heard North American claim that the English School is epistemologically and methodologically unsophisticated, that its key figures are insufficiently self-conscious and self-critical about their mode of engagement with the questions they explore and the answers they present. This is a serious challenge, coming back at the English School so many years after Bull's rather cavalier rejection of what he depicted as an American scientism in IR. The discussion was conducted also partly to elucidate the parameters within which the English School's intellectual pursuit operated. In particular, three issues were raised:

1. On what grounds, given their unanimous stress on the importance of historical knowledge, does the English School think that the study of history sheds light on our present and future in international relations?

2. What is the epistemological nature of their inquiry into international relations, given that it is not meant to be scientific?
3. What exactly is their attitude to the study of norms and values in international relations, given their focus on norms on the one hand and their stated dislike of normative advocacy on the other?

For a school of thought that prides itself upon at least some of its key members' historical erudition, there is a surprising lack of coherent reflection on their part regarding what history is for. But a key message seems to be this: that we should try to enrich our understanding of the present at least in part in the light of our understanding of the past, which a comparative study will reveal to be partly similar to and partly different from what we now are; and we should bear in mind that in speculating about our future options, the past is an indispensable, though not necessarily a sufficient, guide.

As for the second question, it is clear that English School writers have not uncovered any significant causal mechanisms which are present in world politics and which may contribute causally towards some of its recurrent features, such as war, imperialism, exploitation, global inequalities, international cooperation, emergence of relatively stable pockets of peace and solidarity in the world, and so on. English School writers' primary focus has been to make sense of the world of states in the light of the normative assumptions that prevail in that realm of politics. What type of assumptions, or international political culture, obtains helps shape the quality of life enjoyed by states in the world political arena, and the three ideal-types of 'system', 'society' and 'community' enable us to represent a variety of world political circumstances. But what causal mechanisms may transform one kind of situation towards another is not a question that the English School has considered in any depth, although, as will be revisited later, we saw in Chapter 4 a demonstration to the effect that English School writings point to progressive potentials located in states-systems.

As we noted, making sense of the world of states in the light of the normative assumptions prevalent in that realm of politics is a central concern of the English School. This gives one answer to the third question listed above: the School's dominant mode of engagement with the normative dimension of world politics is from the positivist, or anthropological, perspective. This goes hand in hand with some of its earlier writers' hesitancy to get involved in normative questions proper, or substantive moral questions. Their way out is a standard disclaimer that they are only engaged in an instrumentalist inquiry, not into 'what ought to be done', but into 'what needs to be done *if a certain goal is desired'*.

Such a disclaimer is especially pronounced in Bull. But this is disingenuous, given what he actually does in *The Anarchical Society* – to defend the political oragnization of the world as a society of sovereign states as the best practical alternative, currently available, to achieving what he characterizes as the elementary, primary and universal goals of all social life, as well as, be it noted, economic and social *justice*. The difference between this and an explicit moral engagement is paper thin, even non-existent. It is no surprise perhaps that Vincent, following on from here, produced an explicitly normative work – concerning which human rights are most basic and what international obligations follow from this – and Wheeler, following in Vincent's footsteps, wrote a volume, which not only advances a qualified defence of the practice of humanitarian intervention in contemporary international society, but argues passionately for the realization of a more solidarist world, based on dialogue, consent and transnational world public scrutiny. This kind of explicit moral advocacy has long been alien to the English School, but that is not to say that Bull did not advocate; he clearly did in his defence of the states-system.

The problem, however, is not with advocacy itself, but the extent to which the argument, backing the advocacy, is a sound one. Various criticisms were aimed at the reasoning, or the mode of argumentation, on the part of a number of English School contributors to the normative discourse on international relations.

In the case of Bull, the problem lies with his seemingly arbitrary separation between two kinds of values, those of social order, which he held to be objective, and those of social justice, which he presented as subjective; and also with his not very well defended assertion that 'life, truth and property', which he treated as the three elementary, primary and universal goals of all social life, were the objective values of social order. In the case of Vincent, it was noted, the reasoning that brings him to the conclusion that the right to life is the most elementary of all human rights would require closer scrutiny. As for Wheeler, his determination to make a solidarist case as a counterpoise to realism and pluralism seems to have made him adopt at least in part an overly prescriptive tone on somewhat optimistic empirical assumptions. As for Jackson's line that intolerable miseries experienced in less successful states are entirely their own responsibility and that more successful states may expel non-improvers from international organizations and even banish them 'to the outer fringes of diplomacy and beyond' (2000: 312), it neglects the historical origins and contemporary structural causes of the 'failed states' phenomenon, and is unlikely, at any rate, to command wide international support.

English School works have been criticized in a number of respects in the course of the discussion in this volume as well as by others. (1) Although the School offers a set of ideal-types with which to analyse the quality of life present in world politics – international system, international society and world community – it does not give a proper account of how a system can move towards society, or society towards community. (2) Although the School deals with international theories (as a subject-matter), its engagement with this subject is at times seriously flawed, skewing its own theoretical perspective on international relations. (3) Despite its stress on the importance of historical knowledge, its work is still underdeveloped, and its relevance to understanding the present or the speculating about the future is not fully explicated or substantiated. (4) The School tended, especially in its earlier phases, to conceal what amounted to its normative engagement with the subject of world politics, and this has made its work unsystematic and less than comprehensive.

Chapters 4–7 of this volume contain an attempt to address each of these deficiencies in turn. Thus, Chapter 4 argued that although English School writers have not analysed causal mechanisms of world political transformation, it is nonetheless possible to reread their texts constructively, perhaps with the help of some ideas and insights from some outside sources, and extract ideas about progressive potentials present in a states-system that would make possible a transformation of an international system towards a pluralist international society and from there towards a more solidarist one.

Such ideas, deriving from a number of English School writings, include the view that the desire to avoid destructive war would contribute towards imposition of some constraints on the use of force, adoption of a more moderate behaviour in foreign policy, and elementary recognition of the importance of reciprocity. If, through a process of social learning, these conditions lead gradually to mutual recognition among states of the legitimacy of each other's separate existence, we might say that the system of states has become a society of states, though still in a very elementary sense. What is envisaged here, in other words, is a possibility to move out of the international state of nature towards more civil forms of inter-state relations. The possibility is grounded in the states', and especially the more dominant states', appreciation of the cost of living under anarchy – incurred by the mode of life ruled by the need constantly to monitor, outmanoeuvre, dominate or coerce one another – and, their realization that through the use of rules, unspoken initially, but increasingly more formal, a semblance of order, *de jure* and more stable, could emerge for their mutual benefit.

How a society of states in the minimalist sense, where the bases of order are still very precarious, may proceed towards a more solid pluralist society and further along the solidarist path is an intriguing question, which the English School has not addressed explicitly or systematically. Chapter 4 argued, however, that there are some elements in English School writings which can be construed as pointing to a path of progressive transformation. Most importantly, Bull's discussion of the primary/elementary goals of international society was seen to suggest that what makes possible the consolidation of the pluralist society of states is a gradual acceptance of these goals as its common interests, a gradual working out of the rules that help achieve them, and operation of these rules by the states themselves (or their 'co-operation'). This, of course, would not satisfy those who are curious about the causal mechanisms that push states to come to accept these goals as their society's common goals. But it does indicate the path of progress which states must follow if they are to come to engage in more civil interrelations.

This is partly a constitutive claim; to follow such a path *is* to become civil. But, as with any constitutive claims, it is also a prescriptive one; it suggests a path that the agents need to follow to form a more civil social environment. The claim, then, that there is a progressive potential embedded in a system of states to move towards a societal one is one which points to the potential freedom on the part of the agents, located within that structure, to shape their interactions in an increasingly more civil manner. Contrary to the immutability thesis associated with Waltz's structural realism, it is a claim that affirms a human capacity to learn from harmful experiences and improve our conditions.

Still, the English School has often doubted that states can go much further than agree on pluralist rules of coexistence, and feared the negative consequences, in the circumstances they have taken to prevail in the world, of a premature stress on higher goals. They were willing to acknowledge that states learn in the sphere of strategic actions (where they master new techniques for outmanoeuvring or over-powering each other) or in the sphere of communicative action (where they establish principles of coexistence through diplomatic dialogue), but they were certainly not unanimous in accepting the view that they also learn in the moral sphere (where they gradually develop more sophisticated tests for the legitimacy of global political and economic arrangements). Nonetheless, some English School writers have drawn attention to the need and the possibility for international society to move more in the direction of protecting human rights and humanitarian values.

It was noted in this connection that Wheeler in particular gives a brief account of *how* a transition to a more solidarist world may come about. Central to his argument was the idea that those powers which intervene on humanitarian grounds may act as 'norm entrepreneurs' which invite other members of the society of states to take part in a diplomatic dialogue to rethink the classical prohibition of humanitarian intervention and work out tightly defined rules concerning its operation (Wheeler, 2001b: 160ff). One problem, of course, is that norm entrepreneurs may not necessarily be motivated by solidarism. Deterioration of international order is also always a possibility, of which English School writers have been mindful.

Nonetheless, in drawing attention to the possibility of progress towards a more solidarist world, Wheeler and others were gravitating towards the evolutionary vision of international relations embodied in the argument of Kant. Chapter 5 was therefore devoted to demonstrating that, far from being a typical revolutionist in Wight's tripartite classification of international thinkers, Kant should be seen to be located chiefly in the solidarist wing of the rationalist tradition.

This move has, among other things, an important heuristic impact. For it suggests that those who work within the English School tradition of rationalism, or who wish to build on it, could take Kant's writings seriously as their starting point and consider a variety of ways in which they can advance the study of world politics, world history and global ethics. This is to urge those who work within the English School tradition, or on the basis of its achievements, to go beyond its customary (typically Vattelian, 'miserable comforters') threshold of engagement – not the least because the need and the possibility to do so are already perceptible in the writings of the English School. Reoriented in this way, and with a clear self-awareness that Kant, as a political, moral and historical thinker, is one (though, of course, not the only one) of their intellectual ancestors, English School writers can gain considerable intellectual impetus to develop their argument further.

This is not at all to suggest that those who wish to build on the English School should turn utopian. Significantly, as was pointed out in Chapter 6, Kant's own position on humanitarian intervention was in fact similar to that of Jackson. Kant's famous remark that 'from such crooked wood as man is made of, nothing perfectly straight can be built' (Kant, 1963b: 17–18) is reminiscent of the scepticism of Bull and Wight. And his cosmopolitanism was so restrictive that he would not strike us now, by our current standards, as advancing an especially far-reaching cosmopolitan international relations theory. Despite all this, Kant stands for radicalized rationalism because of his fundamental belief in the possibility of progress, and ever closer approximation, towards the condition of perpetual peace, though, we should remember to add, through centuries perhaps of often unrewarded effort (Kant, 1965b: 124).

It was on the basis of this preliminary move that, in Chapter 6, a possibility of a Kant-inspired historical sociology of states-systems was explored. A Kantian historical sociology of states-systems, unlike the Hobbesian one, focusing on the rise and fall of hegemonic powers, would draw attention to a long-term historical process in which visions of the unity of humankind influence the development of states-systems. Although the Hobbesian narrative was more pronounced in the writings of Wight, it was suggested that the Kantian line, too, was discernible.

Inspired by Kant and the works of the British Committee on the Theory of International Politics, therefore, this chapter outlined a research project on the comparative historical sociology of states-systems, and gave an account of its preliminary findings on how far the constituent parts of different international systems have been able to reach an agreement that harm to individuals is a moral problem for the whole of humanity, requiring states, individually and collectively, to endeavour to solve. How far, to use Bull's idiom, have different international political orders contributed to world order by drawing on the idea of a universal community to create mechanisms for protecting individuals and non-sovereign communities from unnecessary suffering?

It was suggested in response to this question that although the potential to develop 'cosmopolitan harm conventions' – those which are designed to protect individuals everywhere from unnecessary harm irrespective of their citizenship or nationality, class, gender, race, sexuality and other characteristics – may have been present in all historical states-systems, the modern society of states has been unique in developing such conventions, or standards of legitimacy, as extensively as it has done. In particular, there have been advances in enlarging the circle of those with equal rights to be free from unnecessary physical violence and cruelty.

There has been significantly less progress, however, in recognizing the right of all human beings to be protected from the disadvantages caused by the operation of the global economic forces or by environmental degradation. Moreover, the modern society of states has become capable of inflicting an unprecedentedly large scale of harm on human beings, leading one to reflect on the dangers implicit in civilizing processes. Here then is one significant illustration of how a comparative historical study, in search of similarities *and* differences between the past and the present, may produce a deepened understanding of our present achievements, possibilities, limitations and dangers.

Finally, Chapter 7 made an attempt to distil from a number of English School texts a list of some key *prima facie* obligations which states should take seriously in their foreign policies so as not only to maintain international order but also to contribute to a more just world society. This discussion was conducted with reference to four ideal-type contexts: relations of states in a bare system of states; interrelations of pluralist states; those of solidarist states; and solidarist states' actions towards pluralist states. The chapter stressed the continuing relevance of Kant's philosophy of international relations to the project of radicalizing rationalism, noting also that Kant had no illusions about the scale of the achievement involved in creating order between states or about the obstacles to adding cosmopolitan harm conventions to the pluralist rules of inter-state coexistence.

Chapters 4–7 of this volume have thus indicated how we might build on the work of the English School, taking their achievements as a point of departure. Many weaknesses remain, and may remain to be noted, in the key classical texts of the English School. Some of these weaknesses may be unique to English School works, others they may share with those stemming from other intellectual backgrounds and traditions. But what the preceding chapters have indicated is one coherent way in which to proceed from where they have left off.

In setting out on this path, a particular attention was paid to what Bull appreciated in Wight's approach: that it embodied a commitment to moving beyond 'those studies of states-systems which view them as determined purely by mechanical factors such as the number of states in the system, their relative size, the political configuration in which they stand, the state of military technology' to a position which concentrates instead on 'the norms and values that animate the system, and the institutions in which they are expressed' (Bull, in Wight, 1977: 17): 'Institutionalism', in this sense, is indeed the common quality of all English School writings, from Manning and Wight earlier to Wheeler and Dunne more recently (Suganami, 2003).

And in advancing further along this path, the project outlined here sought to engage in 'a normatively grounded empirical analysis of the immanent possibility of a radically improved world order' (Chapter 5, p. 168). This, it was acknowledged however, requires a deeper reflection on its epistemological foundations. And, of course, its sociological location and political implications must also be subjected to critical scrutiny on the well-known principle that any theory, or history, contains claims to knowledge which are by someone and for someone (Cox, 1981).

There are therefore a number of deeper issues that remain to be addressed in the project outlined. A central one, however, has to do with the nature of solidarism that is being advocated. It is, centrally, a political attitude which insists that we must not be pessimistically fatalistic about the extent to which progress can be made in international relations, and that we must nurture those potentialities, perceptible in the world, which, when realized, will make it a more orderly and just place. But how are we to distinguish genuine solidarist arguments and policies, which contribute to such ends, from other solidaristic claims that in fact undermine them? In the aftermath of the events of 11 September 2001, the problem presents itself with unusual clarity.

The terrorist attacks, we might suppose, are not an example of genuine solidarism, though the perpetrators may have convinced themselves that they were fighting against American hegemony on behalf of the solidarity of the oppressed. Moreover, in the case of the recent war against Iraq, where the decision to start a war was not endorsed by the United Nations, those who favoured the invasion could and did argue that they stood for the security of the civilized way of life and for the human rights of the Iraqi people themselves, that there was a possibility to act together for these universal ends, but that the vetoing powers of their allies undermined this potential solidarity for peace and justice, and that they were forced therefore to act on behalf of this unrealized solidarist potentiality.

These positions may or may not strike us as genuine cases of solidarism. But they – rather awkwardly for the unpersuaded – appear in principle capable of satisfying the idea of solidarism as formulated above: 'a political attitude which insists that we must not be pessimistically fatalistic about the extent to which progress can be made in international relations, and that we must nurture those potentialities, perceptible in the world, which, when realized, will make it a more orderly and just place'. Now, of course, it would be absurd to suggest that the terrorists were on the side of order. But it is not *prima facie* implausible to argue that undermining the unipolar hegemony of the United States contributes to making the world a more orderly and just place in the long run, and many do in fact hold such a view. Nor is it of course mistaken in principle to argue that removing a tyrannical, erratic and militarized regime contributes to making the world a more orderly and just place.

But the key issue here seems to be the legitimacy of the chosen means. This needs to be brought into the conception of solidarism to protect it against its possible degeneration into a self-serving doctrine. In the two cases touched on here, the means used, and the process through which the choice of the means was authorized, lacked proper consensual legitimacy – in one case rather more starkly than in the other, many would of course argue. This leads to a modified interpretation of solidarism: 'a political attitude which insists that we must not be pessimistically fatalistic about the extent to which progress can be made in international relations; that we must nurture those potentialities, perceptible in the world, which, when realized, will make it a more orderly and just place; and *that in attempting to actualize such potentialities, care must be taken to act on the basis of sound consensual legitimacy*'.

It will of course be asked what constitutes 'sound consensual legitimacy', which is not an easy question. The UN Security Council's endorsement is, of course, neither unconditionally necessary nor necessarily sufficient to prove the presence of such legitimacy, but will count as supporting evidence. The role of the government leaders is to identify and pursue the policy which, in the circumstances, is likely not obviously to contradict the requirement of consensual legitimacy measured in the light of a number of fairly standard indicators, such as preponderant opinions expressed by a wide range of entities in the global, regional, governmental and non-governmental forums.

One implication of this qualification – that care must be taken to act on the basis of sound consensual legitimacy – is this: where a requisite consensus fails to emerge, solidarists-at-heart should be resigned, perhaps temporarily, to take on a pluralist stance. This, of course, is not to turn away from the responsibility to act in such a way that does not hinder the emergence of a more consensual world. Moreover, to act unilaterally against evil when everyone else turns a blind eye towards it may be morally laudable in specific cases. But the danger we now face – and have always faced – is the evil of unilateralism masquerading as solidarism, which any solidarist project must guard against, without, of course, abandoning the quest for a radically improved world order.

Bibliography

Acton, H. B. (1970) *Kant's Moral Philosophy*. London: Macmillan.

Adler, E. and Barnet, M. (eds.) (1998) *Security Communities*. Cambridge: Cambridge University Press.

Akehurst, M. (1984) 'Humanitarian Intervention'. In Bull 1984b, 95–118.

(1992) *A Modern Introduction to International Law*. London: Routledge.

Alderson, K. and Hurrell, A. (eds.) (2000) *Hedley Bull on International Society*. London: Macmillan.

Armstrong, D. (1993) *Revolution and World Order: The Revolutionary State in International Society*. Oxford: Clarendon Press.

Bain, W. (2003) 'The Political Theory of Trusteeship and the Twilight of International Inequality', *International Relations*, 17(1), 59–77.

Barkan, E. (2000) *The Guilt of Nations: Restitution and Negotiating International Injustices*. London: Johns Hopkins University Press.

Barry, B. (1995) *Justice as Impartiality*. Oxford: Oxford University Press.

Bauman, Z. (1989) *Modernity and the Holocaust*. Cambridge: Polity Press.

Baylis, J. and Smith, S. (eds.) (2001) *The Globalization of World Politics*, 2nd ed. London: Oxford University Press.

Beck, L. (ed.) (1988) *Kant: Selections*. London: Collier Macmillan.

Beck, U. (1992) *Risk Society: Towards a New Modernity*. London: Sage.

Bellamy, A. J. (ed.) (2005) *International Society and its Critics*. Oxford: Oxford University Press.

Bending, L. (2000) *The Representation of Bodily Pain in Late Nineteenth-Century English Literature*. Oxford: Oxford University Press.

Best, G. (1994) *War and Law since 1945*. Oxford: Clarendon Press.

Blair, T. (2001) 'Speech to the Labour Party Conference', *The Guardian*, 3 October 2001.

Blundell, M. W. (1991) *Helping Friends and Harming Enemies: A Study in Sophocles and Greek Ethics*. Cambridge: Cambridge University Press.

Bohman, J. and Lutz-Bachmann, M. (eds.) (1997) *Perpetual Peace: Essays on Kant's Cosmopolitan Ideal*. London: Massachussetts Institute of Technology.

Bolis, J. and Thomas, G. (eds.) (1999) *Constructing World Culture: International NonGovernmental Organisations since 1875*. Stanford: Stanford University Press.

Booth, K. (ed.) (2001) *The Kosovo Tragedy: The Human Rights Dimensions*. London: Frank Cass.

Booth, K. and Dunne, T. (eds.) (2002) *Worlds in Collision: Terror and the Future of Global Order*. Basingstoke: Macmillan.

Booth, K. and Smith, S. (eds.) (1995), *International Relations Theory Today*. Cambridge: Polity Press.

Bozeman, A. (1960) *Politics and Culture in International History*. Princeton: Princeton University Press.

Brown, C. (1988) 'The Modern Requirement? Reflections on Normative International Theory in a Post Western World', *Millennium*, 17(2), 339–48.

(1995) 'International Theory and International Society: The Viability of the Middle Way', *Review of International Studies*, 21(2), 183–96.

(1997) *Understanding International Relations*. Houndmills: Macmillan.

(2001) *Understanding International Relations*, 2nd ed. Houndmills: Palgrave.

Brown, C., Nardin. T. and Rengger, N. (eds.) (2002) *International Relations in Political Thought*. Cambridge: Cambridge University Press.

Brown, P. G. and Shue, H. (eds.) (1981) *Boundaries: National Autonomy and its Limits*. Totowa, New Jersey: Rowman and Littlefield.

Bull, H. (1966a) 'Society and Anarchy in International Relations'. In Butterfield and Wight 1966, 35–50, reprinted in Alderson and Hurrell 2000, 77–94.

(1966b) 'Grotian Conception of International Society'. In Butterfield and Wight 1966, 51–73, reprinted in Alderson and Hurrell 2000, 95–124.

(1969) 'International Theory: The Case for a Classical Approach'. In Knorr and Rosenau 1969, 20–38. Originally published in *World Politics*, 18(3), 361–77.

(1972a), 'International Law and International Order', *International Organization*, 26 (3), 583–8.

(1972b) 'The Theory of International Politics 1919–1969'. In Porter 1972, 30–55.

(1973) 'Options for Australia'. In McCarthy 1973, 1–10.

(1977) *The Anarchical Society: A Study of Order in World Politics*. London: Macmillan.

(1979a) 'Human Rights and World Politics'. In Pettman 1979, 79–91.

(1979b) 'The State's Positive Role in World Affairs'. In Alderson and Hurrell 2000, 139–56.

(1980) 'The Great Responsibles? The United States, the Soviet Union and World Order', *International Journal*, 35(3), 437–47.

(1982) 'The West and South Africa', *Daedalus*, 11, 255–70.

(1983a) 'Civilian Power Europe: A Contradiction in Terms?' In Tsoukalis 2003, 149–70.

(1983b) 'The International Anarchy in the 1980s', *Australian Outlook*, 37, 127–31.

274

(1984a) 'The Emergence of a Universal International Society'. In Bull and Watson 1984, 117–26.

(ed.) (1984b) *Intervention in World Politics*. Oxford: Clarendon Press.

(1986) 'Hans Kelsen and International Law'. In Tur and Twining 1986, 321–36.

(1990) 'The Importance of Grotius'. In Bull, Kingsbury and Roberts 1990, 65–93.

(1991) 'Martin Wight and the Theory of International Relations'. In Wight 1991, ix–xxvii. Originally published in 1976 in *British Journal of International Studies*, 2, 101–16.

(2000a) 'International Relations as an Academic Pursuit'. In Alderson and Hurrell 2000, 246–64. Originally published in 1972 in *Australian Outlook*, 26(3).

(2000b) 'The State's Positive Role in World Affairs'. In Alderson and Hurrell 2000, 139–56. Originally published in 1979 in *Daedalus*, 108(4), 111–23.

(2000c) *'The Twenty Years' Crisis* Thirty Years On'. In Alderson and Hurrell 2000, 125–38. Originally published in 1969 in *International Journal*, 24(4), 625–38.

(2000d) 'Justice in International Relations'. In Alderson and Hurrell 2000, 206–45. Originally published in 1984 as *Hagey Lectures*, University of Waterloo, Ontario.

(2000e) 'Natural Law and International Relations'. In Alderson and Hurrell 2000, 157–69. Originally published in 1979 in *British Journal of International Studies*, 5, 171–81.

(2002) *The Anarchical Society: A Study of Order in World Politics*, 3rd ed. London: Palgrave.

Bull, H., Kingsbury, B. and Roberts, A. (eds.) (1990) *Hugo Grotius and International Relations*. Oxford: Clarendon Press.

Bull, H. and Watson, A. (eds.) (1984) *The Expansion of International Society*. Oxford: Clarendon Press.

Burke, P., Harrison B. and Slack, P. (eds.) (2000) *Civil Histories: Essays Presented to Sir Keith Thomas*. Cambridge: Cambridge University Press.

Butler, J. (2004). *Precarious Lives: The Powers of Mourning and Violence*. London: Verso.

Butterfield, H. (1951a) *The Whig Interpretation of History*. London: Bell.

(1951b) *History and Human Relations*. London: Collins.

(1951c) 'The Tragic Element in Modern International Conflict'. In Butterfield 1951b, 9–37.

(1953) *Christianity, Diplomacy and War*. London: Epworth Press.

(1966a) 'The Balance of Power'. In Butterfield and Wight 1966, 132–48.

(1966b) 'The New Diplomacy and Historical Diplomacy'. In Butterfield and Wight 1966, 181–92.

(1972) 'Morality and an International Order'. In Porter 1972, 336–57.

Butterfield, H. and Wight, M. (eds.) (1966) *Diplomatic Investigations: Essays in the Theory of International Politics*. London: Allen and Unwin.

Buzan, B. (1993) 'From International System to International Society: Structural Realism and Regime Theory Meet the English School', *International Organization*, 47(3), 327–52.

(2001) 'The English School: An Underexploited Resource in IR', *Review of International Studies*, 27(3), 471–88.

(2004) *From International to World Society?: English School Theory and the Social Structure of Globalization*. Cambridge: Cambridge University Press.

Buzan, B., Jones, C. and Little, R. (1993) *The Logic of Anarchy: Neorealism to Structural Realism*. New York: Columbia University Press.

Buzan, B. and Little, R. (2000) *International Systems in World History: Remaking the Study of International Relations*. Oxford: Oxford University Press.

Carr, D. (1986) 'Narrative and the Real World: An Argument for Continuity', *History and Theory*, 25(2), 117–31.

Carr, E. H. (1939), *The Twenty Years' Crisis 1919–1939*. London: Macmillan.

(1945) *Nationalism and After*. London: Macmillan.

(1946) *The Twenty Years' Crisis 1919–1939*, 2nd ed. London: Macmillan.

Chomsky, N. (1999) *The New Military Humanism*. Monroe: Common Courage Press.

Cicero (1967) *On Moral Obligation*. Introduction and Notes by Higginbotham. London: Faber and Faber.

Clark, I. (1989) *The Hierarchy of States: Reform and Resistance in the International Order*. Cambridge: Cambridge University Press.

(2003) 'Legitimacy in a Global Order', *Review of International Studies*, 29 (special issue, December 2003, 75–95).

(2005) *Legitimacy in International Society*. Oxford: Oxford University Press.

Clark, I. and Neumann I. B. (eds.) (1996) *Classical Theories of International Relations*. Basingstoke: Macmillan.

Cohen, S. (2001) *States of Denial: Knowing about Atrocities and Suffering*. Cambridge: Polity Press.

Cooper, R. (1996) *The Postmodern State and the World Order*. London: Demos, Paper 19.

Cox, M. (ed.) (2000) *E. H. Carr: A Critical Appraisal*. Basingstoke: Palgrave.

Cox, R. W. (1981) 'States, Social Forces and World Orders: Beyond International Relations Theory', *Millennium*, 10(2), 126–55.

Crawford, N. C. (2002), *Argument and Change in World Politics: Ethics, Decolonisation and Humanitarian Intervention*. Cambridge: Cambridge University Press.

Cummiskey, D. (1996) *Kantian Consequentialism*. Oxford: Oxford University Press.

Dan-Cohen, M. (2002) *Harmful Thoughts: Essays on Law, Self and Morality*. Princeton: Princeton University Press.

Denemark, R. A., Friedman, J., Gills, B. K. and Modelski, G. (eds.) (2000) *World System History: The Social Science of Long-Term Change*. London: Routledge.

Der Derian, J. (1987) *On Diplomacy: A Genealogy of Western Estrangement*. Oxford: Blackwell.

Der Derian, J. and Shapiro, M. J. (1989) *International/Intertextual Relations: Postmodern Readings of World Politics*. New York: Lexington Books.

Derrida, J. (2000) *On Cosmopolitanism and Forgiveness*. London: Routledge.

De-Shalit, A. (1998) 'Transnational and International Exploitation', *Political Science*, 46(4), 693–78.

Donelan, M. (1984) 'Spain and the Indies'. In Bull and Watson 1984, 75–85.

Donelan, M. D. (1990) *Elements of International Political Theory*. Oxford: Clarendon Press.

Donnelly, J. (1998) 'Human Rights: A New Standard of Civilization?', *International Affairs*, 74(1), 1–23.

Doyle, M. (1983) 'Kant, Liberal Legacies and Foreign Affairs Parts I and II', *Philosophy and Public Affairs*, 12(3), 205–35, 12(4), 232–52.

(1986) 'Liberalism and World Politics', *American Political Science Review*, 80, 1151–69.

Dray, W. H. (1957) *Laws and Explanation in History*. Oxford: Clarendon Press.

Dunne, T. (1995a) 'International Society: Theoretical Promises Fulfilled?', *Cooperation and Conflict*, 30(2), 125–54.

(1995b) 'The Social Construction of International Society', *European Journal of International Relations*, 1(3), 367–89.

(1998) *Inventing International Society: A History of the English School*. London: Macmillan.

(2000a) 'All Along the Watchtower: A Reply to the Critics of *Inventing International Society*', *Cooperation and Conflict*, 35(2), 227–38.

(2000b) 'Sociological Investigations: Instrumental, Legitimist and Coercive Interpretations of International Society', *Millennium*, 30(1), 67–91.

(2001) 'Watching the Wheels Go Round: Replying to the Replies', *Cooperation and Conflict*, 36(3), 338–42.

(2003) 'Society and Hierarchy in International Relations', *International Relations*, 17(3), 303–20.

Dunne, T. and Wheeler, N. (2000) 'The Blair Doctrine: Advancing the Third Way in the World'. In Little and Wickham-Jones 2000, 61–76.

Dunne, T. and Wheeler, N. J. (eds.) (1999) *Human Rights in Global Politics*. Cambridge: Cambridge University Press.

Elias, N. (1978) *The History of Manners: The Civilising Process, Volume One*. Oxford: Basil Blackwell.

(1991) *The Symbol Theory*. London: Sage.

(1994) *Reflections on a Life*. Cambridge: Polity Press.

(1996) *The Germans*. Cambridge: Polity Press.

(1998a) 'The Expulsion of the Huguenots from France'. In Goudsblom and Mennell, 1998.

(1998b) 'The Breakdown of Civilization'. In Goudsblom and Mennell, 1998.

(2001) *The Loneliness of the Dying*. London: Continuum.

Elman, C. and Elman, M. F. (2001) (eds.) *Bridges and Boundaries: Historians, Political Scientists, and the Study of International Relations*. Cambridge, Mass.: MIT Press.

Epp, R. (1998) 'The English School on the Frontiers of International Relations', *Review of International Studies*, 24 (special issue), 47–63.

Evans, G. and Grant B. (1991) *Australia's Foreign Relations in the World of the 1990s*. Melbourne: Melbourne University Press.

Evans, M. D. (1994) *Blackstone's International Law Documents*. London: Blackstone Press.

Evans, T. and Wilson, P. (1992) 'Regime Theory and the English School of International Relations: A Comparison', *Millennium*, 21(3), 329–51.

Fawn, R. and Larkins, J. (eds.) (1996a) *International Society after the Cold War: Anarchy and Order Reconsidered*. Houndmills: Macmillan in association with *Millennium*.

(1996b) 'Introduction'. In Fawn and Larkins 1996a, 1–24.

Feinberg, J. (1984) *Harm to Others: The Moral Limits of the Criminal Law*. Oxford: Oxford University Press.

Finnemore, M. (1996) 'Constructing Norms of Humanitarian Intervention'. In Katzenstein 1996, 153–85.

(1999) 'Rules of War and Wars' Rules: The International Red Cross and the Restraint of State Violence'. In Bolis and Thomas 1999.

(2001) 'Exporting the English School?', *Review of International Studies*, 27(3), 509–13.

Finnemore, M. and Sikkink, K. (1998) 'International Norm Dynamics and Political Change', *International Organisation*, 52(4), 887–917.

Fischer, M. (1992) 'Feudal Europe, 800–1300: Communal Discourses and Conflictual Practices', *International Organisation*, 46(2), 427–66.

Fletcher, J. (1997) *Violence and Civilization: An Introduction to the Work of Norbert Elias*. Cambridge: Polity Press.

Forbes, I. and Hoffman, M. (eds.) (1993) *Political Theory, International Relations and the Ethics of Intervention*. London: Macmillan.

Forsyth, M. G., Keens-Soper, M. and Savigear, P. (eds.) (1970) *The Theory of International Relations: Selected Texts from Gentili to Treitschke*. London: Allen and Unwin.

Foucault, M. (1977) *Discipline and Punish: The Birth of the Prison*. Harmondsworth: Penguin.

Fry, G. and O'Hagan (eds.) (2000) *Contending Images of World Politics*. Houndmills: Macmillan.

George, J. (1994) *Discourses of Global Politics: A Critical (Re)Introduction to International Relations*. Colorado: Boulder.

Geras, N. (1998) *The Contract of Mutual Indifference: Political Philosophy after the Holocaust*. London: Verso.

(1999) 'The View from Everywhere', *Review of International Studies*, 25(1), 157–63.

Gerth, H. H. and Mills, C. Wright (eds.) (1948) *From Max Weber: Essays in Sociology*. Routledge and Kegan Paul.

Glaser, C. (2003) 'Structural Realism in a More Complex World', *Review of International Studies*, 29(3), 403–14.

Glover, J. (1990) *Causing Death and Saving Lives*. London: Penguin.

Goldgeier, J. M. and McFaul, M. (1992) 'A Tale of Two Worlds: Core and Periphery in the Post-Cold War Era', *International Organisation*, 46(2), 467–91.

Gong, G. (1984) *The Standard of 'Civilisation' in International Society*. Oxford: Clarendon Press.

Gonzalez-Pelaez, A. and Buzan, B. (2003) 'A Viable Project of Solidarism? The Neglected Contributions of John Vincent's Basic Rights Initiative', *International Relations*, 17(3), 321–39.

Goodin, R. (1985) *Protecting the Vulnerable: A Reanalysis of our Social Responsibilities*. London: University of Chicago Press.

Goodwin, G. L. (ed.) (1951) *The University Teaching of International Relations*. Oxford: Blackwell.

— (1973) 'International Institutions and International Order'. In James 1973a, 156–87.

Goudsblom, J. (1994) *Fire and Civilization*. London: Penguin.

Goudsblom, J., Jones, E. and Mennell, S. (1996) *The Course of Human History: Economic Growth, Social Process and Civilization*. London: M. E. Sharpe Inc.

Goudsblom, J. and Mennell, S. (eds.) (1998) *The Norbert Elias Reader*. Oxford: Basil Blackwell.

Gouldner, A. (1960) 'The Norm of Reciprocity: A Preliminary Statement', *American Sociological Review*, 25, 161–77.

Grader, S. (1988) 'The English School of International Relations: Evidence and Evaluation', *Review of International Studies*, 14(1), 29–44.

Groom, A. J. R. and Light, M. (eds.) (1994) *Contemporary International Relations: A Guide to Theory*. London: Frances Pinter.

Grotius, H. ([1646]1925) *De Jure Belli ac Pacis*. Translated by F. W. Kelsey. Oxford: Clarendon Press.

Haas, P. M., Keohane, R. O. and Levy, M. A. (eds.) (1994) *Institutions for the Earth: Sources of Effective International Environmental Protection*. Cambridge, Mass.: MIT Press.

Habermas, J. (1984) *Theory of Communicative Action, Vol. 1*. Boston Massachusetts: Beacon Press.

— (1997) 'Kant's Idea of Perpetual Peace, with the Benefit of Two Hundred Years' Hindsight'. In Bohman and Lutz-Bachmann 1997, 113–53.

Hall, I. (2001) 'Still the English Patient? Closures and Inventions in the English School', *International Affairs*, 77–4, 931–42.

— (2002) 'History, Christianity and Diplomacy: Sir Herbert Butterfield and International Relations', *Review of International Studies*, 28(4) 719–36.

Hall, R. B. and Biersteker, T. J. (eds.) (2002) *The Emergence of Private Authority in Global Governance*. Cambridge: Cambridge University Press.

Halliday, F. (1994) *Rethinking International Relations*. London: Macmillan.

Hart, H. L. A. (1961) *The Concept of Law*. Oxford: Clarendon Press.

Hasenclever, A., Mayer, P. and Rittberger, V. (1997) *Theories of International Regimes*. Cambridge: Cambridge University Press.

Held, D. (ed.) (1991) *Political Theory Today.* Cambridge: Polity Press.

(1995) *Democracy and World Order: From the Modern State to Cosmopolitan Governance.* Cambridge: Polity Press.

Hill, C. J. (2003) *The Changing Politics of Foreign Policy.* Basingstoke: Palgrave Macmillan.

Hobbes, T. ([1651]1962) *Leviathan.* Edited and abridged with an introduction by J. Plamenatz. London: Collins.

Hobden, S. (1998) *International Relations and Historical Sociology.* Cambridge: Cambridge University Press.

Hobden, S. (1990) and Hobson, J. (eds.) (2002) *Historical Sociology of International Relations.* Cambridge: Cambridge University Press.

Hoffman, M. (1987) 'Critical Theory and the Inter-Paradigm Debate', *Millennium: Journal of International Studies,* 16(2), 231–49.

Hoffmann, S. (1990) 'International Society'. In Miller and Vincent 1990, 13–37.

Hollis, M. and Smith, S. (1990) *Explaining and Understanding International Relations.* Oxford: Clarendon Press.

Honderich, T. (1980a) *Violence for Equality: Inquiries in Political Philosophy.* Harmondsworth: Penguin.

(1980b) 'Our Omissions and Their Violence'. In Honderich 1980a, 58–100.

Hurrell, A. (1990) 'Kant and the Kantian Paradigm in International Relations', *Review of International Studies,* 16(3), 183–205.

(1992) 'Collective Security and International Order Revisited', *International Relations,* 11(1), 37–55.

(1994) 'A Crisis of Ecological Viability? Global Environmental Change and the Nation-State', *Political Studies,* 42, 146–65.

(1995) 'International Political Theory and the Global Environment'. In Booth and Smith 1995, 129–53.

(1998) 'Society and Anarchy in the 1990s'. In Roberson 1998, 17–42.

(1999) 'Power, Principles and Prudence: Protecting Human Rights in a Deeply Divided World'. In Dunne and Wheeler 1999, 277–302.

(2001) 'Keeping History, Law and Political Philosophy Firmly Within the English School', *Review of International Studies,* 27(3), 489–94.

(2002) 'There Are No Rules (George W. Bush): International Order after September 11', *International Relations,* 16(2), 185–203.

Hutchings, K. (1999) *International Political Theory: Rethinking Ethics in a Global Age.* London: Sage.

Ignatieff, M. (2000) *Virtual War.* London: Chatto and Windus.

Jackson, R. H. (1990) *Quasi-States: Sovereignty, International Relations and the Third World.* Cambridge: Cambridge University Press.

(1995) 'The Political Theory of International Society'. In Booth and Smith 1995, 110–28.

(1996) 'Is There a Classical International Theory?' In Smith, Booth and Zalewski 1996, 203–18.

(2000) *The Global Covenant: Human Conduct in a World of States.* Oxford: Oxford University Press.

James, A. M. (1964) 'Power Politics', *Political Studies*, 12(3), 307–26.

(1972) 'The Contemporary Relevance of National Sovereignty'. In Leifer 1972, 16–34.

(ed.) (1973a) *The Bases of International Order: Essays in Honour of C. A. W. Manning*. London: Oxford University Press.

(1973b) 'Law and Order in International Society'. In James 1973a, 60–84.

(1986a) *Sovereign Statehood: The Basis of International Society*. London: Allen and Unwin.

(1986b) 'The Emerging Global Society', *Third World Affairs 1986*, 465–68.

(1989) 'The Realism of Realism: The State and the Study of International Relations', *Review of International Studies*, 15(3), 215–29.

(1993) 'System or Society?', *Review of International Studies*, 19(3), 269–88.

Jellinek, G. (1922) *Allgemeine Staatslehre*. 3rd ed. by W. Jellinek. Berlin: Springer.

Johansen, R. C. (1980) *The National Interest and the Human Interest: An Analysis of U. S. Foreign Policy*. Princeton: Princeton University Press.

Jones, R. E. (1981) 'The English School of International Relations: A Case for Closure', *Review of International Studies*, 7(1), 1–13.

Jones, R. W. (ed.) (2000) *Critical Theory and World Politics*. London: Lynne Rienner.

Kaldor, M. (1999) *New Wars, Old Wars: Organized Violence in a Global Age*. Cambridge: Polity Press.

Kant, I. (1963a) *On History*, edited with an introduction by L. W. Beck. Indianapolis: Bobbs-Merrill.

(1963b) 'Idea for a Universal History from a Cosmopolitan Point of View'. In Kant 1963a, 11–26.

(1965a) *The Moral Law: Kant's Groundwork of the Metaphysic of Morals*. Translated by H. J. Paton. London: Hutchinson University Library.

(1965b) *The Metaphysical Elements of Justice*. Translated by John Ladd. New York: Bobbs-Merrill.

(1970a) 'On the Commonplace: What May Be True in Theory May Be Useless in Practice'. In Forsyth, Keens-Soper and Savigear 1970.

(1970b) *Perpetual Peace*. In Forsyth, Keens-Soper and Savigear 1970.

(1988) 'Idea for a Universal History from a Cosmopolitan Point of View'. In Beck 1988, 320–36.

(2002) 'Essay on Theory and Practice'. In Brown, Nardin and Rengger 2002, 428–32.

Katzenstein, P. J. (ed.) (1996) *The Culture of National Security: Norms and Identity in World Politics*. New York: Columbia University Press.

Keal, P. (1983) *Unspoken Rules and Superpower Dominance*. London: Macmillan.

(ed.) (1992) *Ethics and Foreign Policy*. St Leonards: Allen and Unwin.

(1995) 'Just Backward Children': International Law and the Conquest of Non-European Peoples', *Australian Journal of International Relations*, 49(2), 191–206.

(2000) 'An International Society?' In Fry and O'Hagan 2000, 61–75.

(2003) *European Conquest and the Rights of Indigenous Peoples: The Moral Backwardness of International Society*. Cambridge: Cambridge University Press.

Bibliography

Kelly, P. (ed.) (1998) *Impartiality, Neutrality and Justice: Re-Reading Brian Barry's Justice as Impartiality*. Edinburgh: Edinburgh University Press.

Kelsen, H. (1934) *The Legal Process and International Order*. The New Commonwealth Research Bureau Publications, Series A, No. 1

(1967) *Principles of International Law*. 2nd ed. by R. W. Tucker. New York: Holt, Rinehard and Winston.

Keohane, R. O. (1984) *After Hegemony: Cooperation and Discord in the World Political Economy*. Princeton: Princeton University Press.

(ed.) (1986a) *Neorealism and its Critics*. New York: Columbia University Press.

(1986b) 'Reciprocity in International Relations', *International Organization*, 40 (1), 1–27.

(1989a) 'Closing the Fairness-Practice Gap', *Ethics in International Affairs*, 3, 101–16.

(1989b) *International Institutions and State Power*. Boulder, Colorado: Westview.

(1989c) 'International Institutions: Two Approaches'. In Keohane 1989b, 158–79.

Kiernan, V. (1998) *Colonial Empires and Armies, 1815–1960*. Stroud: Sutton Publishing.

Kissinger, H. (1979) *White House Years*. London: Weidenfeld and Nicholson.

Knorr, K. and Rosenau, J. N. (eds.) (1969) *Contending Approaches to International Politics*. Princeton: Princeton University Press.

Knudsen, T. B. (2000) 'Theory of Society or Society of Theorists? With Tim Dunne in the English School', *Cooperation and Conflict*, 35(2), 193–203.

(2001) 'Beyond the Watchtower? A Further Note on the Origins of the English School and its Theoretical Potential', *Cooperation and Conflict*, 36 (3), 331–3.

Konstan, D. (2001) *Pity Transformed*. London: Duckworth.

Krasner, S. D. (1999) *Sovereignty: Organized Hypocrisy*. Princeton: Princeton University Press.

Kutz, C. (2000) *Complicity: Ethics and Law for a Collective Age*. Cambridge: Cambridge University Press.

Kyle, D. G. (1998) *Spectacles of Death in Ancient Rome*. London: Routledge.

Lamy, S. L. (2001), 'Contemporary Mainstream Approaches: Neo-Realism and Neo-Liberalism'. In Baylis and Smith 2001, 182–99.

Lang, A. F. (ed.) (2003) *Just Intervention*. Washington: Georgetown University Press.

Leaver, R. and Richardson, J. L. (eds.) (1993) *The Post-Cold War Order: Diagnoses and Prognoses*. St Leonards: Allen and Unwin.

Leifer, M. (ed.) (1972) *Constraints and Adjustments in British Foreign Policy*. London: Allen and Unwin.

Lewis, B. (1990) *Race and Slavery in the Middle East: An Historical Enquiry*. London: Oxford University Press.

Linklater, A. (1982/1990) *Men and Citizens in the Theory of International Relations*. London: Macmillan.

(1990a) *Beyond Realism and Marxism: Critical Theory and International Relations*. London: Macmillan.

(1990b) 'What is a Good International Citizen?' In Keal 1992, 21–43.

(1993) 'Liberal Democracy, Constitutionalism and the New World Order'. In Leaver and Richardson 1993, 29–38.

(1996a) 'The Achievements of Critical Theory'. In Smith, Booth and Zalewski 1996, 279–98.

(1996b) 'Citizenship and Sovereignty in the Post-Westphalian State', *European Journal of International Relations*, 2(1), 77–103.

(1998) *The Transformation of Political Community: Ethical Foundations of the Post-Westphalian Era*. Cambridge: Polity Press.

(2000) 'E. H. Carr, Nationalism and the Future of the Sovereign State'. In Cox 2000, 234–57.

(2001) 'Citizenship, Humanity and Cosmopolitan Harm Conventions', *International Political Science Review*, 22(3), 261–77.

(2002a) 'The Problem of Harm in World Politics: Implications for the Sociology of States-System', *International Affairs*, 78(2), 319–38.

(2002b) 'Unnecessary Suffering'. In Booth and Dunne 2002, 303–12.

(2002c) 'Towards a Critical Historical Sociology of Transnational Harm'. In Hobden and Hobson 2002, 162–80.

(2002d) 'The Problem of Harm in World Politics: Implications for a Sociology of States Systems', *International Affairs*, 78(2), 319–38.

(2004) 'Norbert Elias, The "Civilising Process" and International Relations', *International Politics*, 41, 3–35.

Little, R. (1994) 'International Relations and Large-Scale Historical Change'. In Groom and Light 1994, 9–26.

(1995) 'Neorealism and the English School: A Methodological, Ontological and Theoretical Reassessment', *European Journal of International Relations*, 1 (1), 9–34.

(1996) 'Friedrich Gentz, Rationalism and the Balance of Power'. In Clark and Neumann 1996, 210–32.

(2002a) 'The English School's Contribution to the Study of International Relations', *European Journal of International Relations*, 6(3), 395–422.

(2002b) 'International System, International Society and World Society: A Re-Evaluation of the English School'. In Roberson, 2002, 68–85.

(2003) 'The English School vs. American Realism', *Review of International Studies*, 29(3), 443–60.

Little, R. and Wickham-Jones, M. (eds.) (2000) *New Labour's Foreign Policy: A New Moral Crusade?* Manchester: Manchester University Press.

Luard, E. (1976) *Types of International Society*. New York: Free Press.

Lynch, M. (2000) 'The Dialogue of Civilisations and International Public Sphere Theory', *Millennium*, 29(2), 307–30.

(2002) 'Why Engage? China and the Logic of Communicative Engagement', *European Journal of International Relations*, 8(2), 187–230.

Lyons, G. M. (1986) 'The Study of International Relations in Great Britain: Further Connections', *World Politics*, 38(4), 626–45.

Mackie, J. (1977) *Ethics: Inventing Right and Wrong*. Harmondsworth: Penguin.

MacMillan, J. (1995) 'A Kantian Protest Against the Peculiar Discourse of Inter-Liberal State Peace', *Millennium*, 24(3), 549–62.

(1998) 'The Power of the Pen: Liberalism's Ethical Dynamic and World Politics', *Millennium*, 27(3), 637–67.

Makinda, S. M. (2000) 'International Society and Eclecticism in International Relations Theory', *Cooperation and Conflict*, 35(2), 205–16.

(2001) 'International Society and Global Governance', *Cooperation and Conflict*, 36(3), 334–7.

Mandelbaum, M. (1971) *History, Man, and Reason: Study in Nineteenth-Century Thought*. Baltimore: Johns Hopkins University Press.

Mann, M. (1986) *The Sources of Social Power: A History of Power from the Beginning to A. D. 1760*. Cambridge: Cambridge University Press.

Manning, C. A. W. (1936) 'The Future of the Collective System'. In Geneva Institute of International Relations, *Problems of Peace*, 10th series, *Anarchy or World Order*. London: Allen and Unwin, 152–77.

(1951a) 'International Relatons: An Academic Discipline'. In Goodwin 1951, 11–26.

(1951b) 'Report of the General Rapporteur'. In Goodwin, 1951, 27–73.

(1954) *The University Teaching of Social Sciences: International Relations – A Report Prepared on Behalf of the International Studies Conference*. Paris: UNESCO.

(1962) *The Nature of International Society*. London: Macmillan, Bell and Sons.

(1964) 'In Defence of Apartheid', *Foreign Affairs*, 43(1), 135–49.

(1966c) *Collective Selfhoods: An Element in the South West Africa Case, Being the Testimony of an Academic South African*. London: South Africa Society.

(1972) 'The Legal Framework in a World of Change'. In Porter 1972, 301–35.

(1975) *The Nature of International Society*, reissue. London: Macmillan, first published by the London School of Economics in 1962.

Mason, M. (2001) 'Transnational Environmental Obligations: Locating New Spaces of Accountability in a Post-Westphalian Order', *Transactions of the Institute of British Geographers*, 26(4), 407–29.

Matravers, M. (1998) 'What's "Wrong" in Contractualism?'. In Kelly 1998, 108–19.

Mayall, J. B. (ed.) (1982) *The Community of States: A Study in International Political Theory*. London: Allen and Unwin.

(ed.) (1996) *The New Interventionism, 1991–1994: United Nations Experience in Cambodia, Former Yugoslavia and Somalia*. Cambridge: Cambridge University Press.

(2000a) 'Democracy and International Society', *International Affairs*, 76(1), 61–75.

(2000b) 'The Concept of Humanitarian Intervention Revisited'. In Schnabel and Thakur 2000, 319–33.

(2000c) *World Politics: Progress and its Limits*. Cambridge: Polity Press.

McCarthy G. (ed.) (1973) *Foreign Policy for Australia: Choices for the 1970s.* Sydney: Angus and Robertson.

McGrew, A. and Lewis, P. et al (eds.) (1992) *Global Politics: Globalization and the Nation-State.* Cambridge: Polity.

Meron, T. (1998) *Bloody Constraint: War and Chivalry in Shakespeare.* Oxford: Oxford University Press.

Midgley, E. B. F. (1979) 'Natural Law and the "Anglo-Saxon" – Some Reflections in Response to Hedley Bull', *British Journal of International Studies*, 5(3), 260–72.

Miller, J. D. B. (1990) 'The Third World'. In Miller and Vincent 1990, 65–94.

Miller, J. D. B. and Vincent, R. J. (eds.) (1990) *Order and Violence: Hedley Bull and International Relations.* Oxford: Clarendon Press.

Mitrany, D. A. (1966) *A Working Peace System.* Chicago: Quadrangle Books.

Naff, T. (1984) 'The Ottoman Empire and the European States System'. In Bull and Watson 1984, 143–69.

Nardin, T. (1983) *Law, Morality and the Relations of States.* Princeton: Princeton University Press.

Neiman, S. (2002) *Evil in Modern Thought: An Alternative History of Philosophy.* Princeton: Princeton University Press.

Neumann, I. B. (1997a) 'John Vincent and the English School of International Relations'. In Neumann and Waever 1997, 38–65.

Neumann, I. B. and Waever, O. (eds.) (1997b) *The Future of International Relations: Masters in the Making.* London: Routledge.

Neumann, I. B. and Welsh, J. M. (1991) 'The Other in European Self-Definition: An Addendum to the Literature on International Society', *Review of International Studies*, 17(4), 327–48.

Northedge, F. S. (1976) *The International Political System.* London: Faber and Faber.

Nussbaum, M. (1997) 'Kant and Cosmopolitanism'. In Bohman and Lutz-Bachmann 1997, 25–57.

Oakeshott, M. (1974) *Rationalism in Politics and Other Essays.* London: Methuen.

O'Hagan, J. (2002) *Conceptualizing the West in International Relations: From Spengler to Said.* Houndsmill, Basingstoke: Palgrave.

O'Neill, O. (1989) 'Justice, Gender and International Boundaries', *British Journal of Political Science*, 20, 439–59.

(1991) 'Transnational Justice'. In Held 1991, 276–304.

(2000) *Bounds of Justice.* Cambridge: Cambridge University Press.

Onuma, Y. (ed.) (1993a) *A Normative Approach to War: Peace, War, and Justice in Hugo Grotius.* Oxford: Clarendon Press.

(1993b) 'War'. In Onuma 1993a, 57–121.

(1998) *Jinken, Kokka, Bunmei.* Tokyo: Chikuma Shobo.

(2000) 'When Was the Law of International Society Born? An Inquiry of the History of International Law from an Intercivilizational Perspective', *Journal of the History of International Law*, 2, 1–66.

Oppenheim, L. (1905–6) *International Law*. 2 vols. London: Longmans, Green. ([1911]1921) *The Future of International Law*. Translation by J. P. Pate of *Die Zukunft des Völkerrechts* (1911). Oxford: Clarendon Press.

Ortega, M. C. (1996) 'Vitoria and the Universalist Conception of International Relations'. In Clark and Neumann 1996, 99–119.

Paton, H. J. (1953) *The Categorical Imperative: A Study in Kant's Moral Philosophy*. London: Hutchinson's University Library.

Peters, J. and Wolper, A. (eds.) (1995) *Women's Rights, Human Rights: International Feminist Perspectives*. London: Routledge.

Pettman, R. (ed.) (1979) *Moral Claims in World Affairs*. London: Croom Helm.

Pogge, T. (2002) *World Poverty and Human Rights*. Cambridge: Polity Press.

Porter, B. (ed.) (1972) *The Aberystwyth Papers: International Politics 1919–1969*. London: Oxford University Press.

Pouncey, P. R. (1980) *The Necessities of War: A Study of Thucydides' Pessimism*. Princeton: Princeton University Press.

Pufendorf, S. ([1688]1935) *De Jure Naturae et Gentium*. Translated by C. H. Oldfather and W. A. Oldfather. Oxford: Clarendon Press.

(2002) 'On the Duties of Man and Citizen'. In Brown, Nardin and Rengger 2002, 341–8.

Rabinow, P. (1986) *The Foucault Reader*. Harmondworth: Penguin.

Rae, H. (2002) *State Identities and the Homogenisation of Peoples*. Cambridge: Cambridge University Press.

Ray, J. L. (1995) *Democracy and International Conflict: An Evaluation of the Democratic Peace Proposition*. Columbia, SC.: University of South Carolina Press.

Rengger, N. (2000) *International Relations, Political Theory and the Problem of World Order: Beyond International Relations Theory*. London: Routledge.

Reus-Smit, C. (1999) *The Moral Purpose of the State: Culture, Social Identity, and Institutional Rationality in International Relations*. Princeton: Princeton University Press.

(2002) 'Imagining Society: Constructivism and the English School', *British Journal of Politics and International Relations*, 4(3), 487–509.

Rich, J. and Shipley, G. (eds.) (1993) *War and Society in the Greek World*. London: Routledge.

Richardson, J. (2000) *Contending Liberalisms*. Boulder, CO: Lynne Reinner.

Richter, J. (2001) *Holding Corporations Accountable: Corporate Conduct, International Codes and Citizen Action*. London: Zed Books.

Rittberger, V. (ed.) (1993) *Regime Theory and International Relations*. Oxford: Clarendon Press.

Roberson, B. A. (ed.) (1998) *The Structure of International Society*. London: Pinter.

(ed.) (2002) *International Society and the Development of International Relations Theory*. London: Continuum.

Roberts, A. (1991) 'Foreword'. In Wight 1991, xxiv–xxvii.

(1993) 'Humanitarian War: Military Intervention and Human Rights', *International Affairs*, 69(3), 429–49.

(1999) 'NATO's "Humanitarian War" over Kosovo', *Survival*, 41(3), 102–23.

Roberts, A. and Kingsbury, B. (eds.) (1993) *United Nations, Divided World*. Oxford: Clarendon Press.

Roberts, A. and Guelff, R. (eds.) (2000) *Documents on the Laws of War*. Oxford: Oxford University Press.

Rodley, N. (1987) *The Treatment of Prisoners under International Law*. Oxford: Clarendon Press.

Rosenberg, J. (1994) *The Empire of Civil Society*. London: Verso.

Ross, W. D. (1930) *The Right and the Good*. Oxford: Clarendon Press.

Rousseau, J.-J. (1968a) *The Social Contract and Discourses*. London: Dent.

(1968b) *A Discourse of Political Economy*. In Rousseau (1968a), 233–69.

(1970a) 'The State of War'. In Forsyth, Keens-Soper and Savigear 1970, 167–78.

(1970b) 'Abstract of the Abbe de Saint-Pierre's Project for Perpetual Peace'. In Forsyth, Keens-Soper and Savigear 1970, 131–56.

Rowe, C. and Schofield, M. (eds.) (2000) *Cambridge History of Greek and Roman Political Thought*. Cambridge: Cambridge University Press.

Sadowski, Y. (1998) *The Myth of Global Chaos*. Washington, DC: Brookings Institution Press.

Schelling, T. C. (1966) *Arms and Influence*. London: Yale University Press.

Schnabel, A. and Thakur, R. (eds.) (2000) *Kosovo and the Challenge of Humanitarian Intervention: Selective Indignation and International Citizenship*. Tokyo: United Nations University.

Shapcott, R. (1994) 'Conversation and Coexistence: Gadamer and the Interpretation of International Society', *Millennium*, 23(4), 57–83.

(2000) 'Solidarism and After: Global Governance, International Society and the Normative "Turn" in International Relations', *Pacifica Review*, 12(2), 147–65.

Sharp, P. (2003) 'Herbert Butterfield, the English School and the Civilizing Virtues of Diplomacy', *International Affairs*, 79(4), 855–78.

Shaw, M. (1994) *Global Society and International Relations*. Cambridge: Polity Press.

Shinoda, H. (2000) 'The Politics of Legitimacy in International Relations: A Critical Examination of NATO's Intervention in Kosovo', *Alternatives*, 25(4), 515–36.

Shipley, G. (1993) 'The Limits of War'. In Rich and Shipley 1993, 1–24.

Shklar, J. (1984) *Ordinary Vices*. London: Harvard University Press.

Shue, H. (1981) 'Exporting Hazards'. In Brown and Shue 1981, 107–45.

Smith, K. E. and Light, M. (eds.) (2001) *Ethics and Foreign Policy*. Cambridge: Cambridge University Press.

Smith, S., Booth, K. and Zalewski, M. (eds.) (1996) *International Theory: Positivism and Beyond*. Cambridge: Cambridge University Press.

Stamatopoulou, E. (1995) 'Women's Rights and the United Nations'. In Peters and Wolper 1995, 36–48.

Stivachtis, Y. A. (1998) *The Enlargement of International Society: Culture versus Anarchy and Greece's Entry into International Society*. London: Macmillan.

Suganami, H. (1982) 'International Law'. In Mayall 1982, 63–72.

    (1983) 'The Structure of Institutionalism: An Anatomy of British Mainstream International Relations', *International Relations*, 7(5), 2363–81.

    (1984) 'Japan's Entry into International Society'. In Bull and Watson 1984, 185–99.

    (1986) 'Reflections on the Domestic Analogy: The Case of Bull, Beitz and Linklater', *Review of International Studies*, 12(2), 145–58.

    (1989) *The Domestic Analogy and World Order Proposals*. Cambridge: Cambridge University Press.

    (1996) *On the Causes of War*. Oxford: Clarendon Press.

    (1997) 'Narratives of War Origins and Endings: A Note on the End of the Cold War', *Millennium*, 26(3), 631–49.

    (1999) 'Agents, Structures, Narratives', *European Journal of International Relations*, 5(3): 365–86.

    (2000) 'A New Narrative, a New Subject? Tim Dunne on the "English School"', *Cooperation and Conflict*, 35(2), 217–26.

    (2001a) 'C. A. W. Manning and the Study of International Relations', *Review of International Studies*, 27(1), 91–107.

    (2001b) 'Eikoku-gakuha to Hedorii Buru', *Kokusaiseiji*, 126, 199–210.

    (2001c) 'Heroes and a Villain: A Reply to Tim Dunne', *Cooperation and Conflict*, 36(3), 327–30.

    (2001d) 'Alexander Wendt and the English School', *Journal of International Relations and Development*, 4(4), 403–23.

    (2002) 'On Wendt's Philosophy', *Review of International Studies*, 28(1), 23–37.

    (2003) 'British Institutionalists, or the English School, Twenty Years On', *International Relations*, 17(3), 253–71.

Tanaka, A. (2002) *The New Middle Ages*. Translated by J. H. Hoff. Tokyo: The International House of Japan.

Thomas, S. (2001) 'Faith, History and Martin Wight: The Role of Religion in the Historical Sociology of the English School of International Relations', *International Affairs*, 77(4), 905–29.

    (2002) 'A Pilgrim's Progress? Progress, Passion and Hope in Martin Wight's International Thought', paper delivered at the International Studies Association Convention, New Orleans.

Thornberry, P. (2002) *Indigenous Peoples and Human Rights*. Manchester: Manchester University Press.

Thucydides (1972) *The Peloponnesian War*. Harmondsworth: Penguin.

Tilly, C. (1992) *Coercion, Capital and European States, AD 900–1992*. Oxford: Blackwell.

Toynbee, A. (1978) *Mankind and Mother Earth*. London: Paladin.

Tronto, J. (1994) *Moral Boundaries: A Political Argument for an Ethic of Care*. London: Routledge.

Tsoukalis, L. (ed.) (2003) *The European Community: Past, Present and Future*. Oxford: Basil Blackwell.

Tur, R. and Twining, W. (ed.) (1986) *Essays on Kelsen*. Oxford: Clarendon Press.

Van Benthem van den Bergh, G. (1992) The *Nuclear Revolution and the End of the Cold War: Forced Restraint*. Basingstoke: Macmillan.

Vattel, E. (1970) 'The Law of Nations or the Principle of Natural Law'. In Forsyth, Keens-Soper and Savigear 1970.

Vattel, E. de ([1758]1916) *Le Droit des Gens*. Translated by C. G. Fenwick. Washington, DC: Carnegie Institute of Washington.

Verkamp, B. J. (1993) *The Moral Treatment of Returning Warriors in Early Medieval and Modern Times*. Scranton: University of Scranton Press.

Vincent, R. J. (1974) *Nonintervention and International Order*. Princeton: Princeton University Press.

(1983) 'Change and International Relations', *Review of International Studies*, 9 (1), 63–70.

(1984a) 'Edmund Burke and the Theory of International Relations', *Review of International Studies*, 10, 205–18.

(1984b) 'Racial Inequality'. In Bull and Watson 1984, 239–54.

(1986a) *Human Rights and International Relations*. Cambridge: Cambridge University Press.

(ed.) (1986b) *Foreign Policy and Human Rights: Issues and Responses*. Cambridge: Cambridge University Press.

(1990a) 'Grotius, Human Rights and Intervention'. In Bull, Kingsbury and Roberts 1990, 241–56.

(1990b) 'Order in International Politics'. In Miller and Vincent 1990, 38–64.

(1992) 'Modernity and Universal Human Rights'. In McGrew and Lewis et al 1992, 269–92.

Vincent, R. J. and Wilson, P. (1993) 'Beyond Non-Intervention'. In Forbes and Hoffman 1993, 122–30.

Walker, R. B. J. (1993) *Inside/Outside: International Relations as Political Theory*. Cambridge: Cambridge University Press.

Waltz, K. N. (1959) *Man, the State and War: A Theoretical Analysis*. New York: Columbia University Press.

(1979) *Theory of International Politics*. Reading, Mass.: Addison-Wesley.

Walzer, M. (1980) *Just and Unjust Wars: A Moral Argument with Historical Illustrations*. London: Allen Lane.

Warnock, G. (1971) *The Object of Morality*. London: Methuen.

Watson, A. (1982) *Diplomacy: The Dialogue Between States*. London: Methuen.

(1987) 'Hedley Bull, States Systems and International Societies', *Review of International Studies*, 13, 147–53.

(1990) 'Systems of States', *Review of International Studies*, 16(2), 99–109.

(1992) *The Evolution of International Society: A Comparative Historical Analysis*. London: Routledge.

(1997) *The Limits of Independence: Relations Between States in the Modern World*. London: Routledge.

(2001) 'Foreword', 'Forum on the English School', *Review of International Studies*, 27(3), 467–70.

Weber, M. (1948) 'Politics as a Vocation'. In Gerth and Mills 1948, 77–128.

Weller, M. (1999) 'On the Hazards of Foreign Travel for Dictators and Other International Criminals', *International Affairs*, 75(3), 599–617.

Wells, D. A. (1992) *The Laws of Land Warfare: A Guide to the U. S. Army Manuals*. London: Greenwood Press.

Welsh, J. (1996) 'Edmund Burke and the Commonwealth of Europe: The Cultural Bases of International Order'. In Clark and Neumann 1996, 173–92.

Wendt, A. (1999) *Social Theory of International Politics*. Cambridge: Cambridge University Press.

(2000) 'What Is International Relations for? Notes toward a Postcritical View'. In Jones 2000, 205–25.

Wertheimer, A. (1996) *Exploitation*. Princeton: Princeton University Press.

Wesson, R. G. (1978) *State Systems: International Pluralism, Politics and Culture*. London: The Free Press.

Wheeler, N. J. (1992) 'Pluralist and Solidarist Conceptions of International Society: Bull and Vincent on Humanitarian Intervention', *Millennium: Journal of International Studies*, 21, 463–89.

(1996) 'Guardian Angel or Global Gangster: The Ethical Claims of International Society Revisited', *Political Studies*, 44(1), 123–35.

(2000) *Saving Strangers: Humanitarian Intervention in International Society*. Oxford: Oxford University Press.

(2001a) 'Humanitarian Intervention after Kosovo', *International Affairs*, 77(1), 113–28.

(2001b) 'Reflections on the Legality and Legitimacy of NATO's Intervention in Kosovo'. In·Booth 2001, 145–63.

(2002) 'Dying for "Enduring Freedom": Accepting Responsibility for Civilian Casualties in the War against Terrorism', *International Relations*, 16(2), 205–25.

(2003) 'Humanitarian Intervention after September 11, 2001'. In Lang 2003, 192–216.

Wheeler, N. J. and Dunne, T. (1996) 'Hedley Bull's Pluralism of the Intellect and Solidarism of the Will', *International Affairs*, 72, 91–108.

(1998) 'Good Citizenship: A Third Way for British Foreign Policy', *International Affairs*, 74(4), 847–70.

(2001) 'Blair's Britain: A Force for Good in the World?' In Smith and Light, 167–84.

White, H. V. (1975) 'Historicism, History, and the Figurative Imagination', *History and Theory*, 14(4) Beiheft 14, 48–67.

Wiesel, E. et al (1977) *Dimensions of the Holocaust*. Northwestern University Press.

Wight, M. (1966a) 'Why Is There No International Theory?', in Butterfield and Wight 1966, 17–34.

(1966b) 'Western Values in International Relations', in Butterfield and Wight 1966, 89–131.

(1966c) 'The Balance of Power', in Butterfield and Wight 1966, 149–75.

(1973) 'The Balance of Power and International Order'. In James 1973a, 85–115.

(1977) *Systems of States*, Edited by H. Bull. Leicester: Leicester University Press.

(1978) *Power Politics*. Edited by H. Bull and C. Holbraad. Leicester: Leicester University Press.

(1991) *International Theory: The Three Traditions*. Edited by G. Wight and B. Porter. Leicester: Leicester University Press.

(2004) *Four Seminal Thinkers in International Theory: Machiavelli, Grotius, Kant and Mazzini*. Oxford: Oxford University Press.

Wilkinson, D. (2000) 'Civilisations, World Systems and Hegemonies'. In Denemark, Friedman, Gills and Modelski 2000, 54–84.

Williams, N. M. (1986) *The Yolngu and Their Land: A System of Land Tenure and the Fight for its Recognition*. Stanford: Stanford University Press.

Wilson, P. (1989) 'The English School of International Relations: A Reply to Sheila Grader', *Review of International Studies*, 15(1), 49–58.

Wolfers, A. (1962a) *Discord and Collaboration: Essays on International Politics*. Baltimore: The Johns Hopkins Press.

(1962b) 'Amity and Enmity Among Nations'. In Wolfers 1962a, 25–35.

(1962c) 'Statesmanship and Moral Choice'. In Wolfers 1962a, 47–65.

Wolff, C. ([1764]1934) *Ius Gentium Methodo Scientifica Pertractatum*. Translated by J. H. Drake. Oxford: Clarendon Press.

Yost, D. S. (2004) 'Introduction: Martin Wight and Philosophers of War and Peace'. In Wight 2004.

Index

CAMBRIDGE STUDIES IN INTERNATIONAL RELATIONS